AF644727

VIJAYANAGARA

History and Legacy

VIJAYANAGARA
History and Legacy

S. Krishnaswami Aiyangar, et al.

Introduction by: B.M. Pande

Aryan Books International
New Delhi

VIJAYANAGARA
History and Legacy

ISBN: 978-81-7305-168-5

© Aryan Books International

First Published by Aryan Books International: 2000

Reprinted: 2022

All rights reserved. No part of this book may be reproduced or transmitted in any form or by any means, electronic and mechanical, including photocopy, recording or any other information storage and retrieval system or otherwise, without written permission from the publisher.

Published by:

Aryan Books International
Pooja Apartments, 4B, Ansari Road, New Delhi-110 002 (India)
Tel.: 23287589, 23255799; Fax: 91-11-23270385
E-mail: aryanbooks@gmail.com
www.aryanbooks.com

Printed in India

Books That Live!

Aryan Books International was established in 1992. Though it began as a commercial venture, business was only a part of the whole. The primary aim was to bridge the gap between the history taught and the real history of our country, and also to present its lesser known and sometimes deliberately neglected facets. In academia, the legacy of our art, culture and ethos was being undermined to perpetuate a narrative which left us looking weak, soft and lagging behind the so-called progressive West.

It was this narrative that we sought to contest. The journey over the last thirty years has not been an easy one. However, it gives us a sense of satisfaction to have possibly made a small difference by publishing over 750 titles written by the most acclaimed authors in the field. We have specialized in publishing ingenious and outstanding scholarship, both established as also fresh. While we focus on our long forgotten history, we also bring to the fore certain extremely important aspects of Indian art, culture and traditions.

Apart from pioneering content, we also ensure that our production quality remains the best in the business, as we continue with the mission to publish books that **Live Forever**!

We are also aware that this is just the beginning of a long journey. A long road lies ahead. A lot more needs to be said. A lot more needs to be explored. We assure you that we're on it with renewed commitment!

www.aryanbooks.com
@AryanBooksInt

Aryan Books 30 Years International

30 Years of Aryan!

Preface

This volume is being published on the auspicious occasion of the Sexcentenary Celebrations of the Vijayanagara Empire.

The object of the celebrations is to remember with gratitude the rich cultural legacy which the Vijayanagara Empire has bequeathed and the Volume has been so devised as to bring out in relief the political, literary, artistic and religious aspects of the History of that Empire. It is gratifying that the effort has evoked commendable response from scholars of all parts of the country.

This volume owes its existence to the initiative and organisation of Mr. D.P. Karmarkar. All the articles of the volume were reviewed by distinguished orientalist Dewan Bahadur Dr. S. Krishnaswami Aiyangar, who made the work his own and even in the midst of ill-health has devoted precious labour and time to the revision of the manuscripts, and expert supervision of the Volume. It was in the fitness of things that this Volume should have been brought out under the guidance of a veteran scholar who has devoted the best of a whole life to the study of Vijayanagara History. Grateful thanks are due to the Director-General, Archaeological Survey of India in helping to make the Volume tastefully illustrated.

It is hoped that this volume will enable the reader to have some glimpses of the rich cultural achievements of the Great Empire.

Introduction

The Vijayanagara empire represents an important phase in Indian history. It came into existence in the second quarter of the fourteenth century, its rise coinciding with the decline of the Hoysaḷas. The traditional date of the foundation of the Vijayanagara empire is AD 1336 while some scholars date it to AD 1346. It continued to exist till about the middle of the seventeenth century when it finally collapsed.

During its nearly three hundred years existence, four dynasties, the Saṅgama, the Sāḷuva, the Tuḷuva and the Aravīdu held sway over large parts of peninsular India from coast to coast covering Karnataka, Tamil Nadu, Goa and substantial areas of Andhra Pradesh and Kerala. It has rightly been stated that the Vijayanagara empire represents 'the last imperial polity in peninsular India before the British' and is as important for 'clarifying India's cultural evolution for this generation as the Harappan sites were for previous generation'.

The Vijayanagara rulers successfully resisted Muslim inroads into the south India and provided bulwark against their onslaught as is evident from their constant struggle against the Bahmanīs, the 'Ādil Shāhīs, the Nizām Shāhīs, the Qutb Shāhīs and the Barīd Shāhīs. They were also involved in clashes with the Gajapatis of Orissa, the Reḍḍis of Koṇḍavidu, the Valamas of Rachakoṇḍa and other rulers far south; they also undertook successful expedition to Sri Lanka during the reign of Harihara II.

The greatness of the Vijayanagara empire was however due not merely to its political strength but to the all-round contribution that it made and its rich religious and cultural legacy. Notwithstanding their almost continuous engagement in war with their belligerent neighbours, the Vijayanagara rulers bestowed their full attention to religious and cultural matters and architectural activities. Their capital — now represented by Hampi — on the bank of the Tungabhadra was founded by the brothers Harihara and Bukka under the orders of the great sage Vidyāraṇya, the head of the Sriṅgerī-*maṭha* and was named Vidyānagara or Vijayanagara. This great city was spread over an area of more than twenty-five sq. kms; the ruins of the city in the form of temples, shrines and other religious structures, palaces and other secular buildings, fortification walls and gateways, tanks, aqueducts, system of water works and channels, large enclosures and platforms, roads and streets, one of which was 50 metres wide, all bespeak of its prosperity and magnificence. The fame of the Vijayanagara empire and its capital spread far and wide; its rulers had relations with European nations, Africa, West Asia as well as the neighbouring Burma and Sri Lanka. Trade and commerce flourished under the Vijayanagara rulers adding to the royal coffers and also contributed to the prosperity of the empire. Several foreigners have left detailed description of the city of Vijayanagara mentioning about its grandeur in glowing terms. The earliest among these was Nicolo dei Conti, the Italian, who visited Vijayanagara sometime in AD 1420 during the reign of Devarāya I. 'Abdu'r-Razzāq, the Persian ambassador visited Vijayanagara during the reign of Devarāya II (AD 1422-46). In 1504 an Italian, Ludovico di Varthema and later Duarte Barbosa and Domingo Paes visited Vijayanagara respectively in 1518 and 1520 during the reign of Krishṇadeva Rāya (AD 1509-29). In *circa* 1535 came Fernao Nuniz and in 1567 Ceasaro Federici visited the city.

The extant remains at Hampi, comprising both religious as well as secular structures more or less match the description given by these foreign chroniclers. In recent years, these remains at Hampi have been subjected to detailed study and investigation as a national project.

The fame of Vijayanagara however does not rest only on its strength as a great empire or its splendid art and architecture. The all-round contribution that it made to the heritage of India is indeed amazing. Various religious sects like the Kālamukhas, Śaivasiddhānta, Lakulīśa Pāśupatas, Śrī Vaishṇava, Madhvā, the Vīraśaiva or the Liṅgāyats as well as the Jains and others made much progress truly exemplifying spirit of tolerance and religious understanding. The rise of Vijayanagara gave great impetus to Śaivism and the early kings ruled as vice-regents of Virūpāksha, their patron-deity. Later, the Vijayanagara rulers developed partiality for Vaishṇava doctrines; Krishṇadeva Rāya in fact introduced the cult of Viṭhobā into Vijayanagara.

Creativity in literary as well as artistic pursuits made much headway as a result of the patronage given by the Vijayanagara rulers and one finds a large corpus of works ranging from commentaries on religious literature to lexicography, anthologies, philosophical literature, poetry, drama, music, etc. in Sanskrit, Kannada as well as Telugu. While the name of the great Vedic commentator Sāyaṇāchārya stands out for his *Ṛg-veda Bhāshya* and the anthology *Subhāshita-sudhānidhi*, equally important are: Vidyāraṇya or Vidyātīrtha who wrote the biography of Śaṅkara entitled *Śaṅkara-vijaya*, and *Saṅgītasāra*, a treatise on music; Mādhava the brother of Sāyaṇa who wrote *Sarvadarśana-saṅgraha*, *Jaiminīya-nyāya-mālā-vistara* and *Jīvanamuktiviveka*; Irupaga Daṇḍādhinātha or Bhāskara, who lived under Harihara II prepared *Nānārtharatnamālā*, a work on lexicography; Divākara, who was at the court of Krishṇadeva Rāya composed *Pārijātaharaṇa*, *Devīstuti*, *Rasamañjarī* and *Bhāratāmṛta*, based on the stories of the *Mahābhārata*. Lakshmīnārāyaṇa, state musician in the court of Kṛishṇadevarāya wrote *Saṅgītasūryodaya*. Timmanna, another poet in his court composed *Pārijātapaharaṇaṁ*, a Telugu work while Dhurjati and Mallana wrote *Kālahastimahātmya* and *Rājaśekharacharita* respectively; during his reign the *Mahābhārata* was translated into Kannada by Timmanna. Then these was the poetess Tirumalāmbā who composed the *champu* entitled *Varadāmbikā-pariṇaya*.

But it was not merely patronage that the Vijayanagara rulers gave to scholars, poets and others, some of them also composed original works; for instance, Virūpāksha, the son of Harihara II of the Saṅgama dynasty of Vijayanagara wrote two plays *Nārāyaṇavilāsa* in five acts and *Unmatta-Rāghava*, a one-act play. Gopendra Tippa Bhūpāla of the Sāḷuva dynasty wrote *Tāladīpikā* which is a work on the *mārga* and *deśī tālas*. Krishṇadeva Rāya who was a great patron of arts and literature is believed to have composed the work *Amuktamālyadā*.

The present volume contains articles by scholars on the political, literary, religious, social and artistic aspects as well as the history of the Vijayanagara empire and provides glimpses of the rich, all-round achievements of this great empire. It is a seminal work providing the necessary background to the ongoing researches on different aspects of Vijayanagara.

B.M. Pande
Former Director
Archaeological Survey of India

Contents

List of Illustrations

1

The Character and Significance of the Empire of Vijayanagara in Indian History

By

Dr. S. Krishnasvami Aiyangar, M.A., Ph.D., F.R.Hist.S.,
Honorary Correspondent Archæological Survey of India,
Fellow of the Royal Asiatic Society of Bengal.

EARLY MUHAMMADAN EMPIRE AND KHALJI IMPERIALISM

Since the establishment of Muhammadan rule in Delhi early in the 13th century, the new power never ceased in its efforts to extend its authority gradually, first over Hindustan and then across the Vindhya mountains into the Dakhan. The process of the introduction of a new government in place of the old was indeed very gradual, and in the earlier stages it seemed almost imperceptible. When, at the end of the 13th century, what might seem a mere accident led Allaud-din-Khalji to cross the Vindhya mountains in what was, to begin with, a mere raid, opened a new vista before him for conquest, or for bringing the new kingdoms under his own authority, at least to the extent of their resources becoming available for his own purposes. When Allaud-din had finally placed himself on the throne, and had completely reorganised his administration and put it on a satisfactory footing, first for efficient protection against the nomadic hordes pouring in from across the north-western frontier, and for conducting the administration in peace internally, he could think of a further extension in the south. With the experience of the north-west frontier, he seems to have acquired the prudence to modify his dream of emulating the exploits of Alexander the Great, by giving the caution to the generals whom he sent out that their object should not be complete conquest of all the south and simple extension of Mussalman government. He was more anxious that the state of things obtaining in the peninsula should continue to be much as it was, provided only his armies and generals could succeed to the extent of infusing respect for Muhammadan authority, and enabled him, as occasion called for, to draw from the resources of the Hindu kingdoms of the south. So his first step at Khalji imperialism, as it transcended the bounds of Hindustan, was the creation of subsidiary States, not exactly in the sense in which the term is used in British Indian History, nor could the political relations, such as they happened to be, be the same, nor at any rate quite similar. The practical steps taken certainly differed widely. When once the idea was put into practice, with so much success as he obtained, in regard to the two States nearest to him, further extension became a process of natural development. The unsatisfactory character of the hold that he obtained on the distant southern kingdoms however, led to a modification of the policy in his successors, though in principle it remained essentially as he formulated it. But the most efficient amongst his Khalji successors modified it substantially, and gave the first hint of what that policy of extension meant, in the arrangement that he made after the final rebellion of the Yadava ruler of Devagiri, Harapala Deva. After overthrowing the rebellion and putting the ruler beyond power of further mischief by punishing him severely, Mobarak Khalji not only appointed a viceroy in the place of the old ruler, but actually attempted to rivet his hold on the Yadava territory by placing Muhammadan garrisons in salient places under Amirs of his own. That indeed must have opened the eyes of the southern powers, if indeed such an eye-opener was at all needed. After Allaud-din had brought both Devagiri and Warangal under his authority, there were left only two considerable powers in the south, the Hoysala on the plateau with his capital in what is now the Mysore territory, and farther south of him the Pandya with his capital at Madura, but with the territory so extended as to take into it the great bulk of what was the Chola Empire. The position of these powers was such that any attack upon the Pandyas by the Muhammadans can only be either after conquering the Hoysala and reducing him to subjection, or bringing him under a treaty somewhat like the Yadavas of Devagiri, or the rulers of Telingana at Warangal. So far as Allaud-din was concerned, his general Malik Kafur defeated the Hoysala, and managed to bring about his entry into the Khalji imperial system. For the moment the position of the Hoysala was assured and saved from further attack from the Muhammadans. The Muhammadan army could carry its raid southwards and Malik Kafur's raids to the south, as far as Madura and Ramesvaram, seem well attested by the known facts of history. That was the position of the South Indian Powers when the dynasty of the Khaljis was overthrown, that is, when Ghazi Khan Tughlak overthrew the usurper Khusru, and succeeded to the Muhammadan Empire of Delhi.

THE TUGHLAK EMPIRE AND ITS EXPANSION TO THE DISTANT SOUTH

Ghazi Khan better known Ghiyazu-d-din Tughlak had a comparatively short reign, and had to attend to troubles nearer home and effect the reduction of Bengal which had set up in rebellion. Returning from Bengal, he met his death during the reception, whether the death was brought about by design, or as the result of a mere accident. It was his successor, Muhammad who became heir to the imperialistic policy of the Khaljis, and he it was that adopted the policy and developed it further to the extent of carrying his conquests to its natural limits, disregarding the prudent limitation that Allaud-din thought it necessary to impose upon his more forward lieutenants. In the course of the first five years of his rule, Muhammad succeeded in bringing back under his father's authority, and then his own, the territory of Warangal which showed an inclination to throw off the Muslim yoke. An expedition to the more distant south against the Pandya kingdom probably did not meet with success altogether to begin with. But Muhammad was not to be baulked. A subsequent invasion, or two, succeeded in overthrowing the Pandyas completely and admitted of the establishment of a Muhammadan government in Madura. That such a government was established in the southern districts is in evidence in some few inscriptions we have, which mention Muhammad Sultan, in Pudukottai and Ramnad. The very trouble that Muhammad experienced in effecting the conquest, and the natural difficulty of maintaining the hold thus acquired, combined possibly with the rebellion of his own cousin, Bahaud-din Gurshasp, in the Dakhan, made a more central capital than Delhi a necessity of the situation. So Muhammad resolved to make Devagiri the capital as a more centrally situated place for the necessities of his position. It must be remembered that he started it as a moderate, and even prudent measure, by making it his official headquarters and only asking his noblemen, his immediate courtiers, to build for themselves houses there. That took place almost about the same time as his general Jalal-ud-din Ahsan Shah ultimately brought the Tamil country under his authority.

Jalal-ud-din was appointed the first governor of the south in Madura, and the long line of communication had to be maintained even with Devagiri, if not Delhi, by garrisons along the long route. We have definite information that Kaṇṇanūr, a neighbouring village to the Hoysala capital near Trichinopoly, became a Muhammadan cantonment. The garrison at Kaṇṇanūr, on the route to Madura would guard the route against hostile armies. Although we have not got the kind of definite information for other garrison centres along the route, we may take it that he had other salient places where he had garrisons like that. To the Hoysala ruler, who occupied a position of political subordination, and who remained aside of the long line of communication between the new capital of Devagiri and its southernmost viceroyalty, the drift of the policy was clear. His position of subordination was taken advantage of as was clear in the planting of a Muhammadan garrison quite in the immediate neighbourhood of his southern capital. He must therefore have become aware of what was coming on, and took steps accordingly to see that the flood tide did not sweep him out of existence without an effort on his side. In the earliest years of this extension of power of Muhammad, the Hoysala must have felt himself in no such condition as to do anything active to protect himself. He therefore pursued the policy of the cane-reed (*Vētasa-gñyāya*) as one of his records puts it. He bent before the storm and "let the legions thunder past," at the same time not altogether unmindful of what he should do to protect himself. Action must be taken, but it must be taken unobserved. Perhaps he took advantage of the damage that was done to his capital in one of the recent raids of the Muhammadan armies in the South, to make Tiruvaṇṇāmalai his headquarters, and, remaining there, he must have been watching the situation and biding his time, perhaps taking such steps as might enable him ultimately to take advantage of any chance that may offer itself. Fortunately for him, and, unfortunately for the Islamic extension, Muhammad embroiled himself with powerful subordinates of his by unnecessarily mad acts of cruelty against his cousin who rebelled against him in an effort to set himself up on the throne. As a direct result of this, the powerful western governor of Sind and Uch rebelled, and simultaneously the governor of distant Bengal also revolted, as his father's settlement did not please all parties concerned and a rival party was left in power to work the mischief. This was taken advantage of and his governor of Madura declared himself independent also about the same time. These events took place more or less about A.D. 1335, the critical point in the history of the empire of Muhammad Tughlak.

THE HINDU REACTION TO THIS EXPANSION : THE HOYSALA RESISTANCE

Just about that time, South India was in a condition favourable to the spread of Muhammadan conquest in one way. Whether it be under the authority of Muhammad bin Tughlak or independently, the person who held possession of Madura in the Islamic interest could extend his authority almost over the whole of the Pandya kingdom, as the Pandya authority had been completely undermined and left entirely feeble to do anything for itself. The only power worth mentioning was that of the Hoysala, who, though frightened into submission, still had the resources which he might utilise to purpose, if not in a policy exactly of aggression, at least of successful resistance to the spread of Islamic power in the South. The rebellion of Jalal-ud-din of Madura against his liege lord Muhammad in A.D. 1335, would just be the signal for the Hindu power to make an attempt to regain independence, and resist the further incursions of the Muhammadans whenever they should make the next attempt to revive the power of the Tughlak Muhammad in the south. The Hoysala Vira Ballala III probably adopted the policy of the cane-reed deliberately, and, if that policy meant anything, it meant a policy of merely biding one's time. His time had come when Madura cut itself away from the empire. But what was the Hoysala's position at that time for him to take any action in this juncture ? Whatever the Hoysala may have been, he does not appear to have been the craven that historians were accustomed to dub him as. If he found circumstances against him and adopted the policy of bending before the storm, that fact alone cannot make a coward of him. Ever since the first attempt on Dvarasamudra (Halabeid) by Malik Kafur's invasions, he seems to have realised his position to the fullest extent, and was ready prepared to adopt a policy which would leave him alone till he could so develop his resources and take an opportunity whenever it should present itself. The planting of Mussalman garrisons in the districts of the Mahratta country was an indication of what the Islamic power actually meant doing. The revolution in Delhi for the time saved the position. But that offered no guarantee that the danger would not again arise. There was the possibility of a raid by Muhammad bin Tughlak himself in behalf of his father. That proved abortive because of Muhammad's own illness and occurrences at Delhi and in the camp of his father. When Ghiyazu-d-din died and Muhammad had duly installed himself upon the throne, his expansion policy developed, and the establishment of the capital in Devagiri gave a further hint to the Ballala that the danger was coming nearer home, and the actual conquest of his territory would perhaps prove to be the ultimate objective of Tughlak policy. Naturally he should put himself in a position, as far as may be, for efficient defence whenever the attack should come, and one of the steps called for, would be the protection of the vulnerable northern frontier, especially one of the main arteries of communication across the Tungabadra leading into his territory. The citadel of Kampli, only about 2½ miles down the Tungabadra from Hampi, could be utilised to purpose, as in fact it was on previous historical occasions, and even in later British history. With the fortified post of Anegondi on the other side of the river and the strong fortress of Kampli, a short distance to the east, this route was fairly well protected, and, if any strengthening was possible, it was provision against an enemy making use of the ford immediately on gaining possession of Anegondi, the fortified position on the northern bank of the river. It would seem therefore quite natural that efforts should be made to protect the ford on the southern side as well, and possibly steps were taken accordingly; but whatever action was taken, it had to be done secretly and gradually, so that the enemy may not know. This was made the more urgent when in the course of the expedition to the south in A.D. 1327, the army of Muhammad Tughlak made a detour against the Hoysala capital and left it considerably damaged, if it did not make it altogether untenable as the capital of the Hoysalas. The Hoysala vacated his capital and the invading army, which, of course, marched successfully further southwards along the more direct route, took possession of Madura. This led in the first instance to the establishment of a garrison in Madura and the creation of a government there. The rebellion of that government and the establishment of its independence changed the aspect of affairs..

THE GOLDEN OPPORTUNITY

The Tughlak government was in difficulties; but still its hold on the Dakhan was firm. But the hold on South India had been broken by Jalal-ud-din declaring himself independent. What was the Tughlak emperor going to do? From all that was known till then, Muhammad would make efforts certainly to regain his authority. That was made impossible by the simultaneous rebellions in Bengal and Sind, and the immediate possibility of a rebellion in other provinces as well. The opportunity which offered itself to the Ballala ruler was a certain amount of time for deliberating upon a course of action to be adopted in a decisive bid for independence. The very Muhammadan governors were setting themselves up independently. The justification in his case would be all the greater. But the real justification would only be if he could make his position good; once he had set up in rebellion, he was likely to be caught between two fires, the Tughlak attack from the north, and, in that contingency, the actual possibility of an attack in co-operation from the south as well. There was the alternative possibility of his territory being surrounded so long as the line of communication between the Dakhan and the distant south, Madura, remained open. The Ballala therefore made up his mind betimes to provide for the defence of the northern frontier, and prevent communication between the Dakhan government of the Tughlaks and the garrison at Madura so long as it was loyal, and to prevent a combination even when Jalal-ud-din had declared himself independent. He therefore marched down by the highway from Mysore and took his position at Tiruvaṇṇāmalai, which still was his own wherefrom he could operate, when the time came for him to show his hand, effectively in carrying out this particular policy. From A.D. 1328 onwards Tiruvaṇṇāmalai had become more or less his capital. He was almost constantly there devising means and taking measures to carry out the project that was forming in his mind. The rebellion of Jalal-ud-din in A.D. 1335 only indicated the occasion for greater activity on his side. That he was not there doing nothing is in evidence in the remark of Ibn Baṭuta that the Hoysala was trying to effect a surrounding movement to shut in the Muhammadan garrison at Madura by throwing his armies round at salient places along the high road from Tiruvaṇṇāmalai to Ramesvaram. The next seven years were years of activity for the last Ballala in this great effort of his. The chances of success could not have looked very brilliant in A.D. 1335 or very soon after, as the ruler of Madura was himself a capable man and the threat of an attack from the northern side was yet real. It is only when the complicated movements of rebellion developed, and Muhammad got entangled in an utterly hopeless mesh of rebellions and wars within the empire that the Ballala could feel that the time had come for him to make a desperate effort. The fact that an inscription in Chickmagalur says that he annointed his son, in all solemnity in the year 1340, is an indication that he was launching into the southern campaign to do or die, and took steps and made his preparations almost with a view thereto. He was active all over and was gradually closing in upon Madura by beating into it the small Muhammadan garrisons in the various places between Tiruvaṇṇāmalai and Madura. When therefore he was prepared to launch a big attack, his final attack, upon the Muhammadans, there was only the garrison at Kaṇṇanūr which was being besieged by the Hoysala as the next strongest garrison to Madura itself. We find the Hoysala therefore encamped in Trichinopoly at the head of a whole army composed of a lakh and twenty-five thousand troops, of which a Muhammadan contingent of twenty to twenty-five thousand formed a substantial part. He fell fighting in Trichinopoly in A.D

1342, and the Hoysala power suffered possibly the greatest disaster in his death.

THE HOYSALA STRUGGLE ULTIMATELY LEADS TO THE FOUNDATION OF THE EMPIRE OF VIJAYANAGARA

This great event, calamitous in its consequences to South India, brings us to a date six years after the traditional date of foundation of Vijayanagar, A.D. 1336. The question naturally would arise whether it was founded independently of the titular ruler of the locality for the time being, namely, the Ballala, who fell fighting in Trichinopoly. Great efforts have been made, and have not yet ceased, to ascribe this foundation to fugitives from Warangal, and to make that possible and bring it about, the power of the Hoysala had been reduced to insignificance. Ever since the declaration of independence by the Sultan of Madura as against the Tughlak empire of Muhammad, we find the Hoysala active in the central region of South India and the South. It must be remembered that it is the downfall of the Chola power, as the leading power in South India, that brought the Hoysalas down from above the plateau, and their operations against the aggressive Pandyas, who were instrumental in the overthrow of the Chola empire, gave them sufficient prestige and even territory to make them build for themselves a capital not far from Trichinopoly, one of the Hoysala predecessors of the last ruler even made it his habitual residence. But by the time we come to the last Ballala, their dominence in the south had suffered very considerable damage. It was the rivalry between the Ballalas and the Pandyas that paved the way for Muhammadan invasions and subsequent conquest of the two powers in detail. The establishment of Muhammadan garrisons and the foundation of, first, the province of Madura, and then, a separate Muhammadan State there, must have rudely awakened the Hoysala who, from all that we know of him, certainly had not gone to sleep. His activity in the south increased therefore when Muhammad bin Tughlak involved himself in a hopeless tangle of rebellion and dissatisfaction on the whole of his territories in the north, so as to make the Ballala feel almost certain that there was nothing to be feared from that quarter. It was just then that the Ballala should have formed the project of dislodging the Muhammadan garrisons in the south in an effort to bring back, at least, that part of the southern kingdoms that acknowledged the authority of the Hoysalas before. As he was moving carefully onwards in a gradual effort from his central position at Tiruvaṇṇāmalai to dislodge the different garrisons and ultimately concentrate his effort upon the main Muhammadan garrisons at Trichinopoly (Kaṇṇanūr) and in Madura, the tangle of rebellion in the Dakhan and Gujarat was so developing that there was no chance whatever of Muhammad paying any attention to the south. In these circumstances one would naturally expect the Hoysala to take the flood at the time, and so he did. The resources that the Hoysala could put into the field were something magnificent, and, even as against the desperate efforts of the Mussalman garrison in Madura, the Hoysala achieved successes and actually won the battle. It was his death at the moment of the achievement of his ambition that upset his plans and made them fall short of complete success. So far therefore it is quite clear that the Hoysala power was still great and gave Vira Ballala the confidence to try his strength against the Muhammadan garrisons of South India as a whole, while the possibility cannot altogether be excluded of his action bringing down upon himself the wrath, if not the army of Muhammad bin Tughlak, though, for the time being, he had no fear from that quarter.

HOYSALA RESISTANCE IMPOSSIBLE WITHOUT THE EMPIRE

The question then arises whether we could conceive of Vira Ballala adopting this course of action with the territory round his headquarters in jeopardy, or much worse in the hands of hostile feudatories. The northern frontier of the Hoysala was a cause of trouble and anxiety under the successors of the Hoysala Somesvara. The Yadavas were active in their efforts to extend their frontier to the south, and therefore wars on that frontier were pretty common. The Hoysalas probably suffered reverses even, as in fact we have positive evidence of their having suffered these reverses. The position had been, to a considerable extent, restored by the predecessor of Vira Ballala who could be more active on the northern frontier as he detached the southern government and placed it in the hands of his younger brother, so that by the last decade of the 13th century, the position of authority of the Ballala on the northern frontier had been to a great extent restored. A great deal is attempted to be made of the achievements of the chieftain of Kampli, and the documents quoted in authority, apart from the piece of literature bearing upon the question directly, give no date, nor describe precisely under what circumstances the fight took place between the ruler of Kampli and the Hoysala. The Kampli ruler might have fought and might even have won advantages, against the Ballala, and from what we know of the actual circumstances of the position, his achievement must have been earlier than the period which we are now discussing. The fact that the ruler of Kampli felt that he could pass on the fugitive Baha-ud-din for greater safety to the Ballala before launching himself into that forlorn hope of fighting against the angry Tughlak Muhammad, is certain indication that the Hoysala was in considerable power, and could, in the estimation of the ruler of Kampli, give effective protection to the fugitive rebel, Baha-ud-din Gurshasp. Granting therefore that the ruler of Kampli was a valiant man and had snatched successes against Vira Ballala even, it could not have been after A.D. 1327, much less after A.D. 1335. The 1327 invasion must have been in connection with the rebel Baha-ud-din, and the ruler of Kampli must have passed out of existence soon after. In regard to the statement of Ibn Batuta that Muhammad Tughlak sent two of Kampli's officers to govern Kampli, and the attempt at an equation that they were the brothers Harihara and Bukka, it is just possible that the two brothers constituted apostates from Muhammadanism; but, if we are quoting Ibn Batuta for authority, we must also bear in mind that Ibn Batuta speaks of eleven brothers who have been converted to Islam, and at least one of them still remained with Muhammad Tughlak, while all subsequent documents that refer to the Vijayanagar brothers speak of only five brothers as if they were five and no more. Even later when Firishta speaks of the foundation of Vijayanagar, he refers to Kanniah Nayak of Warangal conspiring with the Hoysala. Therefore the Hoysala must have retained sufficient power at the time when Kanniah Nayak of Warangal revolted or thought of setting up against Muhammad bin Tughlak. In none of these Islamic authorities have we a precise date, which only makes the position more complicated. Whether they were men from Warangal or other people nearer home, and whatever be their nationality, Telugu or Kanarese, it would be more in keeping with the trend of historical events of the time to take it, in the absence of any statement to the contrary, that the brothers worked in co-operation, n not in subordination, to Vira Ballala. Other arguments put forward such as the occurrence of an inscription of Harihara dated A.D. 1340, in the Bangalore district without reference to the rule of Vira Ballala, it is possible to quote other inscriptions in that locality itself and elsewhere, where the name of the ruling sovereign is not mentioned in circumstances which leave no doubt that the supreme ruling authority at the time was the Ballala sovereign. The foundation of Vijayanagar as such, apart from the laying of the foundation-stone of the fortress, is the outcome of that policy of the last Hoysala who dislodged the garrisons planted in the course of the southern invasions under Muhammad Tughlak and getting South India free of the Muhammadans.

FOUNDATION OF THE CITY OF VIJAYANAGAR

In regard to the foundation of the city itself, a well provided frontier station was absolutely necessary in the particular locality at all times, but very much more so when Kampli had fallen into hostile hands, and even had been partially destroyed. The time therefore when we should naturally look for an attempt at laying the foundation of the fortified town on the southern bank of the Tungabadra as the main citadel, with Anegondi as an outpost across the river, should have been after the destruction of Kampli by Muhammad bin Tughlak in A.D. 1327 or 1328. Naturally and quite consistently with his policy Vira Ballala could have set about the business secretly at least so far as the Muhammadan powers in the north were concerned. In the laying of the foundation stone of such a fortress, it is perfectly likely that the Hoysala sought and obtained the blessings of the occupant of the Mutt of Sringeri for the time, and that person would have been the pontiff who goes by the name of Vidyātīrtha, not to be confounded with Vidyāraṇya of later fame. While therefore the fortification might have begun somewhat obscurely, and in a small way to avoid notice, it must have reached a stage of completion and might have been announced to the world soon after the rebellion of the Madura Sultan when the Hindu power saw that Muhammad, for very good reasons of his own, left the rebel entirely to himself, almost a confession that he had extended his empire beyond the bounds of his resources. That may be the reason why tradition ascribes the foundation to the date A.D. 1336, although as yet we have no definite evidence that the fort was either founded or completed in that year. The years between A.D. 1335 and A.D. 1342 are years of activity of the Ballalas in consolidating the Hoysala state and putting it on a footing to offer effective resistance against future Muslim aggressions either from the Dakhan or from the empire of Delhi. The Hoysala failing in the effort, those on whom the mantle of administration fell must have shouldered the responsibility, and, after the vital northern frontier was placed under a certain number of officers who were prepared to co-operate and work towards this cause, they would naturally take the leading position. When the last Hoysala, the successor of Vira Ballala, who was crowned in all solemnity as his successor in A.D. 1340, passed out of existence obscurely two or three years after Ballala III, the course becomes clear, and it is these brothers who would stand out as having rendered yeomen service to the empire. What actually were the circumstances of his death, whether he left heirs or no, and who were legitimately entitled to the succession are points upon which we have so far come upon no information of a reliable character. The names of these brothers come to notice prominently only about A.D. 1346 just before the successful establishment of the Dakhan kingdom of Gulburga, but almost simultaneously with the rebellion of the Dakhan governments of Muhammad with no probability almost of their being brought back into the empire owing to Muhammad's pre-occupations in Gujrat and farther west. There seems to be therefore a sequence of events which led gradually from efforts at protecting the Ballala kingdom to ultimately erecting a state which would offer effective opposition and save South India from Muhammadan conquest. That culmination is what is really to be described as the foundation of the empire, the Hindu Empire of Vijayanagar, in the South.

THE CAUSE FOR WHICH IT STOOD

The actual stress of circumstances which brought about this foundation gives us clear indication of the objects which it was intended to subserve if it was to justify its having been brought into existence. The danger was real of Hindu civilisation and culture being completely overwhelmed in the new conquest, and, if Tughlak Muhammad had only succeeded and opportunity had been given to him for putting his imperial ideal into practice successfully, we can well imagine that South India would have been not different in point of character from the north as it is actually at present. South India continues to be, notwithstanding all historical vicissitudes, just the solitary remnant of the Hindu India of old both in spirit and in structure, though time has worked havoc with very many of the features which gave character to the Hindu ideal of society and state. Whether it is all for the good or for evil, is a different question from this. The historical phenomenon is just that. South India declined to be swept away by the advancing tide of Islam, and, what was more, to stand up positively for Hinduism for all that it was at the beginning of the 14th century. The first item of work that this ideal would involve is certainly the clearing of such vestiges of the secular power of Islam from the south. That was not completely done as yet at the date of foundation of Vijayanagar. It meant a further half century of serious work before South India could feel that that preliminary task had been accomplished. The substantial historical event that indicates this ideal is the destruction of the Muhammadan State of Madura and of the garrison in Kaṇṇanūr near Trichinopoly. That done, the next item of work that called for action, constituted the measures that had to be taken actually to prevent further effort on the part, not of Islamic conquerors from the north, though that possibility was not altogether absent, but the much more real danger of advance from the now established Muhammadan State of the Dakhan. As it looked, the chances were that, when North India got out of the confusion, the political confusion of the later years of the reign of Muhammad bin Tughlak, either they themselves would make an effort, or, if they should fail for some reason or another, they would support to the full extent of their power any effort on the part of their cousins in faith, and perhaps even political aspirations, the Muhammadan State established in the Dakhan. This possibility, or rather this constant threat, was removed once Firuz Shah Tughlak resolved upon definitely giving up the policy of expansion, or even interference, in the affairs of the distant Muhammadan kingdom of the South, or of the hostile Hindu powers beyond. This decision happened to be wise at the time, for, if the opposite policy had been adopted, the very existence of the Islamic power in India would have been jeopardised by the invasion of Timur from the north-west which was devastating enough without the southern embroilments which would have resulted naturally from the other policy. As it was, the Islamic power in Hindustan almost collapsed, and had to be revivified by gradual effort from the end of the 14th century till it regained in a great measure its political power in the course of the century following. The problem for Vijayanagar therefore was immediately the keeping of the Dakhan power, the Bahmani kingdom, within limits and guarding against its incursions into what was marked out as Hindu India, just along the Tungabadra-Krishna frontier. Just on the eve of the establishment of the Bahmani kingdom, we hear of the activities of two at least of the five brothers, whose names figure prominently in this enterprise somewhat later. When the first Bahmani king came on an expedition towards his southern frontier to put it on a footing of security, having been assured of Firuz Tughlak's pacific intentions, the names of the three elder brothers of the five, Harihara, Kampa and Bukka are heard of on that very frontier fighting in behalf of the newly established State. That was a time when the successor of Vira Ballala had passed out of existence without leaving much of a vestige of how exactly his fall came about. We cease to hear of the ruler; but these brothers stand before the world shouldering the responsibility which should have been Ballala's at the most vulnerable frontier of the new kingdom. We are therefore left to our own shifts to account for this transformation. To imagine that, in the face of the difficulties that confronted the kingdom of the Hoysalas in the last years, a couple of fugitives, however talented and resourceful, should have come into the Hoysala kingdom and shown themselves, in a very short space, possessed of all the resources of the now defunct kingdom of Vira Ballala without any previous connection with it, seems really too much for belief. The more so if we make the Hoysala kingdom the puny petty State that some of the votaries of the Telugu theory of the origin of the empire would have us believe it was. Apart from the question whether the brothers were of Telugu or Kannada origin, a matter really of no importance, and, at the very best, of only very subordinate importance, the transition would be but very normal if these were the legitimate frontier wardens of the Hoysala kingdom in the days of its power, who assumed a higher responsibility when the central authority, for one reason or another, had passed out of existence. We find them doing what one would normally expect the Hoysala ruler and his officers to do, and it would be too much to expect a power newly come into authority successfully even to attempt to do. When the established kingdom of Vijayanagar rises into view in the years following A.D. 1350 we see the main block of Hoysala territory formed into a certain number of viceroyalties to which are appointed people on whose loyalty confidence could be placed. The three brothers are along the frontier stretching from the West Coast right down to the Bay of Bengal, near Nellore. The Udayagiri Mahārājyam is the easternmost on this frontier under Prince Kampa, the second brother. The middle block of territory, the central block of the Hoysala kingdom dominated by Halabeiḍ and Penugonḍa fortresses, is under the rule of Bukka; the third, but the most capable of the five brothers. The western region including a considerable part of what is nowadays known as the Southern Mahratta country reaching up to the sea, was under Harihara, the eldest of the five brothers, whose name comes into view the earliest. Behind him in a second line of defence is placed the great viceroyalty of Āraga with headquarters at Āraga in the Shimoga District of Mysore under one of the younger brothers. Penugonḍa constituted another important government and that was under the fifth brother. Behind them all was another great viceroyalty with headquarters at Muḷbāgal, and this viceroy had charge of the territory in the south, and, what is really more important, the special charge of having to conduct the war against the Muhammadans commenced and conducted to a considerable stage of advance under the last great Hoysala himself. The details that one gets from a study of the Kamparājavijayam of Gangā Dēvi, the consort of this very prince, describing the glorious career of her husband in classical Sanskrit, give one unmistakably to understand that his was a responsible task, of reclaiming the southern parts, the Tamil part at any rate of the Hoysala kingdom in the best days, for Vijayanagar, and to repair, as far as may be, the damages done to this region by the invasions and the subsequent wars between the Muhammadans and the Hindus. When this campaign of by far the most capable of Bukka's sons had been completed almost as Bukka's reign was drawing to a close, we find Kampana symbolising the re-establishment of the Hindu power by two acts of great significance, the re-establishment of the temple of Śrīrangam in all its glory, and the reconstruction of at least the main part of the great temple at Madura practically razed to the ground during the Muhammadan occupation. These were obviously intended to mark the triumph of Hinduism and its emergence from the devastating flood of warlike Islamic expansion in the south. This glorious prince is described as *Davvarika* the door-guardian of the Hoysala in the Temple Chronicle of Madura datable in the 17th Century. These events give unmistakable indication of the actual purposes of those who fought and fought hard for cause and country throughout. While therefore the five brothers and this one prince Kampa all laboured to bring this about, the kingdom had not yet assumed the compacted form of a united single kingdom. With Kampa's conquest during the period of Bukka's administration, both of Bukka's elder brothers having passed away in the course of years, the time had come for announcing to the world the establishment of the new kingdom, and that fell actually to the lot of the successor of Bukka to do, another son who ruled as the first emperor of the new foundation under the name and style, Harihara II.

Harihara II came to the throne in A.D. 1378. Of course, he had a number of brothers and cousins ; but we do not know that Harihara I left any children, though we do know of one prince who played an important part, and who was the son of Kampana I. However, we have nothing on record to indicate that there was any disturbance at the accession of Harihara II. We may therefore assume that he succeeded peacefully. Harihara had comparatively little work to do by way of conquest, and immediately on accession he could proceed to consolidate the new foundation and stand before the world as the emperor of the newly-founded Hindu empire. So he did, and himself announced to the world in glowing terms the accomplishment of the design which had been working itself through a course of more than half a century. Two of the titles that he assumed happen to be unusual for Hindu monarchs generally. They are " the supporter of the four castes and orders " and " the master in establishing the ordinances prescribed by the Vedas." This last title is now generally affected by the various Āchāryas, such as Śankarāchārya and the other Hindu Āchāryas. While the protection of the " castes and orders " was usually regarded as the duty of the king, the form in which it appears here and the need for announcing it in the form in which it was done, gives it a new emphasis. To these two may be added a third one " Publisher of the Commentaries on the Vedas," which can hardly be regarded as a special function even of a Hindu sovereign. We do not find these titles assumed by even his successors generally. It is therefore clear that the feeling of those who struggled and succeeded in founding the empire of Vijayanagar was that the most cherished items of Hindu culture were in danger of being swept away, that Hinduism and Hindu society itself was in danger. Vijayanagar therefore came into existence (1) for the purpose of saving South India from being completely conquered by the Muhammadans, (2) to save Hindu religion and give it a chance for its natural development, at least in this corner of India without molestation from outside agencies, and (3) to save for India as much of its culture and learning as it was possible to do. With these objects before it, the empire came into being formally under Harihara II of Vijayanagar.

THE FIRST CENTURY OF THE EMPIRE—A PERIOD OF CONSOLIDATION

The first century of the empire, after Harihara set the seal of its foundation by proclaiming himself emperor in the terms indicated, practically coincided with the period of the first dynasty of Vijayanagar. During almost the whole of this period, Vijayanagar was constantly exposed to Islamic aggression from the north sometimes provoked by their own acts, and almost as often without that provocation. The wars were pretty frequent and often fierce. The net result however was that the frontier was efficiently guarded notwithstanding severe reverses suffered by the new empire on two or three occasions. As the wars progressed, the power for resistance of the Hindus increased, and the carrying out of a reorganisation of the armies of the empire under Dēvarāya II assured the effectiveness of the defence of this frontier. During this period of war in the north, the consolidation of the empire of Vijayanagar in the south had been brought about also by extending Vijayanagar authority over the whole of the south. Along with the extension of authority also went a certain amount of reorganisation of the administration, more or less on conservative lines, the main object being to remove such disorders and confusion as crept into the administration during the period of wars, and the gradual introduction of the old order of settled government all through. Even in this department of activity, the culmination was reached under Dēvarāya II in the creation of a 'lordship of the southern ocean' and the appointing of his own right-hand-man Lakkanna, or Lakshmana, to the charge of it. This lordship of the southern ocean could mean nothing more than the exercise of governmental authority and control over the sea which, under Vijayanagar, could have meant no more than the exercise of control and the regulating of trade, etc., overseas, as we have no evidence whatever of Vijayanagar having ever maintained a fleet, such as the imperial Cholas before them had, and perhaps even the Pandyas. The reason for the absence of any naval power under the Vijayanagar empire is probably due to the fact that the sea-going activity had gradually, during this period, changed hands passing from the Hindus to the Muhammadans, a change which began soon after Marco Polo's visit. It is then that we hear for the first time of Muhammadan settlers and Muhammadan sea-going merchants exercising influence at the Pandyan court, so much so that we hear of an Arab merchant holding the position of Customs-General of the principal port of the Pandya country, the sea-port of Kayal. There are numbers of documents made available in which the administrative organisation was brought back to the old footing in places where anarchy prevailed consequent on the recent wars. The work of the first dynasty therefore up to the usurpation by the last ruler, Virūpāksha II, consisted in the efficient defence of the northern frontier and the reorganisation of the administration in the interior. This was naturally to be expected from the rulers who became heirs to the responsibilities of Vira Ballala.

There is one other department of activity for which we have a considerable mass of evidence and that is this. At the very outset of the empire, arrangements had been made to bring together all men of learning whose services were available, and setting them to work to put on record all that was left of Indian learning which till then was habitually handed down from teacher to pupil, although we are not without evidence of recorded literature also. This traditional handing down of learning related mostly to religious learning pure and simple, and the efforts needed were to put it on record to save it from being completely lost. This seems to have been undertaken under Bukka, and Harihara set his stamp of authority on the work, by the assumption of the name "the Publisher of the Commentaries on the Vedas." Mādhavāchārya and Sāyanāchārya, the brothers, and a number of others who co-operated with them were responsible for the vast collection of works bearing upon this subject. This partial activity gradually widened, and showed itself in subsequent periods as a general patronage and cultivation of learning as such, not only in Sanskrit but also in the vernacular languages of the country. We have a number of illuminating examples from among the Vijayanagar rulers and even members of the ruling family. What is more remarkable, works have come down to us written by the ladies at the court, and even royal ladies. Along with all this, went the sedulous promotion of trade and commerce, the mainstay of the financial resources of the empire other than agriculture. There were as many as 300 ports in the period immediately following where a flourishing trade was carried on, naturally bringing in a considerable amount of revenue to the general coffers.

THE FIRST USURPATION AND ITS CONSEQUENCES

It was a junior member of the ruling family of this first dynasty that set the bad example of a usurpation some time about A.D. 1475 or somewhat earlier. That luckily happened to be a period when the neighbouring Bahmani kingdom was also in some confusion owing to internal dissensions and the advancing power of a newly rising dynasty in Orissa. The rise of this new power diverted the attention of the Bahmani kingdom from Vijayanagar, and Vijayanagar happened to be left in peace to indulge in the luxury of this usurpation. This left the empire somewhat weakened by the discord within, and gave the opportunity not exactly for the Bahmani kingdom but for the kingdom of Orissa to take advantage of. The usurper Kapilesvara, and his successor, Purushottama, carried their arms successfully along the coast region down to Rajahmundri first, and took the fortified strongholds of the lower Krishna next. From these salients they were able to extend their territorial authority even into the farther south, attacking Kanchi and extending their authority even into the South Arcot District round about Tiruvaṇṇāmalai. This activity on the part of Orissa seems to have coincided more or less with the first usurpation. These activities began much earlier and furnished ultimately the justification for one of the first generals of the empire to turn out usurper himself, and take the power into his own hands with a view to restore the authority of the empire and recover its east coast territory from those who had almost succeeded in annexing it to their own territories. Of such aggressive neighbours there were two at the time. The Bahmani kingdom which took advantage of the confusion to advance into the Doab between the Krishna and the Tungabadra, and the kingdom of Orissa which had advanced right down the coast to as far south as Tiruvaṇṇāmalai. The great usurper Narasinga justified his usurpation by a successful effort against the Kalinga rulers, and recovered a considerable portion of their conquests in the south. He probably began by doing this first before taking steps to recover the lost possessions of the empire in the river frontier of the Doab. He died before effecting the recovery of the strong fortress in this region; but had the prudence to hand over the authority and this responsibility to his most trusted general and colleague, Narasa Nayaka, although like most fathers he was anxious that his own sons should succeed to the throne. The general Narasa Nayaka seems to have carried out his trust loyally in accordance with the wishes of his master, notwithstanding attempts to damage him both physically and morally. It does not look as though he usurped the empire from the son of his master; but his son who succeeded him in his responsibility had not probably the same consideration for loyalty to the children as he himself had, and the usurpation seems to have taken place under the eldest of his sons, another Narasimha, who succeeded to the throne and ruled for a few years. His accession was the signal for a general rebellion in the empire; but Narasimha had the capacity to bring the rebels to reason in a large number of cases. Then came in the succession, not altogether undisputed, of his younger brother Krishna, by far the greatest ruler of the dynasty, who realised fully the needs of the empire and set forward to do what had to be done to bring the empire back to the position to which his predecessors laboured hard to bring it. So far therefore the dynasty to which he belonged is generally known as the third dynasty, and, under the third dynasty, Vijayanagar was able to establish itself as the empire of the south. The Muhammadan opposition from the Bahmani kingdom had grown feebler, and, almost about the period when the first usurpation of Saluva Narasimha took place in Vijayanagar, the Bahmani kingdom also broke up not by a general rebellion, but by what in effect was almost as good as that. The great governors established themselves in their centres, to the neglect of authority at the centre, and, in the course of the next few years, it was a question of five Bahmani Sultans instead of one Bahmani kingdom. This break up of the central Government was to the advantage of Vijayanagar, and the only enemy to reckon with was the Kalinga ruler of the north. Krishnadēvarāya started with putting down the rebellions in the interior and bringing back to loyalty one State that still remained recalcitrant, that is the Ganga ruler in Southern Mysore. When that was done, and the whole empire had been brought to order, he could set forward on a well-planned, deliberate effort to recover from Orissa all the territory that her kings had taken from Vijayanagar. He succeeded in taking possession of the territory down to the lower course of the Krishna, and, in a glorious march northwards against the ruler, was encamped at Simhachalam and brought his Cuttack contemporary to terms.

UNDER KRISHNA VIJAYANAGAR REACHES ITS ZENITH OF GLORY

This achievement of Krishna set a term to the territorial extent of Vijayanagar and secured for it the assurance of peace on the debatable frontier of the north, as far as such assurance was humanly possible. As far as could be judged from the material at our disposal, Krishna seems to have carried his arms successfully across the Doab and come to some kind of understanding with his Muhammadan neighbours, before his expedition against Orissa, so that for the time being, we may regard the whole northern frontier as having been given the security which the great usurper Saluva Narasimha seems to have considered a prime necessity of the position of the Hindu empire. Returning from this campaign in the north, Krishna is said to have performed an act of public duty for the Hindu religion by setting aside solemnly ten thousand gold pieces for repairs and restorations of the temples in South India which had suffered during the period of Muhammadan invasions. This scheme, very moderate in origin, seems later on to have developed into a general scheme not merely for the restoration, but even for the extension of several of the temples in South India, and their being made live institutions forming an integral part of the life of the Hindus. Most of the big towers, the really large ones, in temples all over the country go by the name Rāyagopuram, in honour as it were of Krishna having initiated the building of the big gateways, and these are found in the most remote and distant places in the south. We need not regard it as directly the work of Krishnadēvarāya himself, but we have to regard it as the outcome of a policy initiated by him on his return from the victorious expedition to the north. Valiant as he was and an active warrior taking part even in the distant wars directly, he seems to have been a man of piety and fell in largely with the beliefs of his countrymen at the time. As another measure of religious beneficence, he removed the image of Balakrishna from Udayagiri when he took the fortress and gave it a shrine within the walls of the imperial capital ; he also constructed a temple, perhaps the most magnificent monument in the city, the Viṭala shrine with a view to housing the image of Viṭala in Pandarpur, which had more than once suffered at the hands of the enemies. It is therefore generally ascribed to him that he built shrines for all those deities in the debatable land to the immediate north of the Vijayanagar territory, to be properly housed and worshipped in the capital. This religious patronage of course widened into patronage of literature and learning generally. Not only did he maintain a court containing a large number of learned men, but he himself made an effort at attaining sufficient proficiency to try his hand at literary work, both in Sanskrit and in Telugu. Some of his successors also achieved distinction in this line. So Krishna's reign marks the grand climacteric in the development of the empire, and the successful achievement of the objects for which it was actually founded. The very organisation of the empire itself reached its completion almost with his reign. He could set himself to investigate the rates and taxes which proved oppressive, and abolished some of them which were regarded as such. Even during his reign we are enabled to see the elements of danger that the empire contained, and so long as these were kept under control by the ruler for the time being, all was well with the empire. Having regard to the facilities of communication in those days, the empire must be regarded as certainly extensive, and was divided into a number of viceroyalties embracing comparatively large blocks of territory. The smaller divisions constituting these viceroyalties have had their own arrangements for government, which were recognised and respected, and even developed to the extent of being very efficient under the Chola empire of the tenth to the fourteenth century. It is this arrangement that actually held notwithstanding the period of confusion following the fall of the Hindu kingdoms and the incursions of the Muhammadan armies following that event. The work of reorganisation of this administration started betimes and reached a high degree of completion under the great Dēvarāya. It had since received development and the viceroyalties grew up to be more or less kingdoms themselves. With such a constitution, the life of the empire would depend upon the loyalty of these viceroys, springing from their realisation of their responsibilities and the direct consequences which were bound to follow in case of a breakup of the imperial authority. With Krishnadēvarāya's achievements, the danger above adverted to had diminished a great deal and there was a considerable feeling of security.

A LURKING DANGER TO THE EMPIRE

A disturbance that was created in the last years of his reign gave clear indication of the lurking danger to the empire. It looks as though Krishna fell ill somewhere about A.D. 1525, and his half-brother Achyuta had to carry on the administration for him. Krishna apparently had children. We seem to hear of a son and a daughter of whom the boy of tender years died about the time. We cannot be certain, from the information we have so far, how exactly the death came about; whether it was an act of assasination or merely a question of natural death. In either case, it seems to have upset Krishna a good deal. Perhaps he managed to get over the difficulty. A little later in his reign two of the most trusted of his viceroys, namely, the viceroy of Madura and the viceroy that held the government over the central block of territory, both rose in rebellion. We cannot be sure which rebellion was the first. The latter ruler went by the title Saluva Nayaka, a Brahman officer of great reputation, who had the fullest confidence of the king. This rebellion however had to be dealt with only at the beginning of his successor's reign, that is, in the reign of Achyuta. Therefore it was probably the latter of the two. The rebellion of the other viceroy Nāgama Nāyaka by name, a distinguished man who had seen service under Krishna's father, and even perhaps under old Sāḷuva Narasinga, a proved veteran, chafed under the interference from headquarters and set up in rebellion, which apparently took Krishna by surprise. The young son of the selfsame viceroy who was at court, holding a responsible position, himself volunteered to lead an expedition to punish the viceroy and bring him back to reason. The young officer proved to be as good as his word and carried out loyally what he undertook to do, and got round his father to the extent of making him submit to the royal clemency. The rebellion by two trusted veterans and confidential officers of the empire showed that the danger to the empire lay in the attitude of the great viceroys. The death of Krishna and the accession of Achyuta to power were not attended by disturbances ordinarily attributable to a disputed succession. The only disturbance that we hear of is the outcome of the machinations of the rebel viceroy who fled to the king of Tiruvaḍi (Travancore) for protection, and there was the threat of an invasion from there into the southern part of the empire. Achyuta was able to march at the head of his army, bring the rebel to book, and put the Travancore ruler on a footing of subordination to the empire. That done, the empire seemed to be at permanent peace. Unfortunately however for the empire, Achyuta relaxed his personal hold on the administration, and let two of his brothers-in-law, who had served him well, to carry on the administration for him. This was irritating to the viceroys. While they were quite willing to put up with the control from the sovereign for the time being, they naturally chafed under the exercise of authority, as they knew it really, by officers of a position like their own, apart from other personal considerations which might have entered into the question. That began the trouble which went on throughout the remaining period of imperial history and ceased only with the downfall of the empire. The administration of the brothers-in-law, both of them bearing the name Timma or Tirumala, and known, with their family prefix, Salakam Timmarazu, managed to make the administration exceedingly irritating to their brother viceroys, particularly those related to the royal family. A rival party sprang into existence led by three brothers, the eldest of whom claimed to be a son-in-law of the last ruler directly or indirectly. The death of Achyuta was the signal for their taking definite action. The young prince, Achyuta's son, who succeeded was overthrown, and a nephew by name Sadāśiva was placed on the throne, the actual administration being carried on by the three brothers. The brothers led by Rama took efficient steps to keep the northern frontier safe and otherwise conduct the administration efficiently.

THE DECLINE OF THE EMPIRE

We have already noted a change that took place in the Bahmani kingdom by its breaking up into five separate kingdoms. Among the southernmost of these five, Bijapur and Ahmadnagar, were in the immediate neighbourhood of Vijayanagar in the north-west. The other Golkonda which also abutted on the territories of Vijayanagar, had on her eastern frontier the kingdom of Kalinga, which still retained a certain amount of power and had to be gradually overcome. Therefore that third State, Golkonda, as it was called, was not quite so actively hostile as the other two, in their relations with the empire of Vijayanagar. These States among themselves cherished ambitions of their own, and these showed themselves in various degrees of activity according to the circumstances of the moment. They often fought with each other for aggrandisement, and sought the assistance of the neighbouring Hindu ruler. Ramarāja, who was now responsible for the policy of Vijayanagar, availed himself of the advantage that these offered, and supported the one party or the other according to the exigencies of the moment. It was generally the rivalry between Bijapur and Ahmadnagar that formed the feature of this struggle. In the course of the struggle the Muhammadan States gradually grew weaker and weaker, and the Hindu power grew the stronger, and after one of these wars the Muhammadan powers saw clearly that they were fighting among themselves only to the advantage of the Hindu power. As the regent Rama had a clear vision of his superiority, he did not always show the consideration that he was accustomed to, to the feelings of his neighbours, thereby demonstrating clearly that he was getting to be rather overconfident of his strength, and perhaps even neglected the precautions which prudence dictated. Occasion was not wanting for the Muhammadan powers to come to an understanding and bring about a combination, and a combined invasion of Vijayanagar territory was the result. The fateful battle that was fought, which historians were hitherto accustomed to call Talikota, happened to be fought on the outward march of the Vijayanagar armies from Vijayanagar towards Bijapur, as offering the best marching route. They fought in a region one march from a place called Tāvarekere marked by the site of a village, as a matter of fact two villages, Rākshasatangaḍi. The capture of Ramarāja and his prompt decapitation by the Nizam Shah of Ahmadnagar was the end of the battle, though the advantage was with the Hindus till this incident happened. The usual disorganisation of the Hindu army followed, and the one of the three brothers who survived, Tirumala, the middle one, retreated hastily to Vijayanagar, and managed to carry off thence a great deal of the wealth that was stored in Vijayanagar and retired for safety to the strong fortress of Penugoṇḍa farther south. The Muhammadan armies advanced into the city of Vijayanagar in a rather leisurely fashion, and were in occupation for a period of six months searching and hunting up for treasure and plunder. A good deal of damage certainly was done in the course of this activity, and the city, though it was standing in its entirety two years afterwards, had become neglected and gradually fell into ruin. It used to be regarded that this battle put an end to the empire. Undoubtedly this battle did vital damage to the empire, but the empire was still intact and could go on for another century almost with a comparatively brilliant epoch of a generation before it got weakened and dismembered-weakened by the constant invasions from the north, and dismembered by the dissatisfaction and rebellion of the viceroys within. That is the sad tale of the end of Vijayanagar, the actual ending of which is marked by the beginning of the Mahratta power in the South.

The battle of Talikota was no doubt badly damaging in its results to the progress of the history of the empire of Vijayanagar, and could have proved easily destructive to the empire altogether. It actually proved quite otherwise as, even after the defeat of the

Hindu army, the Muhammadan rulers did not feel that they could effectively pursue the enemy into his retreat, but left him alone to recouperate himself there. It is easy to understand the reason for this. The alliance among the Muhammadans held together so long as there was a strong enemy to fight against, and when the enemy ceased to be active, naturally the jealousies had more play than any common aim, and therefore the pursuit of a steady policy became impossible. The States that evinced any interest in the affairs of Vijayanagar were the three southern ones, Bijapur, Golkonda and Ahmadnagar. Ahmadnagar really called for vengeance, and she had it; and there was no particular reason that she should interest herself any more in the affairs of Vijayanagar. A Vijayanagar policy therefore became peculiarly a policy to be pursued by the rulers of Golkonda and Bijapur. Both of them could be, to some extent, friendly to, and may even have had a friendly corner in their hearts for, the late ruler. The actual Golkonda contemporary of the battle as well as the ruler of Bijapur at the time were both persons who could feel a certain amount of personal gratitude to the last ruler and might even have pursued a friendly policy, had it not been for certain irritating acts on the part of the ruler of Vijayanagar. As a matter of fact, the whole combination seems to have been engineered by the Nizam Shahi ruler for the time being, and he was satisfied with what had been achieved by the battle. Hence the policy adopted by the Mussalman rulers of the south was one of comparative indifference once the enemy was dislodged from his strong position on the banks of the Tungabadra. Tirumala was clearly allowed to recover himself from the effects of the staggering blow. In the course of the next five years, he had so far recovered that he gained back sufficient prestige even to interfere in the affairs of the Muhammadan states again. What was more, either Tirumala himself at the fag end of his reign or his immediate successor, was able to dispense with the phantom of a titular ruler in the person of Sadāśiva. We cease to hear of him after A.D. 1570. Tirumala was succeeded by his eldest living son Śrī-Ranga and we hear of Muhammadan activities in the northern frontier immediately on his accession. He however managed to hold his own as against them even after having suffered a siege at Penugoṇḍa; and some of the holy places of the Hindus were attacked and even occupied for some time by the Muhammadans, such as for instance the great Vaishnava holy place of Ahobilam. With the growing activities of the Muhammadans in the north, Śrī-Ranga seems to have thought it better to reorganise the empire and put it on a footing of greater efficiency. So the three surviving brothers,

Śrī-Ranga, Rama and Venkaṭa divided the spheres of authority among them, Śrī-Ranga being at Penugoṇḍa, the actual ruler of the empire, had for his sphere of activity the guarding of the most vulnerable frontier, namely, the northern frontier. The next brother Rama was entrusted with the viceroyalty of Śrīrangapatam and the territory dependent thereon extending to the borders of Madura; and lastly Venkaṭa, the next, but perhaps the most capable, made Chandragiri his headquarters and remained there with the charge of all the territory to the south. When Śrī-Ranga passed away, Rama had predeceased him having given cause to some of his powerful feudatories near the headquarters to attack him at Śrīrangapatam and take possession of the territory immediately dependent upon the viceroyalty. This is the foundation of the new kingdom of Mysore, and Raja Odayar, the responsible author of this movement, gradually extended his territory by conciliation and conquest among those in his immediate neighbourhood and built up a small state for himself. Rama Raja having fallen in this struggle, and his two sons having been too young for the responsibility and remaining with their uncle at Chandragiri, Venkaṭa was able to succeed to the whole empire again, and, during the next thirty years and more, he was able to give to the empire a unity and gain back for it much of the prestige that it had before his time. He may be regarded perhaps as the last great emperor of Vijayanagar and had a glorious reign. In the course of his reign, he gave recognition to what was in fact a rebellion by the ruler of Mysore by recognising Raja Odayar as the ruler of the territory that he had taken from Venkaṭa's elder brother round Śrīrangapatam. This was in the year A.D. 1612, and that is the charter of foundation of the kingdom of Mysore, which continues to-day to be under a Hindu ruler maintaining the traditions of Vijayanagar. That was the first dismemberment of Vijayanagar, and the example thus set was certainly not likely to be lost on the other viceroys and their successors, particularly as Mysore tried hard and with success to maintain the status that she had acquired. During the remaining years of his reign hardly more than two or three, Venkaṭa was able to maintain the empire intact, and held his own successfully against the attacks from the north. But his difficulties were the attitude of the great viceroys in the south, and attack from his Muhammadan neighbours of Bijapur and Golkonda in the north. He had to suffer a siege in Penugoṇḍa itself in A.D. 1612 by the Muhammadan armies investing the capital and besieging him there. He succeeded in beating them back with the assistance of the loyal viceroys of whom two stand out prominently, the viceroy of Chennapatna in

Mysore, and the viceroy of Tanjore. Both of these sent active assistance and it is that that turned the scale. The attitude of the viceroys of Gingee and Madura was doubtful, and this attitude of suspicion wanted only the occasion which came with Venkaṭa's death in A.D. 1614. He did not leave behind him a son of his own, but had to will the succession away as it were, to a nephew—son of his elder brother Rama—who stayed with him and even enjoyed the title of 'Chikkarāya' Yuvarāja at the court. One of the premier nobles of the court, Gobbūri Jagga Rāya, who happened to be a brother-in-law of the king, became so badly dissatisfied with this arrangement, because of a putative son to his sister who was one of the queens, that he felt justified in the assassination of the unfortunate successor and the whole of his family. That set the whole empire ablaze. It was a loyal officer at court, Yachama-nayaka by name, who took it upon himself to resist. He managed to smuggle one of the little boys of the five children of the late ruler just before the massacre of the royal family, and with him in his camp he could set up as a loyalist to purpose. He fought and even won a victory against Jagga Rāya and his army, and found the most valuable support in the viceroy of Tanjore who was one of the most powerful at the time. A war was the result in which all the other viceroys, except Mysore, and even a contingent from the Portuguese took the side of the rebel; but the battle fought near Trichinopoly, went against them. This gave a blow more terrible than Talikota. The rebel viceroys stood aloof, and could never be brought under the empire again. Standing aside, Mysore pursued its own policy, and the effort that was made by the last ruler of Vijayanagar to reunite the empire proved futile. He had to be a fugitive and find asylum here, there and everywhere till at last we hear no more of him. This last ruler it was that gave the charter for the foundation of Fort St. George, renewing the one granted just a decade before by his predecessors, to the British East India Company. This was the last Vijayanagar Emperor, Śrī-Ranga III, the last ruler of the dynasty.

Śrī-Ranga came to the throne fully realising that the unity of the empire was absolutely essential to its existance. He made an effort to bring that about by all means in his power. He was even driven to such desperation that he appealed to Shah Jahan, the Mughal emperor, promising to turn Muslim if that were called for, provided the Great Mughal assisted him to gain back his own. That was almost about the end of Shah Jahan's reign. The appeal did not receive the response that it might have. But what indeed was the active cause of the dismemberment of the empire was the advance of the arms of Bijapur and Golkonda under a treaty dictated by Shah Jahan. These two states came to an early agreement between themselves to make as much of a conquest of the territory of the Vijayanagar empire as they could manage to, Bijapur taking all the territory above the Ghats, Golkonda all below. Their repeated aggressions wore off the resources of the empire. The last successful effort of Śrī-Ranga to recover the prestige and even the possessions of the empire was made against the Bijapur forces, under Shahji, the Mahratta in the passes leading up from Gudiyattam not far from Vellore, and the siege that he had to stand within the walls of the fortress was the result of a turning movement by another Bijapur army making a detour and advancing by way of the Changama Pass. He was however ultimately defeated. Bijapur already in possession of the Vijayanagar territories in the East Mysore under the administrative control of Shahji, marched down and managed to take possession of the viceroyalty of Gingee. It is in this desperate position that Śrī-Ranga appealed to Mysore and the Mysore Prince Chikadeva Raja beat back the combined army of the discontented viceroys assisted by even a contingent from Bijapur at a battle near Erode. But the attitude of the southern viceroys of the empire became more hostile in consequence and Śrī-Ranga had to go for protection to Ikkeri, and this time it was that the ruler of Mysore inflicted a defeat upon the allies. That was the last straw. Śrī-Ranga passed into obscurity. A document on silver plates, as yet perhaps of not certain authenticity, has it that an appeal from Śrī-Ranga's queen to Shivaji later on obtained a grant for the maintenance of the royal family of the last Vijayanagar ruler. That was how the end of the empire came, and from subsequent Mughal conquests there stood out Mysore, the Hindu state, and, after the fall of Bijapur, the Mahratta states of Gingee and Tanjore, as the remnants of the glorious Empire.

It will thus be seen that Vijayanagar came into existence under the stress of circumstances, which united the resources of all South India in a common cause against the advance of the Muslim authority in the south. This great effort was successful and South India remained Hindu India for very near three centuries as a consequence of that effort. On several occasions influences were internally at work, and a dismemberment of the empire seemed almost certain. Vijayanagar managed to get clear of all these, and succeeded in maintaining herself till the disloyalty of the great viceroys made it impossible for her to maintain her position, and the empire passed out of existence having had a history of at least three clear centuries of nobly active existence.

2

Vijayanagara Empire: A Synthesis of South Indian Culture

BY

REV. H. HERAS, S.J., M.A.,

Director, Indian Historical Research Institute, St. Xavier's College, Bombay.

AND

MR. V. K. BHANDARKAR, B.A. (HONS.),

Indian Historical Research Institute, Bombay.

IN the first half of the fourteenth century South India witnessed an epoch-making event. It was the foundation of the last great empire of the Hindus of the South—the Empire of Vijayanagara. As its name signifies it was an empire that became victorious after a relentless struggle against superior forces. Founded at a time when everything that a Hindu loved and venerated was on the verge of total annihilation, the empire came into existence over the ashes of the southern kingdoms, and represented the Hindu cause, fought for it, and for over three centuries held sway in the South.

The foundation of the empire came as a blessing. Every Hindu state from the Yādavas in the north-west to the Pāṇḍyas in the extreme south had fallen a prey to the invader's greed for gold. First came the turn of the Yādavas of Dēvagiri. It was a mere accident that opened the flood-gates of invasion. 'Ālā-ud-dīn Khilji to avoid the intrigues at Delhi came to the South and was informed of the fabulous wealth of the Dēvagiri ruler. Having a spirit of adventure and forced by necessity to amass wealth to put his secret plans into action, 'Ālā-ud-dīn captured Elichpur, and later on, Dēvagiri whose Rājā, Rāmacandra was forced to give an enormous sum of money and jewels as tribute. This was the first blow to Hindu isolation of the South. The unimaginable wealth of the State, the utter want of unity among the various Hindu States of the South and, to crown all, the inherent weaknesses of the Hindu armies convinced 'Ālā-ud-dīn and his successors who followed in his footsteps, of the advantage of invading the South.

The above events happened in A.D. 1294 and nearly a decade and a half later, 'Ālā-ud-dīn sent his favourite Mālik Kāfūr to tap once again the riches of the Hindu kingdoms. Rāmacandra was taken prisoner and sent away to Delhi, but was later on released. His kingdom was laid waste ; his capital was captured ; his treasury was emptied and he was forced to pay an annual tribute In 1309 A.D. Mālik Kāfūr again invaded the South. This time it was the turn of the next kingdom on the onward march of the triumphant hordes of Islam towards the extreme South. The Kākatīyas of Wārangal were as rich as the Yādavas, and the fact that these Hindu states were rich was enough to induce the armies of Islam to move. Pratāpa Rudra, the Kākatīya prince, after a heroic resistance, submitted and paid his tribute to prevent his kingdom from annexation, and to retain his religion from molestation.

In 1311 A.D. once again Mālik Kāfūr marched to the South. This time it was the third powerful kingdom of the South—the Hoysaḷa Empire of Ballāḷa III. Resistance to the forces which were actuated at once by a fanatic zeal and an unbridled passion for gold was out of the question. Moreover, the armies of the invader were much superior to the Hindu ruler's emasculated hordes. Ballāḷa III surrendered prudently, gave away a great portion of his wealth, sent his son as hostage for good behaviour and acknowledged the Sultan of Delhi as his overlord. Thus fell the third great empire of the South.

Mālik Kāfūr never halted when greater glory and more wealth was promised. In the extreme south were rich temples and weak though wealthy kings—the Pāṇḍyas, who waged an internecine struggle for the throne. Grasping this opportunity, Mālik Kāfūr, bold and unscrupulous adventurer that he was, led the army into the Pāṇḍya kingdom, plundered the temples, ravaged the territories, massacred the infidels and captured Madura, the Pāṇḍyan capital. Thus fell another South Indian kingdom. Mālik Kāfūr returned to Delhi with 312 elephants laden with the spoils, 12,000 horses, 96,000 *maṇs* of gold, and many boxes of pearls and precious stones.

The fall of those Hindu states marked by unprovoked and unjustified massacre of the innocent Hindus, the plunder of their temples, the imprisonment of their kings, the extortion of their wealth, one after the other, opened their eyes to find a solution for ending this intolerable plight. But there was no power worth the name that could stand up and fight the Hindu cause. Nor was the trouble over ; the worst was yet in store for them.

Muhammad bin Tughlak, a name at which friend and foe alike trembled, came to the throne. As Ulugh Khān before his succession, he had in 1323 A.D. won his spurs at Wārangal by capturing the fort, imprisoning the Rājā, Pratāp Rudra and exacting a heavy tribute. This virtually tolled the knell of the Kākatīya hegemony.

In 1327 A.D., the rebellion of a relative of the Sultan, by name Bahā-ud-dīn paved the way to the complete subjugation of the South. The hitherto unknown and small principality of Kampili suddenly came into the limelight. Actuated by an admirable spirit of protecting those in distress, the king of Kampili gave his sanctuary in his hill-kingdom to the desperate Bahā-ud-dīn. In welcoming Bahā-ud-dīn, Kāmpila invited disaster. Muhammad bin Tughlak sent his generals who took Kampili fort by storm, and in the skirmishes the king, Kampila was killed and eleven of his sons were captured, converted to Islam and sent to the capital.

The rebel, however, escaped to Ballāḷa III who had no scruples for the laws of hospitality when his own fate was hanging in the balance. He gave up the rebel to his fate and saved his empire from extinction.

With the destruction of the Kampili state, the last nail in the coffin of South Indian states was driven, and Hindu independence became a thing of the past. Ballāḷa III was the only king worth the name who survived and from the moment he handed over the rebel to the army of the Tughlak or even before, he made himself active in finding out an auspicious hour for blotting out the struggling Muslim garrisons left scattered in the land by the invaders. He moved from place to place. First it was Dōrasamudra, then Tonnūr, according to tradition, then Aruṇāsamudra or Uṇṇāmale or Uṇṇāmalepaṭṭaṇa, the modern Tiruvaṇṇāmalai, and so on. Finally a time came when he marched from Tiruvaṇṇāmalai with a big army and fought a battle at Kaṇṇānūr, near Śrīraṅgam. Had he understood the true nature of Muslim military warfare, he would have won a great battle and carved for himself a great name in South Indian annals. The Muhammadans fearing the total extinction begged for an armistice and when it was observed shamelessly violated it and fell on the Hindu army. The usual massacre followed, the old king captured, and when all his wealth was extorted from him, he was inhumanly put to death.

The death of Ballāḷa III removed the last prop of Hindu independence. There was not a state worth the name that commanded an efficient army and an influential leader. One after the other the Hindu states had fallen under the scimitar of the Khilji and the

Tughlak. Empires which were considered powerful had passed away, amidst scenes of devastation and massacre. There seemed to be no power to stem the tide of fanaticism and greed for gold. When such was the state in the South, there came into existence a small kingdom out of the smouldering ashes of the kingdoms of the South.

Whatever be the exact relationship between the founders of the Empire and the Hoysaḷas or the Kākatīyas or even the Kampili state, as some claim recently, there can be little doubt that the empire came into existence due to the political upheavals of the time. There never was a kingdom which could wield an influence to weld the conflicting elements in the South. There never was an efficient army to withstand the blows of the zealous invaders. There never was a king to organize a steady and pertinacious resistance to the unconquered army of Islam. It was, therefore, necessary to organize a strong unitary government, put forth determined opposition and thus check the further aggressions of the Muhammadans. If that were done, then Hindu culture would be saved.

It was therefore the intention of the founders to put a strong and impenetrable barrier in a suitable place, organize the people, and then check further inroads of the Muhammadans. The foundation of the empire was not without certain principles which the founders and their successors had in view. It must be remembered that the invaders in their early career had no ideas of territorial conquests but were impelled by a love of gold of the southern kingdoms and the fanatic zeal to spread Islam. They had found that the plunder and defilement of the rich temples of the South would achieve their double object. Hence their stay in the south is signalized by the looting of many temples. To the Hindus of the South it meant religious annihilation. The invaders had not hesitated to kill those who resisted and to convert those who submitted to their fate. In brief, it was religion that was to be first protected and for that a strong centralized government was necessary. The foundation of the empire provided this long-felt necessity. The underlying idea in protecting religion was not only to protect Hinduism as such, but also to protect all the indigenous sects and guarantee peaceful life among themselves. Therefore, we can clearly demarcate two broad principles which actuated the founders to found an empire—freedom of religious worship, free from persecution and molestation ; and freedom from political subjection. It was to assure these two principles that the empire was founded. It was this empire founded on these principles that symbolized all that was best in South Indian culture.

How then can we say that the empire was the culminating point in South Indian History ? As pointed out formerly, in several respects, the empire of Vijayanagara reaches the high-water mark in the cultural history of the South. In the political, religious, social, geographical, architectural and literary spheres it marks the climax of South Indian history. That is why, perhaps, it is said with pride and justification that the empire is the last and the greatest Hindu empire of the South.

To defend Hindu culture a sound political organization was necessary. In South India there was no empire which rightly deserved to be the political representative of the Hindus at a time when all the states worth the name to champion their cause had been put out of existence. Within three or four decades of its foundation the kings of Vijayanagara became the sole and unchallenged masters of a vast portion of the south, from Goa in the west to the mouth of the Kṛṣṇa and a little beyond it, in the east. This extensive empire had to be organized in such an efficient way as to make it proof against collapse in times of danger. In this the emperors were eminently successful. While they carried on the struggles with the enemies of Hinduism in the north the provinces supplied them with a perennial source of revenues to continue their wars. Several times in its early days the emperors failed but in the reign of the *mahārājādhirāja* Kṛṣṇadēva Rāya and even later on till its fall in A.D. 1565, Vijayanagara played the part of an arbiter of South Indian politics. Never was such a conspicuous and important position occupied by any South Indian dynasty.

The empire was founded for the protection of *Dharma*, at least, such is the boast of the founders. In the whole range of South Indian history an instance of an empire founded with the purpose of giving protection to a religion irrespective of different sects, has yet to be discovered. It is this aspect of the foundation that makes the history of the empire of Vijayanagara so unique. Evil having greatly encompassed the earth, so states the Heddase grant of Mārapa, a brother of Harihara I, the founder of the empire, and *Dharma* having found " that he was unable to move about," God was pleased and " caused king Sangama to be born in a great royal line for the help of *Dharma* " (*M.A.R.*, 1929, p. 166). It is therefore the protection of *Dharma*, not Hindu *Dharma* as such, but *Dharma* in general, which had been threatened by an alien enemy. Religion did not mean, according to the ideas held by the founders and their successors, Śaivism alone or Vaiṣṇavism alone, but it embraced all the systems of religious thought. It is this broadminded policy of toleration which is to be admired in the history of the empire. Such a policy was not so successfully followed by any other dynasty before Vijayanagara. It must, however, be admitted that the times were such that the Vijayanagara rulers could not but follow such a policy. This is indeed the truth but one must admit that Hinduism never demanded from its devotees that those who disbelieved its doctrines deserved death. Religious persecution on a vast scale and wars in the name of a particular sect are less frequent, and in fact almost nil, during the Vijayanagara regime than in former days. Such a policy of toleration was laid down in a statesmanlike manner by one of the earliest kings of the empire. When dispute arose between the Vaiṣṇavas and the Jainas, Bukka I according to some records of 1368 A.D. (*E.C.*, II, SB. 136), declared that "there was no difference between the Vaiṣṇava *darśana* (or faith) and the Jaina *darśana*...... If loss or advancement should be caused to the Jaina *darśana* through the *bhaktas* (Vaiṣṇavas), the Vaiṣṇavas will kindly deem it as loss or advancement caused to their (own *darśana*). The Śrīvaiṣṇavas will to this effect kindly set up a *śāsana* in all the *bastis* of the kingdom. For as long as the sun and moon endure the Vaiṣṇava creed will continue to protect the Jaina *darśana*." It is very difficult to find in the various records of South Indian dynasties that ruled the land, an incident that can parallel this. The policy of mutual trust and toleration so admirably expounded by Bukka I in the early and precarious stages of the existence of the empire characterize the religious policy of the rulers who followed him. This aspect of life in Vijayanagara was the admiration of various foreign travellers who visited the empire from its rise to its fall and even later on. One of them, by name Barbosa, states, "The king allows, such freedom that every man may come and go, and live according to his own creed without suffering any annoyance, and without inquiry, whether he is a Christian, Jew, Moor or Heathen. Great equity and justice is observed by all." Religious controversies and bigotry of the 12th and 13th centuries were totally absent from the 14th century onwards, thus assuring to the people a calm and prosperous existence under the ægis of the empire.

It is another boast of the founders of the empire and their successors that they were the custodians of the ancient customs of the land—*pūrvada paddati* or *maryāde*. It is this sense of responsibility that endeared them to the people. So scrupulously and zealously did they respect the established principles of the land that it gave their administration a conservative bias. The founders never deliberately changed the existing structure of government in the villages. If at all the democratic spirit and the local autonomy of the village government was lost, the charge can never be laid at the doors of the founders and their successors; but rather it is due to circumstances absolutely unconnected with the policy of the emperors. The renewal of old grants, the mention of the old names of towns and districts together with the new ones given under the Vijayanagara regime, the retention of the old territorial divisions of the land, the liberty the rulers gave for the circulation of old currency—all these facts illustrate the care with which the emperors managed the empire without injuring the feelings of their subjects and the respect which they showed to the dynasties of old.

The masterly policy of non-intervention followed in religious affairs by the emperors was, with equal force, applied to social matters. In matters spiritual the policy was the protection of *Dharma* understood in its widest sense; in matters social, it was the protection of the various *varṇāśrama dharmas—sakala varṇāśrama dharmagaḷanu pratipālisuvadu—i.e.*, the peaceful observation of the rules of conduct as enjoined by the castes to which one belonged. If at all there was any intervention in social matters on the part of the state, it was because the rulers found that intervention was necessary to guarantee peaceful life. Often state-enforcement of certain local legislation was sought for. In 1425 A.D. the Brahmans of the Paḍaiviḍu *Rājya* (the present South and North Arcot Districts), belonging to the Karnāṭaka, Tamiḷ, Telugu and Lāṭa (Gujarat) sections, met together in the presence of the god Gōpinātha of Arkapuṣkaraṇi, drew up a document stating that those Brahmans who conclude a marriage except by *kanyādāna*, should be liable to punishment by the king and be excommunicated (*S.I.I.*, I, No. 56). Only in such serious matters was interference sought from the king. The record reveals, moreover, the extent of harm done by the dowry system, and the seriousness with which the people regarded it and their attempts to check it under the benevolent rule of the emperors.

A policy of impartiality was followed by the emperors in their encouragement of literature and literary activity. Patronage was extended to all languages—Samskṛta, Telugu, Tamiḷ and Kannaḍa. Under their fostering care, some of the finest works of literature were produced. The sixteenth century especially, when Kṛṣṇadēva Rāya the Great was the emperor, Vijayanagara was the venue of great literary figures. This reign " marks the dawn of a new era in the literary history of South India. Himself a scholar, a musician, and a poet, he loved to gather around him poets, philosophers, and religious teachers whom he honoured with munificent gifts of land and money." (V. Ramanayya, *Studies in the History of the Third Dynasty of Vijayanagara*, p. 420). The emperors of the last dynasty, notwithstanding the fall in their fortune, never hesitated to extend their patronage to the poets and religious teachers of the time. Even the petty chiefs of the emperors took some pride in being patrons to the literary figures living in their *Rājyas*. There were also authors among the emperors and their relatives. Gaṅgadēvi's *Madhura Vijayam* is a fine example of literary composition in Samskṛta and is of immense historical value. Works on music, dancing, drama, grammar, logic, philosophy, etc., found well-deserved praise and encouragement from the kings and their ministers.

In their commercial relations within their empire and outside there is hardly a state in the history of South India that carried so extensive a trade. From Portugal in the west to China in the east the empire of Vijayanagara, for more than three centuries carried on a busy commercial intercourse. Calicut was an important port on the west coast but the empire, according to the testimony of the reliable 'Abdur Razzāq, had "three hundred ports each of which was equal to Calicut." Articles of trade were of a diverse nature, trade having been carried on in rubies, pearls and all kinds of jewels, horses, elephants, silks and all kinds of cotton cloths, spices, drugs, iron, silver, and many other articles. In this connection the political maxims followed by emperor Kṛṣṇadēva Rāya may be found interesting. "A king," so states the Āmuktamālyada (Canto, IV, v. 245), "should improve the harbours of his country and so encourage its commerce that horses, elephants, precious stones, sandalwood, pearls and other articles are freely imported into his country. He should arrange that the foreign sailors who land in his country on account of storms, illness and exhaustion are looked after in a manner suitable to their nationalities. He should set his own favourites to look after the gardens, herds of cattle and mines of the state." In another verse (v. 258) it is stated: "Make the merchants of distant foreign countries who import elephants and good horses attached to yourself by providing them with villages and decent dwellings in the city, by affording them daily audience, presents and allowing decent profits. Then those articles will never go to your enemies." It was this benevolent policy of the rulers that attracted the Arab and Portuguese merchants to the empire. And therefore the words of Barbosa have in them some truth when he says,, "There is an infinite trade in this city, and strict justice and truth are observed towards all by the governors of the country." (Stanley's translation, p. 86).

In the early years of its existence the founders and their successors had to concentrate chiefly on the political defence of the infant state, so that they could not pay great attention to the development of art and architecture. The early style was essentially an imitation of the Karnāṭaka style of the Kadamba period. Temples such as the Gānagitti temple at Hampi and the so-colled Jaina *bastis* savour of the Kadamba style with their horizontal stages of the *vimānas*. With the accession of emperor Kṛṣṇadēva Rāya we have a glorious period in Vijayanagara art and architecture. It was in his period that the well-known Hazāra Rāma Temple was built. " Although comparatively a small building, it is one of the most perfect specimens of Hindu temple architecture of the Vijayanagara period in existence " (Longhurst, *Hampi Ruins*, p. 69). Amidst the ruins of this old capital of the Hindu empire there is perhaps no other building, so ornate in its workmanship and so beautiful in its carvings as to provide a very absorbingly interesting example of Vijayanagara style of architecture to a student of its art and history. The Viṭṭalasvāmi temple is also a good specimen of Vijayanagara architecture. " In spite of the fact that the roof over the magnificent hall," says Longhurst referring to the ruined shrine, " was never completed and that many of its beautiful pillars have been grievously damaged by the destroyers of the city, it is still the finest building of its kind in Southern India, and to quote Fergusson—' shows the extreme limit in florid magnificence to which the style advanced ' " (*Ibid*., p. 126-7). These instances are enough to convince one that the empire of Vijayanagara showed its greatness in South Indian art and architecture as well.

Nor was the empire less in extent and resources than the others that preceded it. In the South, not to refer to the history of the northern dynasties, history consisted of the attempts of the various dynasties to found an empire and their struggles to maintain and extend it. No line of rulers succeeded so well as the emperors of Vijayanagara. Their empire was the most extensive and their resources incredibly limitless. The dynasties that existed at the time submitted to their rule after no great resistance. Foreign travellers speak with admiration and wonder of the resources which the emperors commanded in times of war and the revenues they had in times of peace. " This country is so well populated that it is impossible in a reasonable space to convey an idea of it," so states ' Abdur Razzāq (Elliot, IV, p. 109). " In the king's treasury," continues the Persian ambassador, " there are chambers, with excavations in them, filled with molten gold, forming one mass." Paes and Nuniz, two other chronicles also refer to the revenues of the emperors derived from the provinces. It is unnecessary for us to refer to other authorities, but suffice it to say, that the history of South India can hardly present an example of an empire that can equal the empire of Vijayanagara in its extent and resources.

In the rapid survey of the history of Vijayanagara in its cultural aspect we brought home the point that it stood as the bulwark of Hinduism for more than two and a half centuries. In the protection it afforded to Hindu culture, the encouragement it gave to art and literature, the fostering care with which it looked after the prosperity of its subjects many times harassed, often beaten though always holding their own against the Muhammadans, Vijayanagara affords a noble example of a great empire. Its policy of religious toleration and non-intervention in social affairs deserve the greatest praise. Being an empire founded chiefly for the protection of *Dharma,* it proved to be the asylum of the much-harassed Hindus who looked upon its rulers as the true representatives of all that was noble in Hindu culture. So perfectly did the empire represent the ancient glory of Hinduism, that we can with ample justification say that it stands out as a synthesis of Hindu culture.

3
Hinduism under Vijayanagara Kings

BY

MR. R. RAMA RAO, B.A.,
Assistant to the Director of Archæology, Mysore.

IN no country is religion so closely interwoven with the life of the people as in India. All their habits, usages or laws connected with their daily life, their food, dress, houses, social or political life are greatly influenced by religion. The rise of the Vijayanagara kingdom in the fourteenth century was mainly due to the universal desire felt all over South India among all classes of Hindus to protect their *Dharma* against the inroads of enemies. The only method of protecting their *Svadharma* was believed to be the establishment of *Svarājya* which would be sufficiently strong to maintain itself against the disruptive influences in South India and subdue the enemies of Hinduism and nourish the religious, social educational and economic institutions in the country. We find later that similar ideas of Svadharma and Svarājya influenced the actions of Śivāji and his followers and led to the rise of the Maratha kingdom. Śivāji is believed to have taken Rāmarāya, the Vijayanagara king who was slain in the battle of Tāḷikoṭa (or Rakkasa Tangaḍi) in 1565 as his ideal and worked hard at the establishment of a Hindu kingdom.

India south of the Vindhyas first experienced the horrors of a foreign conquest in 1294 when Allāuddin Khilji, nephew of the Sultan of Delhi invaded the Hindu kingdom of Dēvagiri and exacted a heavy tribute from its Yādava king Rāmadeva. The Mussalman attacks on the Dekhan and south of India followed in rapid succession. His general Malik Kāfur, subdued the Yādavas and the Hoysaḷa Baḷḷāḷa kings of Dorasamudra, and over-ran the whole of the Coromandel Coast, and Muhammadan garrisons were set up at Madura, the ancient Pāṇḍyan capital. The Kākatīya king of Wārangal named Pratāpa Rudra, was defeated and made to pay tribute. During the reign of Muhammad bin Toglakh (1321-1351) the Mussalman conquest of the South was more complete. Devagiri and Wārangal became parts of the Delhi empire. Dorasamudra fell in about 1327-8 and was sacked. The Raja of Kampili near Anegondi was subdued, and his sons were taken prisoners and converted to Islam. Thus the whole of India south of the Vindhyas including Malabār fell into the hands of the Mussalmans about 1336 A.D. and Muhammadan garrisons were set up in important places like Madura. Many cities had been pillaged during the conquest and the temples including the famous Ranganātha temple at Śrīrangam were attacked. It seemed as if the horrors of the foreign occupation in the North would repeat themselves in the South and the religion, honour and property of the inhabitants south of the Vindhyas were in great danger. The rule of the old dynasties, the Kākatīyas, the Hoyśaḷas and the Pāṇḍyas still nominally continued in some places but it was merely a shadow of what it was before.

It was at this time, i.e. in about 1336 that a new kingdom came into the scene as the saviour of Hinduism. Attempts had been made before by the old powers in the South to unite and oppose the Mussalmans, but internecine wars broke out every now and then, and they had found themselves powerless before the invaders. The only way to effectively protect the country against the foreign aggression seemed to lie in the establishment of a strong central kingdom in the South corresponding to the Delhi kingdom in the North. This great task was achieved, to some extent, by the founding of the Vijayanagara kingdom by Harihara I and his brothers in about 1336. He and his successors ruled all the territory south of the Tungabhadrā river for nearly 300 years and saved the Hindu Dharma in all the area from ruin.

It is only natural in the circumstances that the new kingdom of Vijayanagara should have *Svadharma* or *Ārya-Dharma,* the religion and culture of the Hindus as its supreme goal. This also explains the easy conquest of a large country from Bādāmi (in Bijapur District) to Nellore in the east, and the whole of the Maisur State and Malabār and a considerable portion of the southern peninsula by Harihara I and his brothers and generals within 10 years after the foundation of the kingdom. This conquest is testified to by various stone inscriptions of Hariyappa Vodeyer, . . . (Harihara I) : one at Bādāmi dated Ś. 1261, one in Mālur Taluka, Kolar District of Ś. 1268, another in Nellore District referring to the rule of Kampa I, younger brother of Harihara I, another at Gaṇḍasi, Arsikere Taluka, Hassan district of Ś. 1265 which gives imperial titles to Harihara I, another in Tirthahaḷḷi Taluka, Shimoga District dated Ś. 1269, another in Bangalore Taluka referring to the rule of Harihara I and Bukka I dated Ś.1268. It is stated in the South Canara Manual (Vol. I, p. 55) that by A.D. 1336 that Bairarasu Voḍeyars of the west coast had been forced to acknowledge the suzerainty of Vijayanagara and that a fort had been built at

Bārakūru by Harihara I (See the Government of India Archæological Report for 1907-08, p. 236)

The inscriptions and literary evidence which testify to the growth of the Vijayanagara empire also contain clear proofs of the nature of the conquests which were aimed at freeing the country from the rule of the *Turushkas,* and protecting or restoring the ancient temples demolished by them and making grants for the gods and priests and the *Maṭṭs.* Thus the Bādāmi inscription of Ś. 1261 speaks of the gift of Bādāmi to the two thousand (Brāhmans) by the governor Chāmēyanāyaka under the orders of Harihara I. A set of copper-plates at Kāṭavaḷḷi, Sorab Taluk, Shimoga District, dated 1347 A.D. (Epigraphia Carnatica Vol. VIII Sorab 375) describe the rule of Mārappa Voḍeyar, younger brother of Harihara I, and the grant of an *agrahāra* made under his orders by his house minister Mādhavamantrin. Here we are told that in the Kali age, evil having greatly increased, Dharma seeing that it was impossible for it to move about went to the Creator and said, "With only one leg left how can I travel about in the troubles of the Kali age ?" Hearing this the father (Creator) made in the great royal line of which Sailānka (?) was the lord, a king named Sangama. From the king Sangama's wife Kāmāmbikā were born Harihara", etc. This shows that in the reign of Harihara I the idea that the new dynasty arose for the protection of Hindu Dharma was clearly understood by all. Mārappa is stated in the record to have been ruling at Chandragupti (Chandragutti), and that in a successful expedition against the Kādamba king he paid a visit to the sacred place called Gōkarṇa, and while there he bathed in the water of the ocean at the time of the *parva,* pouring a libation to the manes and made gifts to Brāhmans of lands, cows and gold in quantities. And there he also bathed Mahābala with cool water, musk, camphor, sandal and saffron freely and offered golden flowers. We can see from this that the Vijayanagara kings and princes were highly pious and devoted to the performance of *Dharma* as laid down in the Śāstras. Another record belonging to the above minister Mādhavamantrin, the Kuchēra copper-plate grant of 1391 published in J. B. Br. A. S. IV. pp. 115-116 tells us that by the order of the king Harihara II Mādhavamantrin governed Jayantīpura (Banavāse) and subdued Goa and banished all the numerous *Turushkas* infesting that country and set up again Saptakōṭīśvara, and the other ancient deities that had been rooted up and thrown away by them. Next we have the stone inscription at Śringeri dated 1346 A.D. which records a grant of land made for the benefit of the Guru Bhāratitīrtha made and his disciples at Śringeri by Harihara I and all his brothers, Aliya

Ballappa-daṇṇāyaka, Kumāra Sōvaṇṇ Oḍeyar and others. This grant is said to have been made by Harihara I who had conquered the earth from the eastern to the western ocean, in order to celebrate the festival of his victory. This is another proof of the solicitude shown by the Vijayanagara kings for the maintenance of Dharma by liberally endowing the *Maṭṭ* at Śringeri whose *gurus* Vidyātīrtha (who is described in the record as having a form of celestial glory whose friendship gained is never lost) and Bhāratitīrtha were learned ascetics and teachers. Among other princes or generals who helped the cause of Hindu rule under Vijayanagara empire may be mentioned Channappa, son of Mallappa Voḍeyar, younger brother of Harihara II who drove the *Turushkas* from the Ādavāni-durga (Adoni) and kingdom (in Bellary District) (Epigraphia Carnatica XII Kunigal Taluka, 43 of Ś. 1302), and the general Guṇḍa into the flames of whose valour the Yavanas, *Turushkas* and Āndhras fell like moths according to an inscription at Bēlūr, Hassan District (Epigraphia Carnatica V. Bēlūr, 3 of 1397). In the south of the peninsula we learn from the Kamparāyacharitra of Gangādēvi that Kampaṇa, son of Bukka I, marched against the Tuṇḍīra country (Toṇḍamaṇḍala), and after defeating Champarāya and reducing Kāñchī, he proceeded against the king of the *Turushkas* who had his headquarters at Madura. A goddess appeared before the prince Kampaṇa, and, after describing to him the consequences of the Mussalman invasions of the south and the sad plight of the southern country and its temples, exhorted him to extirpate the invaders and restore the country to its ancient glory and presented him with a sword. Kampaṇa then proceeded against Madura and in a battle killed the Sultan ruling in the place. He then made grants to several temples.

The above instances prove that the Vijayanagara kings had as their chief aim the protection of the Hindu *Dharma*. We have now to study the different sects or faiths that comprised the Hindu religion at the time the Vijayanagara kingdom arose, and the treatment accorded to each by the successive sovereigns of Vijayanagara. Traditionally there were four *Samayas* or sects in the country, viz., Mahēśvara (Śaiva), Bauddha, Vaishnava and Ārhata (Jaina), and we find kings and queens and generals taking the title of *Chatus-samaya-samuddharaṇa,* supporter of the four faiths (see Epigraphia Carnatica, Vol. XII, Chiknāyakanhaḷḷi Taluk 13 of 1181 A.D.). Of these Buddhism seems to have had very little influence in the Karnāṭaka. Jainism was still professed by several nobles and merchants and gauḍas, etc.; but it had to struggle hard against the rising popular sects established by Rāmānujāchārya and Basavēshwara and was already waning at the time that Harihara I established the Vijayanagara kingdom. Amongst the Jaina officers of Harihara II was Irugappa-dandanātha who granted Śravana Beḷgoḷa with a tank built by him for the god Gommaṭēśvara (*Śravaṇa Beḷgoḷa Volume of Inscriptions Revised,* p. 64). The king Devarāya I had a Jaina queen named Bhīmādēvi (*Ibid.,* p. 64). The Jaina guru Abhavachandra is called rāya-rājaguru-maṇḍalāchārya in an epitaph recording the death of a gauḍa by *samādhi* in 1415 A.D. in Sorab Taluk, Shimoga District (Epigraphia Carnatica, Vol. VIII, Sorab Taluk 329). Jainism was powerful in the Kaḷasa Kārkaḷa kingdom in the west, and its rulers erected gigantic images of Gōmaṭa at Kārkaḷa in 1432 and at Vēnūr (in South Kanara) in 1603. But except in the west Jainism gradually declined. There was a powerful struggle for supremacy between the Jainas and the followers of Rāmānujāchārya (Śrīvaishṇavas), and the latter persecuted the Jainas very much at the beginning of the reign of Bukka I. Bukka composed the differences between the sects in 1268, and, assembling the leaders of both the sects, placed the hand of the Jains in the hand of the Śrīvaishṇavas and declared that there was no difference between the Vaishṇava and the Jaina creeds. The Śrīvaishṇavas had to appoint 20 servants as a body-guard for the god at Śravaṇa Beḷgoḷa and repair the ruined Jaina temples (*Śravaṇa Beḷgoḷa Volume of Inscriptions,* Revised, Intro. pp. 63-64). This policy of complete religious freedom was the keystone of administration under the Vijayanagara kings and even Mussalmans and Christians who lived in peace were accorded religious freedom during their rule.

Although the kings of Vijayanagara treated all religions with respect and liberality, yet we can see that there were three stages in the history of the religious faiths followed by the Vijayanagara kings. The first stage extends from 1336, the year of the foundation of the empire, according to tradition, up to 1467 when Virūpāksha the last of the Sangama dynasty of kings began his rule. During this period of nearly 100 years the Vijayanagara kings mostly favoured Śaivism or Advaitism. The Kāḷāmukha sect of the Śaivas which stood for the supremacy of the god Śiva, the *Vedic dharmas* and the rules of conduct laid down in the Śāstras for the different *varṇas* (castes) and *Āśramas* (stages of life) was highly respected and patronised. The priests of this sect were learned in all the branches of learning prevalent at the time, and were the great educationists, religious preachers and the managers of the Śiva temples from about the 8th century A.D. Their religion known also as the Nakulīśa Pāśupata, or Lakuṭāgama, has been noticed by Mādhavāchārya in his work Sarvadarśanasangraha, and differed from, to the extent of being opposed to, the Advaita system to which the writers belonged. The title Advaita-bhuja-kuṭhāra has been applied in an inscription at Beḷgāmi in Shikārpur Taluk to Lakulīśvara-paṇḍita, a priest of the Kāḷāmukha school in 1036 (Epigraphia Carnatica Vol. VII, Shikarpur 126). At the time the Vijayanagara history opens Kāśīvilāsa Kriyāśakti was the chief guru of the Kāḷāmukhas. He was regarded as an incarnation of Śiva himself. He is called the *Kulaguru*, family preceptor in religion, of Harihara II in an inscription of 1378. This shows that he was also regarded as a *guru* by Harihara I and Harihara II (Epigraphia Carnatica Vol. V, Channarāyapaṭna Taluk 256). The title Rāyarājagurū-maṇḍalāchārya and Rāyarājagurū-pitāmaha are applied to him in certain inscriptions (Epigraphia Carnatica XI, Davangere 23 of Ś. 1332 of Devarāya I, and Mysore Archæological Report for the year 1912, p. 47. Harihar Plates of Ś. 1320). Mādhavamantri, the governor of Chandragutti, Āraga and Konkaṇa and the conqueror of Goa calls Kriyāśakti as his *guru* both in inscriptions (Epigraphia Carnatica, Vol. VII, Sorab 375, Kāṭavaḷḷi Plates of 1347), and in his work, *Tātparyadīpikā,* a commentary on the *Sūtasamhitā,* a *Pauranic* treatise. This work showed the enlightenment of the Kāḷāmukha gurus. The author quotes not only from *Śaiva Āgamas* like *Mrigēndrasamhitā,* but also from the works of Śankarāchārya, *Bhāgavata Purāṇam* and *Bhagavadgitā.* The last of the inscriptions that refers to Kriyāśakti is the Daṇḍapalle copper-plate grant of Ś. 1332 recording the gift of Kriyāśaktipura near Daṇḍapalle in Chittoor District by the king Vijayabhūpati. In addition to the above kings Harihara II, Devaraja I, Vijayabhūpati, the ministers Mādhavamantri, Muddadaṇḍeśa and Viṭṭhaṇṇa Oḍeyar, governor of Āraga, from 1403 to 1407, were all disciples of Kriyāśakti.

After 1410 we hear very little of the Kāḷāmukha priests. It is possible that the democratic *Lingāyat* sect, (and the enlightened *Advaita* religion ?) absorbed the Kāḷāmukhas and they practically disappear from history.

We may also note here the part played by the Śaiva schools not belonging to the Kāḷāmukha sect. Foremost among them is the Śaiva-siddhānta noticed in the *Sarvadarśana-sangraha.* Its votaries are more numerous in the Tamil Districts of Southern India. The 63 Nāyanārs who sang the praise of the Śaiva centres of pilgrimage in the south in their Dēvāram songs and who were popular preachers and devotees of Śaivism, belonged to this sect. The Śiva-dvijas or Śiva-Brāhmaṇas mentioned as the officiating priests in the

Śaiva temples at Āvani, Kuruḍumale, etc., in Kolar District Inscriptions, probably belonged to this school though to-day their descendants and the Brāhmaṇa priests in all the important Śaiva temples who are also Śiva-Brāhmaṇas profess the religion of Advaitism as taught by Śankarāchārya.

The Vīraśaiva or Lingāyat sect which was promulgated in the Karṇāṭaka by Basavaṇṇa in the reign of Bijjaḷa 1156-1167 was an offshoot of Śaivism. It was influenced by the teaching of the Tamil Nāyanārs. It differed from the older faiths in that it admitted members of all castes (except the Panchamas or Pariahs) to its fold on a basis of complete religious equality and to some extent of social equality. The Vedic ceremonies and rules of conduct were discarded, and worship of Śiva and devotion to Śiva and the *Jangamas* (or Vīra-Śaiva priests) took their place in this sect. On account of these features it attracted to its fold mostly people of other castes than Brāhmaṇas. The work *Channabasava Purāṇa,* a Kannaḍa poem written by Virūpāksha-paṇḍita in 1584 A.D., tells us that Prauḍhadeva Rāya (1419-1446) revered and patronised the *Lingāyat Gurus* Kerasthaḷada Vīraṇṇa and *Guru* Basaveśa, and that he even gave his daughter in marriage to the former. Various miracles are attributed to these *gurus.* The poem also tells us that this religion declined again till the reign of Āravīṭi kings (viz., Aḷiya Rāmarāya and his successors). After this once again great *Gurus* like Gosala, Channabasava, Toṇṭaḍa Siddhalinga propagated the teachings of this sect, and we find many subordinate chiefs of the Vijayanagara kingdom like the Keḷadi Nāyakas, Ummuṭṭur Voḍeyars, Muddagiri gauḍas embracing this Lingayata or Vīraśaiva religion. This poem ends with a prophecy that in the reign of Vīra Vasanta commencing from Kali 4683 (1582 A.D.) the Vīraśaivas would rise to power, and that a minister of that sect would become the minister and restore Kalyāṇa the centre of activities of Basavaṇṇa to its original glory.

ADVAITISM

We shall now go back to the reign of Harihara I, the founder of the Vijayanagara kingdom. In spite of the prevalence of sects, like the Śaiva or Vaishṇava, devoted to the exclusive worship of one god Śiva or Vishṇu and laying great stress on *bhakti* or devotion, as contrasted with *Karma* or action as laid down in the Vedas and Smritis and Purāṇas and Dharma-śastras, or Jñana (knowledge as taught in the Upanishads Vedānta Sūtras, etc., which were all in Sanskrit), the mass of the people still continued to pay homage to all the gods of the Hindu patheon believing them to be the manifestations of the one Supreme Spirit (Paramātman). They also believed in the efficacy of the Vedic rites, or ceremonies performed by the Brāhmaṇas, for increasing the prosperity of the country by causing rain to fall, cultivation to prosper by warding off diseases, etc. The old law of *Varṇāśrama-dharma,* as laid down in the Vedas, *Smritis,* and *Dharma-śāstras* enjoining each caste to attend to its hereditary duties, seemed to them to bring about prosperity and contentment. It is only natural to believe that the school of *Śankarāchārya* (known as the Advaita or Smārta sect) which admitted in worldly life the equality of gods and the efficacy of Vedic sacrifices or ceremonies and Varnāśrama-dharma, should receive the highest support of Harihara I and his immediate successors. Thus although Kriyāśakti was styled *rājaguru,* and treated with great respect, Harihara I, Bukka and Harihara II paid greater attention to the teachings and advice of the Brāhmaṇa scholars of the *Advaita* sect. It was fortunate for the *Advaita* sect that, during the reigns of Harihara I and Bukka I, a towering personality like Vidyātīrtha was the head of the monastery at Śringeri. He was a learned Vedic teacher and is called a Maheśvara whose breath was the Veda by his disciple Sāyaṇāchārya in the Vedic commentaries. He collected around him numerous learned Brāhmans who all became his disciples. Among these may be mentioned Bhāratitīrtha, who was the virtual head of the Śringeri Maṭṭ under Vidyātīrtha, and the author of Vaiyāsika-nyāyamālā treating of the Vedānta Sūtras; Vidyāraṇya successor of Bhāratitīrtha in the Śringeri Maṭṭ and author of Vivaraṇapramēya Sangraha, a work on Advaita philosophy, etc.; Mādhavāchārya, author of a commentary on Parāśarasmriti, a work on Mīmāmsa, and the Hindu calendar (Kāla-nirṇaya); his brother Sāyaṇāchārya, author of a work on Sanskrit verbs and rhetoric, and the Vedic commentaries, etc.; Chauṇḍapa, a disciple, Bhāratitīrtha and author of Prayōga-ratnamālā dealing with ritual, etc. All these have invoked Vidyātīrtha in one work or other composed by them.

In addition to their religious and literary activities Vidyātīrtha and his school actively assisted the early Vijayanagara kings with their counsels in the government of the people. Harihara I showed great regard for Vidyātīrtha by making a gift of lands to the maṭṭa at Śringeri conjointly with his brothers in 1346 A.D. (Epigraphia Carnatica, Vol. VI, Śringeri 1). His successor, Bukka I, went all the way to Śringeri in 1356 to pay his respects to Vidyātīrtha. He also was a disciple both of Bhāratitīrtha and Vidyāraṇya (Mysore Archæological Report for 1916, pp. 56, 59). In an inscription of 1377

Bukka I is called the moon to the ocean of kindness of Vidyātīrtha, and his incarnation for the enjoyment of worldly pleasures (Epigraphia Carnatica, Vol. IV, Yedatore 46). As regards Vidyāraṇya a record of the Śringeri maṭṭa says that Harihara II acquired the empire of knowledge unattainable by other kings by the grace of Vidyāraṇya (Mysore Archæological Report for 1916, p. 58). The Hosahaḷḷi plates of Harihara II dated 1384 describe Harihara as

महानुभावानां क्रियाशक्तिविद्यारण्यश्रीचरणानामुपदेशजनिततत्वप्रकाशक

(J.B.H.S., Bombay, 1928, Vol. I, pp. 1-6).

Mādhavāchārya calls himself वीरबुक्कभूपालसाम्राज्यधुरंधर in his commentary on the Parāśara *smriti*. His brother, Sāyaṇāchārya, was at first attached to the Court of Kampaṇa, younger brother of Harihara I, who ruled in the Nellore District, and later he was connected with an expedition against Champanarēndra, and, after serving under Kampa's son Sangama II, came to Bukka I at Vijayanagara and wrote numerous works including his famous commentaries on the Vedas in which he calls himself at first the minister of Bukka I and later Harihara II. Chauṇḍapa was attached to the Court of Vīrabhūpati, grandson of Harihara II. Outside the school of Vidyātīrtha flourished Śankarānanda whom Vidyāraṇya invokes at the beginning of his works *Vivaṛna-prameya-sangraha* and *Panchadaśi*, and Sarvajña-vishṇu invoked by Sāyaṇa-Mādhavāchārya in his Sarvadarśanasangraha. The Kānchi *Mutt* tradition equates the first with a *guru* of that Mutt of the same name, and a disciple of Vidyātīrtha, and the second with Vidyātīrtha himself. But this tradition is not based on any inscription or contemporary literary work discovered so far.

We may note here that all the political and literary activities of Vidyātīrtha and his school has been generally ascribed to the genius of Vidyāraṇya who is equated with Mādhavāchārya. But some scholars dispute this view of Vidyāraṇya's political work as it is unsupported by contemporary inscriptions and literary works, and as this work of his, first comes to notice in the 16th century in the works of Nuniz, etc. Chief among these is Rev. H. Heras, Bombay. Similarly Vidyāraṇya's identity with Mādhava is questioned as it is opposed to Vidyāraṇya-Kālājñāna and Guruvamśakāvya, and the contemporary literary evidence does not support the identity and is even opposed to it (see my article on the identity of Vidyāraṇya in the Indian Historical Quarterly, Calcutta, Vols. VI and VII). The question cannot be considered here as it is outside the scope of this article.

After the death of Vidyāraṇya in 1386 a grant was made by Harihara II of the *Vidyāraṇyapura agrahāra* in his memory. But beyond a few grants made in the reign of Devarāya II, the Śringeri Mutt did not receive any great patronage from the later Vijayanagara kings.

ŚRĪVAISHṆAVA AND MĀDHVA SECTS

The Advaita school so ably led by Vidyātīrtha and Vidyāraṇya, etc., had to compete with two other schools for power and influence. The Śrīvaishṇava sect founded by Rāmanujāchārya based on the teachings of the Vedas, Smritis and Purāṇas, and also on the Tamil hymns of the Dravidian saints of various castes called Āḷvārs, received support from the Hoysaḷa king Vishṇuvardhana who is believed to have become a convert to this religion in 1116. The great temple of Keśava at Bēlūr was built by the king and entrusted to the Śrivaishṇavas, as the followers of Rāmānujāchārya were called. This religion gradually spread in South India and Mysore. The great family of Perumāḷa-daṇṇāyaka who were the governors of the south of Mysore in the last quarter of the 15th century belonged to this school. But soon however internecine wars broke out between two sects of this school called Tengalai and Vaḍagalai, the first standing for the superiority of the Tamil *prabandhams* (hymns of the Āḷvārs) over the Sanskrit Vedas, of *Prapatti* (self-surrender to God and Guru) over *karma* (daily ceremonies enjoined by Śāstras), etc., while the second stood for the ancient Sanskrit culture and the Vedic ceremonies and the caste system. This weakened the position of the Śrīvaishṇavas for a time. Fortunately for this sect a great teacher called Venkaṭanātha or Vēdānta Dēśika was born in Kāñchī in 1269 A.D. and his teachings of the ancient Śāstras in the sacred temples of Kāñchī, Śrīrangam, etc., his victories over *Advaitis*, and his numerous works in Sanskrit on philosophy and religion, and above all his selfless service in the cause of religion and scrupulous observance of *dharma* as laid down in the Śāstras gave a new impetus to the growth of the religion of Rāmānuja. He is said to have lived till 1371 A.D. In his time the Mussalmans attacked the temple of Śrīrangam, and he was able to organise a party to save the idols thereof and also books including a manucript copy of Sudharśanāchārya's commentary on *Śrībhāshya*. The idols were transferred to various places like Melkote and Tirupati, and restored to Śrīrangam after the Turushkas were driven out. Thus Vēdānta Dēśika was one of those who prayed for and actively co-operated in freeing the south of India from its iconoclastic aggressors. But he did not go to the Court of Vijayanagara, or participate in its political affairs like Vidyātīrtha, and his school. The Tengalai school too had at this time a powerful teacher, Piḷḷai Lōkāchārya, as its guru.

Another sect which was a powerful rival of the *Advaita* school was the *Dvaita* school of Mādhvācharya. This school inculcated, like the Śrīvaishṇavas, the supreme position of Vishṇu as god and the attainment of salvation by man by devotion to him. People of all castes, men and women could get salvation if only they meditated on Vishṇu knowing his supreme qualities and the eternal differences between God, Prakrti (nature) and Souls. In addition to this knowledge and devotion, performance of religious ceremonies or duties according to *Varṇāśrama-Dharma* was enjoined on all. Madhvāchārya flourished from 1238 to 1318. His disciples continued his work. Akshobhyatīrtha, one of his disciples succeeded to the pontificate in 1350, and exercised spiritual jurisdiction for 15 years till 1365. His successor was Jayatīrtha who was the pontiff from 1365 to 1388, and wrote learned commentaries on Mādhvācharya's works. A disputation is said to have taken place in the Court of king Bukka I between Vidyāraṇya, the *guru* of the *Advaita* sect and Akshobhyatīrtha with Vēdānta Dēśika as the arbitrator. Both the Mādhvas and Śrīvaishṇavas state in their works (See Jayatīrtha-vijaya by Vyāsatīrtha, Sankarshaṇatīrtha, etc., and Guruparaṃparāprabhavam and Vedāntāchārya Vaibhava-prakāśam of Doḍḍayācharya) that Akshobhyatīrtha was victorious. But the *Advaitis* claim that Vidyāraṇya was able to stem the opposition of his rivals (see the Introduction to Yādavābhyudaya, Śrīrangam). This disputation could only have taken place before Vidyāraṇya became pontiff of the Śringeri Mutt if the Mādhva chronology is to be accepted. It is also stated that Vidyāraṇya once met Jayatīrtha and appreciating his learning had him taken in a procession on an elephant. The Mādhva *gurus* did not trouble themselves with political affairs till the time of Śripādarāya at the end of the 15th century.

LATER VIJAYANAGARA KINGS AND THEIR RELIGIOUS POLICY

The second stage in the history of Hinduism under the Vijayanagara kings begins from the reign of Virūpāksha (1467-1478). A *Śrīvaishṇava* work named Prapannāmritam by Anantāchārya tells us that this king who had been a Śaiva before like his ancestors became a devotee of Vishṇu, and a disciple of Eṭṭūr Narasinhachārya, a Śrivaishṇava *guru*. It is said that this *guru* freed the spirits of the relations of the king who had been murdered by him from their bondage, and sent them to *Moksha* by expounding the Rāmāyaṇa. It is also stated, in the above work, that his nobles and subjects also followed his example. Virūpāksha was overthrown by Śaļuva Narasinha, his general, who usurped the throne. It is said in a work called Śripāḍarājāshṭaka, a poem of the Mādhva sect, that Vīra Narasinha, son of Sāļuva Narasinha (or possibly Śāļuva Narasinha himself) was freed from the sin of slaying Brāhmaṇas by the Mādhva *guru* Lakshmīnārayaṇa *yogi* called also Śrīpādāchārya. It is said that the king seated the *guru* on his throne and honoured him. His general Narasa-Nāyaka, who later usurped power, and his sons Vīra Narasinha, Krishṇarāya and Achyutarāya who succeeded him on the throne also favoured the Mādhva sect. The great Mādhva *guru* named Vyāsatīrtha, who studied under Śripādarāya, was the pontiff at this time. He changed the policy of his predecessors by openly assisting the kings, Krishṇarāya and Achyutarāya, in their political affairs and popularising the religious teachings of his sect by himself and his disciples, Purandaradāsa and Kanakadāsa, composing songs in Kannaḍa language which soon spread over the whole of the Karnāṭaka. It is said in Vyāsavijaya that he sat on the throne of Vijayanagara at the time of the inauspicious *Kuhu yoga*, and saved the king Krishṇarāya from its evil consequences. The king had him bathed in gold and gave numerous presents. Krishṇarāya was however liberal to all the sects. A *guru* of the Śringeri Mutt named Vidyāraṇya (different from his namesake of the 14th century) received grants of lands from him. A poem named Āmuktamālyadā was composed by the king in Telugu in praise of Ānḍāḷ, a woman-Āḷvār worshipped by the Śrivaishṇavas. The Kāñchi Kāmākshi *Mutt* of the *Advaita* school also received lands from him. Achyutarāya followed the same policy and gave numerous grants to learned Brāhmaṇas of all sects.

The third stage in the religious history of the Vijayanagara kings begins from the reign of Sadāśiva which nominally lasted from 1543 to 1567. But the king became a puppet in the hands of Rāmarāya, his general, who later usurped the title of the king. Rāmarāya and his descendants are classed as of the Āravīḍu dynasty. During the rule of this dynasty which lasted till about 1660, the sect of Rāmānuja gained ascendancy. The kings followed this faith, and numerous chiefs also became converts to that religion, though a few like the Keḷadi Nāyakas were Lingāyats. The family of Tātāchāryas, noted for their piety and learning and liberality, became the royal *gurus* and numerous grants were made to their family and other learned Śrīvaishṇava Brāhmans. The signature at the end of the royal grants was changed from Virūpāksha to Rāma and Venkaṭēśa. But the kings granted perfect religious freedom to all classes of Hindus, and encouraged learning irrespective of religion or sect. The *gurus* of the Mādhva sect Vijayīndra (*C.* 1539 to 1595) and Rāghavēndra (*C.* 1623 to 1671) were honoured, and received grants from the kings Śrīrangarāya I and Venkaṭapatirāya. Krishṇānanda, the head of the Bhāgavata Sampradāya *Mutt* at Muḷbāgal, in Tīrthahaḷḷi Taluka, was granted the village of Surapura by Śrīrangarāya VI in 1661. The numerous local chiefs who were subordinates of the Vijayanagara kings followed the same policy of religious toleration and liberality to temples, *matts*, priests or learned men of all sects or faiths.

4

Telugu Literature under the Vijayanagara Empire

By

Mr. K. Iswara Dutt, B.A.,
Local Fund Auditor, Cocanada.

The bulk and the best part of the Telugu literature which affords the greatest delight to the minds of the Andhras, is the product of direct patronage of Vijayanagara Emperors and their Viceroys. It is equally a striking phenomenon, that the above literature has grown both in volume and variety under each Vijayanagara Dynasty.

The first Vijayanagara dynasty, *viz.*, the Sangama Dynasty, extended its patronage to the Kannaḍa men of letters and Kannaḍa literature and some of them were authors of Kannaḍa poetical works. They did not pay equal attention to the development of Telugu Culture, though half the portion of the Empire consisted of Telugu speaking tracts. But instances were not wanting to show that they did not forget to do their duty in this respect. Bukka I gave a grant of a village of Penchukala dinne, which was named Bukkarāyapaṭnam, to Nāchana Soma, the author of Uttaraharivamśam. The poet is described in that inscription as follows.[1]

याजुषाणां वरेण्याय सकलागमवेदिने
अष्टादशपुराणानामभिज्ञातार्थवेदिने ॥
अष्टभाषाकवित्वश्री वाणी विजतसंपदे
सोमाय नाचनांबोधेः सोमयामिततेजसे ॥

Nāchana is one of the celebrated Teluge poets of the fourteenth century. He is called Sarvajña on account of his great poetical talents. Another poet of equally great merit, Jakkana, wrote Vikramārkacharitram and dedicated it to Siddana, who was a minister of Dēvarāya I. It was also stated therein, that Janna,

1. Epigraphia Carnatica, Volume X. G. D. 46 and Epigraphical Report, Southern Circle for 1907, para. 53.

father of Siddana, was also minister of the above Emperor. *Vikramārkacharitram* describes the exploits of Vikramārka, and was written in pleasing and elegant style.

It was during the reign of Dēvarāya II that the great Telugu poet, the Literary dictator of the 14th century and the Director of Public Instruction (Vidyādhikāri) under the Reḍḍi kings, visited the court of the Kannaḍa Emperor and had the unique honour of being bathed in gold in the court of that Emperor, and he boastfully depicted in the colophon of one of the cantos of *Kāśikhanḍam* written by him. He was introduced to the Royal Court by Chandraśekhara Kriyāśakti, the spiritual teacher of the Emperor and defeated the poet laureate Gauḍaḍinḍima in a literary contest. The triumph of the great Andhra poet Śrīnātha in the court of a Kannaḍa monarch demonstrates the powerful and penerating influence of the Telugu language and the Telugu men of letters in the Court, for which a strong foundation was laid by Śrīnātha, and grew from strength to strength which ultimately culminated in the usurpation of the Vijayanagara court by the Andhras and Andhra culture for nearly three centuries. Vinukonḍa Vallabhāmātya, wrote *Kriḍābhirāmam*. He was the son of Tippa, the keeper of Ratnabhanḍāra of Harihara II. This book depicts in a variety of interesting details, the social life of the Telugu people and the poet lays his scene at Wārangal, the erstwhile capital of the Kākatiyas. In the introductory verses of the book, the poet says that Sanskrit is the mother of all *Deśabhāshas* and that among the *Deśabhāshas* Telugu is the best, which sentiment, is later on solemnly repeated by Krishṇarāya in his monumental work, '*Āmuktamālyadā*'. Though we find that Telugu literature did not flourish under the direct patronage of the Sangama Dynasty, yet, it had its own striking growth during the century in which that dynasty guided the destinies of the Empire, as the few instances narrated above would demonstrate. By the middle of the fifteenth century, the Telugu influence gradually assumed a greater proportion and by the time the Sāḷuva usurper was on the scene, we witness, the Telugu poets singing his praises, acclaiming him as the greatest warrior of the day.

SĀḶUVAS

It was during the hey-day of the usurper Sāḷuva Narasiṁha, that the direct patronage of the Vijayanagara monarch was extended to Telugu letters. Telugu poets flourished in his court, wrote books, and dedicated them to him. The Emperor was a great scholar and he wrote *Rāmābhyudayam* in Sanskrit[2] and patronised Sanskrit poets. Aruṇagirinātha composed *Śaḷuvābhyudayam* and dedicated it to the Emperor. Pina Vīraṇṇa wrote Jaimini Bhāratam in Telugu and dedicated it likewise. The poet describes the pedigree and the power of the Emperor in the introduction of the work, narrates the various conquests and portrays the Emperor as a sturdy soldier and a successful statesman. The same poet composed *Śringāra Śākuntalam.* The poet made a judicious blending of the story in the Bhāratam and that of the great drama *'Abhigñāna Śākuntalam'* of Kalidasa and presented the interesting story to his people. Though the Sāḷuvas ruled the Empire for a short time, yet the contribution to the Telugu literature under their patronage is considerable, when compared with that of the previous dynasty which held sway for a century and a quarter. The influence of the Telugus in the Vijayanagara court became inevitable by this time for the following reasons.

1. The capital of the Vijayanagara Empire was not in the heart of the Kannaḍa country and it was in the border line between the two great linguistic areas even from the beginning of its foundation.

2. The extension of the Empire into the Southern districts and towards the West Coast had always been a hurdle-race for the Vijayanagara monarchs, and this occupation had never been as effective, as that of the Eastern tracts up to the Bay of Bengal.

3. That portion of the Empire comprising the modern Kurnool, Cuddapah and Nellore districts, and some portion of the Anantapur district, which are mainly of Telugu-speaking tracts, had been under the Andhra domination till the extinction of the Andhra Empire of the Kākatiyas.

4. By the end of the fourteenth century, Telugu poets of great eminence, who hailed from those districts produced already a considerable part of the best Telugu literature, and, as a natural consequence thereof, the Telugu muse, not in a surreptitious style but in a stately fashion, made her way into the Royal court of the Vijayanagara and occupied a high pedestal from the commencement of the sixteenth century.

THE TUḶUVAS —THE AUGUSTAN AGE OF TELUGU LITERATURE

It is a simple matter of fact that the Telugu literature under the Tuḷuva dynasty and its successor, the Āravīḍu dynasty, has grown

2. Sources of Vijayanagara History, page 83.

remarkably rich and known for its romantic turn and range of subject. The age of translation drew to a close and the three great *epics* and most of the *purāṇas* were already translated by that time. Even during the period of the early Tuḷuvas, Nandi Mallayya and Ghanṭa Singayya, the two poets jointly translated *Varāhapurāṇam* and dedicated that work to Narasimharāya, the father of Krishṇadēvarāya. He was described as a scion of Tuḷuva family and a great generalissimo of Sāḷuva Narasimha. The two poets translated *Prabodhachandrodayam,* the Sanskrit drama, into Telugu poetry like their predecessor Pina Vīraṇṇa, who translated Śākuntalam likewise. Vīranarasimha, the first Tuḷuva Emperor was not known to have patronised any Telugu poet but to his brother and successor Krishṇarāya that the Telugu literature owes an incalculable debt of gratitude. The age of Krishṇarāya is known as the Augustan age of Telugu literature. The Empire grew in strength and splendour. The Emperor was an accomplished monarch. The Telugu poets from Nannaya (the poet-laureate of Rājarājanarēndra) to Peddana (the poet-laureate of Krishṇarāya) have all from time to time, translated the epics and purāṇas, so much so, that Telugu literature had already become copious in that branch. The needs of the common people were fulfilled in that respect. They wanted a new theme to delight their minds and Peddana was the product of the times. He was called the 'Āndhra Kavitāpitāmaha', the grandfather of Andhra poetry. His influence in the court was so great, and the esteem of the Emperor for him was so enormous, that Krishṇarāya took the poet along with him, in his Kalinga campaigns, and granted Kokata-Agraharam from the banks of the Kistṇā during his march against the Gajapati.[3] Not only was he chosen as a poet-laureate, but also appointed as a provincial subordinate by the Emperor.[4]

Peddana wrote *Manucharitra* which describes the birth of Svārochisha manu. The episode is taken from Mārkanḍēya purāṇa and the poet improved upon it and almost made it his own. From religion to romance, from imitation to imagination, from narration to description and from ethics to aesthetics, the Telugu literature assumed a new shape and had been completely metamorphosed and Peddana was the literary dictator of the day and his work the literary model of the succeeding ages. The Prabandha period in

3. Epigraphical Report, Southern Circle; page 143. (No. 623 of appendix B.)
4. Epigraphical Report from 1921. Para 50. Melpadi Inscription.

Telugu literature was inaugurated with the production of Manucharitra.

The emperor Krishṇarāya was an accomplished scholar, in Sanskrit and Telugu and he wrote his 'magnum opus' *Āmuktamālyadā* in Telugu. In an introductory stanza of that work, he gave a number of works written by him in Sanskrit. The emperor was a staunch Vaishṇava. He described in his work the love of *Āmuktamālyadā* towards Ranganātha, the sacred deity at Śrīrangam. She was brought up by Vishṇuchitta, a pious Vaishṇava Brahman, who prayed the god Śrīranganātha, to accept his lovelorn daughter as his bride and Śrīranganātha graciously married her. But the book is very important to the South Indian historian in more than one respect. The colophons of the work, are veritable goldmines of historical information. He described, therein, all his conquests, concisely and chronologically and revealed himself not only as an emperor-poet but also a great historian. He painted on the canvas of South Indian History, vivid pictures of Vaishṇava customs and manners in the South, and in Canto IV of the work, he gave an elaborate disquisition on political philosophy disclosing his views on general polity. The book is not only an embodiment of deep scholarship but also an emblem of literary craftsmanship. The language is terse and the diction complicated. Kannaḍa words are frequently used :—

In the court of Krishṇarāya flourished the 'Asṭadiggajas,' the eight elephants who supported the world of (Telugu) literature. They were said to be :—

1. Allasani Peddana.
2. Nandi Timmana.
3. Ayyalaraju Rāmabhadrakavi.
4. Dhurjaṭi.
5. Mallana.
6. Pingali Sūranna.
7. Rāmarāja Bhushaṇa.
8. Tenāli Rāmakrishṇa Kavi.

The last three poets did not write any work during the time of Krishṇarāya and perhaps, they were very young in that period. These would be dealt with under the Āravīḍu dynasty.

Next to Peddana, the great poet was Timmana, the author of *Pārijātāpaharaṇam* which was dedicated to Krishṇarāya. It was written in a sweet style and elegant imagery. He described in it the love of Krishṇa towards his pert and jealous spouse Satyā. Himself an ardent lover of that obdurate wife, Krishṇa had to extricate himself from many a delicate predicament to please that queen. Nārada placed him in an embarrassment. He made him present the celestial flower to Rukmiṇi. This evoked jealousy in the mind of Satyā and the story of *Pārijātāpaharaṇam* is the consequence. If Rukmiṇi had to satisfy herself with a single flower brought by Nārada and presented to her by her husband, Satyā had the singular fortune of having the entire tree planted in her palace by her much-devoted husband, and had thus come out successful in the triangular fight between herself, her husband, and Rukmiṇi. It seems that Satyā rudely spurned Krishṇa when he went to her to appease her anger, and Timmana, describes the incident in a very beautiful manner Krishna bore the insult very coolly and is calmly said to have revealed his wife "O dear, I do not mind the kick. But I apologise poignantly that thy tender foot should have ached by coming in touch with my stony head."

Another great poet of the time was Rādhāmādhava Kavi. His original name was Yellaṇārya. But he had come to be known as Rādhāmādhava Kavi after he wrote *Rādhāmādhavam* and pleased the Karṇāṭa Emperor by his exhibition of great poetical talents thereby. He also wrote Vishṇumayavilāsam and Tārakabrahma Rājīyam. The latter was dedicated to Nanja Timmarsu one of the subordinates of Achyutarāya.

Before we complete the development of Telugu literature during the reign of Krishṇarāya we have to make mention of some of the Viceroy-poets of the time. Of them the most important was Nādinḍla Gopa, a nephew of Sāḷuva Timmarsu, the prime minister of Krishṇadēvarāya. Gopa was the governor of Konḍavīdu. He wrote *Krishṇa-Arjunasamvādam*. In the introduction of the work he gave an account of the family. The Nādinḍla family held very important positions of office under Krishṇarāya, and Appa, the brother of Gopa was the Governor of Gutti. Mallana composed *Rājaśekharacharitram* and dedicated it to Appa.

The influence of the Kannaḍa Court and the contact of the Kannaḍa language is felt on Telugu literature. The poets like Nāchanasoma and Pālakurki Somanātha and others used Kannaḍa words in their poetry to some extent and the frequency of such usuage has become more conspicuous in the poetry of the Prabandha period. Krishṇarāya profusely used Kannaḍa words in his work. Not only Kannaḍa words were used but also the Hindustāni or

Persian vocabulary is resorted to, on account of the intercourse with the Mohammadan culture. Peddana used a number of such words in Manucharitra and we can trace them in the later compositions of the Vijayanagara period.

THE ĀRAVĪḌU DYNASTY

Telugu literature from the middle of the sixteenth century onwards shows a distinct departure from that previous age and begins to move abruptly away from the established convention of the period. The change may be sudden but it is a logical sequence and a natural corollary of the changes which had already taken place. From the purāṇas and their entire translation, the poets went a step further. They took simple episodes from the purāṇas and developed them into descriptive stories. This happened till the end of the reign of Krishṇarāya. Afterwards the poets took insignificant relics or little known threads of stories from the purāṇas and wove them into fine literary fabrics. *Vasucharitra* written by Rāmarāja Bhūshaṇa is the literary prototype and pattern of all succeeding Telugu *kāvyas* for nearly two centuries. Poet after poet imitated Rāmarāja Bhūshaṇa in style and sentiment, to such an extent that the later *kāvyas* are generally known as Pilla Vasucharitralu or progeny of Vasucharitram. As the name of the poet indicates, he adorned the court of Rāmarāya, the *de facto* Emperor under Sadāśiva. The story of Vasucharitra is simple. Girikā is a daughter born to Śuktimatī (river) by her husband Kolāhala (Mountain). The child, grew up into a beautiful girl and Vasu, hearing of her captivating charms, falls in love with her. The father of the girl hears of it and finally gives her away in marriage to King Vasu. Though the story is thus very simple, the poet brought to bear upon this trifling theme, a depth of scholarship and an extraordinarily vivid imagination, producing a monumental literary work of a very high order. His idea of a theme for a *kāvya* is stated as follows. "Mere stories of imagination resemble those of false precious stones. Stories of days gone-by are like those precious stones found as they are. But stories of old, embellished with poetic decoration resemble those precious stones which are cut by diamonds." In our opinion, the poet cared both for sound and sense, form and fact, and being a great musician himself, it is said that he wrote Vasucharitra in such a way that the verses can easily be set to music. Incidentally, it may be stated, that he is a non-Brahmin Hindu poet hailing from a middle class family, and from hereafter, we can come across more of his class who are still some of the bright stars that shine in the firmament of Telugu letters. The Brahmin monopoly of Telugu scholarship and Telugu poetry, had a rude shock and we have a host of " chāṭu " verses in Telugu describing wordy warfare between the Brahmin and non-Brahmin poets, who flourished in the Vijayanagara court at this time. The Brahmin poet had always an occasional sting against his brother non-Brahmin poet for his alleged inferior literary output, and Tenāli Rāmakrishṇa, another great poet of the age, figured much in these literary duels. Even the author of Vasucharitra could not escape it, and perhaps he had to fare very badly in such contests.

The next great poet of the age is Pingali Sūranna. He was an exact contemporary of Shakespeare and likewise wrote *Kalāpūrṇodayam,* which resembles the ' Comedy of Errors.' The purāṇa is the sheet anchor of Telugu poetical compositions in some form or other and even Rāmarāja Bhūshaṇa falls victim at times, as he could not but turn to the purāṇa for his theme. But Sūranna broke the shackles of contemporary literary conventions and wrote a new story entirely different from that of any known one either from an epic or a purāṇa. It is an original story by itself. The story of the plot, though very complicated is succinctly stated as follows : Rambhā, the voluptuous dancer in the court of Indra loves Nalakūbara and boasts of her beauty and of her love for him. She thinks that her love towards him is so ardent that none can separate her from her lover. But there is the inevitable Nārada, the divine ambassador, who predicts that Rambhā will soon be disillusioned. A false Rambhā and Nalakūbara will arise in Kalabhāshiṇī and Maṇikandhara, who play the role of 'double' to Rambhā and Nalakūbara. Maṇikandhara becomes Nalakūbara and loves Rambhā. Kaḷabhāshiṇī becomes Rambhā and is loved by Nalakūbara. They fall in love with each other. Thus the false and the true meet with each other and many a comic situation is created. The spell will be broken finally and to their dismay they realise the folly of each other. The whole story is a fine imagination of the poet and *Kalāpūrṇodayam* is still a very entertaining Telugu *kāvya.* The great conspicuous feature of the work is its dramatic character with full of dialogues though it is written in a *prabandha* form. With a little change the whole book can easily be transformed into a drama. The two other works of Sūranna are also worthy of special notice. Rāghavapāṇḍavīya, a *dvarthi* Kāvya, is the second of its kind but best of all such compositions so far available in Telugu literature. Verses are composed in such a way that they are capable of affording two meanings, one applicable to the story of the Rāmāyaṇa, and the other to that of the Mahābhārata, and the story is interwoven in such a way that the whole book carries with it, the two stories in a continuous way. It may be said that it is only a type of literary acrobatism. But the cardinal feature of the composition is its simple, and symphonic style which attracts its reader but not repel him from following the two stories with as little effort as possible. The other work is called Prabhāvati Pradyumnam. Here the story is from the purāṇa, but the fertile brain of the poet furnishes it with a form which is altogether a new one. The story deals about the marriage of Prabhāvati with Pradyumna. The former is the daughter of Vajranābha who is a demon, and whose valour, even Indra could not face. So the Gods conspire to put an end to Vajranābha's power and as none other than demons can enter into the citadel of Vajranābha, Śuchimukhi a swan is created for the purpose and she enters into the palace of Vajranābha. She creates love in Prabhāvati for Pradyumna and speaks of a dramatic troupe of Bhadra. Pradyumna enters into the capital in disguise with the troupe of Bhadra and meets Prabhāvati. Love triumphs over racial animosity. The father of Prabhāvati is killed and she is married to Pradyumna.

The chief characteristics of Sūranna's poetry are (1) the style is simple and euphonic; (2) the plot arrests the attention of the reader; (3) the characters pulsate with life; (4) description is replaced by dialogue, and (5) the whole story can be transformed into drama with a little adjustment.

Another great poet of the age was Tenāli Ramakrishna. He wrote Udbhaṭārādhya Charitram and Pāṇḍurangamāhātmyam and the latter is regarded as one of the Panchamahākāvyas in Telugu. He was known only as a court jester to the common people, but the cultured know him as a great poet of the times. It is said that he was a staunch Śaiva in the beginning but became afterwards an ardent Vaishṇava. He is known for his extraordinary flow of diction and a very terse style.

The volume of Telugu literature under the Āraviḍu dynasty is the product, strange it may seem, of the aftermath of the battle of Tālikōta. Vasucharitram, the best book of the period was composed in 1570 A.D. Though the empire had a political reverse on the battlefield, the banner of the crescent was never hoisted permanently on the fortified walls of the Vijayanagara capitals, though it may be either at Vijayanagara or Penugoṇḍa or Chandragiri. The Mohammadan was never able to have an effective sway over the Hindu soil and so the religious and cultural edifice, which has been so zealously reared and guarded by the Hindu monarchs and their subjects, never gave way to the sledge hammer of the Muhammadan inroads. So much so, the Vijayanagara empire was never conquered on that battlefield and though the capital had to be moved from Vijayanagara to Penugoṇḍa and thence to Chandragiri owing to the exigencies of the times, the court flourished in all its usual splendour. Hence Telugu literature, instead of showing any signs of decay, developed with reinforced vigour.

THE SOUTHERN SCHOOL OF TELUGU POETRY

The Nāyakas of Tanjore and Madura

It will be inappropriate to ignore the development of Telugu literature under the Nāyakas of Tanjore and Madura, who were the viceroys of Tuḷuva and Āravīḍu emperors, when we give a sketch of Telugu literature under the Vijayanagara empire. Whatever may be the political vicissitudes of the two Nāyaka kingdoms, the Nāyakas gave a fillip to the growth of the Telugu literature and they seem to have vied with their masters in this respect. Political decay had already set in and with it social degeneration followed. The viceregal courts became the beehives of the erudite and voluptuous courtesan of the day. The Nāyakas delighted themselves in their company. They revelled in all sorts of aesthetic pleasures and carnivals of the flesh. Literature is naturally the mirror of the times. The Tanjore Nāyakas delighted themselves in theatricals and we find that innumerable Yakshagānams, Koravangis, and Jakkinis written either by Nāyakas or their court poets. The above three named classes of works resemble dramas and though they are not written in the form prescribed for a drama in Sanskrit poetics, yet they contain all the essentials of the drama, with characters and dialogues and scenario. The Yakshagāna is the cardinal feature of the Nāyaka literature. As they are intended for the masses they are composed in simple style, interspersed with song and comic scenes, and it was said that Raghunātha, the great Tanjore Nāyaka composed more than two hundred dramas of the Yakshagāna pattern.[5]

The theme selected by the poets of the southern school, belong to the type of the so-called eternal triangle—wife, husband and lover.

5. We know of an instance where such dramas, were actually staged even during the time Śri Krishṇarāya. A drama called *Tayikunda Nāṭakam* was actually staged. Naṭṭuva Nāgayya and a daughter of Naṭṭuva Timmaya who was a 'pātrī' (temple dancing girl) were connected with the performance of this drama and rewarded with a gift of land. Vide 558 Appendix B. Epigraphical Report for 1916.

The story of Rādhā's love for Mādhava, the elopement of Tārā with Chandra, the illicit love of Indra for Ahalyā, the amorous advances of a step-mother towards a step-son as in the case of Chitrāṇgi, the young wife of the old king Rājanarēndra towards Śāraṅgadhara the son of the king by his first queen, are some of the unedifying themes that were selected by the poets for their plots. The aesthetic tendency of the previous *prabhanda* literature degenerated into an erotic nature. *Śāraṅgadhara charitramu* of Chamakura Venkaṭa kavi, *Ahalyāsānkrandanamu* of Venkaṭa Krishṇappa Nāyaka and *Tārā Śaśānkavijayamu* of Venkaṭapati, are the typical works for illustration of the above tendency.

The chief characteristic feature of the style they employed, is simplicity and symphony and can easily be comprehended by both the scholar and layman. They cared more for the effect than for the form and in most cases disregarded the strict grammatical conventions. The Madura school is known for its largest contribution to prose literature. *Vijayarangachokkanātha* and Ananta Bhūpāla take the lion's share in the matter.

The most noticeable feature of the southern school is the literary democracy of the period. The literary plutocracy is the characteristic feature of the state of Telugu letters, but the southern school established the literary democracy in which, man and woman, Brahmin and non-Brahmin, prince and pauper, master and subject, alike mingled together and contributed to the growth of the literary wealth of the Andhras.

A list of the poets, both major and minor who flourished under each dynasty, with the books written and firms of their publication, is attached to this sketch, which is an indispensable part of the same. The list is elaborate but not exhaustive, but it gives a fair glimpse into the vast range of the subject. The variety and the vastness of the Telugu literature under the Vijayanagara period can easily be judged by the number of the poets and the nature of the works written.

SANGAMA DYNASTY.

Name of Poet.	Caste.	Books written.	Dedicated to or Patronised by	Published by or unpublished.
Nachana Soma	Brahmin	*Harivamśam*	God Hari-hara-nātha of Nellore.	Vavilla Ramaswamy Sastry & Sons, Madras.
Vallabharāya	do.	*Krīḍābhirāmam*		Śringāra Granthamālā Series, Madras
Jakkaṇa	do.	*Vikramārkacharitram*	Siddana, minister of Devaraya.	V. R. S. & Sons, Madras

SĀḶUVA DYNASTY.

Name of Poet.	Caste.	Books written.	Dedicated to or Patronised by	Published by or unpublished.
Pina Vīraṇṇa	do.	1. *Jaimini Bhāratamu*	Sāḷuva Narisiṁha	do.
		2. *Śringāra Śākuntalam*	Venna mantri	do.
		3. *Avatāra-Darpanam*	* * *	Book not available
		4. *Nāradiyam*	* * *	do.
		5. *Makhamāhātyam*	* * *	do.
		6. *Manāsollasasaram*	* * *	do.
		7. *Purushārthaśudhānidhi*	* * *	do.
Manumanchi bhattu		1. *Hayalakshanasāram*	Saluva Kampa	
Duggana		2. *Nachiketupākhyānam*	Gangaya, sometime minister of Sāḷuva Narasimha	V. R. S. & Sons, Madras

TUḶUVA DYNASTY.

Nandi Mallayya Ganta Singayya	Brahmin	*Varāha purāṇam*	Narasimharāya, father of Krishṇaraya	V. R. S. & Sons, Madras
		Prabhodhachandrodayam	Gangaya mantri, sometime minister of Sāḷuva Narasimha	V. R. S. & Sons, Madras
Peddana	Brahmin	1. *Manucharitram*	Krishṇarāya	V. R. S. & Sons, Madras
		2. *Harikathāsāram*		Books not available
Timmana	do.	*Pārijātāpaharaṇam*	do.	do.
Krishṇarāya	Kshatriya	*Āmuktamālyadā*	God Venkaṭeśvara	do.
Yellanārya	Brahmin	*Rādhāmādhavam*	God, Śrī Krishṇa	Zamindar of Kapileśvarapuram, East Godavari
		Vishṇumayanāṭakam	God, Madana Gopala	Madras University
		Taraka Brahma Rājīyam	Nanja Timmarsu, a subordinate of Achyutarāya	Not published
Dhurjati	do.	*Kālahasti mahatmyamu*	God of Kalahasti	V. R. S. & Sons, Madras
		Kalahasti Śatakam		do.
Mallana	do.	*Rajasekhara charitram*	Nadindla Appa, son-in-law of Prime Minister of Timmarsu	do.
Talapaka Chinnanna	do.	*Ashṭamahishi Kalyāṇam*		Not published
Sankusala Narisimha kavi	do.	*Kavi karṇa rasāyanam*	God, Śrī Ranganātha	V. R. S. & Sons, Madras
Rāmabhadrakavi	do.	*Rāmābhyudam*		do.
Nadindla Gopa	do.	*Krishna-Arjuna Samvādam*		
Yerranarya	do.	*Sringāra Malhana charitra*	Kalana Mantri of chundi. The poet says that he intended to dedicate the work to Krishnaraya, but he could not do so.	Śringāra Granthamālā Series, Madras

ĀRAVĪḌU DYNASTY

Name of Poet.	Caste.	Books written.	Dedicated to or Patronised by	Published by or unpublished.
Ramaraju Rangappa	Kshatriya	*Sāmbhopākhyānam*	God, Śrī Ranganātha	Telugu Academy,
Ramaraja Bhushana	do.	1. *Vasucharitram*	Tirumalāraya	V. R. S. & Sons, Madras
		2. *Harischandra-Nalopakhyanam*	God, Śrī Rāma	do.
		3. *Narsaa Bhūpālīyam*	Narsaraju, nephew of Tirumalaraya	do.
Kumara Dhurjaṭi	Brahmin	*Krishṇaraya Vijayam*	Śrī Rāma. The book is written by the request of Tirumala, a cousin of Tirumalaraya.	do.
Pingali Suranna	do.	1. *Kalāpūrṇodayam*	Krishnaraja of Nandyala	do.
		2. *Rāghavapaṇḍavīyam*	God, Virūpāksha	do.
		3. *Prabhāvati-pradyumnam*	Amarana, the father of the poet	do.
		4. *Girijā Kalyāṇam*		Books not available.
		5. *Garuḍa Purāṇam*		
Timmarasu (a nephew of Ramaraya)	Kshatriya	*Paramayogivilasam*	God, Śrī Narasimha of Mangalagiri	
Tiruvengalanatha	Brahmin	do.	The poet says that he was patronised by Venkaṭapathi, brother of Tirumalaraya.	
Rayasam Venkatapathi	do.	*Lakshmivilāsam*	The poet says that he is patronised by Śrīranga Rāya.	
Tatigoppula Mallana	do.	*Chandrabhānu charitram*	He is patronised by Venkaṭa, son of Tirumala.	V. R. S. & Sons, Madras
Charigonda Dharmanna	do.	*Chitrabhānu charitram*	Peddanamatya, a minister of Manabhunatha, a viceroy of Śrīranga Rāya	do.

Chennamaraju	do.	*Chāruchandrodayam* The poet says that he is patronised by Pemmasāni Timmaraju, minister of Śrirangarāya and Venkaṭapatirāya.		
Tenali Annayya	Brahmin	*Sudakshaṇāpariṇayam*	Soma mantri, minister of Konēṭi Rama Raju, one of the grandsons of Rama Raya's cousins	
Andugula Venkayya	Brahmin	*Ramarajīyam*	Kodaṇḍa Rāmarāju, a grandson of Tirumala	
Tenali Ramakrishna	do.	*Pāṇḍu Ranga Māhātmyam*	Viruri Vedadri	V. R. S. & Sons, Madras
Savaram China Narayana Nayaka	Non-brahmin	*Kuvalayasvacharitramu*	Narayana Bhupala, one of the subordinates of Śrīranga Raya and Venkaṭapathi Raya	do.

NĀYAKAS OF TANJORE

Raghunātha Nāyaka.	Kshatriya	1. *Valmiki Charitram*	God, Sri Rama	Amudritandhra Grandha Sarvasvamu
		2. *Sāvitri Charitram*		Chitrada Sringara Granthamālā
		3. *Pārijātāpaharaṇam*		Not published
		4. *Nalacharitram*		do.
		5. *Rāmāyaṇa*		Being published by Telugu Academy
Chamakura Venkatakavi	Brahmin	*Vijayavilasam*	Raghunatha Rāya	V. R. S. & Sons, Madras
		Sārangadhara charitram	do.	do.
Rangarajamma (woman)	Non-brahmin	*Mannārudāsa vilasa nāṭakam*		
		Ushāpariṇayam		Telugu Academy.

NĀYAKAS OF TANJORE (*Contd.*)

Name of Poet.	Caste.	Books written.	Dedicated to or Patronised by	Published by or unpublished.
Vijayarāghava Nayaka	Non-brahmin	*Raghunāthābhyudaya naṭakam*		Not published
		Rajagopalaswamy prabandham		do.
Kalakavi	Brahmin	*Vijayarāghava Vamśavali*		do.
		Rājagopala Vilasamu		do.
Venkatapathi Somayaji		*Vijayarāghava kīrti chandrika vihāramu*		do.

NĀYAKAS OF MADURA.

Name of Poet.	Caste.	Books written.	Dedicated to or Patronised by	Published by or unpublished.
Sesham Venkatapati	Non-brahmin	*Taraśasanka Vijayam*	Seeniah, minister of Vijayaranga Chokkanadha	V. R. S. & Sons, Madras
Errabhupaludu	do.	*Yuvajanahridayanandam*		
Venkaṭa Krishnappa Nayaka	do.	*Ahalya Sankrandanam*	God, Śrī Ranganātha	Śringāra Granthamālā Series, Madras
		Rādhāsantanamu		Not published
		Jaimini Bhāratamu (prose)		Telugu Academy, Cocanada
		Māghamahatyam (prose)		Not published
Nanjarāju	do.	1. *Vishṇupurāṇam*		
Ananta Bhupaludu	do.	2. *Ramayanam* do.		Not published
		3. *Bhagavatam* do.		do.
		4. *Bharatam* do.		do.
		Śrīranga māhātmyam do.		do.
Vijayaranga Chokkanatha	do.	*Maghamāhatmyamu* do.		do.

5

Vijayanagara and Jainism

By

Mr. Shripad Rama Sharma, M.A.,

Professor of History, Willingdon College, Sangli.

The more one studies the history of Vijayanagara the more one realises the "Never to be forgotten" character of that "Forgotten" empire. Much water has followed through the Tungabhadra since Sewell and Suryanarayanrao wrote. Dr. Krishnaswami Aiyangar, Rev. Heras and Dr. Saletore have opened up new vistas and further revealed the vastness of the glory that lies buried among the ruins of Hampi. For lovers of Karnāṭak and the New India that is being born in every province to-day Vijayanagara is no longer a faint memory, but a deep inspiration. The purpose of this sexcentenary Commemoration Volume, I take it, is to throw light upon the myriad faces of that diamond which we call Vijayanagara. I propose, in the course of this article, to focuss the reader's attention on one important aspect, often overlooked, of the glory that was Vijayanagara.

KARNĀṬA DHARMA

Just as in later times the great Shivaji tried to spread *Mahārāshṭra-dharma* in the four corners of his world, so did the rulers of Vijayanagara try to uphold *Karnāṭa Dharma* in the heart of the peninsula in the plenitude of their power. In the eyes of the Mahomedans they were the champions of Hinduism, but in reality, they were custodians of the Karnāṭa tradition. Their conflict with the Moslem kingdoms was political rather than religious; they tolerated Islam within their own jurisdiction, employed Muslims in their own service and patronised them in several ways. Muslims were not hated as Muslims. The same was their attitude towards all other faiths and creeds. Within Karnāṭa itself there were at least three great sects, *Vaishṇava, Vīra Śaiva* and *Jaina,* which claimed the allegiance of vast numbers of its population. These had not always been at peace with one another. History records mutual persecutions—least on the part of the Jains—and the attempts at suppression of the rising by the ruling religion. But a careful reading of history will show that *toleration* rather than *persecution* was in the spirit of our tradition: it is a long history of toleration disturbed by short-waves of persecution, rather than a long history of persecution broken by a few interludes of toleration. And Vijayanagara was no blind champion of a selected creed, but the conservator of our best traditions. Hence it is we find that Muslims and Christians, Brahmins and non-Brahmins, Lingayats and Jains, whether they were in a minority or majority, alike lived in amity being treated with equal tolerance and interest by their rulers. The patronage of the Jainas, set down below, at the hands of the Hindu rulers of Vijayanagara was typical of their general attitude and policy.[1]

BHAKTAS AND BHAVYAS

An inscription of Bukkarāya I dated c. 1368 A.D.[2] states, "During the time of Śri Bukkarāya, dispute having arisen between the Jainas and the Bhaktas (Vaishṇavas), the blessed people (Jainas), of all the nāḍus......having made petition to Bukkarāya ......about the injustice done by the *Bhaktas*, the king, taking the hand of the Jains and placing it in the hand of the Śri Vaishṇavas of the eighteen *nāḍus*, including *āchāryas* of the places,......and declaring (at the same time) that there was no difference between the *Vaishṇava-darśana* and the *Jaina-darśana* decreed as follows :—

"This Jaina-darśana is as before entitled to the five great musical instruments and the *Kalaśa*. If loss or advancement should be caused to the *Jaina-darśana* through the *Bhaktas*, the Vaishṇavas will kindly see as loss or advancement caused to their own (*darśana*) The Śri Vaishṇavas will kindly, to this effect, set up a *Śāsana* in all the *bastis* of the kingdom. *For as long as the sun and moon endure the Vaishṇavas will continue to protect the Jaina darśan. The Vaishṇavas and Jainas are one (body) : they must not be viewed as different.*"[3]

1. "The national movement which gave rise to Vijayanagara," says Dr. Krishnaswami Aiyangar, "was comprehensive and embraced a defence of all that was Hindu against Mussalman—including Jainism which received protection and patronage. The sovereigns' of this family, although each one had his own persuasion, adopted religious compromise as their civil policy."
Some contributions to S. India to Indian culture, pp. 298-299.

2. Epigraphia Carnāṭika, II SB. 344.

3. Cf. "For an empire ruled by one head," said Akbar (according to Bartoli), "It was a bad thing to have the members divided among themselves, and at variance, one with the other. We ought, therefore, to bring them all into one, but in such a fashion that they should be *one* and *all*, with the great advantage of not losing what is good in one religion, while gaining whatever is better in another. *In that way honour would be rendered to God, peace would be given to the people, and security to the Empire.*"
V. A. Smith, Akbar, pp. 211-212.

The details given of the administration of this highly interesting edict seem to show that Bukkarāya was even partial to the *Bhavyas,* as the Jainas were called, and threw the burden of their protection upon his own co-religionists, the *Bhaktas* or *Śrī Vaishṇavas.*[4]

FURTHER ADVANCE OF JAINISM

The advancement of Jainism further under Vijayanagara is illustrated by another inscription at Śravaṇa Beḷgoḷa. It describes Bhīmadēvi, the queen of Dēvarāya I, as a disciple of the Jaina *guru* Abhinava-chārukīrti Paṇḍitāchārya, and records the installation of the image of Sāntinātha in the Mangai Basti of Beḷgoḷa.[5] This instance is the more instructive as it indicates the attitude, not merely of the enlightened kings in the former case, but the active association with Jainism of a queen despite the traditional conservatism of her sex.

The employment of Jainas in high service is perhaps best exemplified in Irugapa—*daṇḍanāyaka* the general of Harihara II. Irugapa appears to have been a staunch Jaina. His father Chaichapa, had been Harihara's general before him, an epigraph[6] on the lamp pillar of the Gāna-gitti (oil-woman's) temple at Hampī speaks of his services to the cause of his religion : he was a follower of Sinhanandi and built the Kuṇta-Jinālaya at Vijayanagara : he is also described as the author of the Jaina lexicon *Nānārtha-Ratnamāla.* Even a distant inscription at Conjeevaram proclaims Irugapa's endowment of a Jaina temple for the benefit of Bukkarāya II, son of Harihara II."[7]

The continuation of the same policy and patronage is amply illustrated in epigraphs scattered throughout the empire of Vijayanagara. For example, in South Kanara, at Muḍabidri an inscription in the *Gurugaḷa* Basti records a grant of Bukkarāya II ;[8] another under Dēvarāya II alludes to the grant of one *Koḷaga* of paddy on every bullock-load coming into the town of Basrūr.[9] Although this ruler is described as " the tree of heaven to the

4. Cf. Heras, the Aravidu Dynasty of Vijayanagara, I p. 539.
5. Epigraphia Carnāṭika, II L.B. 337.
6. Hultzsch, South Indian Inscriptions, I, pp. 156 ft.
7. Epigraphia Indica VII, pp. 115-116.
8. Rangacharya, *Inscriptions of the Madras Presidency,* II Sk. 116.
9. *Ibid.* Sk. 27.

Brāhmaṇas,"[10] he caused a temple (chaityālaya) to be built to the Arhat Pārśvanātha who rules over the empire of all knowledge and who well knew how to proclaim the *Syādvāda-vidyā*, in the *Pānsupāri* bazaar at Vijayanagara."[11]

Last but not the least, might be mentioned the great Ḳrishnadēvarāya endowment among others (both Brāhmaṇical and Jaina) to the Trailokanātha Jinālaya[12] in the Chingleput district.

JAINISM AND FEUDATORIES

Space does not permit further dilation on the state of Jainism in the outlying parts of the empire. There is fascinating evidence in the Jaina monuments and epigraphs of Kārkaḷ and Muḍabidri, for instance, in the South Kanara district. They bear testimony to the progress and achievements of that religion under the Vijayanagara as well as its feudatories, like the Woḍeyars of Kārkaḷ, the chowters of Muḍabidri, the Bangars of Nandvar, the Ajalars of Āldangaḍi, the Mūlars of Bailangaḍi and the Savants of Mulki. This province was distinguished from the rest of Karnāṭak by the name of *Tuḷuva*.

An inscription in the Hosa Basti of Muḍabidri speaks of "Śrīman Muhāmanḍaḷēśvara *Jinadasa* Sālmalla Mahīvallabha as ruler of Tuḷuva comprising *Haiva-Konkan,* adorned with the city of Suvarṇapuri with his capital at *Nagira* which was as it were its tilaka."[13] The rulers of this country are often referred to as "Worshippers of the Three Jewels (Right Faith, Right Understanding, Right Action)" "Implanters of the Flag of Jainism," and "Builders of golden temples, erectors of the golden *Kalaśa*, consecrators of jewelled gold and silver images of Jina, etc."[14] Beautiful descriptions of Jaina centres like Gersoppa and Muḍabidri

10. **Hultzsch,** *op. cit.*, p. 166.
11. *Ibid.*, p. 164.
12. Rangacharya, *op. cit.*, p. 375 ; *Madras Epigraphical Report*, 1901, p. 188.
13. ತೌಳವದೇಶತಿಲಕಾಯಮಾನನಗಿರನಗರಸಿದ್ಧಸಿಂಹಾಸನಾಧಿಪತಿಯಾಗಿ ಸುವರ್ಣಪುರಿಯಿಂದ ಅಲಂಕೃತಮಾದ ಹೈವಕೊಂಕಣರಾಜ್ಯಮಂ ಪ್ರತಿಪಾಲಿಸುತಿರ್ದಂ.

P. Mangesh Rao, *Inscriptions in the Hosa Basti of Muḍabidrī*, Karnaṭak Sammelan Report XII, 1927, p. 158.

14. "ರತ್ನತ್ರಯಾರಾಧಕರುಂ", "ಜಿನಧರ್ಮಸ್ಥಾಪನಾಚಾರ್ಯರುಂ", ಹಿರಣ್ಯಚೈತ್ಯಾಲಯಸ್ಥಾಪನಾಚಾರ್ಯರುಂ", "ರತ್ನಸುವರ್ಣ ರಜತಜಿನಬಿಂಬ ಪ್ರತಿಷ್ಠಾಪನಾಚಾರ್ಯರುಂ". *Ibid.*, p. 160.

are also frequently met with, " Who can describe the charms of the city of Gersoppa ? " asks one ; " full of resplendent towers, palaces, Jaina houses, etc."[15] " Who has the tongue ? " asks another, " to sing the glory of Vēṇupura where women are true to their lords, and men are ever engaged in the study of Jaina *Śāstras* and worshippers find recreation in giving gifts and performing *Pūjā,* and where even children are enthusiastic in their adherence to dharma."[16]

CONCLUSION

This has by no means been either a comprehensive or an exhaustive study of Jainism in the Vijayanagara empire. No mention has been made of either Jaina arts, architecture or literature. These certainly flourished under very benign influences. The wonderful Jaina structures of Muḍabidri and Kārkaḷ in South Kanara belong to this glorious period. Works of the type of *Khagēndramaṇidarpaṇa, Dharmanātha purāṇa, Sabdānuśāsana,* etc., also appear to have been produced by writers of this age. The decline of the Jainas was a concomitant of the decline and fall of Vijayanagara, though Jainism survived for a longer period under its far-flung feudatories. The expansion of Jainism in the Karnāṭak had been due in no small measure to its actual adoption or active patronage at the hands of a great number of Kannaḍa rulers, both great and small, during nearly a thousand years from 200 A.D. to 1200 A.D. The Kadambas, the Gangas, the Chāḷukyas, the Rāshṭrakūṭas, the Kaḷachuris and the Hoysalas among the greater, and the Silāhārs, the Raṭṭas, the Changāḷvas and the Woḍeyars (of South Kanara) among the smaller had all their share in fostering this ancient faith in our province. Vijayanagara took up this tradition like most other traditions at Karnāṭaka and cherished it to the benefit of both itself and Jainism.

15. "ವಿಲಸದ್ಗೋಪುರದಿಂ, ಸುಹರ್ಮ್ಯಚಯದಿಂ, ಶ್ರೀಜೈನಗೇಹಂಗಳಿಂ, ಚೆಲುವಂ ತಾಳ್ದಿದ ಗೆರಸೊಪ್ಪೆನಗರಂ ಕೊಂಡಾಡಲಾರ್ಬಲ್ಲಿರ್ಪೆ". *Ibid.* p. 153.

16. ಬಾಲಕರೆಲ್ಲರುದ್ಗ ಜಿನಧರ್ಮರತರ್ ವರದಾನಪೂಜೆಯೋಳ್ ಲೀಲೆಯನಿರ್ಪ
ಪಾಸಕರ ನಿಂದ್ಯ ಜಿನೋದಕಶಾಸ್ತ್ರಶಾಲಿಗಳ್
ಬಾಲೆಯರಾತ್ಮನಾಥರಿಗನುಕೂಲೆಯರಾಗಿರುತಿರ್ಪರೆಂದೊಡಾ
ನಾಲಗೆಯಾರಿಗುಂಟು ಪೊಗಳಲ್ ನೆರೆವೇಣುಪುರಪ್ರಭಾವಮಂ. *Ibid,* p. 152.

10

6

Vijayanagara Paintings from the temple at Lepakshi *

By

Mr. C. Sivaramamurti, M.A.,

Archæological Assistant, Government Museum, Madras.

In a temple, whose glory has now become a matter of history or a piece of favourite old-time gossip but whose entirely different reality to-day is manifest in its decay and neglected solitude in an unfrequented corner of a district which once formed the heart of a glorious empire that gladdened the people with its smile of plenty that can hardly by us be now imagined, who can but see its shrivelled up gloom and parched desolation, there is on the ceiling almost everywhere a plethora of line and paint revealing the very interesting but little studied art of Vijayanagara that is so important to the student of Indian art who is out to examine the transitions of classical form in various periods right down from the Pallava period and individually the art of that particular period.

Lepākshi, in the Hindupur Taluq of Anantapur district, may now be termed an insignificant village—one of the many hamlets that wear a mournful countenance in that arid district. But, Lepākshi had its day. It was a centre of trade and pilgrimage in the palmy days of the Vijayanagara Emperors when Virūpaṇṇa Naik fostered that town and its surroundings as one of the chiefs representing the emperor. He and his brother Vīraṇṇa Naik were in fact the makers of Lepākshi.

On a small rocky hillock there stands the sacred shrine of Pāpanāśeśvara believed to have been established by sage Agastya, himeslf. The humble cell that sheltered the sacred emblem of Śiva was developed into a temple by the untiring pious zeal of Virūpaṇṇa the worthy son of Nandilakkisetti of Penukonda.

This big structure, whose outer fortifications are now converted by the villagers into a common wall for the rows of miserable buildings that marked the once prosperous town, and the crests of whose mighty towers have slowly crumbled down signifying as it were its fast diminishing prosperity, has yet perched as it is on the low raised hillock Kūrmaśaila the pathetic though noble sight of a mighty old warrior of some ancient race holding up his head in spite of his infirmity (fig. 1).

Inscriptions of the time of Achyutarāya inscribed on the walls of this temple give us some particulars about the place, the holy structure and the pious brothers who enhanced the glory of both.[1] Three shrines are mentioned in the inscriptions. The shrine of Śiva faces that of Vishṇu while further up in the centre is the sanctum of Śrī Vīrabhadra the patron deity of the Naik brothers. They thus form a triangle with a common maṇḍapam in the centre the ceiling of which has on it painted an extraordinarily big figure of Vīrabhadra with his devotees Vīrupaṇṇa beside him.

Speaking of this temple Mr. A. H. Longhurst has made the following observations.[2] "The most interesting and beautiful part of the building is the large hall or maṇḍapa in front of the shrine. This contains over sixty large sculptured stone pillars and a painted ceiling. The central pillars bear almost life-size representations of musicians and dancers, carved with much spirit and freedom, the outer rows being ornamented with equally well executed, but smaller, figures. Unfortunately all the most interesting pillars have been defaced with the usual red and white colour wash. The whole ceiling (including the stone beams and bracket, capitals supporting the roof) was originally painted. Much of the painting still remains, but it is very decayed and damp. The under surfaces of the roof slabs between the cross beams, still contain numerous large paintings of scenes from the Mahābhārata, and the Purāṇas. A few of the figures show a considerable amount of mastery over the arts of drawing and painting. But, taken as a whole, the work is distinctly poor and uninteresting"

During my recent sojourn in the Anantapur district* I visited this temple of which so faithful a picture has been presented by Mr. Longhurst. The most interesting and beautiful part of the building is no doubt the maṇḍapa adjoining the inner gopura and the rather narrow ardhamaṇḍapa. This nāṭyamaṇḍapa is quite a charming piece of work with dancing figures, drummers and divine musicians carved on every pillar. The figures of Brahma playing the drum, Tumburu thrumming the strings of the vīṇa, Nandikeśvara playing the huḍukka, a dance master, one of the immortals, sounding the cymbals, a divine danseuse, may be Rambhā, dancing, and a prominent figure of Śiva in the pleasant ānandatāṇḍava atti-

1. Epigraphical Annual Report. 1912-13.

2. Archæological Annual Report. 1912-13.

* I am thankful to Mr. Kondappa, the President of the Hindu Religious Endowment Board, whose kind help made my tour in Anantapur a success.

tude are amongst the noteworthy sculptures adorning the pillars that beautify the maṇḍapa. It is indeed no fault of Mr. Longhurst that he has not described the inner maṇḍapa between the three main shrines which contains elegant carvings of Gajāntakamūrti, Tāṇḍavagaṇapati, Durgā and two figures of ideal man and woman as conceived by the sculptor. The sanctum is closed for all but Hindus, and had he been inside, the lover of the beautiful that Mr. Longhurst is, he surely would have never missed describing them.

The decay and damp that Mr. Longhurst speaks of in the case of the paintings is only in the narrow corridor to the back of the main shrines. The paintings there are hopelessly decayed and irretrievably spoilt by exposure to weather. These are painted on the roof slabs through the interstices of which rain water has trickled down to spoil the paintings for ever. It is however somewhat of a solace to know that these are not the best of the paintings in this temple. There is something of a tone of irony and sadness in the spectacle presented by the adjoining unfinished maṇḍapa whose sculptured figures, described by Mr. Longhurst as very good in workmanship, from their position on the pillars are the lonely witness of this sad decay.

To the south-west of the temple there is the Somavāramaṇḍapa facing north the cornice of whose facade shows remnants of colour designs signifying the once painted condition of the ceiling which to-day reveals nothing but ugly water stains and swarms of bats that here brood over the darkness and desolation of which they are so significant.

The walls of the small sanctum of Vīrabhadra, the ceiling of the Raghunātha shrine and that of the part of the maṇḍapa adjoining the Śiva sanctuary are full of pictures, which generally escape the eyes of those who do not care to scrutinize every inch of the structure in the hope of discovering some paintings. Those on the ceiling of the Vishṇu shrine are interesting representations of the ten incarnations of Vishṇu painted around the central panel revealing seated Vishṇu.

For one who is more attracted by line and colour than by relief and volume or in other words for one who is interested more in painting rather than in sculpture there is nothing so interesting in this temple as the nāṭyamaṇḍapa and the ardhamaṇḍapa next to it. The paintings that Mr. Longhurst describes as poor and uninteresting are only the larger ones that adorn the maṇḍapa. Those in the ardhamaṇḍapa are really beautiful ones and would do credit to any skilled workman. These are perhaps the ones which elicited the comment that " a few of the figures show a considerable amount of mastery over the arts of drawing and painting". But Mr. Longhurst clubs all the paintings together and says that taken as a whole they are poor and uninteresting. The paintings that adorn the ardhamaṇḍapa should not be clubbed with those of the maṇḍapa for any evaluation of their worth. The former are probably earlier than those of the maṇḍapa and distinctly superior. A master craftsman has been at them and credit should be given for the excellent work he has done.

We find the pendulum swinging to another and more extreme limit in the description of the paintings of the maṇḍapa where extraordinary praise is lavished on performance that does not merit it. " By far the most remarkable feature of this mahāmaṇḍapa, and indeed of the temple itself," says the Gazetteer " are the numerous life-size paintings of scenes out of the Mahābharata, the Rāmāyaṇa and the Purāṇas with which the whole of the roof is covered. They exhibit wonderful mastery over the arts of drawing and colouring. One of the faces possesses the unusual characteristic of appearing to look full at the spectator from whatever point it is viewed." This last is a representation of Krishṇa as Vaṭapatraśāyi and the peculiar feature described in the Gazetteer was shown to me by the kind trustees of the temple as an achievement of the painter who did the work. But I found nothing so attractive about the figure or its looks. In fact, it was one of the many specimens of indifferent workmanship.

Some, though not all, of the figures in the nāṭyamaṇḍapa are drawn with skill and are agreeable to the eye. Though most of the paintings are spoiled and much of the paint fallen off there are some on the ceiling yet in a very good state of preservation. The marriage of Pārvatī, Dakshiṇāmūrti, Rāma's coronation and Krishṇa as Vaṭapatraśāyi are among the pictures. The story of Arjuna's penance forms an excellent theme for a row of pictures and the painter has accordingly shown the various scenes beginning with a representation of Śiva as Sukhāsīna, hunters and sages, Indra presenting a weapon to Arjuna, Śiva coming as a hunter accompanied by his spouse, the boar, the fight over it and the blessing that Arjuna receives from Maheśa. There is a graphic representation of Pārvatī's marriage where many sages and gods like Vishṇu, Vāyu and Agni are shown as important guests. The toilet of Pārvatī before her marriage and the scene of Śiva playing chess with his wife are quite interesting. It is really a surprising thing that here we have a representation of the story of the calf run over by the car of a

Chōla prince and the cow claiming and getting justice dealt unto her, a story which is noted as peculiar to Tiruvālur in the Tanjore district. This and the story of Arjuna's penance seem to be so popular as themes that we find them repeated in the sculptured panels of the Śiva temple at Penukonda.

To the student who studies these paintings from the historical point of view nothing is so important as the representation of Vīrapaṇṇayya and Vīrappa with their train receiving sacred ashes from a Purohita standing before their tutelary deity Vīrabhadra, in whose vicinity is shown Daksha (fig. 2). It gave me great delight when I identified these as the two famous brothers and I at once took a photograph of this figure. Though some of my photographs did not come off all right, it is really fortunate that this has come off fairly successful.

From the dress and especially the headgear which is typically like that of Krishṇadēvarāya (bronze statue) at Tirupati and Chidambaram or that of Tirūmalarāya in Tirupati it is clearly seen that this kind of cap was popular about the time. But as we may see from the painting itself it is only the brothers who as chiefs of some eminence are shown wearing that kind of headgear. The rest of their retinue wear other kinds of turbans. There is a photograph taken by Father Heras of a Vijayanagar chief of about the time of Achyutarāya who has a similar cap on. These point to the fact that the cap is a type for the wear of dignitaries like the Emperor and his nobles.

The most profitable study of paintings typical of the Vijayanagar period is made in the ardhamaṇḍapa where the ceiling is rich in excellent representations of the various forms of Śiva. The first panel of the series shows Śiva rising from the Linga and assuring protection to a number of devotees offering him worship. There is a youth near-by, who, but for the absence of Yama with a noose to torment him might be supposed by us to be Mārkeṇḍēya. Perhaps it is the moment after Yama was repelled that is chosen by the artist. The next shows Śiva dancing over a demon whom he is piercing with his trident surrounded by sages and devotees that adore him. Thanks to Mr. Venkatanaranappa, who arranged for the scaffolding to enable me to reach the ceiling, I copied this (fig. 3) and some other paintings. The poise of Śiva is matched only by the grace of his body ; and, as every student of art knows, it is the rhythm of movement caught in a moment of action and crystallised in a single well-chosen attitude or pose that enhances the artistic interest in a picture. The calm in the placid face of the figure of Śiva in this terrible encounter with evil forces personified in the form of the demon crushed under his foot is a telling suggestion of the mighty glory of the Lord to whom no achievement is so great as to cause the slightest ruffle perceptible in his countenance.

FIG. 3

The third panel shows Dakshiṇāmūrti seated on a hillock under a pair of vaṭavṛkṣas and surrounded by sages who adore him. His hair is done up in the jaṭābhāra fashion ; the vyāghrājina and yogapaṭṭa adorn his person. This panel of Dakshiṇāmūrti is far superior to a similar one on the ceiling of the nāṭyamaṇḍapa and clearly shows how obviously coarser in workmanship the latter is.

The panel coming next shows Śiva in the *anugraha* attitude presenting his paraśu (axe) to Chaṇḍikeśvara, who receives it with the utmost humility. Between them is a funny looking dwarf of a gaṇa blowing a long bugle. Sages and attendants are shown on either side. This is an interesting scene from Chaṇḍeśvara's life and is somewhat unusual the more common representation of his form in sculpture being his seated figure in the Chaṇḍeśānugrahamūrti group where Śiva is shown adorning the head of this great devotee of his with a flower garland.

The fifth scene represents Bhikshāṭana proceeding on his march for alms attended by a gaṇa who carries his bowl on his head. The *ṛishipatnis* are shown offering him food in a state of mind where intense love and passion created by his singularly perfect beauty of form get the better of their usually calm ascetic attitude. The poise of Bhikshāṭana is as noble and majestic as that of the dwarf is quaint and comical. The painter has fully succeeded in his suggestive touches that enhance the obviously beautiful form of the ladies by infusing life palpitating with passion in their breasts. The calm serenity in Bhikshāṭana's general bearing shows off the dignity of the master-painter who was responsible for the piece of work.

Three panels coming after this represent in order Hariharamūrti adored by sages and gods, Śiva with Pārvatī approaching what appears like, and perhaps might be, Mohinī, and a slightly fainter group of perhaps Chandraśekhara with Pārvatī adored by divine beings. The scene coming next shows Śiva as Kalyāṇasundara wedding Pārvatī. There is an assemblage of sages and women. Brahma is shown officiating as priest. It is interesting to compare this scene with the larger one depicting the same theme on the ceiling of the nāṭyamaṇḍapa. The next is a representation of Tripurāntaka attacking the Tripuras from his chariot the wheels of which are the sun and moon and the charioteer Brahma.

One of the finest, if not the best, of the paintings here is the panel showing Śiva (Gangādhara) as Gowriprasādhaka appeasing Gowrī (fig. 4). This is a very delicate theme delicately worked. The whole composition of this picture does credit to the genius of the painter. In this there is a happy blend of action and repose, anger and calm ; also of the straight line and the curve in the lines that form the rhythmic outline of the composition in the simple samabhaṅga of Pārvatī and the complex tribhaṅga of Śiva that already appears to have stepped into the boundary of atibhaṅga. The cause of Pār-

FIG. 4

vatī's vexation is shown in the stream of Gangā flowing down the locks of Śiva where though he hid this his newly-got spouse the unsurmountable devotional power of his bhakta Bhagīratha brought it down willy nilly to the great embarrassment of the one and the angry astonishment of the other. This painting tallies well with the description of Gangādhara as given in the Amśumadbhedāgama and Śilparatna except in some minor details. The general description of Pārvatī and a special feature about her face *virahitānanā* with the look of one "forsaken" is clearly shown. The painter has however taken some liberty in representing Śiva by deviating slightly from the description. The difference is not so much deviation as reversal of the position of hands, feet, and pose of Śiva. The line of the Amśumadbheda "Dakshine pūrvahastam tu varam devyānanāśritam", i.e., "the excellent front right hand (of Śiva) should caress the face of Pārvatī" is the most important part of the description and is missing in the account of Gangādhara in every other Śilpa book. The painter has rightly given prominence to this and shown Pārvatī almost as Khaṇḍitā. The lines that form the contour of the figures herein, the expression in the faces of the divine pair and the general delicacy of treatment are all in perfect consonance with the nature of the theme.

The panel coming next shows Nateśa in the anandatāṇḍava attitude. Śiva as Vṛṣabhārūḍha is painted in the adjacent panel. He is seated on his bull with Pārvatī beside him. The Nandi or bull has one of its four legs on the head of a dwarf. A number of devotees are shown worshipping Śiva. The next panel has a representation of Śiva standing 'as Chandraśekhara" adored by a noble-looking bearded person and a woman with jaṭāmakuṭa painted on either side. These are perhaps Himavān and Menakā. The final panel on this part of the ceiling has a picture of seated Pārvatī with a lily in her right hand. She wears *kuchabandha, kirīṭamakuṭa* and other adornments and is adored by a woman standing in her vicinity. Part of the figure is unfortunately spoilt by weather and part fallen down

So much about the paintings on the ceiling of the ardhamaṇḍapa which are the very best in this temple. On the dark and grimy walls of the shrine of Vīrabhadra there are dim paintings of Śiva (fig. 5) in different attitudes with his attendants. One of the latter (fig. 6) appeared rather interesting being almost like Muchukunda, who is painted over and over again in the temple at Tiruvālūr. Muchukunda was a great king and a greater devotee. He, it is, that is supposed to have brought away from heaven the five figures of Tyāgarāja (Somāskanda) the principal one amongst which is enshrined in Tiruvālūr, the capital of his kingdom. The fact that the story of a cow and its dead calf peculiar to and of local

FIG. 5

FIG. 6

interest at Tiruvālūr is found painted here and sculptured at Penukonda makes me wonder whether this figure cannot be Muchukunda of Tiruvālūr, whose greatness as a Śivabhaktha won him a place in a Śiva temple howevermuch it might be remote from his home. The queer face is characteristic of the conventional way of drawing the monkey so peculiar in all the representations of that animal in the Vijayanagar period a practice which in a more degenerate form continues even to-day.

From the figures reproduced to illustrate some of the points discussed above, it would be quite clear that the painters of the Vijayanagara Emperors had an excellent sense of beautiful form and pose, arrangement of figures to produce good compositions and good colour sense to paint pleasing pictures. The lines have been drawn in sure and unswerving strokes and the curves suggest the facile way in which the brush glided on the surface. The lines that go to form the contours are mute testimonies to the perfect knowledge of the human form that these artists possessed in abundance. Costumes and ornaments in these paintings have a peculiar historical interest here apart from the artistic embellishment that these are intended to add. The portrait paintings of Vīrapanna and his brother with their retinue are most important from this point of view as well. Though the colours used here are quite simple, the entire colour scheme being composed of red, blue, yellow, green, black and white, the differnt shades laid on without any complex blending, bespeak of the taste of the painter. I need not be loquacious about the skill of the Vijayanagara painter at design work, since I expect, and am sure of my expectation, the bit of the scroll of geese to talk more about that (fig. 7). I may just add that the dignified and stately walk of the bird is a *tour de force* with the Vijayanagara artist.

FIG. 7

7

The Vijayanagara Paintings : Late Vijayanagara Paintings in the Brhadisvara Temple at Tanjore

By

Mr. S. Paramasivan, M.A., B.Sc.,
Archæological Chemist, Government Museum, Madras.

I. THE VIJAYANAGARA PAINTINGS

1. Introduction

In speaking of the Vijayanagara paintings, it might appear that one is rather on uncertain ground, for we know so little of them. On the other hand, it was thought that, from the 7th till about the 16th century A.D. the history of Indian painting was almost a blank. But with the discovery of paintings at Śittannavāśal, Kāñchīpuram, Māmaṇḍūr, Ellora, Tirumalaipuram, Tīruvañjikuḷam and Tanjore, it is clear that, so far at least as South India is concerned, there is a continuity of tradition in the art of painting from the 1st till about the 12th century.[1] We do not know what happened to this art afterwards. But we have stray evidence that the art did not die away with the Chola art at Tanjore, and that it survived long after. For, even in the Bṛhadīśvara temple there is superimposed on the beautiful early group of Chola paintings, a later group of paintings of the Vijayanagara period executed during the Nāyak regime. And we find other survivals of the Vijayanagara art in a few other temples in a sadly mutilated condition. The ceiling of the temple at Tiruparuttikuṉṟam, the ruined Chennakēśava temple at Sōṁpalle[2] in Madanapalle taluq of the Chittoor district, the temple at Lepākṣi in the Anantapur district, the Varadarāja temple[3] at Kāñchīpuram and the temples at Hampi and Ānegundi contain pictures representing important scenes from the Jain and Hindu mythology.

Besides these sad remnants that remind us of the glorious days of Vijayanagara art, there is the independent testimony of foreign visitors. Domingos Paes[4] who visited the city of Vijayanagara

1. S. Paramasivan—A Note on the dating of the frescoes in the Bṛhadisvara temple at Tanjore (*Journal of Oriental Research*, Madras, Vol. IX, Part IV (1935), p. 363).

2 The temple was partly destroyed by the Mughals (Vide Archæological Survey Annual Reports 1902-3, page 85).

3. Dr. N. Venkata Ramanayya drew my attention to these paintings.

4. R. Sewell—Forgotten Empire (Narrative of Domingos Paes).

during the days of the king Krishnadēva Rāya (1509-1529) describes the palace of the king, thus :

> " At the entrance to the door outside are two images painted like life and drawn in their manner which are these ; the one on the right is the father of this king, and the one on the left is of this king (Crisnarao). The father was dark and a gentleman of fine form, stouter than the son is ; they stand with their apparel and such raiment as they wear or used to wear. (pp. 284—285);

and again,

> " On this side is designed in painting all the ways of life of the men who have been here even down to the Portuguese, from which the king's wives can understand the manner in which each one lives in his own country even to the blind and the beggars." (p. 286).

From Indian literary evidence, Dr. N. Venkata Ramanayya[5] has come to the following conclusion :

> " It was customary for almost all classes of people to adorn their houses with painted pictures. The favourite subjects which attracted the attention of the artists were usually stories from Hindu mythology for example, the churning of the milk ocean for nectar and the celebration of the marriage of Viṣṇu and Laksmī, the burning of Kāma by Śiva and the latter's marriage with Pārvatī ; the marriage of Nala and Damayantī and the ways of such birds as swans, parrots, etc. These furnished themes for the artists to work upon, probably because the people loved to have the visible representations of these stories in their houses. But these had little or no attraction to the courtesan women, whose company was sought by all fashionable and cultured men. They filled their drawing rooms and bed rooms with amorous pictures representing love scenes from the stories of Rati and Manmatha, Rambhā and Nalakūbara, Urvaśī and Purūrava, Menakā and Viśvāmitra, Gopikā and Kriṣṇa."

There were painters at the court of Venkaṭa Il (1584-1614), says Fr. Heras :[6]

> " Fr. du Jarric states that there were several native painters at Chandragiri ; but these artists could not have approached the

5. Studies in the History of the Third Dynasty of Vijayanagara. (pp. 364-65).

6. The Aravidu Dynasty, p. 486.

standard of the European paintings presented to the king (Venkaṭa II) by the Jesuits."

These independent items of evidence are sufficient in themselves to show that the art of painting flourished in the kingdom of Vijayanagara.

2. Historical

In any attempt to search for paintings of this period, or to assess the proper value and full significance of the few paintings of this period that have come to light, or even to explain the paucity of paintings of this period, one must bear in mind the history of the times, especially of that preceding it. Taking first the Tamil country, it may be stated that, during the middle of the 13th century A.D., the Pāṇḍyas rose to great prominence under king Jaṭāvarman Sundara Pāṇḍya, conquered the whole of the Chola country, which comprised of Tanjore, S. Arcot, N. Arcot, Chingleput and portions of Nellore and Cuddapah districts, expelled the Hoysalas, who held sway over Trichinopoly, Salem and Coimbatore districts and thus they conquered the entire Tamil country. Immediately after the death of Jaṭāvarman, the Muhammadan invasion under Malik Kafur broke up the Pāṇḍyan supremacy effectively. Though the Muslim authority was not firmly established, the whole country was in unsettled condition owing to the frequent Muhammadan invasions. It was during the time of Muhammad bin Tuglak, that the whole of S. India, with the exception of Malabar was subjugated by the Muhammadans and a permanent garrison established at Madura. Soon after, began the troubles for the Sultan Muhammad bin Tuglak, and his kingdom finally broke up. In 1335, Sheriff Hasan Shah, who ruled at Madura, set up in independence. In 1336, the kingdom of Vijayanagara which included a large part of the Telugu country was established. In 1344 the Tellingāṇa broke away under the leadership of Kāpaya Nāyaka. About 1347, the centurians of the Deccan rose in rebellion under the leadership of Zafar Khan, who made himself king of the Deccan, and thus arose the Bahmani kingdom. In 1342, when Ballala III was killed in a warfare with the Sultans of Madura, the Hoysala country passed into the hands of Harihara I and Bukka I of Vijayanagara. About 1360, Kumāra Kampaṇa, son of Bukka I, led an invasion against the Sambuvarāyans, who ruled over the districts of Chingleput, North Arcot and South Arcot, and a few years later against the Sultans of Madura and succeeded in driving them out. By 1380, the Vijayanagara conquest of the south was complete and the empire extended from the river Kṛṣṇā in the north to Cape Comorin in the south and from the Arabian Sea to the Bay of Bengal. In spite of constant conflicts between the kings of Vijayanagara and the Muhammadan kingdoms of the Deccan, the empire finally broke up only long after the Battle of Talikota (1565).

It now seems evident that,

1. From 1272 A.D. till 1382, the whole of S. India was constantly subjected to invasions, especially the Muhammadan ones, and to other political changes.

2. The Muhammadan invasions under Malik Kafur and Muhammad bin Tuglak saw the destruction of many temples, such as those at Chidambaram and Srirangam and other institutions which might have contained paintings. This explains the abrupt break in the art of painting between the Chola and the Vijayanagara periods.

3. If we are to look for the continuity of tradition in art of Indian painting, we have to look for it not in N. India and the Deccan, which were under the sway of the Muhammadan iconoclasts, but in the Tamil and the Hoysala countries, and in those Telugu districts, which were far removed from the Bahmani kingdom of the Deccan, and thus quite uninfluenced by the conflicts between the Vijayanagara and the Bahmani kingdoms. This explains the existence of Vijayanagara paintings in Hampi, Ānegundi, Lepākṣi, Sōṁpalle, Sravaṇa Beḷgoḷa, Kāñchīpuram, Tanjore, etc.

4. On account of the constant hostility between the Hindus and the Muhammadans, and on account of the cultural antagonism between the two races, the Muslim influence could not have affected the art in S. India as it did in N. India under the more congenial atmosphere set up by Akbar which gave rise to a type of Rajaput art, which is a fusion between the indigenous art of India with the Muslim art. Thus any survival of the painting of this period in S. India must be pure and indigenous.

5. The Vijayanagara kingdom is a protest against Muslim invasions from the north, and it was very difficult to foster the art of painting, which requires royal patronage in a peaceful and congenial atmosphere. In spite of this, it was highly creditable that the kings of Vijayanagara embellished their capital with paintings as testified by Domingos Paes and Fr. du Jarric. They also decorated temples with paintings, of which survivals are still to be seen. Probably the art in the very capital met with terrible destruction after the Battle of Talikoṭa.

6. The Vijayanagara kings and the viceroys and the governors under them were great patrons of art. This is revealed unmistakably by the number of temples that they have renovated and the number of temples that they have raised again (for example, the temples at Srirangam and Chidambaram) after their destruction by Malik Kafur and the army of Muhammad bin Tuglak. Many of these temples contain innumerable paintings, and there is hardly a prominent temple in S. India without them.

One might now attempt at the reconstruction of the art of painting of this period, and he has the following data to start from, namely :—

1. The testimony of Domingos Paes testifying to the excellence of the art of painting during the days of Kṛṣṇa Dēva Rāya (1509-1529).

2. Fr. du Jarric has testified to the fact that, during the days of Venkaṭa II (1584-1614 A.D.), the art of painting had degenerated with the result that there was the importation of Portuguese painters, who were encouraged at his court. (What is the cause for the degeneracy of the art between 1509 and 1584 ?)

3. There are the paintings at Lepākṣi (about 1535 A.D.), at Sōṁpalle (middle of 16th century A.D.), at Ānegundi (15th century) and of Virūpākṣasvāmi temple at Hampi. It is very difficult to determine the date of the paintings in the Virūpākṣasvāmi temple, since it underwent renovations a number of times.

4. There are the paintings in the Varadarāja temple at Kāñchīpuram, probably belonging to the time of Kṛṣṇa Dēva Rāya (1509-1529).

5. There is a group of Jain paintings in the Vardhamāna temple in Jina-Kāñchī near Kāñchīpuram, the earliest of them belonging to the times of Harihara II (1378-1404).

6. There are paintings in the Bṛhadīśvara temple at Tanjore and others in many South Indian temples.

Any study of the ancient paintings has three complementary aspects, namely, (1) the historical, archæological and the descriptive, (2) the artistic and (3) the chemical, so that any study could be complete only through the co-ordinated efforts of the historian, the artist and the chemist. This fact has not been so fully realised in India as it has been done in the west, and it may be interesting to know that an American Expedition from the Harvard University is coming out to India to make such co-ordinated studies of some of the important survivals of Indian painting.

3. Recent Studies of Vijayanagara Art

In spite of these difficulties in the way of studying Indian paintings properly, Mr. T. N. Ramachandran of the Archæological Survey of India has written an excellent monograph[7] on the temples at Jina-Kāñchīpuram and described all the paintings in the Vardhamāna temple. But no artist has made a thorough study of the style and technique as such, nor any chemist investigated into the technique of the painting process. Mr. C. Sivaramamurti of the Madras Government Museum has made tracings of some of the paintings in the temple at Lepākṣi and studied them from an artist's point of view. Dr. N. Venkata Ramanayya has noted some paintings in the Varadarāja temple at Kāñchīpuram, and he has been very much struck by three scenes, namely, some dancing figures : a man with drawn bow standing in front of a woman, probably, Rāma and Tāṭakā : a figure seated on a parrot, perhaps Manmatha. He has seen Mr. Sivaramamurti's tracing's from the Lepākṣi paintings and he tells me that, from the point of view of technique and style, the paintings in the Varadarāja temple are far superior to Lepākṣi paintings. He is also of opinion, that the paintings in the ruined temple at Ānegundi, of which only two heads remain compare very favourably with the paintings in the Varadarāja temple. I have seen these Lepākṣi tracings through the kindness of Mr. Sivaramamurti and the Vijayanagara paintings in the Bṛhadīśvara temple at Tanjore. The former are far superior to the Tanjore paintings in expression and in the graceful sweep of the lines. There is nothing in the Tanjore temple to remind one of the marvellous paintings of birds at Lepākṣi. There are other paintings at Lepākṣi, which are relatively crude and compare with the Tanjore paintings. A study of the paintings on the ceilings of the Virūpākṣasvāmi temple at Hampi—if there are remnants still left—is likely to reveal the condition of the art of painting in the very capital of the Vijayanagara empire which should have had the best artists under the fostering care of the emperors. For the same reason, the paintings at Ānegundi are equally important. There might be paintings in the temple at Taḍpatri and at Penukonda. It

7. Tiruparuttikuṉṟam and its temples (Bulletin of the Madras Government Museum—New Series—General Section Vol. I, Part III, 1934).

is absolutely essential that in reconstructing the art of painting of this period, no study could be more helpful than the paintings in the Virūpākṣasvāmi temple and in the temple at Ānegundi. Unless more exhaustive studies are possible in the near future before the few paintings of this period, disappear through the ravages of time, it may not be possible to say anything definitely.* But one can now tentatively divide the Vijayanagara art of painting into three rough groups, namely :—

Group I. Under this group come the paintings that existed in the city of Vijayanagara when Paes visited it. To this group can be added the paintings at Ānegundi and in the temple of Varadarāja and probably those in the Virūpākṣasvāmi temple at Hampi.

Group II. The paintings at Lepākṣi and Sōṁpalle. They belong more or less to the same period in the opinion of Dr. Venkata Ramanayya. They are not so perfect as the paintings under Group I. It may be very useful to study the paintings on the ceilings of the mukha maṇḍapam at Sōṁpalle temple. These paintings represent scenes from the Rāmāyaṇa.

Group III. A degenerate type of art such as existed perhaps during the days of Venkaṭa II and in the 16th and 17th centuries. The paintings in the Bṛhadīśvara temple come under this group which, in a more degenerate form is found in many S. Indian temples.

It is probable that the first group of paintings might have had some characteristics in common with the classical art of Indian painting, examples of which are to be seen as late as the 12th century in the Chola paintings at Tanjore. These three groups of paintings roughly occupy a period of about three centuries, that is, from the 15th to the 17th centuries. But what happened to the art from the 12th

* Some critics hold the view that the art of painting—when examples of it are few or none at all—could be reconstructed from a study of contemporary sculpture. Though a comparative study of contemporary sculpture and painting is highly useful, though the study of sculpture might reveal some important sidelights on contemporary paintings, the art of painting can never be properly reconstructed from a study of sculpture alone. The essential difference in the medium of expression of the two arts should never be ignored. In sculpture, especially with the hard stones and metals used in S. India, there is rigidity and resistance to the free expression of the finer and delicate feelings of the artist. In the other medium with its softness and flexibility, the brush glides with ease in quick response to those very feelings. While it is difficult to give those delicate touches in the one, it is far easier in the other. These facts should never be ignored.

to the 15th century ? We have no means of knowing it. Did the art meet with a sad fate when the armies of Malik Kafur and Muhammad bin Tuglak came to the south ? Did Vijayanagara art suffer much in the conflicts between the Vijayanagara empire and Bahmani kingdoms, so that the best type of classical art of Vijayanagara was swept away ? Are there paintings in the temple at Taḍpatri and at Penukonda partly filling the gap ? These are problems worthy of attention, for, classical art such as one sees as late as the 12th century in the Chola paintings, requires royal patronage and could not have disappeared so suddenly. It is likely that with the disappearance of the Chola rule and the consequent rise of the Vijayanagara empire, the classical artists, or such of those that survived the results of Malik Kafur's and Muhammad bin Tuglak's invasions, got the patronage of the Vijayanagara kings, who were the only Hindu kings in the south. They embellished the capital with their paintings, the qualities of which have been well testified to by Paes and others. Those artists perhaps met with a sad fate in the massacre at Vijayanagara that followed the battle of Talikoṭa. Or, with the change of the capital and the troubles that rose in the empire with the battle of Talikoṭa, these artists were utterly neglected and they disappeared. Otherwise, it is very difficult to explain the absence of good paintings of this period in the country.

II. LATE VIJAYANAGARA PAINTINGS IN THE BṚHADĪŚVARA TEMPLE AT TANJORE

1. Introduction

These paintings were executed in 1646-1647[8] during the days of king Vijayarāghava Nāyaka of Tanjore. Before we proceed to discuss these paintings, it is necessary to consider whether they can rightly be called the true representatives of the Vijayanagara art, even though they are not of the best type. To some artists and art critics, the chapter on Vijayanagara history and art closes with the battle of Talikoṭa in 1565 A.D. and no Vijayanagara art exists after that date. It may be shown from facts of history that the kingdom of Vijayanagara flourished even till about the middle of the 17th century and its influence was well felt. Let us take the testimony of scholars. Speaking of Venkaṭa II (1584-1614), one of the Vijayanagara emperors of the Āraviḍu dynasty, who came to

8. S. Paramasivan—A Note on the dating of the frescoes in the Bṛhadīśvara temple at Tanjore (*Journal of Oriental Research*, Madras, Vol. IX, Part IV (1935), p. 363.)

the throne about twenty years after the battle of Talikoṭa, Fr. Heras[9] says:

> "Venkaṭa II is the most illustrious sovereign of this dynasty, who checked the Muslim raids in the north, subdued the turbulent Nāyaks in the south, caused the Rajas of Mysore to be firmly established in their realm strengthened his power by an alliance with the Portuguese and fostered literature and fine arts throughout his vast dominions."

and again, Fr. Heras says:[10]

> "Fine arts were likewise fostered by him (Venkaṭa II) a fact which gives an aesthetic sidelight on his interesting character."

Speaking of the next emperor, Rama II (1616-1630), Fr. Heras[11] says:

> "We have inscriptions from the beginning of his reign and coming from almost all the corners of the empire in which he is generally acknowledged as the lawful Rajādhirāja of Vijayanagara."

These inscriptions belong to about the first quarter of the 17th century and are from such distant places as Uraiyur (Trichinopoly District), Dindigal (Madura District) and from such districts as Coimbatore, Chingleput, Nellore, Kolar, etc. These facts clearly show that the influence of the Vijayanagara emperor was felt even as late as 1630, when these distant places claimed him as their sovereign. It is quite clear that, if the emperor was acknowledged over a wide area, the arts and crafts of the emperor's court should have had their influence in the south. It was more so at the court of the Nāyak kings of Tanjore. Till the very end, they were very faithful to the emperors. At a time when, due to the machinations of Jagga Rāya, Rama II had great difficulty in getting to the throne, he could always count upon the loyalty and help of the Tanjore Nāyaks. Again, when Śrīranga III, the last emperor of Vijayanagara tried to regain his empire in the south and met with the stoutest opposition from Tirumalai Naik of Madura, it was the timely intimation given by the Tanjore Nāyak that was of great help to him.[12] This emperor seems also to have lived near Tanjore. Thus

9. The Aravidu Dynasty—Introduction, p. XV.
10. Loc. cit. p. 511
11. H. Heras—Rama Deva Raya II, an unknown emperor of Vijayanagara —*Journal of B. & O. Research Society*, Vol. XVI (1930), p. 139.
12. R. Sathyanatha Aiyar—History of the Nāyaks of Madura, p. 127.

none can doubt the fact that the art of painting under the Nāyaks should have been greatly influenced by the art in the court of Vijayanagara kings. Further the unbroken line of Nāyaks, who were originally born and brought up in Vijayanagara should have continued all the original traditions of the Vijayanagara art, which they brought with them when they first came to Tanjore. If theme and subject-matter are good tests, the theme and subject-matter at Tanjore are the same as those mentioned in Telugu literature bearing on Vijayanagara art. The art at Tanjore is crude because, even by the time of Venkaṭa II, the art had degenerated according to the observations of Fr. du Jarric.

Of all the Vijayanagara paintings, those in the Tanjore temple are very important to the student of the history of Indian painting. There is an earlier group of paintings in this temple, belonging to the Chola period. They are both very different in technique and style, and it is worth while studying not only the difference, but also the probable causes that led to this difference.

2. The Brhadisvara Temple.

The Bṛhadīśvara temple at Tanjore was built by the great Chola king Rājarāja (985-1014 A.D.). Simple in its design and stupendous in its proportions, it represents a glorious period in the history of not only Indian art and architecture, but also of Indian painting.

The main shrine of the Bṛhadīśvara temple occupies almost the centre of the western half of the inner court, which is about 100 feet square. The *Vimāna* which rises over it to a height of nearly 200 feet dominates the entire structure. "The boldly moulded basement, the huge monolithic Nandi, the simple and tasteful-bas-reliefs and decorative motifs on the *Vimāna* and the ballustrades, the graceful sculptures in the niches on the sides of the *Vimāna* and the fine chiselling which marks the entire work, including the lettering of the various inscriptions, are not equalled by anything known in S. India. Viewed from any angle, the effect produced by the whole of this wonderful structure is pleasing and impressive."[13]

Surrounding the central shrine or the *garbhagṛha*, and immediately underneath the *Vimāna,* there runs a very dark passage or *Prākāra.* This passage is divided into 15 compartments. All the walls of these fifteen compartments, with the exception of three, contain paintings. There are thin coats of the lime plaster over the stone walls of the compartments with the Nāyak or late Vijaya-

13. K. A. Nilakanta Sastri—The Cholas, p. 232.

nagara paintings on them. These are examples of folk art which, in a decadent form, are found in many temples in S. India. In some of the compartments, notably four in number, the Vijayanagara paintings have peeled off or been removed by art-enthusiasts, and have revealed an inner and nobler layer of Chola paintings of the classical type of Indian art underneath.

3. The Vijayanagara Paintings in the Temple.

The attention of the public has so far been drawn to the earlier layer of Chola paintings by Mr. S. K. Govindaswami.[14] The outer layer of the Vijayanagara paintings has not received the attention due to it, probably because the beauty of the Chola paintings has drawn away all the attention to itself and the former has suffered by contrast.

The subject-matter of the Vijayanagara paintings may be briefly stated thus :—

1. There are scenes from Tanjore Sthalapurāṇa in profusion such as the annihilation of the Asuras, including Tañjan (after whom the city of Tanjore is named) by Devi and Viṣṇu in the role of Ānandavalliamman and Nīlameghaperumāl.

2. There are scenes from the lives of Śaiva saints such as Kaṇṇappar and Chaṇḍīśvara.

3. There are scenes from Hindu mythology such as the churning of the ocean of milk, various things that came out of it, Śiva drinking poison, Dakṣa's sacrifice and the advent of Vīrabhadra and Rāvaṇa lifting up Mount Kailāsa.

4. There are representations of Hindu gods and goddesses such as Brahmā, Viṣṇu, Śiva, Kirātamūrti, Ūrdhvatāṇḍava Naṭarāja, Bikṣāṭanamūrti, Bhairava, Dakṣināmūrti, Śūlapāṇi, Kailāsanātha, Umāsahita-Chandraśekhara, Lakṣmi Devi, Śrī Devi, Bhū Devi, Gaṇapaṭi, Śakti Gaṇapaṭi, Subrahmaṇya and Shaṇmukha.

5. Miscellaneous scenes of general interest are present in large numbers, such as worship of Śiva, both in the Lingā and the human form, attendants, worshippers, life of a sage, fighters, kings (perhaps the Nāyaks of Tanjore) with their names written below in Telugu characters.

14. The frescoes of the Bṛhadīśvaṛa temple at Tanjore—*Journal of Annamalai University*, Vol. II (1933), No. 1, p. 1.
Chola Painting—*Journal of Indian Society of Oriental Art*, Vol. I (1933), p. 73.

These paintings, though highly conventional, though less happy and far less perfect than the Chola paintings, are still as important as the latter to the student of Indian art. They depict the dress and jewels of the 17th century. They mark a growing interest in the study of Sthalapurāṇa. They represent a period of decadence that affected the art of painting at Tanjore.

4. The Nayak Art.

It is said that Indian painting is an art not of mass as in the West, but of pure line, depending for its expression on the grace and swiftness of the outlines. The artist analyses all the manifold complexities of human form, chooses the essentials and portrays them in simple, yet graceful lines. He gives expression to the faces of his subjects through the marvellous sweeps which he employs. Thus this technique is a wonderful visualisation of a rounded object translated into lines. It is marvellous how he achieves this through simple lines, without resorting to the mass effects through colours. In the artistic portrayal of form and expression, this line technique requires handling by a great artist with the genius of a master-mind. Such is the technique that characterises the art at Śittannavāśal and Ajanta and the Chola art.

The Vijayanagara art in the temple stands as a contrast to this high idealism, which characterises the classical art of India. It stands as a contrast to the grace of form and the beauty of rhythmic lines of the Chola art. Though the Vijayanagara artist has adopted the line technique, it is lacking in the genius and skill of the Chola artist. Though there is some expression in the figures, the line has lost its old graceful sweeps and suffers very much in comparison with the Chola paintings. Along with the crudeness of the line technique, the colours too are hot and heavy and quite unpleasing. These qualities mark the beginning of degeneracy of art in S. India.

5. The Technique of the Painting Process.

The technique adopted by the Vijayanagara artists at Tanjore is one of *fresco-secco*[15] or painting in lime medium on plaster. It consists in mixing the pigments with lime water and applying it to the dry plaster on the wall. This method stands in contrast to the Chola one, which consists in mixing the pigments with water and applying it over the wet plaster. In other words, the technique

15. S. Paramasivan—Nature, Vol. 137, May, 23, 1936, p. 867.

adopted with the Chola paintings is one of *fresco-buono* or true fresco.

The entire Vijayanagara stucco is so thin that it measures only from 2.4 to 3 m.m. in thickness. It is composed of three layers. The bottom one consists of rough lime plaster and is about 1.5 m.m. thick. Over it is a smooth plaster about 0.6 m.m in thickness with the paint film thereon. The rough and the smooth plaster vary in thickness in different places.

From the results of complete analysis,[16] it is clear that the artists have taken particular care to remove all the traces of impurities. Such deleterious impurities as clay, gypsum, and soluble salts of potassium and sodium are present in such minute quantities, that their presence may be ignored. It is quite possible that the artists used some sort of a 'pit' lime. They probably allowed the lime to remain well soaked in water in a pit, when the latter removed all the soluble impurities from the former and slaked it well.[17]

Plaster does not set well if some inert material like sand is not added to it. The Vijayanagara plaster contains only sand as an inert material.

So far as the pigments are concerned, the Nāyak artists have used black, especially for the outlines, white, yellow, red, brown, blue, green as primary colours and yellowish green, light blue and bluish green as mixed colours. For white they have used lime, lampblack for black, ochres for yellow, red and brown, lapis lazuli, especially in an impure state for blue and terre verte for green and a mixture of these for the other colours.

In many places, the Vijayanagara stucco and the paint film are loosely bound to the wall and the plaster, respectively, so that, when tapped, they fall off. It seems that the lime used as the binding medium with the pigments was of a poor quality, or somewhat carbonated or not well slaked. These defects are absent from the Chola paintings.

It may be necessary to point out other points of difference between the methods of execution of the Chola and the Vijayanagara paintings at Tanjore. It has already been said that the Chola tech-

16. Nature Loc. cit.

17. This subject being technical cannot be discussed at length here. The results of my investigation are in the course of publication.

nique is one of true fresco and that of the Vijayanagara paintings fresco-secco. The fomer consists in mixing the pigments with water and applying it over the wet plaster. Since the paintings must be done before the plaster dries up in the true fresco process, the technique requires a dextrous and a swift hand on the part of the artist. In the fresco-secco process such as is adopted with the Vijayanagara paintings, the painting can be done even on the dry wall. Thus there is no need to hurry through the work and consequently no such high artistic qualities are necessarily required as in the true fresco process. Great artists always prefer true fresco to fresco-secco process. Just as the style of the Vijayanagara paintings in Tanjore exhibit a certain degeneracy as compared with the Chola paintings, the fresco-secco process adopted by the former marks a degeneracy in the technique of the process of painting as compared with the high artistic qualities and skill required under the true fresco process. The five centuries that separate the Chola art from the Vijayanagara art at Tanjore marks a period when slow decadence set in not only over the art of painting, but also in the technique of the process of painting.

In conclusion, the writer wishes to express his best thanks to Dr. N. Venkata Ramanayya and Mr. M. Somasekhara Sarma for giving many helpful suggestions in the course of this work.

8

The Coinage of the Vijayanagara Dynasties

By

Mr. R. S. Panchmukhi, M.A.,

Office of the Superintendent for Epigraphy, Southern Circle, Madras.

(1) Historical introduction; (2) Coinage before the Vijayanagara period-punch-marked silver coins; Āndhra coins; Padmaṭaṅkas—punch and die systems; specific coins—weight of a gadyāṇa: a comparative statement; (3) Innovations introduced by the Vijayanagara power; (4) Types and symbols; (5) Legends: language and alphabet; (6) Weights and metals; (7) Denominations of coins: gadyāṇa—varāha—pon—pagoda; śuddha-varāha-ghaṭṭi-varāha—doḍḍa-varāha; chakrā-gadyāṇa; pratāpa—māḍa or māḍai; kāṭi, chinnam, paṇa, hāga—kākiṇī, tāra (silver), jital (copper), paṇa (copper), kāśu (copper), etc., (8) Mints.

I

After the overthrow of the Chāḷukyas of Kalyāṇi in the last quarter of the 12th century A.D., the Yādavas of Devagiri and the Hoysaḷas of Dvārasamudra rose to power and divided among themselves the western part of the empire, the portion in the east falling to the share of the Kākatiyas and other minor dynasties of the Telugu country. The Yādavas came into direct conflict with the neighbouring power the Hoysaḷas and constant warfare between them is attested by the existence of a great number of hero-stones recording such fights in the border land, found in the Hāvēri and the Rāṇibeṇṇūr Talukas of the Dharwar District. The sway of the Yādava monarchs Mahādēva and Rāmachandra was recognised in the north Mysore towards Shimoga while the Hoysaḷas under Ballāḷa III had maintained their territory in the east upto the Anantapur District where his inscriptions are discovered. Though it is not possible to ascertain the suzerain power at this period in the Bellary District round about Hampi—Hastināvatī (Ānegondi), it seems probable that this part of the country was held by Mummaḍi-Siṅgeya-Nāyaka and his son Kampiladēva who paid homage to the Yādava banner. The exploits of Kampila are described in some detail in the historical poems *Paradāra-sōdara-Rāmana-charite* and *Kumāra-Rāmana-sāṅgatya* which seem to contain a genuine account of historical facts based upon old chronicles. Kampila's conflicts with the Hoysaḷa, Kākatiya and Gajapati kings are narrated and his desperate attempt to crush the Muhammadan power at Delhi which had overthrown the old Hindu kingdoms of the Dekkan ended disastrously for his own principality. The fall of Kaṁpila's kingdom left no hope in the bosom of a Hindu chief to assert his power in these unsettled political conditions. But in the short interval, the circumstances had shaped themselves so favourably for the rise of a new Hindu power that the central authority of the Muhammadans at Delhi began to grow weak by the revolt of its officers who, throwing off their allegiance attempted to establish their independence (Elliot, *C. S. I.*, p. 90). This opportunity was hailed by the two sons of Saṅgama namely Harihara I and Bukka I who had been the State officers under Kaṁpila and proclaimed themselves kings in the ancestral territory of Kaṁpiladēva. Their kingdom was first confined within the limits of the Hoysaḷa country and in course of time comprised the whole strip of land between the three oceans excepting the small Muhammadan States in the Dekkan that had arisen in the early part of the 14th century A.D. This new power, having enlisted the sympathy and good-will of all the Hindu Chiefs of Southern India, was soon recognised as a paramount authority not only in the Kannaḍa and the Telugu countries but also in the Tamil land, although it had to meet with opposition at the beginning from the local Hindu Chiefs of the Chōḷa country; for Gaṇḍaragūḷi Māraya-Nāyaka the *Pradhāni* of Kaṁpaṇa is stated to have defeated and taken captive Veṉrumaṉkoṇḍa Sambuvarāya (*M. E. R.*, 1919, p. 103, para. 36, No. 267 of 1919 dated Śaka 1285). The Hindu culture which had been swept away by the overgrowing influence of the Muhammadans having been revived under the kings of the Vijayanagara empire, their royal emblems naturally comprised the outstanding gods of the Hindu pantheon, viz., the Boar-*avatāra* of Vishnu, Hanumān, Garuḍa, and Siva-Pārvatī. In course of time, these multiplied themselves numerously according to the king's proclivities towards Śaiva or Vaishṇava religion. But the principal family insignia continued to be the boar and the tutelary deity Śiva-Pārvatī or Virūpāksha of Hampī, as can be gathered from the seals of copper plate grants and the numismatic hoards of the period. The kingdom of Vijayanagara had a lengthened career of over 300 years being subjected to the rule of three families one succeeding the other, namely (1) the Saṅgama dynasty; Sāḷuva usurpation, (2) the Tuḷuva family and (3) the Āravīḍu or Karṇāṭa dynasty. In 1565 the Vijayanagara army under Rāmarāja the usurper was crushed by the combined forces of the four Muhammadan principalities of the Dekkan and the power of Vijayanagara was shattered. Tirumala, the brother of Rāmarāja attempted to restore the family but finding it impossible retired to Penukonda. The descendants of the true line finally took shelter from the storm of Muhammadan invasion at Chandragiri from which hill-fort Śrī-Raṅgarāya is stated to have handed over to the English the site of modern Madras together with the privilege of coining money on the condition that the English would preserve on their coinage " the representation of that deity who was the favourite object of their worship " (Marsden's *Numismata Orientalia,* part II, p. 739).

II

The earliest indigenous coins of India are mostly in silver, very few specimens being found in copper. They are found all over India and have been discovered in large numbers in the primitive tombs or kistavans of Southern India. They are called *purāṇas* or eldlings. They are of all shapes, oblong, angular, square, or nearly round with punch-marks on one or both sides. To understand the significance of the several symbols struck by punches on the obverse of these coins is by no means easy with the material at our disposal and the subject deserves a detailed study with reference to the numerous similar symbols found in ancient sculptures in the eastern as well as the western countries. D. B. Spooner (*Arch. Surv. Report,* 1905-6), R. D. Bhandarkar (*Ibid* 1913-14, pp. 210-13; 220-226) and E. H. C. Walsh (*J. B. O. R. S.,* 1919) are of opinion that the punch-marks on the obverse of the eldlings of all classes were put on by one authority rather than at different times. H. W. Codrington (*Ceylon Coins and Currency,* p. 16), on the other hand, holds that " these archaic coins were probably issued by local authorities—money-changers and merchants—and were submitted by them for the approval of the local king or governor, whose stamp appears on the reverse, the punch-marks on the other side, once blank, being those of the successive money-changers through whose hands they passed in the course of circulation." But a passage from Visuddhimagga by Buddhaghōsha (5th century A.D.) which appears to record a genuine tradition based on early works favours the former view when it states that " the goldsmith knows, by handling a *kahāpana* in which village or market town or city or mountain or river bank, it was made and by which craftsman." This seems to show that the punch-marks found on the obverse were the characteristic symbols of the mints where the coins were struck. It is, however, not possible to account for the existence of groups of symbols not in one particular order, which in some cases overlap each other.

Next in chronological order come the Āndhra coins which form a separate group by themselves, and by their types, symbols, metals and weight standards, they exhibit more a characteristic of Northern coinage than Southern. They are generally cast in moulds and are stamped with symbols of a Buddhist character. The obverse bears the figures of a lion or horse or elephant, etc., and the reverse has often the Buddhist cross or wheel to which the name of Ujjain symbol has sometime been given. The coins weigh from 35 to 560 grains in the order of reduplication as 35-70-140-280-560.

After the Āndhras to the advent of early Kadaṁbas (5th century A.D.), the history of coinage is shrouded in darkness as no specimens are found for that period. To the mints of the Kadaṁbas is assigned the origin of the *Padmaṭaṅkas* which have a lotus in the centre round which are four punch-marks of smaller *padmas*. The earliest authentic instances of the Chāḷukya coins are discovered in Siam and on the shore of the Island of Ramri, which are attributed by Elliot to Maṅgaleśa or one of his predecessors before the siege of Banavāsi, when the conqueror struck by the beauty of the *padmaṭaṅkas* adopted them as his model in substitution of the ruder type which formerly prevailed in the Chāḷukya mint (*C. S. I.*, p. 67). The *padmaṭaṅkas* were current in the Dakhan till the 14th century A.D. even though the new system of striking coins with a die had been introduced into South India during the Āndhra period. In course of time the punch was slowly abandoned as it involved a tedious process of striking the symbol or letters by recourse to different punches every time a new symbol was to be introduced. The coins of Jagadēkamalla and Chāḷukyachandra (Śaktivarman) of the Chāḷukya dynasty exhibit different features from the earlier ones. Some of them bear the figure of a boar in the centre with the king's name punched round about at the circumference. They are generally cup-shaped and the use of double punch or die is discernible from the depression observed on both sides of the coin. This punch system appears to have continued even during the Yādava period (*J. A. S. B.*, Numismatic Supplement, No. XXXIX (1925), pp. 6 ff.). The Hoysaḷa coins, on the other hand, were the production of a pure die (Elliot, Nos. 90-91, pl. III). The coins of the Kākatiya dynasty are very rare. Elliot thinks that "their cognizance appears to have been a bull couchant which is seen on several of the seals." He says that a copper coin had on the obverse a bull couchant and on the reverse the legend which is tentatively read as *Śrīmat* . . . ka . . . Kākati . . . Pratāpa Ru . . . etc. But R. S. R. Ayyangar has described some coins of this dynasty in which the figures of a lion are found in and round the centre (*J. A. H. R. S.*

Vol. I). From the seals of copper-plate grants of this family (*M.E.R.*, 1922, p. 122), the Ēkāmranātha inscription (*Ind. Ant.* Vol. XXI, p. 200) and the *Pratāparudrīyam* by Vidyānātha (V. 10) we learn that the emblem of the dynasty was a boar. It is not known from what source Elliot got the information that their emblem was a bull.

We are not in possession of details regarding the denominations of various coins current in the Pre-Vijayanagara period. But the epigraphical evidence tends to show that gadyāṇa, nishka, paṇa, hāga, dramma and dharaṇa were the most common coins under currency. Money was one among many of the media of exchange in ancient India and so the coinage was not divided into several denominations or fractions in the early period. It is worth while considering the weight standard of the gadyāṇa issued by the respective rulers before the Vijayanagara empire :

1. Buddhist coins (globular with traces of punch-marks on both sides) Bidie, Fig. 1.	Wt.	51·945	grains.
2. Chāḷukya coins :			
Bidie, Pl. I, Figs. 3 and 4 with the figure of a boar.	"	58·225	"
Elliott, *C. S. I.*, Pl. I No. 9.	"	66	"
3. Eastern Chāḷukya			
C. S. I. (Elliot)	"	65·9	"
Cat. Coin. I. M. Vol. I. (Smith), p. 313.	"	65·5	"
A large thin plate Rājarāja (1022-1063) *Ind. Ant.* Dec. 1896, No. 25	"	66·5	"
4. Kadaṁba (latter)			
C. S. I. (Elliot)			
Nos. 66	"	54·5	"
67	"	58·525	"
68	"	60·3	"
5. Hoysaḷa			
Elliot (*C.S.I.*)			
Nos. 90	"	61·75	"
91	"	63	"

6. Yādava

Padmaṭaṅkas	between 58 and	
	„ 59·2	„
(grouped under early anonymous coins in *C.C.I.M.*) (Smith), Num. Suppl. to *A.S.B.* No. XXXIX, pp. 6 ff.	„ 57·25	„

(Elliot No. 88 bearing Garuḍa on the obverse described under this dynasty probably belongs to the Silāhāras of Konkan whose emblem also was Garuḍa.)

7. Lingayat pagodas

Bidie Pl. I, Fig. 8 (14th century) }	„ 51·025	„
C.C.I.M. (Smith), p. 318. }	„ 50·85	„
half pagoda	„ 27	„
The Dom. Embl. and Coins of the South Indian dynasties, p. 18		
pagoda	„ 52	„
half „	„ 26·5	„

8. Kākatiya

One gold coin of Gaṇapaṭi (J.A.H.R.S., Vol. I., p. 139)	„ 56·25	„
Gold fanam, *C.S.I.* (Elliot, No. 93).	„ 6·6	„

The Chōḷa and Pāṇḍya gold pagodas weigh between 50·6 grains and 61·5 grains. (*The Dom. Embl. and Coins of the South Indian dynasties,* p. 38 f. and p. 48).

From the foregoing brief survey, the following points emerge :—

1. Both punch and die were used to coin money.

2. The shape of the coins which in the earliest specimens was of great variety became cup-shaped in the Chālukyan period and regularly circular later on.

3. The obverse bore the royal emblems and the legend which was usually the king's name or his *biruda,* and the reverse was plain. In the case of the later Kadaṁba and Hoysaḷa pieces, the obverse had the emblem and the reverse the legend.

4. The coinage was limited in its variety.

5. The weight of the pagoda was not standardized though in the majority of cases it ranged between 50 and 60 grains.

III

With the advent of the Vijayanagara power, the mintage became more regulated. The matrix was adopted to the exclusion of the punch. A uniform weight standard of the pagodas was introduced, the shape and metallic value of the different coins were fixed and the coinage in general was subdivided into several denominations. Among the administrative reforms of Mādhava, the prime minister under Harihara II, may be mentioned the improvement of the mint and the introduction of the Nāgarī alphabet in the public records and on the legends of the coins (Elliot, *C.S.I.*, p. 95). From the *Parāśara-Mādhavīya,* a copious commentary written by Mādhava on the text of the *Parāśara-Smṛiti,* it may be gathered that Harihara issued an order that taxes should be paid in money instead of in kind. This led to the coining of several fractions to suit the requirements of administration. Nāgarī began to be freely employed in the legends though the language was Kannaḍa. The multifarious symbols found on the obverse afford rich material for the study of the political, religious and historical events that happened in the periods of the respective kings that issued the coins.

Bidie observes that " it is a curious fact that the *Venetian Sequin,* which used to circulate freely on the Malabar coast, and the *Ducat* which also found its way to Madras are very nearly of the same weight as the pagoda " (*Pagoda or Varāha coins of Southern India,* p. 35). According to Prinsep (*Useful Tables,* pp. 43-44) the *Venetian Sequin* weighs 52·40 grains, *Ducat* 53·50 grains and the *Star Pagoda* 52·40 grains. It is interesting to find that the Vijayanagara pagoda also weighs between 50·65 and 52·912 grains, the heaviest being that of Sadāśivarāya (Bidie, pp. 41-45). Elliot has figured a gold coin of Śrī Krishṇarāya which weighs 119·7 grains. This is evidently a double pagoda which is a rare specimen of its kind in the pagoda collection of South India.

IV

" In Indian numismatics, there seems to be no permanent distinction between ' type ' and ' symbol.' In regard both to their origin and their use, they probably had much in common and the terms are often applied to the same designs according to the relative position of predominance or insignificance which they seem to occupy on a coin." (*C.I.C.B.M.* by Rapson, Article 139). A study of the types and symbols attains a paramount importance in the case of coins whose assignment to a particular king or family becomes impossible for want of the legend or the king's name on their reverse. In some pieces, only the emblems are observed to the exclusion of the legend, in which case a knowledge of the various types and designs would be of immense help in locating their period and mint. The following classification of the emblems on the Vijayanagara coins (gold and copper) may be made :—

First dynasty :—
1. Hanumān and Garuḍa in different poses.
2. Bull with a sword.
3. Elephant ; elephant and king.
4. Umāmahēśvara ; Lakshminārāyaṇa ; Sarasvatī-Brahmā ; Lakshmi-Narasiṁha (Akola series).

Second dynasty :—
1. Lion.
2. Veṇkatēśa.
3. Umāmahēśvara.
4. Bālakṛishṇa.
5. Bull.
6. Garuḍa.
7. Gaṇḍabhēruṇḍa.
8. Lakshmī-Nārāyaṇa.
9. Durgā, seated.

Third dynasty :—
1. Śrī Rāma.
2. Conch and discus.
3. Garuḍa.
4. Boar.
5. Elephant.
6. Bull-couchant.
7. Veṅkaṭēśa—with or without consorts.
8. Hanumān.
9. Veṅkaṭēśa (Gaṇḍikōṭa).

From this general tabular statement, it may be remarked that the first dynasty, though Śaiva in its faith favoured the Vaishṇava religion while the second and the third dynasties were pre-eminently the adherents of Vaishṇavism. These symbols may be arranged according to the kings who employed them in their mint, as follows :—

FIRST DYNASTY

Harihara I.
1. Hanumān (*Hanumantarāyi* Varāha).
2. Garuḍa.

Bukka I.
1. Hanumān.

Harihara II.	1. Umāmahēśvara.
	2. Lakshmī-Nārāyaṇa.
	3. Sarasvatī-Brahmā.
	4. Bull.
Bukka II.	1. Bull.
Dēvarāya I.	1. Umāmahēśvara.
	2. Lakshmī-Nārāyaṇa.
	3. Bull.
Rāmachandra.	1. Elephant.
Vijayarāya I.	1. Bull.
Dēvarāya II.	1. Elephant.
	2. Elephant and king fighting.
	3. Umāmahēśvara.
Vijayarāya II.	1. Elephant.
Mallikārjuna	1. Elephant.

The founders of the Saṅgama dynasty, Harihara I and Bukka I issued their coins with the representation of Hanumān embossed on them which are called the *Hanumantarāyi Varāhas.* One or two coins with the Garuḍa symbol are also figured in the (*M.A.R.* 1932). The adoption of the Hanumān type was perhaps intended to commemorate their connection with Kishkindhā the capital of the monkey-king Sugrīva, which was a source of inspiration in building the empire, and the Garuḍa type was a reminiscence of the Yādava hold in the territory, in which they first began to rule. The Hanumān type may also indicate the alliance political or otherwise, of Harihara I with the Kadambas whose flag had the representation of Hanumān. The adoption of the Vaishṇava as well as the Śaiva symbols on the obverse indicates the catholicity of vision of Harihara II who, as his name suggests was a follower of Śaivism. With Dēvarāya II, the elephant die was introduced in the Vijayanagara mint. This is explained by his being an adept in elephant-hunting and his assuming the biruda *Gajabēṇṭekāṛa.* His coins especially the copper issues, bear a representation of the scene of fight between the king and a wild tusker elephant which was ultimately tamed down by the powerful strokes of the spear with which the king was armed, (*M.A.R.*, 1932). The elephant device was continued by his successors, though Śiva-Pārvatī was still found on the gold issues of the period.

The coinage of the Sāḷuva kings is not known by any specimens now extant. The coins of the Tuḷuva family of which Kṛishṇadēvarāya was the most powerful monarch are represented in the gold and copper collections of the Madras and Mysore Museums and the numismatic cabinet of Rao Bahadur S. T. Srinivasagopalachari, M.A., M.L., Madras. The coin figured by Wilson contains on the obverse a representation of the *Narasiṅga-avatar* and on the reverse the legend in Kannaḍa characters, 'Ṅarasiṁha' (Elliot, *C.S.I.*, p. 95). Another coin which bears the name Śrī Pratāpa Narasiṁha' on the obverse and which has been wrongly assigned to Hoysaḷa Narasiṁha may possibly be an issue of Vīra Narasiṁha, as the prefix Pratāpa is peculiar to the Vijayanagara kings. Kṛishṇadēvarāya's coins may be classified under the following types from the variety of devices found on them :—

1. Veṅkaṭēśa.
2. Śiva and Pārvatī.
3. Bāla-Kṛishṇa.
4. Bull
5. Garuḍa.

These devices would at once show that Krishṇadēvarāya was under the Vaishṇava influence though he continued the Śiva-Pārvatī type out of regard for the family deity. With his brother Achyutarāya comes into prominence the use of the device Gaṇḍabhēruṇḍa on the obverse of both gold and copper coins. Sadāśivarāya revived the Garuḍa type along with the Lakshmi-Nārāyaṇa, though he was a Śaiva.

The kings of the Āraviḍu family were great adherents of the Vaishṇava religion as can be surmised from their names and their family god Veṅkaṭēśa of the Tirumalai hills. The devices on their coins are specified below :—

Tirumalarāya :—
1. Śrī Rāma.
2. Conch and discus.
3. Garuḍa.
4. Boar.
5. Elephant.
6. Bull,
7. Vishnu and Lakshmī seated, with the king's hands folded.

Śrī Rangaraya :— 1. Veṅkaṭēśa.

Veṅkaṭarāya I.	1. Veṅkaṭēśa—standing as at Tirupati.
	2. Garuḍa.
	3. Hanumān.
Śrī Raṅgarāya II.	1. Bull-couchant.
Veṅkaṭa II.	1. Veṅkaṭēśvara with consorts.

It may be noted that the third dynasty continued to have the same tutelary deity Śiva and Pārvatī throughout their political career, for, as noticed above, the last king Śrī Raṅgarāya is stated to have conferred upon the East India Company the right of coining money on the stipulation that the latter should stamp the figure of Śiva-Pārvatī on their coins.

V

The next point to be considered is the legend on the reverse of the coins, and the script in which it is couched. The earliest coins available to us belonging to the post-Āndhra period do not bear any legend on the obverse which is on the other hand, occupied by some punch-marks or floral designs ; the reverse having the punch-struck *padmas* or a boar. The first known coin that bears the king's name is that of Kubja-Vishṇu-varddhana of the eastern Chāḷukya family (*C.I.M.*, Vol. I, Pl. XXX, and *Ind. Ant.* Vol. XXI, Dec. 1896, No. 34) who is mentioned by the *biruda* "Vishamasiddhi" in archaic Telugu-Kannaḍa characters. In the subsequent periods, the coins of the later Chāḷukya, Hoysaḷa and Silāhāra kings contain the king's name written in Kannaḍa characters while some specimens of the later Kadaṁbas and Yādavas show it in Nāgarī. It is noteworthy that the founders of the first Vijayanagara dynasty, viz. Harihara I and Bukka I have used the Kannaḍa alphabet of the Hoysaḷa period which as distinct from the Telugu characters, exhibit in spite of their general likeness some peculiar features which are characteristic of Kannaḍa. The adoption of the Kannaḍa legend and the emblems of Hanumān and Garuḍa by the first two kings tends to prove that the family had greater affinities with the Kannaḍa language and Karṇāṭaka where the Kadaṁbas with the Hanumān flag and the Yādavas with the Garuḍa ensign had held sway for about two centuries prior to their rise. In a Tamil epigraph from Guḍimaṅgalam in the Coimbatore district (No. 136 of *M.E.R.* for 1916) dated in Śaka 1458, Mahāmaṇḍalēśvara Valaiyadēva-Mahārāja 'who was the right arm of the king' i.e., Achyutarāya, signs his name at the close, in Kannaḍa characters and language. Though his titles indicate a Chōḷa origin, he appears to have adopted the State language for his signature. This shows that the language of the royal family was Kannaḍa. It may be noted in passing that Nāgarī was gradually substituted for Kannaḍa in coins during and after the reign of Harihara II.

VI

The basis of the metric system in the North Indian coinage was the *rati* seed whereas in South India, Kaḻañju and Mañjāḍi were requisitioned for the purpose. In course of time, the metal pieces cut to the weight of these seeds were substituted for the seminal units, whose weights varied according to usage in different parts of the Dakhan and South India. In Mahārāshṭra and Konkan, the heavy gadyāṇa, weighed 72 grains. In the Tamil country, the Kaḻañju of 20 Mañjāḍi was equal in theory to the same weight. Between the two *Kannaḍa* light gadyāṇa was of the same weight as the coin of the name, i.e., 50-52 grains. The monetary system of the country behind Goa and South and North Kanara districts followed that of the up-Kannaḍa country. The coins usually bore the same name as the weights as for example, the *gadyāṇa, dharaṇa,* etc. The metals of which the early coins were composed mainly lead, copper, potin, silver and gold, the last being found in very few cases. The earliest punch-marked coins are all of silver and the gold issues of the type are as hitherto known, very rare. With the advent of the Kadaṁbas and the early Chāḷukyas, the currency of South India consisted chiefly of gold and copper. Gold, silver and copper were alike used for coinage in the subsequent periods down to the time of the East India Company.

VII

During the Vijayanagara period, the coinage was divided into numerous varieties both in gold and copper. From a study of the stone and copper documents, it may be observed that the following principal coins were under currency :—

Gold :—	1. Gadyāṇa, varāha, poṉ or pagoda.
	2. Pratāpa, māḍa or māḍai.
	3. Kāṭi.
	4. Paṇa.
	5. Hāga.
Silver :—	1. Tāra.
Copper :—	1. Paṇa.
	2. Jital.
	3. Kāśu, etc.

Regarding the coinage of Dēvarāya II, a contemporary report of Abdur-razak (A.D. 1443) informs us that he issued the following pieces :—

Gold :—	1. Varāha.
	2. Partab = ½ varāha.
	3. Fanam = ⅒th partab.
Silver :—	1. Tar = ⅙th fanam.
Copper :—	1. ⅓ tar.

This report is meagre and does not exhaust all the coins in the series. The value and mutual relationship between the several pieces issued by the Vijayanagara kings may be determined to some extent by a study of the contexts in which they occur in the records.

Gadyāṇa, Varāha, Pagoda.	These terms denote the same coin (the Karkal inscription of Bhairava II, Śaka 1508, *Ep. Ind.* Vol. VIII, p. 130).

It weighs about 52 grains and is generally known as 'pagoda.' The word gadyāṇa occurs in the North Indian inscriptions also (Kuruspal stone inscription of Sōmēśvaradēva, Śaka 1019, *Ep. Ind.* Vol. X, p. 37). According to Yājñavalkya (Chapt. III, 258), a Gadyāṇaka is a weight equal to 32 guñjas or approximately 62 grains. Subsequently it began to be used in the sense of a coin weighing about 60-65 grains which was ultimately standardized at 50-52 grains during the Vijayanagara period. This coin was also known by the name Varāha a name which persisted in the South Indian coinage from the time of the western Chāḷukyas down to the period of the East India Company. The coin owes its name to the *varāha-lāñchchhana* of the Chāḷukyas who first adopted it in their mint. This testifies to the influence which the monetary system of the Chāḷukyas exercised on the Vijayanagara coinage. In the gold coins of the first dynasty, no representation of the boar is traced so far. Tirumala and Śrī-Raṅga of the third dynasty have struck this figure on the gold pieces. The copper hoard, however, exhibits several specimens which bear this representation together with a sword on the obverse. There is one type of coins which is very common, but the figure on which is variously called Durgā, Vārāhī or Vishṇu's boar incarnation. It may be noted that the figure has a divine face and two hands. This coin is usually called the Durgī-varāha. The Vijayanagara pagoda in general is described by foreign visitors thus :— " It is coined in certain cities of this kingdom of Narasiṅga

. . . this coin is round and made in a mould " (Barbosa). " It bears impressed on it on one side two images and on the other the name of the king who commanded it to be struck " (Paes). " These pardai . . . have two devils stamped upon one side of them and certain letters on the other " (Varthema). There are three varieties of this coin, viz.: (1) Ghaṭṭi-varāha (*S.I.I.*, Vol. IV, Nos. 274, 279), (2) Doḍḍa-varāha (*Ibid.* Vol. VII, p. 108) and (3) Śuddha varāha. The last is the same as varāha or gadyāṇa of 52 grains. The relationship between the doḍḍa-varāha and ghaṭṭi-varāha is not known. No. 198 of *M.E.R.* for 1922 which is a document of the Tamil country shows that 140 poṉ were equivalent to 100 ghaṭṭi-Veṅkaṭarāyan varāhaṉ. From *Ep. Carn.* Vol. VI. Mg. 48, it is learnt that ga. 775 connotes the money 7 honnu and 5 haṇa, thus indicating that the terms gadyāṇa (varāha) and honnu are interchangeable. Since 100 ghaṭṭi-varāha = 140 poṉ, the ratio between the two coins may be deduced at 7: 5. Doḍḍa-varāha appears to have been a coin of a still higher value. It may be noted that the coinage of the East India Company contained the following copper fractions: *duḍḍu* (= 3 pies), ghaṭṭi-duḍḍu (a coin of account = 4 pies) doḍḍa-duḍḍu (= 6 pies) which, except the second, are still in circulation in the Bombay-Karnāṭak. The ratio between the duḍḍu and ghaṭṭi-duḍḍu works out at 7: 5.25 which is approximately equal to the one arrived at between varāha and ghaṭṭi-varāha. Whether ghaṭṭi-varāha was actually a coin issued from the mint or only a coin of account it is not possible to say. Two copper-plate inscriptions, (*M.A.R.*, 1931, Nos. 9 and 10) dated respectively in Śaka 1506 and 1507, however, mention the coin as *nijaghaṭṭi-varāha-gadyāṇa.* Doḍḍa-duḍḍu is double the value of the ordinary duḍḍu of 3 pies. On this analogy, it may be suggested that doḍḍa-varāha was double in weight and value of the ordinary gadyāṇa. We have got only one rare instance of this doḍḍa-varāha in the double pagoda of 119.7 grains weight issued by the Tuḷuva king Kṛishṇadēvarāya which is figured in *Elliot's Coins of Southern India,* Pl. III, No. 112. According to Varthema who visited the Vijayanagara court in 1504 a gadyāṇa was equal to 20 paṇas, whereas Abdur-razak gives it only 10 paṇas...... (Elliot: *History of India,* Vol. IV, p. 109). From this, it may be gathered that the former's *gadyāṇa* was the doḍḍa-varāha while that of the latter was an ordinary *gadyāṇa* The coin *chakra-gadyāṇa* (*S.I.I.*, Vol. IV, No. 262) belonging to the reign of Achyutarāya, was probably a coin with the symbol of *chakram* impressed on it. This is probably the same as the chakra-varāha which occurs in the *Nellore Inscriptions* which is equated with kuruka-varāha = Rs. 4 (*Nellore Inscriptions*: Glossary of Technical terms). There is again the expression kāṭi-gadyāṇa usually found in the inscriptions of South Kanara, whose relationship with the varieties mentioned above is not clear. *S.I.I.*, Vol. VII. No. 298, which enumerates the coin as kāṭi-gadyāṇa 27 honnu, kā. ga. 5 honnu tends to show that kāṭi-gadyāṇa is equivalent to honnu (= poṉ, varāha or pagoda). But from Nagar 69 (*Ep. Carn.* Vol. VIII.) dated in Śaka 1385, it is apparent that 4 kāṭis went to make one varāha.

The next coin after gadyāṇa was pratāpa. We come across gold coins of the Vijayanagara period which are half and quarter of the pagoda in weight. The half pagoda (Elliot: Nos. 96-99, p. 102) was probably known by the name pratāpa. Even to-day, a villager is accustomed to value varāha and pratāpa at Rs. 4 and Rs. 2 respectively in money accounts, though the coins have become long obsolete. The quarter pagoda (there are several specimens in the Madras Museum, see also *Ind. Ant.* Vol. XX, Nos. 7 and 8) was designated as kāṭi. A copper-plate grant of Vīra Bhūpati-Voḍeya dated in Śaka 1309 (*Ep. Carn.* Vol. XI, Moḷakalmuri No. 31) registers a gift of 400 pratāpa-gadyāṇa which might be a coin half of the varāha. The Tamil Māḍai (*Ep. Ind.* Vol. VII, p. 132; Māḍai = 5 paṇam) and the Telugu *Māḍa* are probably the counterparts of the Kannaḍa Pratāpam, (= Rs. 2 or Re. 1-12-0: *Nellore Inscription,* Glossary). Pratāpa and Kāṭi are fresh addition to the gold coinage of the Vijayanagara period. It may be mentioned that the prefix *pratāpa* is applied first to the name of Harihara II, his predecessors being called Vīra Harihara I and Vīra Bukka I.

From No. 172 of App. C. of 1916 which is a royal order to Śrīgirinātha of Chandragiri to remit the jōḍi of 131 poṉ (varāha) and 6¼ paṇam or 1316¼ paṇam, it is clear that 10 paṇam made up one poṉ (= gadyāṇa). This ratio is confirmed by several records (A.D. 1112, 1215 and 1407) coming from Mysore and Bombay-Karnāṭak (*Ep. Ind.* Vol. XIII, p. 58, *Ep. Carn.* V, Arsikeri 51, *Ibid* IV, Heggaḍadevanakoṭe 62, respectively). But according to an inscription of Krishṇadēvarāya dated in Śaka 1444 which states that ga. 397 63+ga. 3762+ga. 42 were equal to 477 gadyāṇas, 5 paṇas went to make one gadyāṇa. Similarly an inscription at Hariharapur in the Kadur district (*M.A.R.* 1932, No. 42, pp. 209-10) dated in Śaka 1340 during the reign of Dēvarāya II tells us that 17 gadyāṇa and 11 paṇa made up 18½ varāha which gives the value of about 5 paṇas to a varāha. It is not clear whether the *gadyāṇa* mentioned here was the pratāpa-gadyāṇa which, as stated above, was half the value of śuddha varāha. An inscription (*S.I.I.* Vol. IV, No. 274) belonging to the reign of Achyutarāya mentions a coin called *chinna* whose value is not known. The *Nellore Inscriptions* (Glossary) states that *chinnam* is is both a weight and a coin, the latter being ⅛th of the pagoda or 7 annas. From *S.I.I.*, Vol. VII, No. 348, which gives the equation ga. 102 – 1 + ga. 22 – 0 = ga. 125, it is apparent that the Vijayanagara mint issues a coin eight of which made up a gadyāṇa. This was evidently the chinnam referred to above. The next coin in denomination after paṇa is a hāga which was ¼th paṇa. This was also called a kākiṇī as remarked in the *Śivatatvaratnākara* in the verse.

सा काकिनी ताश्चपणश्चतस्रः । (IV Kallōla, IV Taraṇga.)

This coin is stated to have been current in the north एतत्पद्यद्वयेनोक्तमानमुत्तरदेशजम् . Compare in this connection the Līlāvati of Bhāskara (quoted in *Ep. Carn.*, Vol. IV, p. 31) according to which 4 Kākiṇi made one paṇa.

The only silver coin known to us of this period is figured by Hultzsch, in *Ind. Ant.*, Vol. XXV, p. 318. It belongs to Pratāpa-Dēvarāya and bears on the obverse the figure of an elephant. Tāra as a coin occurs frequently in the inscriptions of South-Kanara. According to Abdur-razak, it was equal to ⅙th fanam while *taurh* as reported by Mahaun (*Account*, J. R. A. S., 1896, p. 344) was $1/15$th fanam, and *Tare* was equal to $1/16$th fanam according to Varthema. The last two might represent the same coin whereas the first appears to be a different coin higher in value. It may be noted that the term *tāra* is found in Kauṭalya's *Arthaśāstra* in the passage तारमुपशुद्धं वा ॥ in the book dealing with Mints, etc.

The copper issues of the Vijayanagara mint are vast and present a fertile field for the study of different types. Abdur-razak's report refers to only one coin namely *jital*. The *Parāśara-Mādhava* (III, p. 26) and the Mitākshara (II, 99 (i) 215) bear ample testimony to the existence of *paṇa* as a copper coin. Besides these, Kāśu was another coin of copper whose actual value varied according to different localities. In the representative copper collection in the Madras Museum and in the private cabinet of Rao Bahadur S. T. Srinivasagopalachari, M.A., M.L. (Madras), I have seen several varieties whose actual value has yet to be determined. From references contained in the South Indian Inscriptions, it appears that *kāśu* was a gold, silver and copper coin of different values.

VIII

While touching upon the punch-marked silver coins, I have remarked above that the several groups of symbols struck on them represented the characteristic marks of the different mints in the country. This testifies to the existence of private mints under the supervision of the State. It is worthy of note that one of the officers under the king was the Superintendent of taxes on mints (*achchu-pannāyad-adhishṭhāyaka*). During the Vijayanagara period several private and State-managed mints must have existed and references to these may be found in the expressions Bārakanūru gadyāṇa, Maṅgalūru-gadyāṇa, etc., which show that Barakūr and Maṅgalūru in South Kanara contained mints. In some of the coins, the mints are indicated by a letter on the obverse such as Ne (for Nellore), Ma (for Madura), etc. There are certain coins of the first Vijayanagara dynasty in which the letters *Dē* and *A* are found on the obverse in addition to the legend on the reverse (*Ind. Ant.* XXIII, p. 24, fig 1, XXV, pp. 303-5, Nos. 12, 13, 23, etc., and XX, p. 302, Nos. 9-10). They may perhaps be the abbreviations of the names of places where the coins, were minted. A noteworthy point in the Vijayanagara mintage is that some of the subordinate chiefs were empowered to coin money in their own name as for example the *Lakhamaṇa-Daṇṇāyaka* type. The multifarious types of coins issued by one and the same sovereign may also suggest the existence of a number of mints in the country each of which was furnished with a die or dies of a particular symbol such as an elephant, a bull or Umāmahēśvara, etc. Barbosa, writing about 1516 states that " it (pagoda) is coined in certain cities of this kingdom of Narasiṅga and throughout all India they use this money, which passes in all those kingdoms " (*Ceylon Coins and Currency* ; p. 91). From Elliot's *C.S.I.*, No. 78, which has on the reverse the Kannaḍa word *Nakara* below the figure of Hanumān, it may be surmised that commercial bodies such as the Chambers of Commerce, etc., were also authorised to coin money. The Vijayanagara coins are found all over South India and Dakhan. It is interesting to find that at Bassein in the Akola district of the Central Provinces, a large hoard of gold issues from the days of Harihara to the days of Achyutarāya have been unearthed which has led some scholars to the inference that the Vijayanagara mint had been established at so distant a place as the Central Provinces where their supremacy must have been acknowledged (M.A.R. 1932)

Though it has no direct bearing on the subject under discussion, mention may be made here of the so-called medals or the *Rāma-ṭaṅkas* which were issued by Tirumala and his successors of the third dynasty. There is a good number of varieties in the *Ṭaṅkas* of different sizes and of various shapes, which deserves an independent study by the numismatists.

My sincere thanks are due to Dr. Gravely, and Mr. T. G. Aravamuthan, who ungrudgingly showed me the coins, and got their plaster casts prepared.

The following coins are arranged in the plates (pp. 104 and 112) :—

1. Punch-marked silver coin.
2. Chālukya Jagadēkamalla.
3. Chālukya Rājarāja.
4. Hoysala.

FIRST DYNASTY

5. Harihara I (pagoda).
6. Bukka I (pagoda).
7. Harihara II (pagoda).
8. Harihara II (half pagoda).
9. Dēvarāya (pagoda).
10. Dēvarāya (half pagoda).
11. Devarāya (quarter pagoda).

SECOND DYNASTY

12. Narasarāya (probably Vīra Narasiṁha) (half pagoda).
13. Narasarāya (half pagoda).
14. Krishṇarāya (Durgā seated) (pagoda).
15. Krishṇarāya (Durgā seated) (half pagoda).
16. Achyutarāya (double headed eagle) (varāha).
17. Achyutarāya (double headed eagle) (half varāha).
18. Sadāśivarāya (varāha).
19. Sadāśivarāya (quarter pagoda).

THIRD DYNASTY

20. Tirumala I (pagoda).
21. Tirumala I (half pagoda).
22. Venkaṭa I (pagoda).
23. Venkaṭa I (half pagoda)
24. Venkaṭa II (half pagoda).
25. Krishṇarāya (double pagoda) (from Elliot's *C.S.I* pl. III, No. 112).

For want of leisure, I could not examine other gold specimens and several varieties of copper coins stored in the cabinet. They are not represented in the plates.

9

Shahaji's Relations with Vijayanagara

By

Mr. D. B. Diskalkar, M.A.,

Curator, Historical Museum, Satara.

Mahārashtra and Karṇāṭaka have almost always been under one imperial rule from early times to a very late period, the centre of power being generally towards the Karṇāṭaka. The Chāḷukyas, early and later, and the Rāshṭrakūṭas were purely Karṇāṭaka dynasties and the Yādavas belonged to Mahārāshṭra. Even the Muhammedan Bahmani rulers and most of the succeeding Sultans belonged more to Karṇāṭaka rather than to the Mahārāshṭra. It was only in the Marāṭā period that Karṇāṭaka had a separate political existence generally subordinate to Mahārāshṭra, and the foundations of the Mahārāshṭra power in the Karṇāṭaka were laid by Shahaji at the cost of the Vijayanagara empire.

Soon after the overthrow of the great Yādava rule in 1312 which comprised almost the whole of the present Mahārāshṭra and the Karṇāṭaka, two kingdoms were founded in its place. One was the Hindu kingdom of Vijayanagara founded in 1336 A.D. and the other was the Muhammedan Bahmani kingdom founded in 1347 at Gulbarga. As their centres of activities were not very far from each other it was natural for them to come in conflict very frequently for the spread of their power, just as the Peshwa and the Nizam who founded their families almost at the same time, and not far from each other, did in modern times. The Bahmani's flourished considerably specially in Mahārāshṭra exterminating or subduing with wonderful tact and vigour the local Hindu chiefs. They would not allow the Vijayanagara king to rule independently who consequently always found his existence precarious. The hard and continuous struggle for independence against severe odds maintained by the Vijayanagara kings for more than three centuries is almost unparalleled in Indian history only to be compared with that of the Udaipur family in Rajputana. The five Sultanates into which the Bahmani kingdom was subsequently divided continued the fight with unabated vigour. When they found that they could not subdue Vijayanagara singly they united their strength and gave a shattering blow to it in the famous battle of Taḷikōṭa or rather of Rākshasatangaḍi. Vijayanagara could not get a Hindu ruler to help and save it. But the Vijayanagara family could not be wiped out of existence. It soon restored itself to something of the position it had held before, and began to rule from a new place at Penugoṇḍa. Even this it could not do peacefully. The Bijapur Sultan from the west and the Golconda Sultan from the east with united strength, continued to invade the Karṇāṭaka and 'ultimately seized the heritage of the recently shattered empire of Vijayanagara and crushed its numberless, disunited, mutually jealous, and warring Hindu feudatories across the entire Indian peninsula.'

Shahaji's connection with Karṇāṭaka, and subsequently with Vijayanagara began in these Bijapur campaigns, and was continued to his death. Changing his allegiance at least four times before, just to the Ahmednagar Sultan, then to the Bijapur Sultan (1625), again to the Ahmednagar Sultan (1628), then to the Moghal emperor (1630), again to the Ahmednagar Sultan (1632), he went over to the Bijapur Sultan in October 1632, whom he served to his last although in December 1647 he had for a time thought of taking service with Golconda.

Soon after his joining the service, Shahaji was ordered by the Bijapur Sultan to proceed to the Karṇāṭaka in the autumn of 1637 and help Randulla Khan, chief commander in reducing Vīrabhadra the Nāyaka of Ikkēri. This he did to the satisfaction of the General and the Sultan. Next year Shahaji accompanied Randulla Khan to Karṇāṭaka and took Bangalore from the Nāyak of the place, and was placed there to organise and carry on the government of the conquered provinces. In his third campaign against Kange Nāyaka of Basavāpaṭan in 1639 Randulla Khan was joined by Shahaji, who exhibited great valour in defeating the Nāyaka. Randulla returned to the capital leaving Shahaji to govern the province. About the year 1642 during Shahaji's absence at Bijapur the Nāyak rulers in the Karṇāṭaka revolted and threw off their allegiance to the Sultan. In the following year therefore the Sultan sent a large army under Mustafa Khan—as Randulla had died in the meanwhile—and ordered Shahaji to help him. They subdued the several chiefs and established again the Sultan's power over them.

About this time Śrīrangarāya III began to rule at Chandragiri the remnant of the old Vijayanagara empire from 1642. Just at this time the definite treaty between the Muhammedan States of the Deccan and Moghal emperor set free the States of Bijapur and Golconda to continue more vigorously their aggressive policy in the south. Śrī-Ranga therefore pursued a vigorous policy of bringing about the union of all the feudatories and their loyalty to himself. When Mir Jumla, the Golconda general, advanced towards Vellore against the emperor he was defeated and had to go back. Upon this Bijapur and Golconda thinking that the rising power of the Hindu emperor would be harmful to both of them joined their forces and marched against Vellore. Finding his position untenable against the combined armies, the emperor sent an ambassador to Mustafa, the Bijapur general, and tried to detach him from Golconda. But this he refused to do. It is also said that he requested Shahaji to intercede for him with Mustafa, but Shahaji's words fell on deaf ears. At last Vellore was invested and the emperor submitted and agreed to pay 50 lakhs of gold pieces and 150 elephants as indemnity (1646). Next year the combined armies marched towards Jinji with Shahaji as the assistant of Mustafa. Jinji was besieged. Mir Jumla for some reason or other left the siege only to be conducted by the Bijapur troops. Mustafa suspected Shahaji of treason and put him into fetters. After the fort was captured on 25th December, 1648, the Bijapur general took Shahaji to Bijapur, where however he was released on 16th May, 1649, upon his undertaking to continue to be loyal and sent back to Bangalore. In 1651, when a contest took place between Bijapur and Golconda on the point of the division of the territories conquered jointly, Shahaji had to fight with Mir Jumla. Sufficient information is not obtainable of the further connection of Shahaji with the Vijayanagara emperor. It is seen that Mir Jumla, the Golconda general conducted regular operations against the emperor and Shahaji against his feudatory chiefs. In 1656 the emperor is seen to have recovered a good deal but just the next year he was severely defeated by Mir Jumla who even took his capital Penugoṇḍa. The Raj fled to Chandragiri and began to rule from there. In 1657 when Muhammad Adilshaha died and his minor son came to the throne the Nāyakas of the Karṇāṭaka revolted. The Sultan sent Mulla Muhammad and Shahaji against them. Shahaji tried to capture Tanjore and Trichinopoly in 1659, but was repulsed. In 1661 however he was successful in capturing Tegnapatan and Porto Novo. In 1663 he was imprisoned on the suspicion that he was becoming unruly but was released in a short time. In 1663 finding that the Nāyak of Beḍnūr had revolted against the Sultan, Shahaji marched against him and subdued him. While he was returning from this expedition he met an accidental death on the way on 23rd January, 1664.

It will be seen from the above account that the whole of Shahaji's later career from 1637 to 1664 was occupied in helping his master the Bijapur Sultan, in his conquests of the Karṇāṭaka, and in depriving the last Vijayanagara emperor, Śrīrangarāya, of his possessions ultimately to bring him to total extinction. His relations with Vijayanagara are seen to be all along unfriendly though he was a Hindu. To what extent he was responsible in bringing about the ruin of Vijayanagara depends upon the answer to the question what position he had occupied at the Bijapur court. The Hindu accounts like the *Shiva Bharata, Rādhāmādhavavilāsachampu* and the Brihadīśvara temple inscription give him most of the credit, if not the whole, of conquering the Karnāṭaka while the Muhammadan accounts like the *Muhammadnāmā* and the *Būsatin-z-sulatin* show that Shahaji was not the 'supreme army chief, nor even the commander of an independent division, but only one of the many Bijapuri generals serving under the eyes and orders of the Muslim *generalissimo*'—Sir Jadunath Sarkar who believes more in the Muhammadan sources and Dr. S. Krishnaswami Aiyangar who thinks otherwise have discussed this point in detail in the *Modern Review* of July 1929 and in the *Journal of Indian History* of August 1930 respectively. I am inclined to accept generally the arguments of the latter scholar when we see the actual results of the Bijapur conquests of the Karṇāṭaka in the regular foundation of a Maratha kingdom and the colonisation of the Marathas in the Karṇāṭaka which was not possible if Shahaji had been only one of the leading Sardars of the Sultan. Dr. Krishnaswami says,—'Judged by the combined evidence of all the sources of history, Shahaji the Mahratta appears to have been a man of ability both as a soldier and as an administrator. He first played an important part in the conquests of the various petty states of the Karṇāṭaka for Bijapur. Slowly but surely he was able to build up from out of the conquests a pretty big government for himself certainly under the authority of his masters at Bijapur to begin with, but gradually to become more or less entirely his own (pp. 214-15).'

If this line of arguments is accepted we must say that Shahaji was responsible to a great extent in first conquering the different Karṇāṭaka States and in bringing about the ruin of Vijayanagara. He was no doubt the greatest Hindu general in those days whose help could have saved Vijayanagara for some more years. But throughout his career we never find in him any higher ideas of nationality or religion. The only aim of his life seems to be to work for his master and aspire for his favours. It is true that Shahaji is not to be singled out and condemned for this kind of mentality. In fact we find most of the Hindu princes of the time doing the same. Even the feudatory princes of Vijayanagara acted against each other and against him. It has been shown above how Shahaji frequently changed his allegiance. There is no doubt that he had to do so because his services were not properly appreciated. Even Bijapur whom he served the longest and to his last imprisoned him twice on suspicion of treason, and we find Shahaji sometimes expressing utter disgust for his service. If Shahaji had left the cause of Bijapur and had taken up that of Vijayanagara the history of the Karnāṭaka could have taken a different turn. The foundation of the Maratha power in the south which he laid by his Bijapur service could as well have been laid by the Vijayanagara service.

10

What Sivaji and the Maratha State owed to Vijayanagara *

BY

MR. T. S. SHEJWALKER, B.A.,

Bharat Itihasa Samshodhak Mandal, Poona.

" IT was Akbar's vision of empire that has to be regarded as perhaps the root cause of the rise of the Marathas to political power, and it may equally well be regarded that the collapse of the Hindu empire of Vijayanagara was as much of a contributory, as the Mughal advance in the Dekhan, to the rise of the Marathas as a nation and as a political power in the seventeenth and eighteenth centuries," wrote Dr. S. Krishnaswami Aiyangar in a contribution he made to the Śivāji[1] Tercentenary volume in 1930. Three years earlier Mr. A. Sankara Rao had written in his article[2] " Hindu India from Tāḷikōta to Śivaji's Rise " that " Śivāji and successors were the true successors of the Vijayanagara rulers and the Hindu revival after Tāḷikōta combined with the reactionary policy of Aurangazeb gave a tremendous impetus to the rise of the Maratha power . . . when circumstances made it the only possible alternative for a self-respecting nation to assert itself." Earlier still, Dr. Krishnaswami had hinted that Śivāji's coronation and his southward expedition into the Carnatic " had in it the idea of reviving the Hindu empire of the South " and " the ambition to stand before Aurangazeb as the acknowledged successor of the emperors of Vijayanagara."[3] It was good that two non-Maratha students of history should have said so, for the Maratha thinkers had very early hit upon the same idea and one historian,[4] who began writing a history of the Marathas for the period 1300 to 1600 A.D. had (unconsciously perhaps) found himself writing a history of Vijayanagara mainly based on Sewell and (what is still more important), called it " *Mahārāṣṭra-Mahōdayācha Poorvaraṅga* " or the First Part of the Great Rise of Maharashtra. And all this is as it should be, for History in its correct sense knows

* The author spells Shivaji as Śivaji and Shahaji as Śahaji.

1. *Sivāji-Nibandhāvali,* Part II—p. 27.

2. Quarterly Journal—Andhra Historical Research Society—Vol. II—No. I—p. 57.

3. *Nāyaks of Madurā*—Editor's notes—pages 27, 134, 177.

4. The late Mr. N. K. Gadre—wrote it first in the magazine *Saraswati-Mandir*—1905.

no revolution in human affairs, every event being the effect of a previous cause, which in its own days was the effect of a previous event in History. Great men like Śivāji who are supposed to be epoch-makers are themselves the product of their times, which are not of their own creation. But for a certain ordering of previous events of which the epoch-maker makes full use to fashion his own creation and mould his destiny, no advent of a new age is ever heralded in history.

Now, to begin our investigation into the thesis "What Śivāji and the Maratha State owed to Vijayanagara", the first question that will occur to the superficial reader of History is "How possibly can there be any connection between Śivāji and Vijayanagara, two facts separated by three generations of time". The city of Vijayanagara was abandoned as the capital in 1567 and Śivāji saw the light of the day only in 1630. The only connection that can be thought of between Śivāji and Vijayanagara is that his father Śahāji "does certainly appear as having been mainly responsible for the destruction of the empire of Vijayanagara," as tersely put by Dr. S. K. Aiyangar in reviewing[5] the life of Śahāji by Dr. Bālkrishna. When Śivāji went to the Madras Coast in 1677, it was to conquer territories from the kingdom of Bijapur and not from Vijayanagara which had ceased to exist.

So far so good. A matter of fact historian like Sir Jadunath Sarkar thought it "incredible that a born strategist like Śivāji could have really intended to annex permanently a territory on the Madras Coast".[6] "It was merely to squeeze the country of its accumulated wealth and return home with the booty" to replenish his treasury gone empty by coronation expenditure on a lavish scale (in foolish feeding of worthless Brahmins, etc.) that Śivāji made the hazardous adventure of leaving his none-too-safe tiny kingdom and setting out on a trek of thousand miles and more ! ! ! It could not occur to this "Primus in Indis" that a "born strategist" like Śivāji should have prescience to provide for the safety of his new kingdom, knowing as he thoroughly did the political currents of South India during the latter part of the seventeenth century, not to speak of higher idealism with which his whole life was permeated and without understanding which no historian, however learned, can hope to present an intelligible biography of the great hero. We shall presently have occasion to explain this subjective side of

5. *Journal of Indian History*—Vol. XI—p. 404.
6. *Sivaji and His Times*—Second Edition—p. 352 note.

Śivāji's life. But before we do that we must look to the effects produced by the impact of Vijayanagara rule on Maratha life and mind.

It is a well known historical trait of Hindu mind that it is not political. We never thought of politics unless it forced itself on our attention. In this we markedly differ from the Greeks and the Romans and their cultural heirs even at present, lost as we have our independence. The same was true during historic epochs. The rest of India seems to have slept silent when Sindh was islamized in the eighth century. The same attitude continued when the Punjab was annexed by Muhammad of Ghazni. Two centuries later the whole of Northern India was conquered, but we of the Dekhan do not seem to have stirred. At last Malik Kafur carried sword and fire from Devagiri to Madura and one Hindu kingdom after another toppled down like a house of cards. Then we had to think and think furiously of the problem of our national independence and of the preservation of our age-long culture. The first Hindu State which made a successful stand in this national struggle was the Empire of Vijayanagara. The line of policy pursued by that empire was the line—modified of course by the exigencies of time and further experience—continued by the Great Śivāji in his successful career after the passing away of that " Never-to-be-forgotten Empire "

But where could Śivāji have imbibed the policy of Vijayanagara ? For an answer to this question we must understand the mind of the Maratha populace in general at the beginning of the seventeenth century and study the particular influences brought to bear on Śivāji's mind. Although Maharashtra was not able to throw off the Muslim yoke as Vijayanagara had done, it had not submitted to the foreigner tamely either. The Bahmani Dynasty was not able to establish its rule over Maharashtra all at once.[7] Its rule at first only prevailed in the central plain. Its hold on mountainous regions of the Western Ghats was not established during the first century of its rule. In the north the Raja of Baglan and the Raja of Jawhar, in the centre the Rajas of Rairi and Khelna, and in the south the Chief of Kudal, etc., were more or less independent for a long time. The Southern Konkan for a century or so seems to have been under the direct rule of Vijayanagara[7a] ruling

7. *Bombay Gazetter*, Vol. I—Part II—p. 30.
7a. *Ibid*, Vol. XI—P. 142.

from Khārepatan and it is mentioned at least in one place[8] that its rule extended up to the river Narmada along the Sahyadri range. That Vijayanagara served as a backing force to every discontented petty chief is clear from the family Bakhar of the Brahmin Sardesai of Sangameshwar in the Raṯnagiri District, whose members, it is mentioned, five times resorted to Vidyanagara for help against the armed forces of local robber chieftains and got Vijayanagara officers appointed to rule over those regions from Khārepatan.[9] The title Nayak assumed by these Sardesais and still appended to their names in local correspondence also seems to be of Vijayanagara origin. The cultural influence of Vijayanagara is found mentioned in a curious manner. When after the terrible Durgadevi famine at the end of the fourteenth century the whole of Maharashtra plain was depopulated for 30 years, a certain Brahmin, Dādo Narasinh by name, of Atharva Veda and Bhālanjana Gotra, came from Vidayanagar to Karad,[10] and, with the permission of the Pādshah of Bedar, helped in the re-cultivation and re-population of the land. In this work, the Bedar Sultan had sent a certain white (Turkish) khojā or eunuch of his to accompany Dādo Narasinh as his accredited representative and so the Brahmin came to be called the black khojā, probably on account of his colour. Their work seems to have been so much appreciated by the populace that their names, the Black Khojā and the White Khojā, became household words, as is to be seen from the 15th and 16th century Marathi papers. That the said Brahmin should have come from Vijayanagara speaks volumes and shows the superiority of the southern empire over its northern neighbour in revenue and colonization matters, the two basic things affecting the mass of the population in a predominently agricultural country like India.

When Śivāji was sent back by Śahāji from Bangalore to Poona in 1641 at the age of twelve,[11] he was accompanied by confidential servants of Śahāji who were all trained in that part of the territories of Vijayanagara which was its kernel and were hence saturated with the traditions of that empire. It is clear from the accounts of Sanskrit poets[12] that Śahāji's Court at Bangalore was, a miniature edition of old Hindu Courts, and not modelled after the Muslim court of Bijapur or Ahmednagar, where Śahāji acted as king-maker

8. *History of Sardesai Family*—Vol. I. p. 43 (Marathi).

9. *Ibid*, Vol. I—pages 43-44.

10. *Shiva-Charitra-Sāhitya*—Vol. I. Introduction page 5 (Marathi).

11. *Sabhāsad—Life of Sivaji*—p. 6 (Marathi).

12. *Rādhā-Mādhava-Vilas-Champu*—Chapter VII; and *Shiva-Bhārata*—Chapter IX (both Sanskrit).

for some time. Śivāji himself, it seems, was residing at Bangalore for some two years at least, during the most impressive years of a precocious boyhood, viz., his tenth and eleventh years. It is well known that he was saturated with the tales from Mahābhārata and Rāmāyan and aspired to be guided thereby. Can we expect such a mind to remain uninquisitive as to the history of the territories surrounding his place of residence, especially when his father was conquering those territories from the heirs of Vijayanagara, lawful or otherwise? We can take it almost for certain that Śivāji's mind had become full of tales of Vijayanagara, of the exploits of its heroes and the cultural work of its learned men like Vidyāraṇya. The fame of 'Rāma Rāja Kānaḍā' and the historic battle of 'Rākshastāgdi' had spread far and wide in Maharashtra, as we can judge by the existence of Marathi Bakhars[13] on the subject and the casual mention of his name elsewhere. Śivāji must have imbibed the contents of such works, to be sure. Subjectively speaking, it seems clear to us that Śivāji's ideal was formed in the shadow of Vijayanagara.

If we do not accept this last conclusion we leave a great part of Śivāji's life unexplained, not a very edifying thing for a historian to do. We cannot account for his intense and sincere religiosity bordering on mysticism in any other manner, mysticism that made the man as we know him. Time no doubt brings forth its men, but it is also true that men—at least great men like Śivāji—are formed by their innermost convictions, convictions which through mystic alchemy are almost turned into instincts. Similarly we cannot make his conduct at Bijapur as a boy[14] or in the Diwan-i-Aam Court of Aurangazeb[15] as a full grown man intelligible unless we understand the indelible impress of the contrast left on the mind of the boy Śivāji—contrast between a Hindu court with a full-statured free Hindu ideal of life and the vicious Mohammedan court full of murderous designs between man and man, in the unmanning shadow of which Śivāji had for the most part grown. The ineffacable contrast made the man, formed his life's ideal and ushered in his destiny as the Resuscitator of the Hindu race and the Defender of the Hindu Faith.

His voraciousness in imbibing Hindu scriptures; his punctiliousness in following the tenets of Hindu Religion; his enthusiasm

13. B. I. S. Mandal—II Annual Conference Papers—Pages 168-181.
14. *Shiva-Digvijaya-Bakhar* (Marathi).
15. Sarkar—*Sivaji*—Pages 158-160.

in attending, when possible, the religious sermons; his humble submission to the religious preceptors; his generosity in endowing the edifices of God and the Brahmanical seats of learning; his faithfulness in proceeding, at great inconvenience and risk sometimes, to the shrines of deities to perform religious rites and offer devotion; and last but not least, his religious frenzies and his secret communion with the goddess Bhavāni; all these speak of the man Śivāji and bear witness to the make-up of his mind. If you do not try to understand and explain these, you leave the man un-understood and his life-work unexplained. Now all this he could have imbibed and cultivated only in truly Hindu surroundings and at which place had he the best opportunity and possibility to do it in early life, but at Bangalore and the surrounding parts (which it was quite possible for him to visit in his father's or brother's company) where Hindu life was still flowing in its pristine purity, unimposed upon by foreign domination as in Maharashtra after Muslim rule of three centuries and more? That Maharashtra could not have enthused him in those days with the vision of living Hinduism is clear to those who have read the works of Rāmdās, Śivāji's guru in after-life, who describes in stirring phrases the woes that had befallen his people under the rule of persecuting zealots like Shah Jahan, his son Aurangazeb and Mohammed Ādilshāh of Bijapur. This cultural superiority of the South continued even after the Marathas had become free and strong enough (militarily) to conquer a large part of India under the Peshawās. It is to be seen acknowledged, for example, in an intimate personal letter[16] of the Peshawa Bālāji Bājirao to his friend Nānā Purandare, from Mysore, a century later. To what cause can a historian attribute this lasting cultural superiority, but to the rule of Vijayanagara for three centuries?

We believe the above discussion is sufficient to convince any unprejudiced reader as to what Śivāji owed to Vijayanagara. But a materialistic historian may exclaim "Yes, but all this is subjective. Where is the objective evidence for what you talk about."

For objective data we have to go back a little earlier than Śivāji's times. We have already said that every discontented chief in the Bahmani kingdom looked for support across the Tungabhadra. This fact had always stayed the hands of tyranny beyond a certain limit in the Bahmani kingdom. The tacit moral support kept the ideal of freedom in Maharashtra still burning, it did not extinguish it as in North

16. *Rājwade* Vol. VI—Page 267—No. 160.

India amongst the Rājputs, who were completely submerged by the overwhelming flood of Mohammedan invasions and who could not hope to get any succour, moral or material, beyond their borders. The Rājputs had therefore unwillingly to reconcile themselves to the Mughal rule. Not so the Marathas. Under the Bahmanis they wielded a great influence both in the civil and military administration of the land. They had imposed their language on the administration to a goodly extent. By playing off the parties at the Muslim courts against each other, they were slowly but surely coming to the top. Śahāji was an instance of this type. He had hoped, it seems, at least in early life, to be able to control Muslim courts by loyal co-operation. But he knew ultimately to his cost that this was impossible. So in later life he tried the ideal of keeping himself aloof from the central government and busied himself in carving out for himself a semi-independent principality at Bangalore. In this he was eminently successful, as is clear by recent studies of his career. In doing this, he had to incur the odium of being disloyal, treacherous and self-seeking, but ultimately he triumphed and got what he aimed at. Nay more. He could give Śivāji a start. It is now clear to all Maratha scholars of the subject—by the work of Rājwade, Khare, Divekar, and last but not the least, Mr. D. V. Apte—that the credit of founding the Maratha State must be divided between the father and the son. The work of the above-mentioned scholars has now been incorporated for the most part in the work of Dr. Bālkrishna of Kolhapur, in English and the curious reader may turn to his work for the elucidation of this point.[17]

Nor is this the conclusion of Maratha scholars only. Dr. S. K. Aiyangar has arrived at the same conclusion independently after a detailed study of southern sources as well. Not only that but he also noticed "the remarkable service in the preservation of Hindu Culture and Religion, which ran great risk of extinction by the fanatical policy of Bijapur"[18] rendered by Śahāji in occupying the territories which would otherwise have become Mohammedan jahgirs. But the learned doctor did not emphasise the real nature of the disloyalty, treason and selfishness of Śahāji. Śahāji acted as he did on account of his experience of three Muslim States, viz., Ahmednagar, Bijapur and the Mughal. The conviction which dawned upon him was that, an independent Hindu State must be created if the Hindu race and religion were to be preserved. The policy of co-operation and assimilation was tried and had been

17. *Sivaji, The Great*, Vol. I, Part I.—Śahaji.
18. *Journal of Indian History*, Vol. XI, page 404.

found wanting. So he had to act in furtherance of his well-considered conclusion. So he had to pursue the course of double-dealing even when it entailed personal humiliation and suffering. In order to save his son at least this same experience, he managed to keep him away from direct service under anybody and so laid the foundation of his greatness in so far as it was in his hands. Śivāji was the product of the bitter concentrated Maratha experience, of three centuries of direct Muslim rule, and experience to which the Southern States had not been subjected. The contribution of the Marathas to other parts of India was the transmission of this conviction born of long periods of suffering.

Unfortunately there was no effective medium to transmit this idea to others but that of conquest. There was no new political discovery commensurate with the new ideal. Śahāji's aim is clear from the policy he followed. He never completely destroyed any Hindu chiefship. In this he followed his own policy even when it clashed with that of the Muslim commander, his official superior. Thus it is noted that he reinstated Vīrabhadra of Bednur on his throne, though his kingdom had been completely annexed by Ranadullah Khan.[19] Similarly he gave Tarikere to the chief of Basavapaṭṭan, Māgaḍi to the Kempe Gauḍa of Bangalore, Ānekal to the Hoskote chief, Ratnagiri to the Sira chief, and so on after annexing their fiefs.[20] Lewis Rice notes the beneficial effects of this far-sighted and humane policy on the land in general. This same attitude of Śahāji, of not crushing out of existence any Hindu chief, brought on him the suspicion of his Muslim superiors when he exhibited it in the important case of Śrī Ranga Rayal, the last representative of the empire of Vijayanagara. For gaining his end, he not only sided with Śrī Ranga but also tried to bring political pressure of Golkonda to bear on the matter, by accepting the service of Golkonda himself. In this attempt he was betrayed by the king of Golkonda who divulged the secret to the king of Bijapur. This brought on Śahāji the odium of treason and put him into fetters and imprisonment. All the same, this move was not able to save Śrī Ranga either.[21]

Śahāji got himself freed from this predicament by the valiant efforts and cunning diplomacy of both his sons, Śambhāji and Śivāji,

19. *Shiva-Bhārata*—Chapter XI—Verse 6. (Sanskrit).

20. *Mysore and Coorg Gazetteer*, Vol. I (1877), p. 237.

21. Abdullah Qutbshah's letter mentioning Sahaji's petition—*Modern Review*, Vol. XLVI, page 12.

acting in the south and north respectively. This proved the wisdom of Śahāji in keeping his two sons engaged separately one in the Carnatic and the other in Maharashtra, though acting in concert to gain the common ends. Śivāji had this valuable past experience at the back of his mind when he started to conquer the Madras Coast. He wanted to preserve this important strategical advantage for his sons, by appointing his eldest son Śambhāji to rule the south and his younger son, Rajaram, to rule the Maratha country.[22] Though his intention was foiled by the cussedness of Śambhāji, his ideal succeeded in the end when Rajaram got shelter at Jinji after fleeing from the Maratha country. Incidentally it may be noted that the Rāni of Bednur, a kingdom saved by Śahāji from extinction, screened Rajaram from Aurangazeb's generals when they pursued him upto the jungles of Bednur, a noble service rendered on a most critical occasion in the life of the Maratha State.[23] Verily, a good deed is never wasted, only we do not know when, where, and in what manner it bears fruit.

We have said something above as to the contribution which the Marathas wanted to make to the political stock of other parts of India, a contribution in the form of convictions as to the main lines of policy to be followed by the Hindus all over India. The first and the foremost of these convictions was about the unassimilability of the Muslim Theory of the State with the age-long ideals of the Hindus. This conviction was born of bitter experience and not out of speculative theory. Throughout his life a servant of the Muslims in theory, Śahāji still could maintain a sturdy sense of self-respect, take pride in his Rajput[24] origin in the face of his sovereign and offer himself to be relieved from service if the sovereign so desired, even at the advanced age of sixty, because he was fortified by this conviction. On the other hand, Śrī Ranga Rāyulu, born of a family of Emperors and actually occuping a revered throne as he was, could think of saving his lands for himself by descending to the level of a Jahgirdar of the Mughal empire and if that were not sufficient, by accepting Islam[25] himself with all his family and dependents, because he had had not the experience and conviction of Śahāji. This contrast in the behaviour of these two contemporary

22. Ṣabhāsad—*Life of Sivaji*—page 78. (Marathi).

23. *Śivatattvaratnākara*—*Kallōlo* VIII—*Taranga* VIII in *Sources of Vijayanagara History*, page 363.

24. This is all to be found in a very important letter of Sahaji to the King of Bijapur—printed in *Shivakālīn-Patra-Sāra-Sangraha*—No. 710 (Marathi).

25. Sarkar—*Aurangazib*—Vol. I—page 249 (1st edition).

political figures in the same field shows wherein lay the weakness of Vijayanagara (meaning by this designation all the land south of the river Tungabhadra) and the political advance of Maharashtra, weakness which endangered the independence of the south while the strength of the Marathas was conquering inch by inch the lost ground of independence. Bijapur's intervention in the politics of the south was an invited intervention. While Śahāji was thinking of betaking himself to the south to breathe the free air of Hindu independence, Kenge Hanuma[26] of Basavapaṭṭan, Channaya of Nāgamangala and the renowned Tirumala Nāyak[27] of Madura were resorting to the Muslim courts of Bijapur and Golkonda, and seeking their intervention in the internal politics of the Vijayanagara Empire. Herein we find the irony playing its role in history. While the actions of the Vijayanagara secession States were destroying the Hindu independence in the south, they were also laying the foundation of a new Hindu empire. But for the sequence of events, it seems doubtful if the Maratha State could ever have started on its career, or if by chance started, would have survived in the end. Thus the remark of Dr. S. K. Aiyangar, " That the collapse of the Hindu empire of Vijayanagara was a contributory cause to the rise of the Marathas as a nation " (quoted at the beginning of this essay) does not seem to be wide of the mark.

Lest it may be misunderstood that the trend of the above discussion places the Marathas, in comparison with the southerners, on an unduly high pedestal, it is necessary to bear in mind that all the Marathas had not in Śivāji's times become either nation-minded or religion-minded. Śivāji had to use force to enforce his regime. He had to kill Baji Ghorpade and Chandrarao More. There were more Marathas serving under Aurangazeb and Adilshah than under Śivāji. But a goodly proportion of the Marathas had become ripe to receive Śivāji's advice and to follow his lead. That was the difference. Even in the times of the Peshawas, a good proportion of the Marathas were serving the Nizam.

The South supplied the Marathas with the sinews of war. Tribute and plunder collected by Śahāji, Śivāji and their generals made it possible for the Maratha State to come into existence and maintain itself as a going concern. After Śivāji, Śambhāji was able to defend the Maratha State against the simultaneous attacks of the Mughals, the Siddis of Janjira and Portuguese, because Śivāji

26. *Journal of Indian History*, Vol. IX—page 204 (Dr. Aiyangar's Article).
27. *History of Nāyaks of Madura*—page 128.

had left the treasury full with gold brought from the Madras Coast and Harji Raje Mahadik, his viceroy at Jinji, was sending monies from that quarter. Rajaram maintained himself as well as the Maratha State with revenue from the same sources. All this was possible because Vijayanagara rule had left those regions prosperous and full of treasures. The social organization evolved under the ægis of Vijayanagara seems to have been so perfect that society could recoup itself in a short time after the "Legions' thunder had passed away." Even in the 18th century under the Peshawas, the southern expeditions were always a paying proposition, while the northern ones led to insolvency. This cause was a bone of contention at the court of Shāhu, between his Peshawa Bajirao I and his *Pratinidhi* Shripatrao. The Peshawas Balaji Bajirao and his son Madhavrao maintained themselves by expeditioning to the south. All this phenomenon cannot be accounted for unless we admit the peculiar recouping power of the south perfected by a good social organization, which was the permanent legacy of that venerable empire, Vijayanagara.

We have said enough, we think, to prove what the Marathas owe, in an objective sense, to Vijayanagara. Now to return to the charge of Sir Jadunath Sarkar that Śivāji never wanted to annex the Karnatak to his kingdom and establish a permanent empire there, that "gold, and not land, was his chief object,"[28] Francois Martin of the French East India Company supplies the proof as to even the intention of Śivāji in invading the Madras Coast. Martin notes that "Śivāji sent some Brahmins to all the villages in the country for governing them, the number of these scamps who had followed Śivāji for trying to get some employment is something amazing, they counted more than twenty thousand."[29] Can any one after reading this sentence maintain that "gold, and not land was his chief object"?

What could occur to M. G. Ranade three decades ago with only Duff and Maratha Bakhars as his materials, does not occur to Sir Jadunath, even after thirty years' research in Indian History. "As if he had the prescience of coming events, Śivāji by his conquest and alliances, formed a new line of defence in Southern India in the Kaveri valley, to which he could retire in case of necessity," Ranade wrote in his "Rise of the Maratha Power." But that was perhaps the work of a "Nineteenth century Dakshina Brahman Chauvinist" and so mere fiction born of florid imagination or at

28. Sarkar—*Sivaji*—page 309 (3rd edition).
29. *Foreign Biographies of Sivaji* by Sen, p. 297.

best mere guess-work! So also another arch Dakshina Brahman Chauvinist, this one of the 20th century,—wrote 14 years ago, on the authority of a " fulsome adulation of Śahāji and the boy Śivāji " (i.e. Radha-Madhava-Vilasa-Champu) that half the credit of founding the Maratha State should go to Śahāji the father of Śivāji. Most thought it pure fiction then. But now it has been proved to be true by scholars like Dr. S. K. Aiyangar who are not " Maratha Nationalists." Now which is better, the " fiction " of the above-mentioned type or " a really first-class piece of work," " full of research," " treated in the right way and in the right spirit," " equipped with first-hand knowledge," as is Sir Jadunath's " Śivāji " certified to be, by such unimpeachable scholars as Henry Beveridge, Richard Temple and Vincent Smith ? Let the reader decide after going carefully through what we have said above and consulting oneself, the original sources mentioned, if necessary.

Śivāji not only wanted to found a permanent Hindu empire on the ruins of Vijayanagara, as is clear by Martin's reference quoted above, but also wanted to run that empire in the interest of the agriculturist ryot, the great mass of population in India. Though Martin terms the Brahmins who were sent by Śivāji to govern the Madras Coast villages as " scamps," he had further on in his narrative to write, " It must, however, be admitted, that the Brahmins were more careful in making the lands profitable than those under the government of the Mohammedans had appeared (to us) to be. A number of places around Pondicherry, covered with brambles and brushwood only, of which nobody thought (anything), was reclaimed and these have produced well since."[30] Can there be any better testimony as to the aim of Śivāji in conquering new territories in the south ?

When Śivāji started for Golkonda *en route* to the Madras Coast he had already taken the Qutb Shah into his confidence, in fact that State had already become tributory to Śivāji, who diplomatically allowed it to be called monetary help. Śivāji's diplomat Niraji Raoji had, it seems, entered into an offensive and defensive alliance with the Qutb Shah through the friendly Hindu medium of his Vazir, the famous Brahmin Mādaṇṇa, " who wanted to render some service to his religion," (evidently by helping Śivāji in his expedition to the south), according to Martin.[31] As Bijapur had, through the agency of the Regent Bahlol Khan, become subservient to the Mughals who

30. Sen—*Foreign Biographies of Sivaji*, p. 341.
31. *Ibid*, p. 262.

wanted to conquer the whole of the Dakhan, in sheer self-defence. Golkonda and Śivāji united and resolved to conquer and divide the Bijapur territories between themselves. Śivāji called on the Bijapur Sardar Māloji Ghorpade to leave Bijapur service and come over to Golkonda, though his father Baji Ghorpade had been killed by Śivāji.[32] This was in pursuance of his policy of uniting the Marathas in one cause, that of checking the Muslims. If that was impossible, Śivāji thought of controlling Bijapur through the agency of a Hindu Prime Minister, as he was doing in the case of Golkonda through Mādaṇṇa, and for this post he had selected no other man than Ākaṇṇa[33] Mādaṇṇa's brother. It will be seen from this account how far-sighted Śivāji was in meeting the Mughal danger from the north by creating a Hindu empire in the south, an empire which would incorporate within itself both Bijapur and Golkonda, either by alliance, or failing that, by conquest. This was also the policy of Aḷiya Rāma Raya, the immortal hero of Tāḷikōta or Rakkasgi-Tangaḍgi. Because Śivāji wished to stand forth as a successor of Vijayanagara, he selected as his imperial coin the gold *hona* in imitation of Vijayanagara[34] and did not copy the rupee of the Mughals though it was becoming the current coin of India as a whole then. For the same reason he continued the practice of donating villages and cash from the treasury to learned Brahmins and the shrines of Hindu deities on the Madras Coast. A number of these grant papers have been published in Marathi from the Peshawa State-records by Parasnis and Mavji. His grant, indited on silver-plate, to Tirumalaraya and Ramaraya, the two sons of Śrī Ranga Rāyulu, the last nominal emperor of Vijayanagara, who died a fugitive in the west country (probably Bednur), though in its present form spurious, still appears to be, as remarked by Dr. S. K. Aiyangar, correct in substance from the sentiments expressed in it. Incidentally it may be noted here that it contains the grant, not of two villages as written by Dr. S. K. Aiyangar,[35] but of eight small divisions of the country, probably containing a hundred villages or so.

This lengthy discussion, we hope, has by now made clear to the reader the debt, both subjective and objective, which Śivāji and the

32. Āpte—*Itihāsa-Manjari*, p. 97.

33. Sarkar—*Aurangazib*, Vol. IV, p. 150.

34. *Progress Report of the Archæological Survey of India—Western Circle,* for the year ending 31st March, 1919—p. 48.

35. Aiyangar—*Some Contributions of South India to Indian Culture*, p. 313.

Maratha State owed to Vijayanagara. Let us also hope, that the remembrance of this fact will in future, if it has not done so in the past, go to unite the hearts of the Marathas with those of their southern brethren.

11

Theories Concerning the Origin of Vijayanagara

By

Dr. B. A. Saletore, M.A., Ph.D., (Lond.),
Sir Parashurambhan College, Poona.

I

THE ALLEGED TELUGU ORIGIN

Since the publication of my *Social and Political Life in the Vijayanagara Empire,* writers on Vijayanagara history have given expression to views concerning the origin of that empire which, although by no means either original or promulgated for the first time, have nevertheless been based on statements which require a careful examination. These theories are, to be brief, a reorientation of the old Telugu origin of the founders of Vijayanagara which has ceased to be an historical fact. We shall first deal with the fallacious arguments put forward by the advocates of this theory, and then adduce more proof in support of the undisputed fact that the sons of Sangama were entirely of Karnāṭaka origin.[1]

It is maintained by a recent writer that the Vijayanagara rulers of the Sangama family were of Telugu stock. The arguments advanced by this writer may be summarised thus: —

1. Vijayanagara was not built by Ballāḷa Deva III. This statement rests on three premises: (a) Hampe and the adjoining region was outside the Hoysala kingdom; (b) the Yādavas were in possession of the territory around Hampe; and (c) the rulers of the principality of Kampili succeeded the Yādavas in this region.[2]

2. The ruler of Kampili was Harihara Rāya I. This statement rests on the following considerations: (a) Vijayanagara arose out of, and was identical with Doravaḍi; and (b) the ruler of Kampili was Harihara Rāya I.[3]

1. Read Saletore, *Social and Political Life in the Vijayanagara Empire*, I. pp. 34-39 for arguments advanced till now in regard to the Karnāṭaka origin of the founders of the Vijayanagara kingdom.

2. Venkata Ramanayya, Vijayanagara, *Origin of the City and the Empire*, pp. 16-22, 43, 45. (Madras, 1933).

3. *Ibid*, pp. 99 seq.

3. Harihara Rāya I was a relative of Kanyā Nāyaka of Warangal, and hence was of Telugu extraction. To support this argument, the writer assures us that (a) Kanyā Nāyaka became independent; (b) one of his relatives apostatized from Islām, and revolted at Kampili, and (c) that this relative was no other than Harihara Rāya I.[4]

4. To substantiate further these arguments, the writer tells us that the crest and the administrative divisions of the Vijayanagara empire were borrowed from the Kākatīyas of Warangal.[5]

These arguments have no basis in history. But we shall deal with them in turn.

1. *Vijayanagara was not built by Vīra Ballāḷa III.* There is nothing new in this statement. We have conclusively shown that it was Bukka Rāya I who built the city of Vijayanagara.[6] The main point in this set of arguments centres round the assertion of the writer that the region around Pampā or Hampe was not in the possession of the Hoysalas. "The successors of Ballāḷa II seem to have gradually lost their hold upon the territory in the Bellary district . . . Therefore, it may be said that the Hoysala power in the Bellary district became practically extinct after the death of Narasimha II and that the Yādavas firmly established themselves in the place of their rivals."[7]

This would mean that from A.D. 1220 (the last date of king Ballāḷa II) till the time of Vīra Ballāḷa III (A.D. 1291—A.D. 1342), the Hoysalas had nothing to do with the region around Hampe. One single instance of a Hoysala king who gave a grant to the Virūpākṣa temple of Hampe is enough to demolish this view. It is that of king Someśvara who, as the inscription to the right of the north *mahādvāra* of the Virūpākṣa temple of Hampe informs us, in A.D. 1236 gave to that temple some grant of money.[8] Since Karnāṭaka kings

4. *Ibid,* pp. 20-21.
5. *Ibid,*
6. Saletore, *op. cit.,* I, pp. 101-106. The erroneous nature of the arguments of this writer is seen when we notice that he asserts that Harihara Raya I built the city of Vijayanagara, and named it after his spiritual adviser Vidyāraṇya Śripāda. Ramanayya, *ibid,* pp. 51-52.
7. Ramanayya, *op. cit.,* pp. 20-21.
8. *Mysore Archæological Report* for 1920, p. 33. Dr. Ramanayya seems to be aware of Somēśvara Dēva's presence at Hampe. He refers to an inscription dated A.D. 1236 found at Hampe. *Ibid,* p. 18. Since the evidence of this record violates all the assumptions he has built, probably he does not utilize it! B. A. S.

never gave grants of money or lands to temples outside their kingdom, we may safely assume that Hampe was within the Hoysala kingdom in A.D. 1236.

While the statement of the Yādava kings having succeeded to the Hoysala hegemony over certain parts of the Karnāṭaka, for the time being, is no doubt historically accurate, it is entirely erroneous to maintain that the principality over which the king of Kampili ruled was in any way connected with the Vijayanagara kings or the Kākatīyas of Warangal.

2. This point will be better understood when we examine the validity of the next main argument brought forward by the writer *viz.*, that the *ruler of Kampili was Harihara Rāya I.* The writer asserts that Vijayanagara arose out of Doravaḍi, that the ruler of Doravaḍi fought with Vīra Ballāḷa III, and that this ruler was Harihara Rāya I.[9]

We are afraid that the writer has altogether got himself lost in the history of the principality of Kummaṭa over which the king of Kampila ruled, and which principality of Kummaṭa included Doravaḍi. We prove the latter statement by a stone record dated A.D. 1280 which informs us that the general Cauṇḍarasa, under the Yādava king Rāmacandra Deva, was killed in a battle with Mummuḍi Singeya Nāyaka who was then at Doravadi in the Kurugōḍunāḍu.[10] This Mummuḍi Singeya Nāyaka was no other than the grandfather of Rāmanātha, the hero of the story of *Paradāra Rāmana Kathe,* and the king of Kummaṭa.[11]

Without entering into this intricate point further, it may be said that it is historically erroneous to maintain that the Hoysala ruler Vīra Ballāḷa III had nothing to do with Doravaḍi. For a *vīragal* found in Hosakōṭe, Jāla hobḷi, Nagar tāluka, Mysore State, clearly tells us that in the course of a campaign against Kampila Deva, Vīra Ballāḷa marching with all his army upon Kapila (Kampila) Deva, left him in Baḷaha, and then (on the date specified) marched on to Doravaḍi and ruled over there. (*Ballāḷa Dēva*

9. Ramanayya, *ibid*, pp. 80-81, 91, 99. On page 167-168, Dr. Ramanayya writes that the modern Darōji was the ancient Doravaḍi. How he came to derive thus the name of Doravaḍi is not understood. For the ancient name of Doravaḍi was Doravaḷi which is mentioned in A.D. 1212. *Ep. Carnatica*, VIII. Sb. 309, p. 54.

10 *Epigraphia Carnatica*, VII. Intr. p. 37, Ci. 24, p. 182

11. *M. A. R.* for 1929, p. 45.

Rāyanu tattina samasta-sauvaraṇe sahita Kapila Dēvana mēle naḍadu Baḷahadalli biṭṭali munde (date) Doravaḍige etti naḍadalli). The date of this *vīragal* is given thus:—*Śaka varsa 1242 Raudri samvatsarada C'aitra* Ba. 1 Śa. which corresponds to A.D. 1320 March, Tuesday, the 25th, the week day however not corresponding.[12] The success which crowned the arms of the Hoysala ruler was complete, as the epigraph conclusively proves. We may well assume that after this battle of Doravaḍi, that centre passed into the possession of Vīra Ballāḷa III. Unless the contrary is proved, we may take this to be a fact.

As for the other arguments brought forward to back up the entirely gratuitous assumption that Vijayanagara arose out of Doravaḍi, and that Harihara Rāya I was the ruler of Kampili—Doravaḍi principality, it is enough to note merely that these and similar statements have been based on altogether untrustworthy copper-plate grants which we have examined elsewhere.[13] Further, it is said by the writer that Harihara Rāya I was subordinate to the Delhi Sultan, that the former was converted into Islām from which he apostatized, that Bukka Rāya had a Muhammadan son, and that Kampili was granted to Harihara Rāya I by the Delhi Sultan.[14] These arguments need not be taken seriously, since they contain no historical truth in them whatsoever.[15]

3. We now come to the third group of arguments of the writer. He asserts that *Harihara Rāya I was a relative of Kanyā Nāyaka of Warangal,* that he ruled over the territory which Kampila had ruled before him, and that he was a Telugu by descent.

In addition to the facts which we long ago advanced against this fallacious theory,[16] we may observe the following which further

12. *E. C.* VIII. Nr. 19, pp. 129, 351; Swamikannu Pillai, *Indian Ephemeris,* IV, p. 242. It may be objected that Rice's interpretation of the phrase *Doravaḍige etti naḍadalli* does not mean that Vīra Ballāḷa was ruling there, but that he merely encamped in that place, or that he merely attacked his enemy at Doravaḍi. The latter is permissible, but when we note that in the battle Vīra Ballāla's general Kūruka Nāyaka killed Kampila Deva's general Kakkala Deva, although he himself lost his life in the encounter, then, we may justify Rice's interpretation given to the phrase *etti naḍadalli.* B. A. S.

13. Saletore, *S.P. Life,* I. pp. 90-100.

14. Ramanayya, *op. cit.,* pp. 54, 95-96, 95 n. 101, 129.

15. Saletore, *ibid,* I. pp. 31 seq.; *Indian Historical Quarterly,* VIII. pp. 768-770.

16. Saletore, *Journal of the Bombay Historical Society,* III. pp. 106 seq. where we pointed out the futility of maintaining such arguments, while deal-

demolishes the alleged relationship between the sons of Sangama and the Kākatīya rulers. It is argued that the sons of Sangama waged wars against the Hoysalas, that Ballappa Daṇṇāyaka was an enemy of Bukka Rāya I, that the latter captured Sosevūr, the birthplace of the Hoysalas, and that Bukka Rāya was the same as Sangama whom the writer makes Bukka Rāya's grandfather ![17] The dynastic relationship which existed between the Hoysala House and the family of the sons of Sangama has been amply proved by us elsewhere ;[18] and no value need be attached to statements which allude to the animosity between the sons of Sangama and the Hoysalas, because it never existed.

4. To substantiate the above wrong inferences another set of erroneous statements is made. This relates to the *similarity between the boar crest and the administrative divisions of the Vijayanagara rulers* and *the crest and the divisions of the Kākatīya rulers*. It is maintained that the founders of Vijayanagara borrowed their well-known Varāha crest from the Kākatīyas, for no other reigning family made use of it at the time of the birth of the new kingdom of Vijayanagara.[19]

The similarity is outwardly reasonable but it is dangerous, since it leads us to ridiculous inferences. The fact that one royal family has the same seal or crest as another does not necessarily mean that the origin of the former is to be traced to the latter. Diverse royal families *that never* belonged to the same stock had a common crest. Thus the tiger crest was common to the Pallavas, the Choḷas, and the Hoysalas.[20] If we are to follow the reasoning of the writer who maintains that the Vijayanagara rulers were of the same stock as that of the Kākatīyas, then, we must conclude that the Choḷas, the Hoysalas, and the Pallavas belonged to the same stock ! This would be merely absurd.

Indeed, the absurdity of this method of reasoning is apparent when we note another example. The symbol of Hanumān was common to the Yādavas, the Kadambas, and the Vijayanagara rulers, as Dr. Krishna has amply proved.[21] Now, Muhammad Alī Walajah,

ing with an earlier work of the same writer in which he brought forward the same erroneous theory but with the aid of different arguments.

17. Ramanayya, *ibid*, pp. 132-135, 139, 142 seq. 146.
18. Saletore, *Indian Antiquary*, LXII. pp. 1-3, 11.
19. Ramanayya, *op. cit.*, pp. 103-110.
20. Burnell, *Elements of South Indian Palæography*, pp. 106-107. (2nd ed.)
21. *M. A. R.* for 1932, p. 78.

the Navāb of Arcot, too, had the symbol of Hanumān on his coins.[22] According to the fallacious analogy mentioned above, the Navāb of Arcot belonged to the family to which the Yādavas, the Kadambas, and the Vijayanagara rulers belonged! It is useless to continue this point further.

Unless there is some kind of positive evidence to substantiate one's statement that Vijayanagara rulers actually borrowed from, or were indebted to, the Kākatīyas in the matter of having their crest, it is wrong to say that the Karnāṭaka rulers of Vijayanagara were in any way grateful to the Telugu kings in the fourteenth century for their crest.

On the other hand, it may reasonably be maintained that since the sons of Sangama were of Karnāṭaka stock, they had recourse to the Varāha crest of the Chālukyas whose memories, as we have elsewhere pointed out, lingered on in the Vijayanagara Empire,[23] without having borrowed it from the Kākatīyas with whom they had nothing in common whatsoever.

As for the argument that there is a similarity in the divisions of the Vijayanagara Empire and those of the Kākatīya kingdom, it is entirely erroneous to say that the latter in any way influenced the former. All available evidence proves that the Vijayanagara rulers but continued the rich traditions of Karnāṭaka and the Tamil lands in this matter of dividing their Empire into the various provinces which we have dealt with in detail elsewhere.[24]

It is futile, therefore, to entertain these wrong conceptions which violate all the known facts concerning the sons of Sangama and their intimate relationship with the Hoysala ruler Vīra Ballāḷa III. If the Telugu origin of the rulers of Vijayanagara were an established fact, one cannot understand why, for instance, in A.D. 1347, only one year after the foundation of the kingdom of Vijayanagara, the Brahmans, who received grants of villages at the hands of prince Mārappa, one of the brothers who founded the kingdom of Vijayanagara, should have been styled as people coming from the Āndhradeśa, and not as Brahmans hailing from " our own country the Āndhradeśa."[25]

22. *M. A. R.* for 1932, p. 78.
23. Saletore, *S. P. Life*, I. p. 36.
24. Saletore, *ibid*, I. pp. 287 seq.
25. *M. A. R.* for 1932, pp. 164-166.

Further, we cannot understand, too, why, as we shall mention later on in the course of this paper, had the founders been of Telugu stock, their family deity should have been called Virūpākṣa of Hampe and their pleasure garden the Hemakūṭa hill.

Moreover, the anti-Telugu propensity of the early Vijayanagara rulers is seen in the distinctive *biruda* which they used in regard to the Telugu kings. An undated stone inscription of Harihara Rāya II, for instance, calls him " a lion to the scent-elephant that is the Āndhra king."[26]

Finally, we may note that even so late as A.D. 1571 when a really great Telugu dynasty (the Āravīṭi family) controlled the destinies of the land, the Vijayanagara emperor Tirumala calls himself as one " adorning the golden throne of the Karnāṭa."[27]

It is not basing one's statement on wrong data that one can strengthen the case for the Telugu origin of the founders of Vijayanagara, but by citing other and more substantial, although historically inaccurate, claims which we may enumerate in the following manner. For instance, one may assert on the evidence of the Portuguese historian Faria y Sousa that Bukka Rāya was a Telugu chieftain. This Portuguese historian gives an abstract of a copper-plate grant said to have been discovered in Mylapore in which " Boca " (Bukka) Rāja is said to have been the son of Campula Rāja and grandson of Atela Rāja.[28]

Secondly, in the *Vidyāraṇyakālajñāna* and in another work called *Pitāmahasamhitā* we are told that the two brothers Harihara and Bukka were at first employed under Vīra Rudra (deva of Warangal), as his treasury guards, and on his being defeated by the Muhammadans, went to Rāmanātha (of Kummāṭa) to serve as his treasury officers. What caused them to leave his service is not stated. (But in another part of the *Vidyāraṇyakālajñāna* it is stated that Rāmanātha was killed by the Sultan's soldiers, and that Harihara and Bukka were taken prisoners). We next find the brothers waging wars with Vīra Ballāḷa III. At this stage came Vidyāraṇya who favoured them, and in the next war they overcame Vīra Ballāḷa and occupied his territory.[29] It seems as if we are to attach some weight to these statements, especially when we observe that the

26. *Ibid* for 1929, p. 194.
27. E. C. XII. Tm. i. p. 2
28 Faria y Sousa, *Asia y Portuguesa*, II. pp. 229-230. (Stevens).
29. *M. A. R.* for 1929, pp. 101, 108, 109, 110, 115, 116.

authors of *Śivatattvaratnākara*, *Keladinṛpavijaya*, and *Chikkadevarāyavaṁśāvaḷī*, works of the seventeenth and the eighteenth centuries A.D., repeat the above details with some modifications.[30]

Neither the Portuguese historian nor the authors of the *Vidyāraṇyakālajñāna* can be relied upon on historical grounds. Faria y Sousa's testimony is by no means reliable in this instance. This historian wrote his great work somewhere in the latter half of the sixteenth century A.D. As regards his chronological veracity, one little detail is enough to discredit his statements pertaining to the parentage of the founders of Vijayanagara. He tells us that it was in A.D. 1220 that Bukka Rāya founded Vijayanagara.[31] Obviously the other statement relating to the Telugu origin of the sons of Sangama is equally untrustworthy, in spite of the Portuguese historian assuring us that it was embodied in a copper-plate grant. It may well be that that particular grant was forged to get some concession either from the Portuguese themselves or from the Vijayanagara viceroys stationed at Mylapore.[32]

Now we turn to the *Vidyāraṇyakālajñāna* and the *Pitāmahasaṁhitā*. In the first place, it may be observed that these were not contemporary accounts but later productions, almost of the age in which the *History of Portuguese Asia* was composed by Faria y Sousa. Dr. Krishna, who has made ample use of these documents, is inclined to date them in A.D. 1580 and after.[33] Secondly, these works were not the composition of one man but of different persons.[34] Thirdly, their prophetic vein and ultra-Vīra-Śaiva tendency which is their most prominent feature, detracts from their merit as documents of historical value.[35] Fourthly, the *Vidyāraṇyakālajñāna*, upon which the *Pitāmahasaṁhitā* is based, is said to have been composed by Vidyāraṇya Śrīpāda, but it gives a connected account of the Vijayanagara Empire till the days of Veṅkaṭapati Deva (A.D. 1586—A.D. 1615).[36] Finally, these and other allied accounts connect the building of the city of Vijayanagara by Harihara Rāya I with Vidyāraṇya Śrīpāda. This goes entirely against the impartial evidence of contemporary stone epigraphs of the reign of the sons of Sangama which we have cited elsewhere.[37]

30. *M. A. R.* for 1929, pp. 101, 108, 109, 110, 115, 116.
31. Saletore, *S. P. Life.*, I. p. 107.
32. Read *ibid*, I. p. 136, and *ibid* n. 2. for further evidence to show that Faria y Sousa is not always reliable in his accounts. B. A. S.
33—36. *M. A. R.* for 1932, p. 101.
37. Saletore, *Journal of the Andhra Historical Research Society*, IX, pp. 39-42.

Hence the sixteenth century works *Vidyāraṇyakālajñāna* and the *Pitāmahasaṁhitā* must be dismissed as untrustworthy sources of information for events that took place two centuries earlier.

Here we may note one little point which requires elucidation. When exactly did the Vijayanagara rulers of the first dynasty begin to have intimate relations with the Telugu nobles ? There is every reason to believe that the sons of Sangama were fully aware of the difficult political situation which faced them not only in the Karnāṭaka but in the Telugu land as well ; and that they gave patronage to Telugu scholars almost from the commencement of their political career. We shall cite the evidence of a Telugu scholar whose ancestors were in the service of one of the founders of Vijayanagara. The latter seemed to have imbibed their animosity against the Telugu kings from the Hoysalas themselves, whose last great figure, Vīra Ballāla III is called in A.D. 1340 " a Rudra of the last deluge to the Telungu Rāya," in an inscription found in Khader Sāheb's field at Voḷagerehaḷḷi, Bangalore tāluka.[38] This may be compared to the *biruda* of Harihara Rāya II given above. Nevertheless, matrimonial alliance between the early Vijayanagara rulers and the Telugu nobles began only in the reign of the same Vijayanagara king. This is made out from an undated stone inscription in the fort of Puṣpagiri near Haḷebīḍ, which records some grants for the god Ōrangal (Warangal) Vīrabhadra of the Nakhareśvara temple by Vīra Harihara Mahārāya's son-in-law Pullakhaṇḍa Siddharāja.[39] Obviously such matrimonial relationship, it may not be wrong to presume, was the result of political necessity.

II

THE KURUBA ORIGIN OF THE FOUNDERS

The other theory which I have likewise explained in my *Social and Political Life in the Vijayanagara Empire*, is that relating to the Kuruba origin of the sons of Sangama.[40] In addition to the statement of poet Lingaṇṇa, the author of *Keladinṛpavijaya*, which I cited in the same work,[41] the following may also be noted. Basava Rāja in his *Śivatattvaratnākara* gives a fanciful derivation of the word *Oḍeyar* which the founders assumed, and connects it with *meṣapāla* or shepherd. Dr. Krishna who mentions this statement of Basava

38. *E. C.* IX. Bn. 110, p. 22.
39. *M. A. R.* for 1908, p. 14.
40. Saletore, *S. P. Life*, I. pp. 11, 25, 40.
41. Saletore, *ibid*, I. p. 82. n. 2.

Rāja, also remarks that the author of *Chikkadevarāyavaṁśāvaḷī*, a work written during the reign of the Mysore king Chikkadeva Rāja (A.D. 1672—A.D. 1704), also repeats the same tradition in regard to the Kuruba origin of the sons of Sangama.[42]

While all these later notices only confirm our statement that the founders of Vijayanagara were of indigenous origin, they cannot be accepted as valid unless contemporary evidence is forthcoming to substantiate them. Here a doubt arises whether we have to refer the beginnings of the founders of Vijayanagara to the Kuruvanka family the ruler of which Ēca of Pervvayal governed over the principality of Navilanāḍ in A.D. 1057.[43] This district of Kuruvanka figures so late as A.D. 1530 when it is said to have been a *sthaḷa* belonging to the Sātigrāma-sīme.[44] In A.D. 1719 it is called a *sthaḷa* in the Hoysala country.[45] But since in none of these and other records referring to Kuruvankanāḍ, there is the slightest reference to the origin of the sons of Sangama, and since there is no evidence anywhere to show that particular favour was shown to that district by the later Vijayanagara rulers as having been the place of origin of their illustrious ancestors, we may dispense with the notion that Kuruvankanāḍ had anything to do with the sons of Sangama.

III

THE KARNĀṬAKA ORIGIN OF THE FOUNDERS OF VIJAYANAGARA

All available evidence only confirms the Karnāṭaka origin of the founders of Vijayanagara which we have proved elsewhere on the most substantial grounds.[46]

(a) *Kampili was not the original home of the sons of Sangama.* We shall restrict ourselves to a few points in addition to those we have mentioned in our works regarding the Karnāṭaka origin of the rulers of Vijayanagara. Firstly, we may begin with the alleged relationship with Kampili. Bearing in mind the criticism we have levelled against the Hindu and Muhammadan accounts that

42. *M. A. R.* for 1932, p. 109, and *ibid*, n. 3.
43. *E. C.* IV. Hg. 18, p. 69.
44. *Ibid*, V. Cn. 187, p. 206.
45. *Ibid*, XII. Tm. 46, p. 12.
46. Saletore, *S. P. Life*, I. pp. 38-39; *Indian Historical Quarterly*, VIII. pp. 526 seq.

have traced the beginnings of Vijayanagara to Kampili,[47] we may observe the following in regard to the prinicipality of Kampili. There is nothing whatsoever in the inscriptions concerning Kampili, discovered so far to connect that principality with Vijayanagara, and to justify one's statement that the sons of Sangama were anti-Hoysala in feeling. On the other hand, the available evidence proves in unmistakable terms the bitter animosity which rulers of Kampili showed against the Hoysalas, the initial victories which the latter won over the last great Hoysala king Vīra Ballāḷa, and the final victory which he scored over them towards the end of his eventful reign.

The history of Kampili is to be traced to about the eighth century A.D. A *vīragal* found at Bissanahaḷḷi in the Duggasandra hobḷi, Muḷbāgal tāluka, tells us that when the Ganga king Śrīpuruṣa was ruling, his son Duggamāra Eṟeyappa was placed over the Kuvaḷalanāḍ Three Hundred and the Gangavāḍi Six Thousand, and that on the army going to Kampili, Paṇḍappa, son of Komāla, died in the battle. Duggamāra made a grant for the relatives of the hero. On valid grounds this *vīragal* has been assigned by Rice to *circa* A.D. 750.[48] In A.D. 1022 Jagadekamalla Noḷamaba Pallava is said to have been ruling from Kapili which is evidently an error for Kampili.[49] Rāja Rāja Choḷa is said to have destroyed the palace of the Chālukyas (Śaḷikkiyars) at the *nagara* of Kampili surrounded by fragrant gardens, in a record dated A.D. 1046.[50] In Śaka 976 (A.D. 1054) the Western Chālukya king Someśvara Deva I is said to have ruled from Kampila.[51] Ten years later (A.D. 1064) the Western Chālukya king Viṣṇuvardhana Mahārāja Vijayāditya, son of Trailokyamalla, was ruling over the Noḷambavāḍi Thirty-two Thousand from his residence at Kampili.[52] In Śaka 990 (A.D. 1068) Jayasingha Deva of the same family ruled over the same and other provinces from his capital of Kampili.[52-a]

Thus we find that from the middle of the eighth century A.D., till the latter half of the eleventh century A.D., Kampili was either

47. Saletore, *S. P. Life*, I. pp. 31-33.
48. *E. C.* X. Mb. 255, p. 131.
49. *Ibid*, XI. Intr. p. 11, Mk. 10, p. 91. See also Saletore, *Journal of the Bombay Historical Society*, III, p. 111 where the history of Kampīli has been briefly traced from this date onwards.
50. *E. C.* IX Du. 75, p. 84.
51. *561 of 1915.*
52. *E. C.* XII, Mk. 29, p. 95.
52-a. *514 of 1915.*

directly ruled over by the Karnāṭaka kings or by one of their prominent feudatories.

In the twelfth century A.D., however, Kampili with its stronghold of Kummaṭa became the objective of Hoysala aggrandizement to which it finally succumbed. The main reason why this principality with its almost impregnable fortress of Kummaṭa,[53] was attacked by the Hoysalas is because its rulers sided with the Yādavas of Devagiri, the traditional enemies of the Hoysalas. The first Hoysala ruler who conquered Kummaṭa was the great Viṣṇuvardhana Dēva. The stone inscription found near the Vīrabhadra temple at Haṭna, Nāgamangala tāluka, and dated A.D. 1178, relates that along with other famous fortresses Viṣṇuvardhana Deva conquered Kummaṭa " with a frown."[54]

Notwithstanding the fact that the earliest prominent ruler of Kummaṭa, Mummuḍi Singeya Nāyaka, as we have related above, slew the Yādava general Chauṇḍarasa in A.D. 1280, yet, as the following incidents amply prove, it seems certain that the Kummaṭa principality ultimately took the side of the Yādavas against the Hoysalas. Probably the earlier aggressive designs of Viṣṇuvardhana Deva himself were partly responsible for thus overthrowing Kampila into the arms of the Yādavas. However that may be, a stone inscription found at Harihara, Dāvaṇagere tāluka, and dated A.D. 1300, informs us that in the reign of the Yādava king Rāmachandra Deva, the village of Harihara was regranted by Mummuḍi Singeya Nāyaka's son Khaṇḍeya Rāya to Viṣṇu."[55]

The Kummaṭa-Hoysala relations culminated in the reign of Vīra Ballāḷa III, with the final destruction of the principality of Kummaṭa at the hands of that great ruler. A *vīragal* found in the Rameśvara temple at Bāgavāḷa, Hoḷē-Narsīpura tāluka, and dated A.D. 1303, gives us the following information :—That when Vīra Ballāḷa Deva's sister's husband (*maiduna*) Someya Daṇṇāyaka was governing from Bemmaturudurga (modern Chitaldoorg), Kampila Deva, the general of the Seuṇa (Yādava) army, marched against Hoḷalakere whither Someya Daṇṇāyaka went with his army, fought with Kampila Deva but lost his life in the encounter.[56] This battle of Hoḷalakere seems to have been important, for it is described in

53. Read *M. A. R.* for 1929, p. 38, n. 9 for an account of its position.

54. *E. C.* IV. Ng. 70, p. 130. In the *Channa Basava Purāṇa* (63, 77), we are told that Kampila, son of Mummuḍi Singa, occupied the fortress of Hosamaledurga, etc.

55. *E. C.* XI. Dg. 26, pp. 36-37.

56. Not found in the Ms.

another *vīragal* found at Chiṭṭanahaḷḷi, Krishnarājapet tāluka, and likewise dated A.D. 1303.[57]

Evidently Vīra Ballāḷa Deva was not going to tolerate the growing strength of Kampila Deva. Hence we find definite reference to the wars which that Hoysala ruler waged against Kampila Deva. A stone inscription discovered at Kallumaṭha, Kuḍli village, Shimoga tāluka, gives the following account of the personal activities of the Hoysala king. When having started with the sound of war drums, sounding the march, king Bhūdhara Ballāḷa (i.e., Vīra Ballāḷa Deva) with a view to destroy the pride of the *Mahāmaṇḍalika* Khaṇḍeya Rāya, Svayambhū Nāyakācārya, Pingaḷa Rāya *Mīseyara Gaṇḍa,* and their protector (*rakhapāla*) Kampila Deva came with his army and encamped at Siruguppe, Kampila Deva with his army went against Ballāḷa Deva and fought against the latter so as to win the praise of the whole world. In this battle too the Hoysala monarch was worsted, for the incomplete epigraph ends, thus commemorating the death of the Hoysala general Cambeya Daṇṇāyaka :—" When Ballāḷa was on that occasion looking at the two sides of his army, Cambeya Daṇṇāyaka with his brother-in-law Sakki Sāhaṇi, came out and having promised . . ."[58]

War again had to be declared against Kampila Deva who had killed two Hoysala generals. We gather this from the above cited Hosakōṭe *vīragal* dated A.D. 1303, which describes the signal victory which the Hoysala general Kūruka Nāyaka won, although he himself was killed in action.[59]

Now that the third Hoysala general was killed in the battle against Kampila Deva, the Hoysala ruler had to send another army against that enemy. This time the Kummaṭa prince was killed. We gather this from another *vīragal* found at Nāgalāpura, Mayisandra hobḷi, Tipṭūr tāluka, and dated A.D. 1325. It informs us that when Ballāḷa Dēva was in Dōrasamudra, his great minister Becheya Daṇṇāyaka and Singeya Daṇṇāyaka marched against some one, who was evidently the general of Kampila Deva. And Singeya Daṇṇāyaka and Becheya Daṇṇāyaka pierced and slew Kampila and others (*Becheya daṇṇāyaka-Singeya-daṇṇāykaranu mūdalsi Kampila modalanīṟidu kodu.*[60]) This final victory over Kampila terminated the relations between the Hoysalas and the Kummaṭa princes.

57. *M. A. R.* for 1912, p. 45.
58. *Ibid,* for 1923, p. 119.
59. *E. C.* VIII. Nr. 19, *op. cit.*
60. *E. C.* XII. Tp. 24. p. 130. Nañjuṇḍa (A.D. 1525) attributes the fall

There is nothing in the above records relating to the history of the kingdom of Kampila to suggest in the least that the sons of Sangama were in any way connected with it.

(b) *The Family Priest of the sons of Sangama was a Karnāṭaka priest from a Karnāṭaka centre.* One great reason to which the advocates of the Telugu origin of the founders of Vijayanagara fondly adhere is the alleged part Vidyāraṇya Śrīpāda is said to have played in the foundation of the great mediæval Hindu Empire. That this is entirely unhistorical we have sufficiently proved, both on contemporary epigraphical and literary grounds, elsewhere.[61] Here it has been shown that the family priest of the founders was a *rāja-guru* who belonged to the Kāḷāmukha order hailing from one of the centres in the Karnāṭaka.[62] One or two facts may be added here to support our statements. Harihara Rāya II and Deva Rāya II continued to be under the spiritual guidance of Kriyāśakti Dēva. A copper-plate grant hailing from Dharwar, and dated A.D. 1379, calls Kriyāśakti Mūrti the *guru* of Harihara Rāya II.[63] Another copper-plate dated A.D. 1378 styles the same teacher as *rāja-guru-pitāmaha,* and says that Harihara Rāya II was " a worshipper at his feet."[64] A stone inscription found at Someśvara, Mangalore tāluka, and dated Śaka 13(64) Dundhbhi, Caitra Śu. 1 (A.D. 1442, March, Tuesday, the 13th) informs us that the *rāja-guru* of Dēva Rāya II was Kriyāśakti Deva Oḍeyar.[65]

If in spite of all this evidence one believes in the story of Vidyāraṇya Śrīpāda having helped Harihara Rāya I to build the capital,[66] one merely exchanges fact for fiction.

of Kummaṭa to the invasion of the South by the Delhi Sultan. According to him Rāmanātha fell fighting while defending Hosamaledurga. *M. A. R.* for 1929, p. 47.

61 .Saletore, *S. P. Life.*, I. pp. 108-112.

62. Saletore, *J. A. H. R. S.* IX. pp. 33-42.

63. *M. A. R.* for 1918, p. 51. Mr. R. Narasimhacharya identified this Kriyāśakti Mūrti with his namesake mentioned in earlier records as the *guru* of Mādhava Mantri. *Ibid,* for 1912, p. 48. In a later Report, he identified Kriyāśakti Ācārya with Candrabhūṣaṇa-deva Oḍeyar. *M. A. R.* for 1918, p. 34.

64. *M. A. R.* for 1912, p. 47. cf. *Ep. Report of the Southern Circle for* 1924-25, pp. 88-95.

65. *467 of 1928* ; Swamikannu, *Ind. Ephm.* V. p. 86.

66. Mr. S. Srikanthaya still adheres to this legend. *Q. J. M. S.* XXVI. pp. 180-226 ; 232-235.

(c) *Feudatory Families and Generals under Ballāḷa Deva III and the sons of Sangama.* One more argument which decidedly proves that the founders of Vijayanagara were of Karnāṭaka stock is that relating to some of the prominent feudatories and generals of the last Hoysala ruler, who, having themselves been pillars of the Hoysala power, acquiesced in the new government of the sons of Sangama without a murmur.

Of the feudatory families we shall select only two—one to which Mayileya Nāyaka belonged, and the other from which the well-known Eḷahankanāḍ *prabhus* hailed. In regard to the family of Mayileya Nāyaka, we have already adduced sufficient proof to show that the members of his family and he himself transferred their allegiance from the Hoysalas to the sons of Sangama without any commotion whatsoever.[67] Our statements in regard to this family are further proved by the fact that Mayileya Nāyaka who, as shown by us, was under Ballāla Deva III in A.D. 1340,[68] continued to be under Bukka Rāya in A.D. 1348.[69] Mayileya Nāyaka's younger brother Yōjeya Nāyaka was under the same ruler in A.D. 1359.[70] Mayileya Nāyaka's son Deveya Nāyaka is mentioned under the same ruler in A.D. 1376.[71] Another son of Mayileya Nāyaka called Kōṭeya Nāyaka served under the same Vijayanagara ruler in A.D. 1386.[72]

The other feudatory family that served both the Hoysalas and the sons of Sangama was that of the well known Eḷahankanāḍ *prabhus*. A few facts concerning this family will make our statement clear. It is enough to trace its history from A.D. 1308 onwards when Mudeya Allappa Daṇṇāyaka was placed over the Eḷahankanāḍ principality under Ballāḷa Deva III.[73] In A.D. 1328 Eḷhanka was under the same monarch.[74] A grant was made to the god Keśavanātha of Hōjāla in Eḷahankanāḍ in A.D. 1340 when Ballāḷa Deva III was in his capital at Uṇṇāmulaipaṭṭana.[75] Honnamarāya Nāyaka,

67. Saletore, *I. H. Q.* VIII, pp. 527-528.
68. *Ibid*, p. 527.
69. *E. C.* IX. Dv. 50, p. 80.
70. *E. C.* IX. Nl. 23, p. 33.
71. *E. C.* IX. Bn. 132, pp. 24-25. This Tamil record has some chronological irregularities. *E. C. ibid*, p. 24, n. (1).
72. *Ibid*, Bn. 139, p. 26.
73. *Ibid*, Bn. 136, p. 25.
74. *Ibid*, Db. 14, p. 63, Dv. I. p. 74.
75. *Ibid*, Dv. 54, p. 80.

son of Chikka Bayireya Nāyaka, the Eḷahankanāḍ *prabhu*, made a specified grant in A.D. 1342 when the same ruler was ruling from the same capital.[76] In A.D. 1345 Vīramāji Hiritya Pemmaya Nāyaka was evidently placed over the Eḷahankanāḍ principality by Ballāḷa Deva III, although it is not stated so in the epigraph.[77]

This principality like the one under Mayileya Nāyaka readily acknowledged the hegemony of the sons of Sangama. In A.D. 1348 the great Eḷahankanāḍ *prabhu* Bairi Deva is mentioned along with Mayileya Nāyaka, in a record already cited in connection with the latter, as making a grant in conjunction with a number of farmers, to some specified person.[78] Eḷahankanāḍ Allāḷa Jīya's son Taṇṇiyappa was the recipient of a specified grant in A.D. 1363 when Bukkaṇṇa Oḍeyar was in the city of Mūḷbāgal.[79] The Eḷahankanāḍ *prabhus* were conspicuous in later Vijayanagara history too, but this is outside our purpose.[80]

The history of one great Hoysala general who served under the new masters, the founders of the Vijayanagara dynasty, is enough to add to the evidence we have already cited relating to the status the latter occupied in the land as the legitimate successors of the Hoysala rulers. It is that of Baicheya Daṇṇāyaka. This great minister was the senior house minister (*hiriya maneya pradhāni*) of Ballāḷa Deva III, as is related in a *vīragal* dated *Śaka varuṣada 1240 Kāḷāyukta samvatsarada Puṣya* Śu. 10 Sō. (A.D. 1319, January the 2nd Tuesday, the week day not corresponding), and found in the Pañchalingeśvara temple at Hanagaravāḍi, Honnāli tāluka.[81] In A.D. 1328 he is called Baicheya Daṇṇāyaka Chamūpa, under the same monarch.[82]

This Hoysala general took service under Bukkaṇṇa Oḍeyar. We prove this by three records—one which is to be assigned to the reign of Bukka Rāya himself, and two others of a later period which ex-

76. *E. C.* IX. Bn. 21, p. 7. See also Bn. 34, Dv. 46, dated in the same year, pp.

77. E. C. IX. Dv. 3, p. 74.

78. E. C. IX. Dv. 50, p. 50, *op. cit.*

79. E. C. IX. Bn. 81, pp. 16-17. See also Dv. 58 of A.D. 1382 which evidently falls within the Vijayanagara period. *Ibid*, p. 81.

80. E. C. V. Cn. 241, dated A.D. 1432 ; p. 226 ; E. C. IX. Ma. 54, dated A.D. 1529, p. 58.

81. E. C. VII. Tl. 117, p. 178 ; Swamikannu, *Ind. Eph.* IV. p. 240.

82. E. C. XI. Cd. 4, p. 3.

pressly state that Baicheya Daṇṇāyaka was under Bukka Rāya. The first is a damaged and incomplete *vīragal* found in the Iśvara temple at Vighnasante, Noṇavina hobḷi, Tipṭūr tāluka. It relates thus :— *Maleyāḷara kūḍe kāḷaga Kasava Nāyakara maga sitara gaṇḍa* . . . *kāḷaga kādu* (*date specified*) . . . *svarada kāḷagadalu śrīmanu mahāmaṇḍalika Rāuttara rāyara gaṇḍa bhāśege tappuva rāyara gaṇḍa śrī Vīra* . . . *Voḍeyara maga* . . . *Bayicha daṇṇāyakaru Maleyāḷara mēle* (stops here).

Rice translates the record thus :—" In the war of . . . *the Mahāmaṇḍalika* (with other epithets) Vīra Voḍeyar's son Baicheya Daṇṇayaka, marching upon Maleyāḷa."[83]

The correct rendering of the above *vīragal* would be the following :—" In the war against the people of Maleyāḷa, (some one who had the *biruda* of) *sitara gaṇḍa* (and who was) the son of Kasava (Keśava?) Nāyaka fought (*kādu*), and (obviously lost his life), when (with titles) Śrī Vīra (Bukkaṇṇa Oḍeyar's) son (*vīra* . . . *Voḍeyara maga*) was ruling. Baicheya Daṇṇāyaka marched against Maleyāḷa."

We prove that this record refers to the reign of Bukkaṇṇa Oḍeyar from the *birudas* given to him—*Mahāmaṇḍalika, Rāutta Rāyara Gaṇḍa, Śrī—Bhāśege tappuva Rāyaragaṇḍa, Vīra* . . . *Oḍeyar*. The last four were the distinctive *birudas* of Harihara Rāya I and of his illustrious brother Bukkaṇṇa Oḍeyar.

The date is given thus :—*Hēmalamba samvatsarada Māgha Śud(dh)a* 15 *Maṁ. vāra* which corresponds to Śaka 1280, and the date works out to A.D. 1358 January, the 25th, Thursday, the week day not corresponding.[84] This *vīragal* falls within the reign of Bukka Rāya (A.D. 1353—A.D. 1377).[85]

The two later records which confirm our assumption are the following : the Chennakeśava temple record of Bēlūr dated A.D. 1414, and the Rameśvaram temple inscription found at Kūḍli, Shimoga tāluka.

Of these the first one is important. It gives the descent of Baicheya Daṇṇāyaka thus (*Baicheya daṇṇāyakara pūrvvānvaya-guṇa*

83. *E. C.* XII. Tp. 45, p. 51, text p. 144.
84. Swamikannu, *Ind. Eph.* IV. p. 318. Rice is incorrect when he doubtfully assigns this record to *circa* A.D. 1237. *E. C.* XII. p. 45. n. 1.
85. Rice, *Mysore and Coorg from the Inscriptions*, p. 112.

kathanuṃ)—at first Harihara Oḍeyar (who is called in this later record *śrīmad rājā-dhirājam dharaṇī-pālakam*, etc.) gave Baicheya Daṇṇāyaka the rank of minister with honours (*śrī Baicheya Daṇḍe-śage nija-sachivam kōvidaṃ putra mitra stomam bāpp-embinaṃ sajji-naru pogaḷvinaṃ durga-bhaṇḍāra-rājya-premaṃ kai-sarvinaṃ mudrikeyam oḷaviniṃ paṭṭamam kaṭṭi koṭṭam*). And that king's younger brother Bukka Rāya entrusted him with equally responsible state duties (*ā Harihara nṛpara anujaṃ mahā-vallabha-nṛpaṇoḷ-and atiśayadiṃ bēha bahu-rāja-kāryamaṃ mahā-vaibhava ina*. . .*Baicha Dāṇḍādhiśam*).[86]

There is one difficulty here : In the same record Baicheya Daṇ-ṇāyaka is mentioned as the minister of Deva Rāya in A.D. 1414. This minister of Deva Rāya gave some specified grants to the god Chennakeśava of Bēlūr.

Now, we have identified Baicheya Daṇṇāyaka with the minister who having been under Ballāḷa Deva III, afterwards took service under Bukka Rāya I. Is it possible that Baicheya Daṇṇāyaka lived from A.D. 1319 and earlier till A.D. 1414 ? That seems hardly cre-dible, since it would mean that he lived to a ripe old age of 100 years and more!

On the other hand, there can be hardly any doubt that Ballāḷa Deva III's great minister had taken service under Bukka Rāya I. This is again confirmed by the Rameśvara temple record of Kūḍli which explains our difficulty. In this record dated A.D. 1431 we have not only the confirmation of the fact of Baicheya Daṇṇāyaka's having been the minister of Bukka Rāya, but also an explanation as to who the other Baicheya Daṇṇāyaka was mentioned in the above record hailing from Bēlūr. The latter Baicheya Daṇṇāyaka was the grandson of the first Baicheya Daṇṇāyaka. Thus the record from Kūḍli relates:—Formerly (*purāṇārtha*) under Bukka Rāya was the great minister Baicheya Daṇṇāyaka (his praise given), whose son was Mangappa Daṇḍādhipa, his son, famous as the king of Māhiṣmaṭī, was Baicheya Daṇṇāyaka, whose son was Rāyaṇṇa Rāya, the great minister of Deva Rāya, placed over the Āraga kingdom in A.D.1431.[87] The second Baicheya Daṇṇāyaka is again mentioned in a record assigned to *circa* A.D. 1420 as the great minister (*mahā-pradhanam*) of Deva Rāya.[88]

86. E. C. V. Bl. 14, p. 47, translit. 107.
87. E. C. VII. Sh. 71, p. 27.
88. E. C. V. Bl. 14, p. 47.

It is no wonder that the sons of Sangama, whom the feudatories and generals of the Hoysalas thus readily acknowledged as the rightful successors of the Hoysalas, should have been intimately associated with the Karnāṭaka country. This alone explains why in two trustworthy copper-plate grants issued under the seal of and by the prince Mārappa, and both dated A.D. 1347, the following is said,—" Their (of the four sons of Sangama, Mudappa having obviously died in A.D. 1346) family deity being Virūpākṣa worshipped by all the gods, their garden canal the sacred Tungabhadrā, resembling the Ganges, their pleasure hill (*viharana-śikharī*) the Hemakūṭa mountain, covered with the shadows of peaks, their sporting pond being the Pampāsaras lake—this was their great fortune."[89]

Another copper-plate grant also issued by the same son of Sangama is identical with the above, although it was given to different donee. It relates thus:—" Their (of the four sons of Sangama) family god, the guru of all gods, the god Virūpākṣa, for merit, the Tungabhadrā like the stream of the Ganges, bordered with pleasure gardens; their house filled with women, their pleasure garden, the Hemakūṭa mountain (which Rice incorrectly translates as their *stronghold,* when the original clearly says *viharaṇa-śikharī*) for sport the Pampa lake—great was their fortune!"[90]

It was only their profound sense of responsibility as successors to the rich heritage of the Hoysalas that made the founders themselves give extraordinary prominence to the royal city of their great predecessors—Dōrasamudra. The Hebbasūru copper-plate grant dated A.D. 1346 tells us that after " becoming great " " with the assistance of Vidyātīrtha," Bukka Rāya " freed from enemies a hundred royal cities counting from Dōrasamudra," ruling thereby an empire that was perfect in seven parts (*tasmād Dōrasamudra gaṇanam sad-rājadhānī śatam kṛtvā rājyam akaṇṭakam sa nayatas saptānga samvardhitam*).[91]

Further, in an undated stone inscription found in the Sakkarepaṭṭaṇa, recording the erection of a monument in memory of a Jaina *guru* named Lakṣmisena Bhaṭṭāraka, at Hosapaṭṭana, by Māyaṇṇa and Mākaṇṇa, it is related that the town of Hosapaṭṭana was the face of the goddess of the kingdom of Vīra Bukka (*intī-Hoysala-bhūvibhu-Lakṣmī-lapanamuṃ śrī vīra Bukka rāja sāmrājya ramā*

89. *M. A. R.* for 1929, pp. 160, ll. 24-27, 166.
90. *E. C.* VIII. Sb. 375, pp. 65-67.
91. *E. C.* IV. Yd. 46, p. 58, text 51.

ramaṇīya vilāsa-darppaṇōpamaṃ enisi sogayisuva Hosapaṭṭaṇa-doḷu).[92]

Then again, in a copper-plate grant discovered at Hosakōṭe, Pāvagūḍu tāluka, and dated A.D. 1447, it is said that through Sangama was the lady of the Karnāṭa country able to wear her ear-rings (*i.e.*, not allowed to be without a lord—to be a widow) (*Sangamo nāma bhūmipālo guṇattaraḥ yena Karnāṭa deśa śrīs sthira tāṭaṅkavaty abhūt*).[93]

(*d*) *Literary Evidence to prove the Karnāṭaka origin.* Indeed, nothing demolishes so much the alleged Telugu origin of the founders of Vijayanagara as the fact of a Telugu author in the time of Deva Rāya II calling Bukka Rāya I a *Karnāta kṣitīpa.* This is gathered from the Telugu author Vallabharāya, who was placed as governor of Vinikonda (Krishna district), under Prauḍha Deva Rāya. In his Telugu work called *Krīḍābhirāmam* (which was a Telugu rendering of a Sanskrit work on dramaturgy called *Premābhirāmam* written by Rāvipāṭi Tripurāntaka at the court of the Gajapati king Pratāparudra II), Vallabharāya clearly says that his great grandfather Chandra, served as a minister under the *Karnāṭa ksitīpa* Peda Bukka, *i.e.*, Bukka the Elder (Bukka Rāya I).[94]

The Karnāṭaka origin of the founders thus once again proved by a Telugu poet, who was intimately connected with the dynasty founded by the sons of Sangama, was never questioned even in the days of Kṛṣṇa Deva Rāya the Great, whose benevolent rule looked upon the Telugus and the Kannaḍigas with equal care and affection. Hence Lakṣmīnārāyaṇa in his *sangītasuryodaya* speaks of Kṛṣṇa Deva Rāya as one who belonged to the *Karnāṭānvaya.*[95]

(*e*) *The Fiction of Vidyāraṇya having helped Harihara Oḍeyar.* The pivot upon which the theory of all those who maintain that in A.D. 1336 Harihara Oḍeyar I founded the city of Vijayanagara rests, is the alleged part played by Vidyāraṇya Śrīpāda of the Śringeri *maṭha.* To the overwhelming evidence which completely disproves this, and which we have utilized elsewhere,[96] we may add the following hailing from the Śringeri *maṭha* itself. One of the arguments we have adduced to maintain our contention is that Vidyā-

92. *M. A. R.* for 1927, pp. 61-62.
93. *E. C.* XII. Pg. 67, pp. 27, 384.
94. Aiyangar, The Sources of Vijayanagara History, p. 56, v. 7.
95. Kuppuswami Sastri, Triennial Catalogue of Skt. Mss., V. P. I, p. 6605.
96. Saletore, *S. P. Life,* I. pp. 101 seq.; Saletore, *J. A. H. R. S.* IX. pp. 39-42, *op. cit.*

tīrtha Svāmi preceded Vidyāraṇya Śrīpāda in the pontificate of Śringeri, and that therefore, the latter could not have been in the neighbourhood of Hampe in the year A.D. 1336 or even in A.D. 1346. Even in the later work, the historicity of which we have discussed above called *Vidyāraṇyakṛti* incorporated in the *Vidyāraṇyakālajñāna*, it is clearly stated that Vidyāraṇya was the disciple of Vidyāśaṅkara also called Vidyātīrtha.[97]

We may note by the way two little points here. One is that relating to the person who was responsible for inducing Vidyāraṇya Śrīpāda to comment on the *Śrauta Sūtras.* This person was the minister Chauṇḍappa, disciple of Kriyāśakti, the *guru* of the founders of Vijayanagara. This is related by Chauṇḍapārya himself in his work *Prayogaratnamālā.*[98]

Another trifling point is that relating to Vidyāraṇya himself. He commanded the Vijayanagara viceroy Yadugiri Virūpākṣa Rāya, son of Bukka Rāya, in A.D. 1378, to make a grant, when, according to our calculations, he was already the head of the Śringeri *maṭha.*[99]

(*f*) *Evidence from Numismatics.* Dr. Krishna has drawn the attention of scholars to the symbols of Hanumān and Garuḍa on the Vijayanagara coins. In his very useful work on the *Deccan Numismatics* published in his *Annual Report for* 1932, Dr. Krishna with his usual thoroughness and skill has brought out the remarkable identity between the symbols of Hanumān on the coins of Harihara Rāya I and on those of the Kadambas, and between the Hanumān and Garuḍa symbols of the same ruler and those of the Yādavas.[100] This detail only adds to the mass of other more solid evidence which conclusively proves that the sons of Sangama were Karnāṭaka in orgin and in bravery.

97. *M. A. R.* for 1932, pp. 105, 106. On the latter page Dr. Krishna has an interesting note on Vidyātīrtha.

98. Kuppuswami Sastri, Triennial Report of Sanskrit Mss. for 1910-11 and 1912-13, p. 1050.

99. *E. C.* VI. Kp. 30, p. 81. Opinion now seems to be that Mādhava Vidyāraṇya himself was a Kannaḍiga. For it is related that Lakṣmīdhara was the son of the sister of Mādhava. Vidyāraṇya of the Kannaḍa-kula. Memoirs of the Archæologcial Survey of India, No. 13, pp. 15-18. 38 of 1888-1899. Cf. Kunduri, The Kanarese Origin of the Vijayanagara Empire, Part II, pp. 10-11.

100. *M. A. R.* for 1932, pp. 77-78. Dr. Krishna's remark that there was a currency in the Vijayanagara kingdom in about A.D. 1350 illustrates indeed the fact that from the very inception of the kingdom, it was financially strong. B. A. S.

12

Vijayanagara and Vidyaranya

By

Mr. S. Shrikantaya, B.A., B.L.,
Secretary, Mythic Society, Bangalore.

On the rocks above the Hampi temple, close to a group of more modern Śiva Temples, is to be seen a small shrine built entirely, roof as well as walls, of stone. Everything about this little relic, says Sewell, proves it to be of greater antiquity than any other structure in the whole circuit of hills. It looks like a building of the Twelfth Century A.D. It is quite possible that the shrine may have been used by a succession of recluses, the last of whom was the great teacher Mādhava. If we stand on that rock and imagine, he continues, all the great ruins visible from thence, the palaces and temples, the statues and towers and walls, to be swept out of existence, we have around us nothing but nature in one of her wildest woods—lofty hills near and far formed almost entirely on the farther side, where dwelt the chiefs of Anegondi and was just such a one as would have been chosen by the ascetics of former days who loved to dwell in solitude and isolation amid scenes of grandeur and beauty. We shall in all probability never know, concludes Sewell, whether this hermit, whose actual existence at the time is attested to by every tradition regarding the origin of Vijayanagara, was really the great Mādhava or another less celebrated sage on whom by a confusion of ideas his name has been foisted. For, some say that Mādhavāchārya lived entirely at Śringeri.

The present tiny hamlet of Hampi and its vast picturesque and interesting ruins, situated not far from Hospet in the Bellary District are reminiscent of a great Empire of the Hindus, established about 1336 A.D., as a bulwark against Muhammadan aggression and for the preservation of the Hindu religion and Dharma. Its origin and establishment were not born of any attachment to any particular form of Hinduism. It was a comprehensive movement, taking into its fold all forms of the Hindu faith including the prevalent forms of Jainism and other religious beliefs of a nondescript character, for the preservation of Hindu Dharma, free from the onrush of the proselytising Muhammadans and to provide for it a peaceful home. In this great work, a number of prominent men played a part, and at Vijayanagara all the varying faiths had their *maṭhas* established, receiving the patronage of the Kings.

The strength of the Hindu civilisation was manifested in the culmination of the national efforts for the preservation of the Indian religion. Like the love of country with the enemy at the gate love of religion takes hold when it is fiercely attacked from without: such a love appeared in the Karnataka Country in the early half of the fourteenth century, long anterior to the development of the national idea in Europe. The old Hindu temples and *maṭhas* fostered such a spirit as powerful social, economic centres for these movements, besides providing religious inspiration. These were corporations where co-operation of the people of the locality aided with royal patronage, was possible and there the people had the courage to give independent advice, unhampered by mercenary considerations and because of the source of such advice, the difficulty of opposition to it was great, if not impossible. These were therefore common meeting grounds for the Ruler and the people, providing opportunities for a cordial and healthy co-operation in the interests of the State. To recall the words of Vincent Smith, the influence exercised by Śankara, Rāmānuja and the other Southern sages on the whole country from Cape Comorin to the recesses of the snowy mountains is the best evidence of that inner unity of Hindu India, which survives the powerful disintegrating forces set in motion by diversity in blood, manners, customs and political allegiance. It was this unity which brought about the foundation of the Vijayanagara Empire which we are now commemorating six centuries after its birth.

This subject is still of entrancing interest and the great question is, who founded that Empire of Harihara and Bukka which changed the political fortunes of South India for two centuries and contributed in a remarkable degree towards the evolution and development of religious thoughts in Hindu India ?

The origin of Vijayanagara may not have been a miracle and it is not necessary to consider in this short paper the political vicissitudes of the several South Indian Kingdoms in the fourteenth Century or the part their rulers may have played in the establishment of the Vijayanagara Empire. We need not consequently proceed to discuss whether Harihara and Bukka were Muhammadan vassals sent to subjugate Ballāḷa III, whether they were guards of the treasury of Pratāpa Rudra Dēva of Wāraṇgal, whether they came from Kaṁpili or Anegondi ; much less whether Ballāḷa III himself was responsible for the foundation of the Vijayanagara Empire. It will be sufficient for our purpose to refer to the political map of South India in the beginning of the second quarter of the fourteenth century. (1) The Kingdom of the Yādavas of Deogiri was a regular Muhammadan Province, paying tribute to the Sultan of Delhi (2) The Hoysaḷa Ballāḷas of Dōrasamudra had been twice defeated, their Capital was destroyed and a Ballāḷa, either Ballāḷa III or his son, very probably Ballāḷa III himself who had been taken as a hostage to Delhi, had returned. (3) The Kākatīyas of Wāraṅgal had suffered eclipse, their kingdōm having become a Muhammadan appanage. (4) The Pāṇḍyas in the far South were feeling the pressure of the Muhammadan invasions and there had been a Muhammadan garrison at Madura. (5) In the Muhammadan Sultanate itself, the period was of profound significance. While a revolt was suppressed, its causes were not removed and it was liable to break again. Besides, Muhammad's proceedings frightened the rājās as well as the Muhammadan armies in the Deccan which broke into mutiny. There were also revolutions elsewhere.

It was at this great juncture that the powerful Hindu confederacy of the South was organised with the avowed object of turning the Muhammadans out of South India. This eminently successful Campaign resulted in the Hindu Empire of Vijayanagara, whose Court and whose Capital were a marvel to ambassadors from all parts of the civilised world.

Who is Vidyāraṇya and what part did he play in the foundation and establishment of this great edifice ?

The *guru* of Vidyāraṇya was Vidyāśaṇkara. Vidyāśankara was a great and unique personality who occupied the *guru-pīṭha* of the Advaita *Maṭha* at Śringeri at the time. He was the son Śāraṅgapāṇi, also called Sarvajña Vishnu and came from Bilāraṇya. He revived the influence of the Śringeri *Maṭha,* then on the wane. He was surrounded by Mādhava, Bukka, and Bhārati Yati, amongst others. This chief of the *yogis,* the worshipper of the Goddess Śri Chakra adorned the *pīṭha* for seventy-three years, established during that period eight Sannyāsis like the Ashṭa Diggajas in all parts of the Country in the *pīṭhas* which he created and then in his old age spent fifteen years in severe penance under the foot of the Himalayas. He was fond of *lambika yoga* and versed in Brahma *Vidya.* Of his disciples, Vidyāraṇya was one of the foremost. This ascetic dweller at Śringeri is credited by tradition with the foundation of the Vijayanagara Empire and the Vidyāraṇya tradition has come to be believed by all. I do not propose to enter into a discussion here about this tradition but will content myself by furnishing a brief summary of the facts available concerning this tradition.

The relations of the Hoysaḷa Ballāḷas and of Harihara and Bukka after them with the *Gurus* of Śringeri were most cordial. Large grants were made to Śringeri. Vidyāraṇya's influence at the Court of Vijayanagara was beyond dispute. Bhārati Tirtha of Śringeri exercised considerable influence there and he was being approached for blessings and guidance on important occasions. Sāyana and Bhōganātha were very influential in the Vijayanagara Empire. The Vidyāraṇya tradition, connecting Vidyāraṇya with the foundation of the Vijayanagara Empire, according to Nellore, Kolar and other grants is supported by the accounts of foreign travellers, literary and inscriptional references and in the *grama paddathis* collected by Buchanan. Suryanarayana Rao's date finds an echo in the earlier account of Buchanan. Nuniz and Paes refer to the assistance rendered by Vidyāraṇya in the foundation and indeed, the capital appears to have been known as Vidyānagara at first. Keeping aside the controversy regarding the identity of Vidyāraṇya with Mādhava for a moment and assuming the two to be the same, the celebrated scholar Mādhava, it is said, besides experience and talent, may have contributed in other ways towards this great undertaking. For the *Gurus* of Śringeri were at that time, according to Wilson, apprehensive of the increasing number of *Jangamas* and of the approach of the Muhammadans. It would not be unreasonable to suppose that the wealth and influence of the Śringeri Mutt were placed at the disposal of Harihara and Bukka. For the Hindu religion was in danger, Hindu towns were overrun and their temples plundered and Muhammadan tyranny and ruthless slaughter were inducing people to change their religion. This inconoclastic zeal of the foreign invader was full of ominous portents. For instance, when Śriraṅgam was captured and sacked by the Muhammadans in 1327 A.D., the image was taken for refuge followed by Pillai Lokacharya to Tirupathi. Vēdānta Dēśika himself was a refugee in Satyamangalam. Sectional differences were forgotten and leaders of Hindu religious movements were internally opposed to heretics and anxious to protect Hinduism itself. Vēdānta Dēśika, Akshobhya Tirtha and other religious leaders united in supporting Vidyāraṇya who by his statesmanship and political foresight utilised his supreme influence in this accomplishment.

Vidyāraṇya may have been ordained as a Sannyasin in A.D. 1331 and continued till A.D. 1386. Vidyāraṇya was the disciple of Vidya Śankara, the King of ascetics. Sāyana and Mādhava were the commentator and the reviser of the vedas. They were well known for fluency in speech and Mādhava was the greatest of the *Gurus*, whose *Guru* was Vidyaśankara. The name Sāyana was perhaps the family or surname of the house to which Mādhava belonged and it was like the gem *Kaustubha* of the milky ocean. With Śrimati for his mother, the reputed Māyana as his father and Sāyana and Bhōganātha as his brothers born in the Bhāradvāja gotra, Yajus Śakha and belonging to Baudhāyana sutra is Mādhava who is Sarvajña. Mādhava was one of the eight disciples ordained by Vidyaśankara for the eight Mathas established by him. Vidyāraṇya was the name given to him by Śankarānanda and he was established near Virupākṣa on the banks of the Tungabhadra where the proud Madhvas were in the ascendant and had to be humbled. The name of Vidyāraṇya is not found in the Śringeri list of Dr. Hultzch, prepared from the collections in the possession of Jambunatha Bhatta of Tanjore, but in the Śringeri list of Mr. Seshagiri Sastry which was found in the Matha, and said to be authentic and reliable. Vidyāraṇya is the " twenty second " becoming guru at Śringeri in 1331. We may make a guess that Sacchidānanda referred to in the list might be another name for Vidyāraṇya, in which case that Vidyāraṇya was also a guru at Śringeri may be confirmed. What is important from these considerations is that the lists in all the Mathas refer to the glory of Vidyāraṇya. The *Puṇyaślokamanjari*, *Gururatnamala* and *Suśama* as well as the *Guruvaṁśakāvya*, *Rājakālanirṇaya* and *Vidyāraṇya Kālajñāna* while differing concerning the identity of Vidyāraṇya, nevertheless confirm the tradition that Vidyāraṇya was the founder of the Vijayanagara Empire.

Vidyāraṇya was born about 1268 or 1296 (according to an inference from Devyāparadha śloka). He was not only the spiritual preceptor but the bearer of the burden of sovereignty of Bukka. He was a minister under the early Vijayanagara Kings. He was the hereditary preceptor and minister of Bukka I and was comparable as Brihaspati to Indra. The importance and rise to fame of Śringeri was contemporaneous with the foundation of the Vijayanagara Empire and may be considered sufficient to warrant the Vidyāraṇya tradition. Vidyā Śankara secured a high status to the Matha and he was specially honoured and revered by the early Vijayanagara Kings. In 1356 when Bukka visited Śringeri extensive land grants were made to the Matha. When Vidyāraṇya's presence was required at Vijayanagara a *nirūpa* was secured from the Śenior Śrīpāda to Benares. In 1346 a great grant was made to Śringeri on the occasion of the festival of the Vijayanagara Empire. After getting a nirūpa, Bukka visited Śringeri with Vidyāraṇya to whom he made a grant. A *Kavita* at Śringeri refers to the death of Vidyāraṇya at Hampi in 1386. A grant of the same year relates to a gift of lands to Vidyāraṇyapura to commemorate Vidyāraṇya. In an unfinished inscription Vidyāraṇya is eulogised as the supreme light incarnate. It cannot therefore be said that fabrication of fables were attractive to religious recluses because of their knowledge of what they call absolute reality. The traditions contained in the grants even where the grants are palpable forgeries cannot be summarily rejected. Naturally the forgeries would relate to the operative portions of the grants and not to the preambles and some of the grants are to be found in Śrivaiṣṇava temples and in possession of persons other than the disciples of the Śringeri Matha. It is interesting to observe that all these grants made by the Vijayanagara Rulers to Śringeri or to others are continued to this day. We have so far referred to contemporary references, traditions, inscriptions, concerning the Vidyāraṇya myth and drawn some attention to certain literary references. The latter might be multiplied to show that the tradition relating to the foundation of Vijayanagara by Vidyāraṇya is continuously believed in the annals of *Hanḍe Anantāpuram, Koyiloḻugu, Pārijātapaharaṇam* of Nandi Thimmanna, *Achyuta-rāyā-bhyadayam* of Rajanatha, *Vardāmbika Pariṇaymu* of Tirumalāmba, *Sivatatvaratnākara* of Basavarāja, *Chikkadēvarāyavaṁśāvali* of Tirumala Arya, all confirm the tradition.

G. R. Subrahmayya Pantulu writing on the Augustan age of Telugu literature says that traditions are agreed on Vidyāraṇya's part in the foundation of Vijayanagara. Kittel and Fleet confirm the identification of Vidyānagara with Vijayanagara. C. R. Krishnamacharlu who dwells on the religion of the Vijayanagara house refers with approval to the traditional beliefs attributing the creation of the Empire and the construction of the capital to Vidyāraṇya. Krishna Sastri refers to the famous Śringeri inscription relating to the visit of Harihara and Bukka and others to Śringeri in 1346 and regards that grant as bearing out the traditional connection claimed in later records for the teachers of this religious institution with the rise of the New Empire and the foundation of Vijayanagara. For the joint donation indicates the undivided interest of the teachers in the building up of the great Empire. In the correspondence and grants to be found at Śringeri the reference to Vidyānagara is continued and the *Gurus* are described as Vidyāraṇyapādapadmārādhakas and Karṇāṭaka Simhāsanapratisṭhāpanāchāryas. As Sir Subrahmanya Iyer says, the influence exercised by Mathas as centres of learning on the religious and other literature of the Country cannot be denied. The varied and well-known contributions made thereto by the famous Vidyāraṇyasvāmi of Śringeri Śāradā Math or under his auspices are the most conspicuous examples of this kind. There is scarcely a branch of learning considered by Hindus as important to which Vidyāraṇya or the scholars who gathered round him did not make valuable contributions and it is to his commentaries that the modern world owes its knowledge of the traditional meaning of the oldest of the sacred books, the Ṛgveda.

With the advent of Vidyāraṇya, Śringeri became a State within a State, and its Guru a Rajaguru with a Royal position. Titles and honours and the regalia of the State multiplied. *Agrahāras* and temples and endowments and worships created a profound impression. Instead of remaining a calm centre of learning, study, contemplation and penance, it became a State with Officers to collect revenue and manage its affairs. The importance of this stronghold of the Advaita Philosophy thus increased day after day.

Mādhavāchārya known to the World as Vidyāraṇya may be described as the Establisher of the Karṇāṭaka Empire of Vijayanagara, associated with the great Advaitic School of Philosophic thought, of which he was the Great Teacher and the foremost exponent, as hereditary and chief Minister of the Vijayanagara ruler, bearing the burden of sovereignty and as one of the greatest commentators the world has ever known. This great Statesman and Empire Builder did not construct a Military or a Commercial Empire but a Hindu Empire. His political philosophy was of a rarely practical type and in a period of political and religious turmoil, he created and ushered into existence a powerful Hindu Empire. Mādhava is an extraordinary character ; his fame increases with the march of time and develops into an enigma : exact and extensive knowledge of the Vēdas was his : he was excellent in Brahmavidya : there is none to compare to him in learning. His encyclopædic knowledge enabled him to comprehend the Vēdas in their true light and his mastery over the subtleties of accent, his acquaintance with the nature, origin and significance of the archaic forms in which the Vēdas greatly abound, his deep learning in the Vēdaṇgas, his capacity for the perception of the subtle and the indefinite and his understanding of the Hindu mode of thought and writing are unequalled. Such was the sage for whom his great admirers have erected a seated figure of Vidyāraṇya with the hand in the pose of Vyākhyāna Mudrā in front of the image of the ancient Śri Chakra at Hampi. Vidyāraṇya was more than a Royal personage and the founder of an Empire, perhaps entitled to wear the Udarabhanda and Jaṭāmakuṭa, the attributes of Īśvara himself. South Indian Hindus ought to pay homage to the memory of the great sage Vidyāraṇya who founded the Vijayanagara Empire and preserved the ancient religion of the Hindus. The Vijayanagara Empire has vanished but may the ideal of its founder and the Dharma upon which it was based continue for ever and for ever. May Hinduism prosper !

13

Establishment of the Vijayanagara Rule in the Tamil Country

BY

MR. V. VENKATASUBBA AIYAR,
Epigraphical Assistant, Madras.

ALIEN rule may be established either by conquest or by slow degrees with the consent of the people governed. The latter may be said to be the claim of the Vijayanagara rule established in the Tamil country by a people speaking a different language, with its capital away from the Tamil land and depending on its own rank and file for the administration of this region. The one outstanding feature of this rule was that, though it embraced the whole of the Tamil districts from the traditional limits of Vēṅgaḍam (Tirupati) and Conjeevaram in the North right down to Cape Comorin in the South, it met with no opposition worth the name in the land. No local risings or plots marred its inauguration, and the opposition that it met with later came only from its own generals and subordinates and not from the people of the land. Three main causes greatly contributed to its success, viz., (1) the substitution of the Vijayanagara rule in the Hoysaḷa kingdom, (2) the political situation of the land prior to the advent of the Vijayanagara rule and (3) the Muhammadan invasion of South India.

From time immemorial the Tamil land was exclusively governed by the Chēras, the Chōḷas and the Pāṇḍyas, but prior to the establishment of the Vijayanagara rule in this region, the Hoysaḷas had also come in for a share by establishing their capitals first at Kaṇṇaṉūr (Trichinopoly district) and then at Tiruvaṇṇāmalai (North Arcot district) in the Chōḷa country. The Hoysaḷa monarchs Vīra Narasiṁha and his son Sōmēśvara were related by matrimonial alliances with the royal Chōḷa and Pāṇḍya families with the result that their influence was felt throughout the length and breadth of the Tamil land. When the Chōḷa king Rājarāja III was imprisoned by his rebel chief Kōpperuñjiṅgadēva at Śēndamaṅgalam in the South Arcot district, Vīra-Narasiṁha, his father-in-law defeated the rebel and rescued the king. Vīra-Sōmēśvara is called *māmaḍi* (uncle or father-in-law) by Māṟavarmaṉ Sundara-Pāṇḍya II and the former, according to his Bangalore Plates,[1] is stated to have

1. *Ep. Ind.* Vol. IX, pp. 226-228.

'founded Kaṇṇanūr to please himself in the Chōḷa country which he had acquired by conquest.' Though Sōmēśvara's possessions in the Tamil country did not extend beyond the Trichinopoly and Tanjore districts in the south, there are inscriptions in the Tinnevelly district dated in the reign of Māṟavarman Sundara-Pāṇḍya II referring to grants made and temples built in the name of the king's *māmaḍigaḷ* Vīra-Sōmēśvara, at his own request. By the increasing interest taken by these two Hoysaḷa monarchs in the affairs of the Tamil land, a portion of the Tamil country imperceptibly passed on to them, so that when Sōmēśvara died, the Hoysaḷa dominion was split up into two portions between his two sons, the Tamil districts going to Rāmanātha and the Karnāṭa portion to Narasiṁha III. The Chōḷa king Rājēndra-Chōḷa III was also ruling side by side with the Hoysaḷa Rāmanātha and we find in portions of the Tanjore district the sovereignty of both these kings being acknowledged by the people.[2] On the destruction of the Hoysaḷa capital Dōrasamudra by Mālik Kāfur in A.D. 1310, Ballāḷa III transferred the seat of his government to Tiruvaṇṇāmalai (North Arcot district) in the Tamil country. When, therefore, Bukka's son Kampaṇa II called the 'door-keeper' of Ballāḷa III in the local chronicles of Madura, established the Vijayanagara rule in the Tamil country, his regime appeared as if it was a continuation of the Hoysaḷa rule when he actually carried on and succeeded in the mission for which his master had sacrificed his life.

Roughly the Hoysaḷa territory in the Tamil land included portions of the Tanjore and Trichinopoly districts and the Koṅgu country including the adjoining region round Tiruvaṇṇāmalai. Excluding the Chēra territory in the extreme corner of the Peninsula, the remaining portion of the Tamil country was mainly held by the Chōḷas and the Pāṇḍyas. But by the time when Bukka and Harihara established their new kingdom at Vijayanagara, the Chōḷas had exhausted themselves, leaving the Pāṇḍyas powerful not only in their own territory, but further north into the Chōḷa country, even as far as Nellore where Jaṭāvarman Sundara-Pāṇḍya I (A.D. 1251-1271) performed his 'anointment of Victors.' Māṟavarman Kulaśēkhara (A.D. 1268-1311) also claims to have conquered Malai-nāḍu, Śōnāḍu, the two Koṅgus, Īḻam and Toṇḍaimaṇḍalam. But, among the several principalities set up on the defunct Chōḷa Empire, that of the Śambuvarāyas came to dominate the Toṇḍaimaṇḍalam region comprising the modern Chingleput, North and South Arcot districts in the beginning of the 14th cen-

2. *An. Rep.* on *South Indian Epigraphy* for 1930-31, p. 45.

tury A.D. The Śambuvarāya chiefs started first as officers under the Chōḷas, but during Pāṇḍya domination, Kulaśēkhara-Śambuvarāya bowed before the storm and accepted the overlordship of Jaṭāvarman Vīra-Pāṇḍya. Veṉṟumaṉkoṇḍa Śambuvarāya (acc. A.D. 1322) and Rājanārāyaṇa Śambuvarāya (acc. A.D. 1337) ruled independently in the Toṇḍaimaṇḍalam region, so that when the new government was established at Vijayanagara, the Śambuvarāyas under the above mentioned two chiefs and the Pāṇḍyas under Jaṭāvarman Vīra-Pāṇḍya (A.D. 1296-1342) were chiefly governing the whole of the Tamil land.

Of the different principalities into which the Vijayanagara kingdom was divided, the Muḷuvāyi-rājya included Koṅgu *alias* Vīraśōḻa-maṇḍalam,[3] while the Udayagiri-rājya touched the northern fringe of the Toṇḍaimaṇḍalam region. Sāvaṇṇa-Oḍeya, the son of Kampa I was ruling at Udayagiri-paṭṭana about Śaka 1273 as ' the lord of the eastern ocean.'[4] In the Tamil region, his inscriptions are dated from 4th[5] to the 16th[6] regnal years. Since the 4th regnal year corresponded to the Cyclic year Vikṛiti (=Śaka 1272), he must have counted his reign from Śaka 1269. His inscriptions are found at Tiruppālaivaṉam[7] (Ponneri taluk), Tiruvoṟṟiyūr[8] (Saidapet taluk), Neyyāḍipākkam[9] (near Conjeevaram) and Kāḷahasti[10] (Chittoor district). Udayagiri-rājya on the southern side must, therefore, have bordered on the territory of Śambuvarāya. About Śaka 1278 there seems to have been some insecurity in the region round Tiruvoṟṟiyūr near Madras, in the regime of Śāyaṇa-Oḍeya, consequent on the negligence of duty on the part of the *agambaḍiyārs* of the chief of Paḍuvūr, with the result that dacoities and disturbances became common. As many as 48 of the *agambaḍiyārs* were taken to task for their neglect.[11] This disturbance seems to have extended beyond the Udayagiri-rājya to Kalavi[12] in the North Arcot district, which was then under the Śambuvarāya chiefs.

3. A. R. No. 143 of 1915.
4. A. R. Nos. 500 and 503 of 1906.
5. A. R. No. 357 of 1923.
6. A. R. No. 214 of 1901.
7. A. R. No. 357 of 1929.
8. A. R. Nos. 213 and 240 of 1912.
9. A. R. Nos. 213 and 214 of 1901.
10. A. R. No. 188 of 1903.
11. A. R. No. 240 of 1912.
12. A. R. No. 110 of 1921.

These chiefs were not powerful enough to put up any determined opposition to the extension of the Vijayanagara rule into their own territory, and it was therefore easy for Gaṇḍaragūḷi Mārāya-Nāyaka, the son of Sōmayya-Daṇṇāyaka, the *pradhāni* of Kampaṇa II to capture Veṉṟumaṇkoṇḍa Śambuvarāya as also Rājagambhīraṉmalai, to celebrate which event, the victor constructed in Śaka 1285[13] a *gōpura* in the second *prākāra* of the Śiva temple at Kuḷattūr (identical with Maḍam in the South Arcot district). In the previous year, i.e., Śaka 1284, we find Sōmayya-Daṇṇāyaka issuing an order of Rājanārāyaṇa-Śambuvarāya,[14] which shows that the latter had been subdued and was a vassal of Kampaṇa II. Since Sāḷuva Maṅgu, the general of Kampaṇa II, styles himself *Śambuvarāya-sthāpanāchārya*,[15] it is clear that Veṉṟumaṇkoṇḍa-Śambuvarāya was first defeated and then set up again as a vassal of Kampaṇa II. Since Rājanārāyaṇa-Śambuvarāya had also the title of 'Veṉṟumaṇkoṇḍāṉ',[16] the Śambuvarāya chief captured by Gaṇḍaragūḷi Mārāya-Nāyaka must be Rājanārāyaṇa himself, and this incident probably took place about Śaka 1284 towards the close of Rājanārāyaṇa's reign.[17] The subjugation of Rājanārāyaṇa automatically extended the Vijayanagara empire as far as the South Arcot district in the South.

A fratricidal war at Madura about the beginning of the 14th century brought in a Muhammadan invasion from the North into South India in response to a call from Sundara-Pāṇḍya against his brother Vīra-Pāṇḍya for obtaining the Pāṇḍya throne. Two centuries earlier, i.e., about A.D. 1168 a similar situation arose, when Parākrama-Pāṇḍya and Kulaśēkhara-Pāṇḍya fought for the same throne, each securing foreign help, so that the Chōḷa and the Singhalese forces were ranged on opposite sides to decide this question, which eventually ended in the subordination of the Pāṇḍya power

13. A. R. No. 267 of 1919.

14. A. R. No. 226 of 1916.

15. Sāḷuva Tirumalaiyadēva-Mahārāja in Śaka 1372 (A. R. No. 448 of 1922) and Sāḷuva Saṁgamadēva-Mahārāja in Śaka 1408 (A. R. No. 594 of 1902) also claim this title. Since the Śambuvarāyas were not in power then, these chiefs must have claimed it from Sāḷuva Maṅgu.

16. A. R. Nos. 48 and 201 of 1921 and 499 of 1926.

17. Rājanārāyaṇa came to the throne in A. D. 1337 and his highest regnal year was 32 (A. R. No. 137 of 1916). If he had accepted Vijayanagara overlordship in Śaka 1284 (= A. D. 1362), he must have continued as a vassal for seven years. His records during these seven years are very few and only two have so far come to light, dated in the 28th and 32nd years (A. R. Nos. 177 and 137 of 1916).

to that of the Chōḷa. The price for seeking outside help in the present instance was a heavy one for, after accomplishing their purpose, the Muhammadans, seeing the favourable political situation of the country, made frequent raids therein and finally established themselves in South India with Madura as their capital, from where as many as eight rulers carried on their government for about half a century. According to *Madurait-talavaralāṟu* a Tamil work giving the history of the temple at Madura, the Muhammadan rule in that place lasted from A.D. 1324 to 1371, which fact is also corroborated by the *Kōyiloḻugu* another Tamil work recording the donations made to the Raṅganātha temple at Śrīraṅgam in the Trichinopoly district, with this difference that the latter places the commencement of the Muhammadan rule three years later, i.e., A.D. 1327. The coins of the Sultans of Madura are dated from A.H. 730 to 779, i.e., A.D. 1329-30 to 1377-78. However, a stone record from Iṉṉambūr[18] in the Tanjore district marks the period of anarchy under Muhammadan rule in South India as 40 years. Whatever might have been the exact period of this rule, people were anxious to get rid of it, because it was characterised by cruelty, loot and massacre.

The immediate effect of the capture of Madura by the Muhammadans was to drive out the Pāṇḍyas from this place to seek shelter in the extreme corner of their territory in the Tinnevelly district. The influence of their rule was felt at Śrīrangam, Śaḍaiyampāḷaiyam[19] (in the Coimbatore district), Tiruvāmāttūr[20] (in the South Arcot district) and even as far North as Tiruvoṟṟiyūr[21] (in the Chingleput district). The *Madurait-talavaralāṟu* mentions the complete destruction of the temple at Madura by the Muhammadans and states that the people of this place, however, managed to remove the images of the gods in the temple to Nāñji-nāḍu in Southern Travancore for safety. One of the Sultans of Madura then laid siege to Śrīrangam and plundered it. There was a wholesome massacre of the Hindus, in which some of the Vaishṇava leaders of the place died including Sudarśana Bhaṭṭa the author of *Śrutaprākāśika,* a commentary on the *Vēdānta-sūtras* and saint *Āḷagiya-Nayinār.* Many others including Vēdānta-Dēśika and the sons of Sudarśana-Bhaṭṭa mentioned above escaped with their lives. The image of god Raṅganātha was, on this occasion, secretly removed to Tirupati

18. A. R. No. 322 of 1927.
19. A. R. Nos. 135 and 136 of 1920.
20. A. R. No. 434 of 1903.
21. A. R. No. 203 of 1912.

in the Chittoor district under the escort of the Vaishṇava teacher Piḷḷai-Lōkāchārya, who, however, died on the way. A number of inscriptions in the Tamil country refer to the defilement of temples and the miseries suffered by the people during the Muhammadan rule, so that when Kampaṇa II, son of Bukka I and the 'door keeper' of the great Hoysaḷa monarch Ballāḷa III destroyed this rule, he was hailed as a saviour of the Tamil land. The hardship suffered by priests during the cruel rule of the Muhammadans of Madura and the relief that they experienced when Kampaṇa II destroyed them are also noticed in a record[22] from the Ramnad district. Before Kampana II Ballāḷa himself had attempted the task but unluckily failed: Kampaṇa, however, was eminently successful in this attempt, which brought practically the whole of the Tamil country under his control. The conquest of Madura and the defeat of the Muhammadans provided a theme for an epic poem, *Madhurā-Vijayam* by Gaṅgādēvī one of the wives of Kampaṇa.

When the Vijayanagara rule was established in the Hoysaḷa kingdom, the capital was again changed from Tiruvaṇṇāmalai to Dōrasamudra, thence to Hosapaṭṭaṇa and finally to the newly constructed town of Vijayanagara. For administrative convenience, the new empire was split up into a number of principalities, some of which were placed under viceroys and princes of the ruling family and others were governed directly by the rulers themselves. This policy of governing the vast territory through royal viceroys, which had been successfully adopted in the Pāṇḍya country by the Chōḷas in the 11th century, greatly contributed to the solidarity of the Empire. The Tamil land was made a separate principality called Rājagambhīra-rājya and Kampaṇa II was the first viceroy placed in charge of it.

While Kampaṇa was the governor of the Rājagambhīra-rājya, his father Bukka I was ruling from Vijayanagara. Only three records which can be definitely attributed to Bukka I are found in the Tamil districts, two[23] from the Chingleput district dated in Śaka 1298 and 1272 and the other[24] from the North Arcot district dated in the cyclic year Rākshasa, corresponding to Śaka 1297. These do not give any information about the king. But the bulk of the records of his son Kampaṇa are found in the North and South Arcot and Chingleput districts, though a few are also found in Ramnad, Salem

22. A. R. No. 64 of 1916.
23. A. R. Nos. 255 of 1901 and 378 of 1929.
24. A. R. No. 468 of 1925.

and Coimbatore districts and the Pudukkōṭṭai State. His records are dated in Śaka 1274[25] to 1296.[26] It has been pointed out above that Kampaṇa must have subjugated Rājanārāyaṇa Śambuvarāya by Śaka 1284. Between Śaka 1274 and 1284, Kampaṇa must have had a restless time in defeating the Śambuvarāya king and the Muhammadans of Madura, establishing order and introducing the new regime in the land, because in Śaka 1284 a gift was made to the temple at Tirukkōyilūr (South Arcot district) for the pacification of the king's fatigue[27] *Kampaṇa Oḍēyar tirumēṉi āyāsa-śānti.* A record from Tirukkaḷākkuḍi[28] in the Ramnad district dated in the 31st year of Māṟavarman (Jaṭāvarman ?) Vīra-Pāṇḍya states that 'the times were Tulukkaṉ (Muhammadan) times and that Kampaṇa-Oḍeyar came on his southern campaign, destroyed the Muhammadans, established ORDERLY GOVERNMENT throughout the country and appointed many *nāyakkaṉmār* for inspection and supervision in order that the worship in all temples might be revived and conducted regularly as of old.' By Śaka 1287 Kampaṇa felt his position so secure in the land that he styled himself as "the conqueror of Rājagambhīra-rājya, ruling from his permanent throne (*sthira-siṁhāsana*)."[29]

In the task of administering the Rājagambhīra-rājya, *Mahāpradhāni* Sōmappa or Sōmayya Daṇṇāyaka greatly assisted Kampaṇa. When order and safety were restored in the country, the Brahman *daḷavāy* Goppaṇa took the image of Raṅganātha back from Tirupati where it was removed for safety, and installed in its original place at Śrīraṅgam in Śaka 1293.[30] He also seems to have accompanied his master in the latter's campaign against Muhammadans, since a record from Śrīraṅgam refers to his conquest of the Tulushkas.[31] In Tamil records he is generally called Gōppaṇaṅgaḷ.[32] *Śambuvarāya-sthāpanāchārya* Sāḷuva Maṅgu-Mahārāja was another general under Kampaṇa. Treasurer Viṭṭappayaṉ,[33] *aḍaippam* Nāgappa,[34]

25. A. R. No. 297 of 1919.
26. A. R. Nos. 267 of 1912 and 282 of 1903.
27. A. R. No. 351 of 1921.
28. A. R. No. 64 of 1916.
29. A. R. No. 18 of 1899.
30. *Ep. Ind.* Vol. VI, p. 322 ff.
31. *Ibid.*
32. A. R. Nos. 33 of 1890 and 183 of 1918.
33. A. R. Nos 28 of 1890 and 309 of 1912.
34. A. R. Nos. 89 of 1889 and 200 of 1921.

adhikāri Tuṇaiyirundanambi Koṅgarāyar[35] and *Karaṇikka* Apparaśar[36] also assisted the king in establishing the new rule in the Tamil land. Though this rule extended to the extreme southern corner of the Peninsula, the Tinnevelly region was ruled by the Later Pāṇḍyas, practically as independent monarchs from the 14th to the 17th century. But Tiruvaḍi-rājya, i.e. Nāñji-nāḍu in the South Travancore country, later on came under the influence of this rule. In the time of Kṛishṇadēvarāya, *Karaṇikka* Maṅgaraśayyar[37] was given charge of this region about Śaka 1435. Sāḷuva-Nāyaka next held it about Śaka 1446.[38] The Tiruvaḍi king was defeated by Salaka Timmarāja, the brother-in-law of Achyutarāya for harbouring the rebel Sāḷuva-Nāyaka. In the time of Sadāśiva, Śūrappa-Nāyaka was superintending the region about Śaka 1468.[39] When the Tiruvaḍi king tried to extend his dominions as far as Tuticorin in the east, Rāmarāja Viṭṭhala was directed to chastise the ambitious ruler when the latter was compelled to acknowledge the overlordship of the Vijayanagara sovereign. Rāmarāja thereafter gave this province as an *amara-nāyakam* to Viśvanātha-Nāyaka,[40] after which it gradually slipped out of the control of the Vijayanagara rulers.

Besides the Tiruvaḍi-rājya, the Vijayanagara power was also felt in Ceylon. In the Ālampūṇḍi Plates,[41] Virūpāksha, the son of Harihara II is said to have conquered, among other kings, the ruler of Siṁhaḷa and presented the booty to his father. Probably this was only a boast, because neither Virūpāksha's nor Harihara's (II) inscriptions are found beyond Trichinopoly district in the South. However, Harihara II claims to have 'levied tribute from Ceylon,'[42] which was adopted as a title by almost all his successors. Lakkaṇa-Daṇṇayāka-Uḍaiyar 'the lord of the Southern ocean' and the minister of Dēvarāya II fitted out a cavalry with the express object of destroying Iyāḻpā[ṇam], Napaṭamanam and Īḻam and for the success of this expedition, an endowment was made as *samudra yātrā dāna*[43] to the temple at Tirumāṇikkuḻi in the Cuddalore taluk of the South Arcot district. The endowment made in this connec-

35. A. R. No. 195 of 1912.
36. A. R. No. 18 of 1899.
37. A.R. No. 429 of 1908.
38. A. R. No. 118 of 1897.
39. A. R. No. 41 of 1922.
40. A. R. No. 17 of 1912.
41. *Ep. Ind.* Vol. III, p. 224 ff.
42. A. R. No. 375 of 1917.
43. *S. I. I.* Vol. VII, No. 778.

tion to the temple at Tirumānikkuḻi suggests that the fleet carrying the cavalry to Ceylon might have started from Cuddalore or some port closeby. The success of this expedition was the cause of Dēvarāya assuming the title *Īḻam-tiṟai-koṇḍa* (one who levied tribute from Ceylon) which we find in No. 144 of 1916 from Nāyar in the Chingleput district. Nuniz also mentions that Dēvarāya received tribute from Ceylon. The *Sāḷuvābhyudaya* states that the king of Ceylon was anxious to secure the friendship of Sāḷuva Narasiṁha. Poṉṉambalanātha Toṇḍaimān the chief of Arantāngi and a vassal of Kṛishṇadēvarāya claims to have collected tribute from Ceylon in seven days.[44] This is too short a time within which Poṉṉambalanātha could have achieved this feat and, it is possible that the reference is only to a successful expedition to Ceylon to collect some arrears of tribute on behalf of his overlord Kṛishṇadēvarāya. The father of Sadāśiva, viz., Raṅgappa-oḍeyar also claims to have received tribute from Ceylon,[45] while Sadāśiva himself is said to have looted Ceylon in Śaka 1486.[46]

The administration of the Tamil country underwent a slight modification during the time of the Vijayanagara rulers. The temple as a social unit gradually ceased to function. In pre-Vijayanagara period this institution took a great interest in the civic administration of the land. It advanced money to people in times of necessity, purchased lands for the common benefit of the village, assisted the administration in realising its revenues by offering to purchase the lands of the defaulter and in a variety of ways acted for the common weal of the village. The need for local assemblies which played a great part in Chōḷa times was not felt in the new regime. The democracy of the Chōḷa administration gave place to an absolute monarchy based on military strength with the objective of unifying the resources of the country against the Muhammadan advance into the South. In this task the Tamilians also seem to have contributed their share as when, for instance, a Brahman named Āpatsahāya of Tirukkaḍaiyur in the Tanjore district took part in the war against Raichur,[47] and another person named Tiruchchiṟṟambala-Bhaṭṭa followed Rāmarāja to Tiruvaḍi and fought for him from Anantaśayanam to Mudgal.[48] The change in the administration is also reflected in the inscriptions, because in the pre-Vijaya-

44. *Ep. Ind.* XXI, p. 121.
45. A. R. No. 1 of 1919.
46. A. R. No. 451 of 1905.
47. A. R. No. 47 of 1906.
48. A. R. No. 140 of 1895.

nagara period, the donors mentioned therein were mostly common people, whereas they were invariably nobles or officials in the later period.

A number of new offices such as *pārapattiyam*,[49] *aṭṭavaṇai*,[50] *amaram*,[51] *karaṇikkam*,[52] *adhikāram*,[53] *rāyasam*,[54] *aḍaippam*,[55] *vāśal-karaṇikkam*,[56] *mugappāvāḍai*,[57] *avasaram*,[58] *vāśal*,[59] *nāyakam*,[60] etc., were created. All these offices were remunerated by grants of land as also by a levy[61] specially collected for this purpose from the people. A record from Tiruvaṇṇāmalai[62] gives the receipts of the *pradhāni* as (1) *kai-vilai* (2) *kiṟaiyam* (3) *ūḻiyam* and (4) *uluppai*. Some of these and other taxes pressed hard on the people and instances are on record of people deserting their villages to escape the excessive taxation[63] levied by their masters the *Kannaḍiyas*,[64] by which term the rulers were evidently known to the Tamilians. There have been abuses in the collection of taxes by the officials themselves, which, when brought to the notice of the king, were promptly put down. A record from Tiruveṇṇainallur[65] in the South Arcot district mentions the evil practice of ministers collecting presents from all the ryots at the commencement of each reign. This practice was put down in Śaka 1368 by Vijayarāya. When the taxes *jōdi* and *śūlavari* on certain villages which had been re-

49. A. R. No. 256 of 1894.
50. A. R. No. 366 of 1912.
51. A. R. No. 449 of 1913.
52. A. R. No. 13 of 1922.
53. A. R. No. 418 of 1919.
54. A. R. No. 418 of 1919.
55. A. R. No. 216 of 1906.
56. A. R. No. 84 of 1923.
57. A. R. No. 318 of 1909.
58. A. R. No. 172 of 1918.
59. A. R. No. 648 of 1919.
60. A. R. No. 30 of 1890.
61. The following taxes collected from the land indicate the income of the Vijayanagara officials: *adhikāra-jōḍi* (55 of 1897), *adhikāra-poṉ* (200 of 1892), *adhikāra-vardhanai* (538 of 1922), *rāyasa-vardhanai* (538 of 1922), *daṇṇāyakar-magami* (510 of 1921), *karaṇikka-jōḍi* (*S. I. I.* Vol. II, p. 119), *pradhāni-jōḍi* (55 of 1897) etc. The officials Jōḍi Koṇḍama-Nāyaka (338 of 1918) and Jōḍi Pāppu-Nāyaka (14 of 1918), judging from their names, appear to have been responsible for the collection of *Jōḍi* in the land.
62. A. R. No. 565 of 1902.
63. A. R. Nos. 246 and 50 of 1916.
64. A. R. No. 247 of 1916.
65. A. R. No. 476 of 1921.

mitted by Kṛishṇadēvarāya already had not been given effect to, three persons from Tirukkaḍaiyūr in the Tanjore district proceeded all the way to Vijayanagara to bring the matter to the notice of the king, who forthwith redressed their grievances. There is also an instance on record that for exacting *jōḍi* from the village Tiruppanaṅgādu (North Arcot district) when it had been excused in favour of the temple, Vīra Narasiṁharāya-Nāyaka who was responsible for this misappropriation, fled to Tiruvaḍi to escape punishment.[66] But Achyutarāya punished with a stern hand the miscreant as well as the Tiruvaḍi king who harboured him. The importance of checking the excesses of their subordinates though far away from the seat of government was well recognised by the new rulers.

Thus at a time when the Tamil people were weak and disunited and actually trembling under the Muhammadan regime set up in their midst, the establishment of the Vijayanagara rule, unified the land, terminated the reign of terror and gave a strong but benevolent government to their country.

66. A. R. No. 253 of 1906.

14

Krishna Raya, The Man

BY

MR. K. RAGHAVACHARLU, M.A., B.L.,
Vakil, Coconada.

THE age of Krishṇa Rāya was a great epoch in medieval South Indian History. It was an age of Renaissance in arts and has been rightly called the 'Augustan Age' of Telugu Literature. With the possible exception of Aśoka, Samudragupta and Harsha Vardhana, Hindu India had not witnessed a parallel of the benevolent rule of that mighty Emperor. His name has become a household word in South India and so has that of his renowned and old minister Timmarasu or Appāji. And as usual, the biographical details of his life are few, and had it not been for the famous chronicles of Nuniz and Paes and Vernacular books like Rāyavāchakamu, it would have been a complete blank to us. History, real History has not flourished in the Indian soil. Stray works like the Rājataraṅgiṇi or Vikramānkadeva Charita do not disprove the statement. What little we know of the dynastic lists of our kings or of their personal or public life, has to be gleaned from works like the Purānas, travels as of Hieun Tsang or Fahien, and chronicles as of Nuniz or Paes. Epigraphical, archæological or numismatic evidence is of immense value and the *praśastis* or eulogies of the Sovereigns in Sanskrit or Vernacular works come to our aid now and then in constructing the history out of our crude materials.

Krishṇa Rāya was a great Emperor and beloved of his people. Tāmil, Telugu and Canarese people have vied with each other in claiming him as their Rāyar, Rāyalu or Rāyaru. The Telugu or Canarese Origin of the Empire has added an impetus to the claims. His reign has lasted from 1509-1530 A.D. and his vast Empire extended from the remote Poṭnūru in the Vizagapatam District to Ummattūr and Śivasamudram in the Mysore Territory.

The personality of Krishṇa Rāya has come down to us in the significant words of Paes 'The king is of medium height and of fair complexion and good figure, rather fat than thin; he has on his face signs of small-pox. He is the most feared and perfect king that could possibly be, cheerful of disposition and very merry. He is one that seeks to honour foreigners and receives them kindly, asking about all their affairs whatever their condition may be. He is a great ruler and a man of much justice '.[1] Tradition accords well with the description given by the Chronicles and bestows him with a fine personality and good physique. He was at the time of his coronation about 20 years according to Nuniz[2] and the above description of Paes is corroborative of the same. An anonymous verse in Telugu which gives the Saka year 1409 or 1487 A.D. as the year of his birth also points to the same conclusion.

Young as he was, Krishṇa Rāya was a good athlete. He delighted in wrestling and horse-riding. The *Manucharitra* (VI—123) mentions that the fine build of his body was due to physical exercise (*Vyāyāma*) and the Pārijātāpaharaṇam (VI—92) refers to his skill in horse-riding as equal to that of Nakula of the Pāṇḍavas. Ere the day dawned, he would smear himself with oil and gallop on horse-back till the body became dry. Paes narrates a slightly different version : 'The King drank a Quartilho of oil of Gingelly before daylight and anoints himself all over with the said oil ; he covers his loins with a small cloth and takes in his arms great weights made of earthenware and then taking a sword, he exercises himself with it till he has sweated out all the oil and then he wrestles with one of his wrestlers. After this labour he mounts a horse and gallops in one direction and another till dawn for he does all this before daybreak. Then he goes to wash himself......' We are much indebted to the Chronicle of Paes which has removed all shadow of doubt from the minds of Historians like Sewell and enabled them to give glowing accounts of his personality. His powerful personality, his prowess in war, courage and fearlessness are amply demonstrated by the innumerable campaigns which he led in person in the first half of his rule. A veritable Coeur de lion he was to the foreign powers in the North. He was cheerful of disposition and merry, kind and generous to friends and foes alike. Paes further adds that he was subject to sudden fits of rage, we can only take it to refer to the imperious nature of the sovereign whose word was law. An interesting anecdote is narrated in Rāyavāchakamu as to how the king, displeased at the supreme control of all affairs in the kingdom by Timmarasu, left the city one day and rested in a temple to the north and how he was admonished by the old and veteran minister and brought back to the city.[3] It is also assumed that he was haughty and overbearing and that

1. Sewell's *Forgotten Empire*, page 246-47.
2. Do. p. 315.
3. *Rāyavāchakamu*, pp. 36-41 (Published by the Telugu Academy, Cocanada.).

this quality of the Vijayanagara Sovereigns was to a great extent responsible for the downfall of the Empire ; but this lacks cogent evidence. He is said to have demanded from the Adil Shah as a condition of peace that the latter should kiss his feet. It is incredible to believe that the generous and noblehearted Krishṇarāya would behave in such a manner in respect of a fallen foe. An equally unbelievable story has been given credence to by Nuniz[4] that the king sent word to Vīrabhadra, son of the Oriya Monarch and asked him to fence with a commoner in the arena and that the latter, out of regard for his noble lineage and birth, stabbed himself with the sword and died. How totally incredulous is the story can be gathered from unmistakable epigraphical evidence that Vīrabhadra Gajapati was a governor of Malaga Beṇṇūr Sīma and that he was honoured by the titles of Draviḷa Manḍalēśwara and Mahārāya.[5] The very Āmuktamālyadā of Krishṇarāya and Manucharitra allude to the capture of Vīrabhadra and the Pārijātāpaharaṇa (Canto 1-21) further mentions that he was spared and treated with courtesy, thus supporting the Epigraphical evidence available to us. The generosity of Krishṇa Rāya is further amplified by the fact that after his conquest and subjugation of Ummattūr, the nobles of the place were reinstated as vassals. This is consistent also with the conduct of a sovereign who was trying to establish peace in his dominions and frontiers and preparing himself for the final struggle with the Muhammadan powers on the North. A further example of his generous and humane treatment of a fallen foe is given by Nuniz in his description of the battle of Rāchoḷ (Raichur). The Muhammadan troops were chased to the banks of the river and killed in countless numbers. The king out of compassion ordered the troops to retire and even when his captains advised him to complete the work of destruction of all his enemies, he would not accede to their proposal.[6] His presence of mind on the battlefield even while his armies were being pursued by the enemy and his ultimate bid for victory have been well described by Nuniz.[7] It has been mentioned that even shortly before his death he planned a campaign against the Adil Shah of Bijapur for the capture of Belgaum and the latter on hearing of the arrival of the king fled.[8] The Rāyavāchakamu which describes the king's conquests and exploits

4. Sewell—pp. 319-320.
5. Refer *E. C. XI* Dig. 107, p. 71, also *Arch. S. R.* (1908-09) p. 178.
6. Sewell, pp. 339-40.
7. *Ibid*, p. 338.
8. *Ibid*, p. 361.

in war upto the year 1516 A.D. furnishes us with much material corroborating the accounts of the Chronicles and inscriptions. The Telugu works Manucharitra and *Āmuktamālyadā* compare his prowess in war to a spreading fire.

As regards his queens and children, the materials are equally scanty. The inscriptions mention his two Queens Tirumaladevi and Chinnādevi. Paes mentions that Krishṇadeva Rāya had twelve lawful wives and that three of them were regarded as principal ones.[9] The copper images of the two Queens, Tirumala and Chinnādevi are found in Tirupati[10] and as Tirumalamba occupies the right side of the king, it has been supposed that she is the first queen.[11] The *Āmuktamālyadā* mentions the three queens, Tirumala, Annapūrṇā and Kamalā. Paes further mentions that one of the queens was the daughter of the king of Orissa. *Krishṇarāya vijayamu* of Kumāra Dhūrjaṭi calls her Tukkha while Rāyavāchakamu calls her Jaganmohini.[12] In the introductory verses to the commentary on Prabodhachandrodaya by Nadinḍla Gopamantri, a nephew of the minister Timmarasu, she is called Bhadra. We have not at present material enough to decide whether this Oriya queen was Annapūrṇā or Kamalā of *Āmuktamālyadā*. Mr. K. V. Lakshmana Rao was inclined to the indentification of the daughter of Orissa king with Annapūraṇā.[13]

Tradition in Orissa mentions that an earlier ruler of Kalinga carried off a princess of Vijayanagara and married her at the intercession of his minister, and, if so, the campaign of Krishṇarāya and his marriage with Gajapati's daughter was a return courtesy. The tradition prevalent in the Andhra Country points out that as there was a suspicion about Krishṇarāya's Kshatriya lineage, she plotted against his life, and the life of the king was saved by Timmarasu and, having been abandoned by him, she lived near Kambham. It is also said that she composed the five verses now known as Tukkha Panchakam[14] and was later in her life reconciled to her lord through the intercession of the old minister Timmarasu. The non-mention of the queen in Epigraphical or other evidence supports the story to some extent. Nuniz further tells us that Krishṇarāya imme-

9. *Ibid*, p. 247.
10 A. S. R. 1910-11, Plate XXVI facing p. 188.
11. Introduction to *Rāyavāchakamu*—p. 23, by Mr. J. Ramayyapantulu.
12. *Rāyavāchakamu*—p. 109.
13. *History of India*—Muhammadan period.
14. *Sources of Vijayanagar History*, pp. 143-44.

diately after his accession married a courtesan of younger days called Chinnādevi and built Nāgalāpur in her honour,[15] but one has to remember that the mother of Krishṇarāya was Nāgāmbika and the city should be presumed to be so called in her memory rather in honour of the courtesan princess.

The account of Nuniz mentions a son of Krishṇarāya by name Tirumalarāya who was anointed as king even at the age of six years.[16] He died by poison and the king charged his minister Saluva Timma, his son Timmappa and brother Govindaraja with the crime, put them in prison and ultimately blinded them. If the chronicle were true, it was a most pitiable end to the renowned career of Timmarasu, the minister. He was the right hand man of the emperor and known by the pet name of Appāji. Historians have discredited the testimony of Nuniz on various grounds. An inscription in Tirumalarāya's name in 1524 A.D., one of Saluva Govindaraja in 1529 A.D., paucity of material to conclude in favour of Krishṇarāya's abdication or Saluva Timma's treason and the lack of tradition in relation to such an important occurrence in the life of the emperor have pointed to a contrary view. It might be that Tirumalarāya died young and Achyutarāya seized the throne. A number of Achyutarāya's inscriptions in the closing years of Krishṇarāya's life associate him with sovereignty. As to whether Krishṇarāya had other sons, we have no authentic information. Even at the time of Krishṇarāya's accession, the chronicle refers to an attempt on his life by his brother Busbal Rao or Vīra Narasimha.[17] We do not know whether the above incident refers to a plot by Achyuta for the throne.

Krishṇarāya had two daughters one of whom married Rāmarāya and the other Tirumala of the Āraviḍu Dynasty. Nothing more is known about them than that their names were Tirumalāmbā and Vengalāmba. Tradition, however, in the Telugu Districts mentions a daughter Môhanāngi, who was the author of a work called Mārīchīpariṇayanam. The work is not available, nor is her identity known.

The cultural aspect of Krishṇarāya's life is best seen from his patronage of arts and letters, his munificient endowments to temples and religious institutions and gifts to learned Brahmans, and his

15. Sewell, p. 363.
16. *Ibid*, p. 359.
17. Sewell, p. 315.

attachment to Dharma and justice as exemplified in his work *Āmuktamālyadā*. The chroniclers vie with each other in describing the artistic and cultural greatness of the Vijayanagara Empire and the ruins of Hampi proclaim the same in unmistakable terms to the whole world. The splendour of the capital began to attract foreigners even so early as A.D. 1375. Besides being the patron of letters, he was himself an author of many works in Sanskrit and Telugu. No less than five works in Sanskrit are referred to in *Āmuktamālyadā* and another called *Jāmbavatī Kalyāṇa* now in the Oriental Manuscripts Library, Madras, is ascribed to him. He had around him a galaxy of Telugu poets and the place of honour was given to Peddana. His love of art and humility can have no better exposition than is found in the stray verses ascribed to Peddanārya wherein the king is described as having lifted the poet's palanquin on his shoulders and adorned with his own hands the poet's ankle with a *Kavigaṇḍā Peṇḍēra*. No higher honour could have fallen to the lot of any other poet. The poet laureate was further honoured with the governorship of a district. The works *Manucharitra* and *Pārijātaharaṇa* were dedicated to Krishṇarāya. His minister Timmarasu wrote a commentary on the Champu Bhārata of Agastya and Gopamantri his nephew, a commentary on *Prabōdhachandrōdayam* in Sanskrit and Krishṇārjuna Samvādam in Telugu.

An interesting question is raised in this connection as to whether Krishṇarāya was a Telugu or a Kannaḍa emperor. The origin of the Vijayanagara Empire has had rude shocks at the hands of historians and the opinion now prevalent leans to a Kannaḍa origin but this does not solve our question. The third dynasty—that of the Tuluvas—was not in any way connected with the previous ones by blood. The Āravīḍu dynasty was connected with the family of Krishṇarāya by marriage, the brothers Ramarāya and Tirumala having married his daughters Tirumalāmba and Vengalāmba. Works like the *Chikkadevarāya, Vamśāvali*[18] refer to Rāmarāya as belonging to a Telugu family (ఆంధ్రకులది రామరాజం) Rāmarāya and his brother Tirumala were patrons of Telugu Poetry. The Telugu *Varāha Purāṇa* was dedicated to Narasa Nayaka, the father of Krishṇarāya and *Jaimini Bhāratamu* to Sāḷuva Narasimharāya, his king.

The patronage of a particular language by the king is quite different, from composing a long poem in that language. It is not

18. *Sources of Vijayanagar History*, p. 302.

known why Krishṇarāya should have written in the Telugu language alone and leave his own language. Greater still, the encomium showered on the Telugu Language in Verse 15 Canto I of *Āmuktamālyadā* gives a place of honour to Telugu among the vernaculars. The distinction drawn in the previous verse between Telugu Rāya and Kannaḍa Rāya can only mean that Krishṇarāya was lord of the Kannaḍa country while the God by tradition was the lord of the Telugu country. The other works of Krishṇarāya were all composed in Sanskrit ; Kannaḍa was given the go-bye which would not have been the case if he was a Kannaḍa by birth. At any rate, his family if Kannaḍa should have been so domiciled in Telugu atmosphere as to adopt Telugu as its mother tongue for a very long period. The above is only by way of suggestion. To whatever country Krishṇarāya really belonged, it is an honour and a distinction to both, nay, still more to the whole of India. The kingdom of Vijayanagara has all along comprised the Kannaḍa country in the west and the Telugu country in the East. Its capital was near Bellary which partakes of the nature of a bi-lingual centre. No wonder that the illustrious sovereigns of such a country have been claimed with equal fervour by both the parties.

Equally important is the question of his religion. His work *Āmuktamālyadā* however has an indispensable Vaishnava colour about it and might be presupposed to indicate the leanings of the writer. His patron was Venkaṭanātha of Tirumala. Copper images of himself and his two queens adorn even to-day the precincts of the temple. His benevolent munificience finds an expression in all temples from Simhāchalam in the north to Rāmeśvaram in the South. The Krishṇa and the Hazāra Rāmaswāmi Temples were built and the construction of the Viṭhala Temple commenced in his reign. A beautiful image of Krishṇa is said to have been brought from Udayagiri after his eastern campaign and tradition has it that he brought the image of Viṭhal from Pandharapur. The Monolithic Narasimha statue was a work of his days. But Krishṇa Rāya was not a religious bigot. Jainism and Hinduism seem to have flourished side by side. The Gopura of the Virūpāksha temple was constructed by him. The *Vallabhāchārya charitam*[19] mentions that the king honoured Vallabha with *Kanakābhishēkam* when the latter visited his court in his youth. The Tamil Navalar Charitai refers to the restoration of the images of two Nāyanmārs.[20] The

19. *Sources*—p. 154.
20. *Vide* extract in *Sources*, p. 155.

Vyāsa Yogi Charitam of Somanātha claims the patronage of Krishṇarāya to the Mādhva cult and the position of Rājaguru to Vyāsarāya.[21] The toleration and even active support of all religions has been a significant factor in the reigns of great Hindu Monarchs. Besides the Capital city was so situated as to admit a convergence of various religious sects from different directions. The temples belonging to various sects in close proximity to each other in the ruins of Hampi amply demonstrate the religious toleration of the Vijayanagara Emperors.

The political and economic outlook of Krishṇarāya as a sovereign can be inferred to some extent from canto IV of *Āmuktamālyadā*. It has been said that the maxims narrated therein are merely copies of earlier rules on the subject in *Śukraniti* and similar treatises and that it is not safe to assume that the monarch lived upto these ideals. But one can safely assert that the maxims should have had his approval and active support. They seem to have emanated from the sound wisdom and practical experience of the writer. So far as internal administration is concerned, the protection of his subjects, the observance and enforcement of Dharma, and a harmonious blending of clemency with justice seems to have been his object in life. 'A king should divide his income into four parts, use one part for extensive benefactions and for enjoyment, two parts for maintenance of a strong army and one part to be added to the treasury.'[22] This explains the innumerable architectural monuments and temples of his days and the fabulous wealth of the State and the Capital. The efficiency of the army was such that his name was a terror to all adjacent powers. He was able to bring to the field of battle an infantry 600,000 strong, a cavalry of 60,000 and 2,000 elephants. The accounts given by Feristah, Abdul Razzaq, Paes and Nuniz not only confirm the strength of the army but even mention larger figures. Warfare was medieval and the sovereigns should have long ago realised the importance of a strong army which according to the author of *Śukraniti* was the source of prosperity to the Kōśa (treasury) and Rāshṭra (country). A significant verse in *Āmuktamālyadā* runs thus 'The expenditure of money which is utilised in buying elephants and horses, in feeding them, in maintaining soldiers, in the worship of gods and Brahmins and in one's own enjoyment can never be called an expenditure.'

21. Saletore's *Social and Political life in the Vijayanagar Empire*, Vol. I. pp. 260, 261, 263.

22. *Āmuktamālyadā*, Canto IV, Verse 238.

Political maxims and conduct depend upon the exigencies of the times. They may sound to us moderns like Machiavellian but they were inculcated with great foresight and circumspection. The methods adopted by so-called civilised nations in the modern world are no better and ethics seems to have no place where the preservation and protection of an Empire is concerned. Systems of espionage at home and abroad, creation of schisms and rival parties, friendship with neighbouring powers, the hill tribes and foreigners, and similar methods have been in vogue ever since the dawn of civilisation. The *Śukraniti*, the *Arthaśāstra* and other treatises proclaim the same.[23] Krishṇarāya was consolidating his power and Empire by his campaigns. They were not actuated by motives of aggrandizement. The Raichur Doab on the one hand and the territory south of Krishṇa to Nellore on the other were from time to time changing hands. The first half of his reign was spent in the consolidation of the Empire and the second to works of peace, promotion of the prosperity of the country, architecture, literature and the fine arts. An anicut across the Tungabhadra, the irrigation system in the country, the extraordinary number and size of the tanks dug for irrigation purposes demonstrate the care with which Krishṇarāya and his predecessors endeavoured to promote the wealth and agricultural resources of the country. A Brahman hierarchy is said to have existed during the days of Krishṇarāya and it is no wonder in view of their accomplishments as generals, statesmen and litterateurs. In all matters, he was consulting his ministers and generals though ultimately his views alone prevailed. Among the ruins of Hampi are shown some underground chambers wherein he held his consultations.

His generosity towards the people, his dependents and poets was immense. At the time of Vasantōtsava every year, he bestowed presents on the poets.[24] A number of times he performed the *Tulūpurushapradāna*[25] and weighed himself against gold and pearl.[26] The king's balance on the road by the river leading away from the Virūpāksha temple is said to be the place where he weighed himself in gold. On fitting occasions, he was rewarding his ministers and

23. For the political maxims of Krishṇarāya refer the article of Mr. A. Rangaswami Saraswati, B.A., on the subject, wherein the translation of *Āmuktamālyadā*, Canto IV, pp. 205 to 284 is also given. The translation I have adopted is his.

24. *Pārijātaharaṇa* I—p. 139.

25. *Rāyavāchakamu*—pp. 113, 114.

26. *Pārijātaharaṇa* V—p. 109.

officers with presents. The great Appāji after the Kalinga War was made to sit on a carpet and bathed in gold and precious stones.[27]

His palace was called the Malayakūṭa and the emperor's seat was in another palace called Bhuvana Vijaya (the conqueror of the world).[28] He was wearing a simple dress preferably white embroidered with roses of gold and a diamond garland on his neck.[29] On his head he was wearing a cap of brocade covered with a piece of fine silk. The shoes were either pointed or of the sandal pattern of the present day. Paes concludes the sketch of Krishṇarāya with the highest eulogy that can be bestowed on any monarch ' So gallant and perfect is he in all things.' A pen picture of the great emperor in all its diverse aspects is bound to be incomplete. Well might Nature proclaim to the world for all ages " Here was a man."

27. *Rāyavāchakamu*—p. 114.
28. *Pārijātaharaṇa* II—1 ; V—110; refer *Manu Charitra* I—13.
29. Paes in *Sewell*, pp. 251-52.

15

Krishnadevaraya of Vijayanagara and the Vitthala Image of Pandharapur

By

Mr. G. H. Khare, M.A.,
Bharat Itihasa Samshodhak Mandal, Poona.

In Mahārāshṭra among the public in general and the devotees of the God Viṭṭhala in particular, there is current one story which says that once Rāmarāya, the king of Vijayanagara came to Pandharapur to have the *darśana* of Viṭṭhala. At that time he was so much pleased with the *darśana* that he entreated the God to accompany him to Vijayanagara. The God having acceded to his wish on certain conditions, Rāmarāya managed to carry the Viṭṭhala image to his capital and there installed it in a temple specially built for the purpose. The Marāṭhā devotees being much afflicted by the absence of the image at Pandharapur requested one Bhānudāsa, a devotee from among them, to bring back the image and to this the latter very gladly consented. Accordingly he went to Vijayanagara, propitiated the god and persuaded him to return to Pandharapur. In the meanwhile through some misunderstanding, the king, being enraged, was on the point of hanging Bhānudāsa, when, owing to a miracle and the warning from the God, the king allowed the removal of the image and Bhānudāsa brought it back to Pandharapur. Such is the general outline of the story though there are some deviations here and there.[1]

This story is narrated at length by the following four old Marāṭhā writers (I) Viṭṭhalakavi of Bīd, who flourished about the year 1679 A.D. (II) Keśavasvāmin, who was alive in 1682 A.D. (III) Mahīpati, who wrote his two works *Bhaktavijaya* and *Bhaktalīlāmṛta* in the third quarter of the 18th century and (IV) Bhīmasvāmin, who lived in 1798 A.D.[2]

Of these four writers Bhīmasvāmin's account is based, as expressed by himself, on mere oral tradition.[3] Mahīpati asserts that he has written nothing out of his own imagination, but has based his

1. *Bhānudāsa* by Justin E. Abbot, appendices I-V.
2. *Ibid*, introduction, p. 1.
3. *Ibid*, p. 7.

account on the works of previous writers. He names two such books: *Santacharitra* (*Bhaktamāla* ?) of Nābhāji and *Bhaktacharitra* (*Santamālika* ?) of Uddhavachidaghana.[4] Unfortunately the first does not even refer to Bhānudāsa[5] and the second alludes to him only by name.[6] It follows, therefore, that Mahīpati must have used some other sources. What could possibly be the other sources? I think he must have largely drawn upon the accounts of Viṭṭhalakavi and Keśavasvāmin who were prior to him in age. For we know of no other works than those of the two mentioned above.

The date of Bhānudāsa is not finally fixed as yet though it is generally believed that he was born in śaka 1370 (1448 A.D.) and lived till śaka 1435 (1513 A.D.)[7]. This means that even the earliest biographers of Bhānudāsa were not contemporary with him but lived at least about 175 years after his demise. Besides they were not historians in the sense we use the word at present, and it is but quite natural that their accounts should abound in discrepancies, deviations. anachronisms, etc.

All these biographers state that Rāmarāja managed to remove the image to Vijayanagara. But if we accept the date of Bhānudāsa as correct, then the incident in question must have happened some time before śaka 1435 (1513 A.D.), *i.e.*, about 30 years before the ascendancy of Rāmarāja to power which took place in śaka 1465 (1543 A.D.),[8] or perhaps in the beginning of Krishṇarāya's reign. Then the mention of Rāmarāja must be a mistake. If we take the allusion to Rāmarāja to be true, then we must make Bhānudāsa live at least 30 years more. But in that case we will have to face another difficulty with regard to the age of Ekanātha, the great-grandson of Bhānudāsa, whose accepted date is śaka 1470-1521 (1548-1599 A.D.).[9] Then the period for two generations, *viz.*, of the grand-father and the father will be only five or six years which is unreasonable. Thus it will be seen that there is irregularity and anachronism in the narration of this story.

But the pity of the question is that though Ekanātha in the introduction to his well-known work Bhāgavata, refers to a mira-

4. *Ibid*, pp. 2-3.
5. I have examined only that edition of *Bhaktamāla* printed in the Jagadishwar Press, Bombay, in 1914
6. *Bhānudāsa*, Introduction p. 2.
7. *Mahārāshṭra Sārasvata*, 1919 Edition, p. 100 n.
8. *Historical Inscriptions of Southern India*, p. 250.
9. *Mahārāshṭra Sārasvatā*, pp. 99-113.

culous incident, in the life of his great grand-father, is silent on the present marvellous incident.[10] Had he believed in the truthfulness of the incident he would have been careful to note it. But as he has not done so, the natural inference would be that he either did not believe in the story or he did not know it at all.

At Vijayanagara there is the well-known temple of Viṭṭhala or Viṭṭhalasvāmin under the care of the Archæological Department about which a report of the same Department states that 'It was begun by Krishṇadevarāya in 1513 and the work was carried on by his queens and successors Achyuta and Sadāśiva. However the temple was apparently never finished or consecrated. In all probability the work was stopped by the destruction of the city in 1565.[11] In support of the above statement we find in the same report a reference to a tradition, the gist of which can be given thus, 'But the God having come to look at it (the temple) refused to move, saying that it was far too grand for him and that he preferred his own humbler home.'[12] From this it becomes evident that according to the opinion of the Government Archæologist who has made the above remarks, the temple in question was never completed and consequently no image was installed there.

But if we examine the inscriptions about this temple that have come to light, they tell us altogether a different story. I give at the end the summary of such inscriptions in a tabulated form in order that the readers may have a fair idea about their contents.[13]

The list clearly shows that these inscriptions which range from śaka 1435 to 1486 (1513-1564 A.D.) prove beyond doubt that during all these years there was one Viṭṭhala image in the temple and its daily worship was in full swing with all pomp, show and magnificence; no question whether the temple was finished or not.

Now we have a very interesting piece of information about Krishṇarāya. In śaka 1435 (expired, *i.e.*, 1513 A.D.) this king invested the territory of Gajapati Pratapārudra and after vanquishing him pursued him up to Udayagiri. He captured the town and some of the relatives of Pratapārudra whereafter he returned back

10. Bhāgavata by Ekanātha, chapter 1, pp. 131-134.

11. Archæological Survey of India, Annual Report for 1922-23, p. 67.

12. *Ibid.*

13. Inscriptions of the Madras Presidency, Vol. I, pp. 302-306; the numbers given in the first column are the same as given in the above volume.

to Vijayanagara with a fine image of Bālakrishṇa which he found in a temple at Udayagiri. At Vijayanagara he erected for this image a large temple—resembling that at Udayagiri in general plan and installed the image in it. Both the image and the temple can be seen this day though in a mutilated and neglected state.[14]

In śaka 1442-43 (1520-21 A.D.) a battle was fought between Krishṇarāya of Vijayanagara and the Sultan of Bijapur, Ismail Adilshah in which the latter sustained a crushing defeat at the hands of the former. But before and after the incident there was perfect peace between the two powers. During that period it was quite possible for Krishṇarāya to remove the Viṭṭhala image of Pandharapur to Vijayanagara.[15]

In support of this possibility, evidence can be brought forward. Vādirājatīrtha, a Mādhva saint, who was nearly contemporaneous with Krishṇarāya has left for us a work Tīrthaprabandha written about śaka 1493 (1571 A.D.) which refers to many holy places and in which we find the following interesting verse[16]

चौर्यान्मातृनिबद्धचारुचरणः पापौघचौर्याद्बुधै-
र्बद्धस्त्वं पथि पुण्डरीकमुनिना जारेति संबोधितः ।
तुङ्गातीरगतोसि विठ्ठल भियेर्व (वा) न्याकृतिर्वाञ्छितं
वेत्तॄणां यदि मे न दास्यति (सि) तदा वत्सं स्थितिः कथ्यते ॥

The third line of this verse clearly states that Viṭṭhala had gone to the banks of Tungabhadrā, *i.e.*, to Vijayanagara. But in it also occurs the word *Anyakrtih* which is to be construed with Viṭṭhala and which may mean that Viṭṭhala went to Tungabhadrā in another

14. I. M. P., p. 308, No. 364; pp. 312-13, Nos. 392-93 and 419; ASIAR for 1916-17, part I, p. 14; Historical Inscriptions of Southern India, p. 239; South Indian Inscriptions, Vol. IV, Nos. 254-55; Archæological Survey of India, Southern Circle, Annual Report for 1916-17, pp. 27, 28; the image in question is in the Madras Government Museum for the present.

15. *The Cambridge History of India,* Vol. III, p. 435, *Ferishta* by Briggs, Vol. III, pp. 48-50; History of the Ghorpade family of Mudhol (in Marathi), pp. 165-167; Appendix A, pp. 23-28; here an original Persian farman issued by Ismail 'Adilshah and referring to his deplorable condition has been published.

16. *Annals of the Bhandarkar Oriental Research Institute,* Vol. XVII, pp. 204 n. 3, 207-210.

form. In that case the natural inference will be that the Vijayanagara image of Viṭṭhala was different from the Pandharapur one. But unfortunately we do not know the exact year in which the above work was composed. After the battle of Rakkasagi-Tangaḍāgi there was a general molestation of the Vijayanagara temples in which the original Viṭṭhala image might have been broken and Vādirājatīrtha might be referring to a new image installed there since then. But the question must remain unsettled till we know the exact date of the composition of Tīrthaprabandha and till we find the real image or images consecrated in the temple.

In this connection, I may bring to the notice of readers that Dr. C. Narayana Rao of Anantapur (Madras) seems to claim that he has found the Viṭṭhala image which was worshipped in the above temple. Let us then hope to know more about this question after his very interesting article[17] is published.

But in the present state of evidence, I conclude, that while there is every possibility of Krishṇarāya's carrying the said image of Pandharapur to Vijayanagara, there is very little probability of its having been retaken to Pandharapur and installed there in its original place.

17. *Summary of Papers.* Eighth All-India Oriental Conference, Mysore, p. 114.

APPENDIX.

Inscriptions in the Viṭṭhala Rāya temple at Vijayanagara.

No.	Details of date.	Donor, etc.	Details of donation, etc.	Objects of donation, etc.
337	Ś 1436 Śrīmukha.	Krishṇadēva and his two queens.	One gold plate worth 991 pagodas; 25 silver lamps, 200 cows, 4 villages.	For the worship of Viṭṭhala-deva.
338	” ”	Krishṇadēvarāya.	The village Lingapuram in Tekkalakoṭa and other gifts.	
344-45	Ś 1438 Dhātu.	”	Erection of a 100 pillared Maṇḍapa.	
339	Pramādi (thi)?	”	Devasamudra and four other villages in Rayadurg taluq.	
340	Vyaya.	”	Bhadraseṭṭihaḷḷi, Śāyanapuram, etc., and the taxes on boats of the Tunga-bhadrā.	
316	Ś 1452 Vilambin.	Hiriya Timmappa and Rāgavappa.	Established the Kalaśas and presented golden plates.	Offering.
317	Ś 1453 Khara.	Achyuta-mahārāya.	Gold.	
322	” ”	Tālavāka Tirumalayya.	Some gift.	
342	Ś 1455 Jaya.	Musolamaḍugu Venkaṭarāju Timmarāju.	The tax of 300 pagodas in his own village and some other lands at Samudram, Anantapuram, etc.	
318	Ś 1456 Jaya.	”	Some gift.	For the merit of king Achyuta and the prince Chikkarāya.
346	Ś 1457 Manmatha.	Chikka Timmappa.	200 pagodas.	Daily offerings.
341	Ś 1458 Durmukhi.	”	”	”
319	” Durmukhi.	Nayuḍu.	100 pagodas.	For the merit of the king and Chikkarāya.
315	Ś 1461 Vikārin.	Achyuta Mahārāya.	Ānandanidhi.	To make Kubēras of Brahmanas.
320	Ś 1465 Śobhakrit.	Tirumala Tātāchārya.	Naṭṭur village, land, etc.	For God Viṭṭhala.
326	Ś 1466 Krodhin.	Konēṭi Timmarāya.	Two villages.	For the benefit of his father Konḍarāja.
327	Ś 1476 Ānanda.	Udayagiri Timmarāja.	Tirumalāpuram village worth 600 pagodas in revenue.	The erection of a Maṇḍapa.
328	” ”	With the consent of Aḷiya Rāmappayyadeva.	Gold.	
321	Ś 1480 Kālayukta.	Sadāśivadeva.	One village.	
343	Ś 1483 Durmati.	Konēṭi Konḍarāju.	Ten *Koḷagas* of land at Rāmasāgaram in Kampli District.	
325	Ś 1485 Rudhirōdgārin.	Viṭṭhala Dānamavārulu.	Twelve *Koḷagas* of land at Rāmeśvaram.	For God Viṭṭhala.
336	Ś 1486 Raktākshi.	Śrīnivāsāchārya.	The village of Mukkundi Agraharam.	”

16

Some Aspects of Art during the Reign of Krishnadevaraya, The Great

By

Mr. R. N. Saletore, M.A.,
Bombay.

I. PAINTING

During the reign of Krishṇadeva Rāya painting reached a remarkable state of realism. In the Ivory Room which Paes saw, he beheld the evidence of such craftsmanship which evoked his attention. " On the same side " he explains " is designed in painting all the ways of life of the men who have been here even down to the Portuguese, from which the king's wives can understand the manner in which each one lives in his own country, even to the blind and the beggars."[1] This reveals the range of topics which attracted not only the queens but even the painters.

The walls of certain chambers within the palace were painted. Paes himself witnessed this custom. When going through the palace he found this : " Above this chamber, was another, smaller and with nothing in it save only that it was gilt and painted." Then again he found that room, the walls of which had carvings of amazons and was likewise beautified : " They had begun to paint this chamber, and they told us that it had to be finer than the others, and that it was to be all plated with gold, as well the ground below as all the rest."[2] This tradition of wall-painting must have permeated even into the temples because patches of red and yellow paint are visible even to-day in some of the temples of Vijayanagara. That such was the practice during the times of Krishṇadeva Rāya there is little doubt. Speaking of a 'canopy' evidently a *manḍapa* before a shrine, Paes did not fail to observe even this feature. " All this " he says referring to the sculpture " is also gilded and has some red colour on the under-sides of the leaves which stand out from the sculpture."[3]

1. Sewell, *A Forgotten Empire,* p. 286.
2. Sewell : *Ibid,* p. 287.
3. *Ibid.*

The royal Secretariat too was similarly adorned. "Thence he (the king) goes to a building made in the shape of a porch without walls, which has many pillars hung with cloths right up to the top, and with the walls handsomely painted, it has on each side two figures of women very well made."[4]

Even recesses were painted. "At the end of this house continues Paes, referring to a dancing hall about which more will be written later on, "is a painted recess where the women cling on with their hands in order better to stretch and loosen their bodies and legs . . ."[5] Most probably this was a sort of gymnasium used specially for ladies.

Besides this, painting was utilised to adorn even animals. Paes noted this during the Annual Review of the troops. "The elephants in the same way" he narrates "are covered with caparison of velvet and gold with fringes, and rich cloths of many colours, and with bells so that the earth resounds; and on their heads are painted faces of giants and other kinds of great beasts."[6]

This creative instinct made the Vijayanagara painters more realistic in the sense that they strove to imitate natural forms and colours. This can be verified by examining the observation of Paes once again, for he was fortunate enough to see the statues of Krishṇadeva Rāya and his father. These were placed at the entrance leading to the king's residence. "At the entrance of this door" Paes explains, "outside are two images painted life-like and drawn in their manner, which are these; the one on the right hand is of the father of this king. The father was dark and a gentleman of fine form, stouter than the son is; they stand with all their apparel and such raiment as they wear or used to wear when alive."[7] This practice, of raising such statues, being of long standing, was certainly known to Vijayanagara craftsmen. The torsos of a king and a queen can be seen even to-day within the *prākāra* of the Achyuta Rāya's temple at Vijayanagara. Secondly, the *repoussé* copper statues of Krishṇadeva Rāya and his two queens at Tiruvaṇṇāmalai substantiate this assertion. Moreover the later statues of Tirumala, Venkaṭa I and his queen duly confirm the fact that this tradition of statue-making was continued after Krishṇadeva Rāya. Perhaps the best illustration of this tradition of realism can even now be seen in the Thousand Pillared *Manḍapa* of Tirumala Nāyaka,

4. Sewell, *Op. Cit.*, p. 250.
5. *Ibid*, p. 289.
6. *Ibid*, p. 277.
7. *Ibid*, p. 285.

whose forefathers were of course Vijayanagara feudatories, where Tirumala and his nine ancestors stand, with their consorts with patches of reminiscent paint, reminding the visitor that after all, the provincial governors only followed the fashion started at the capital.

II. ARCHITECTURE

Architecture too in this period reached an excellence which perhaps, it never achieved either before or after. It is known that Krishṇadeva Rāya was a great builder, and among the temples which he built, the great Krishṇaswāmi temple, erected in A.D. 1513, after his successful eastern campaign, the Hazāra Rāma commenced in the same year, and the Viṭṭalaśwāmi temple are the most memorable.

The material used for constructing these shrines was the rough and unyielding granite of the locality. Of course the soft black stone, which can be seen in the House of Victory, for example, was also utilised, but the former was more commonly used. Probably on account of its great weight this stone was not employed in raising the *vimāna* of temples during this period, for the top-heavy temple would have been a perpetual danger.

Krishṇadeva Rāya's *pradakshiṇā*, for instance, of the Viṭṭalaśwāmi temple in no way resembles the *pradakshiṇā* of the Chenna Keśava temple at Beḷur of the Hoysaḷās, who were the political predecessors of the Vijayanagara emperors. The square *pradakshiṇā* in this case, strangely enough, is much lower than the ground floor of the *sukhanāsi* and the *garbhagriha*, and but for an opening or two, would be in total darkness. To this *pradakshiṇā* there are, of course, two entrances. But this was not always the case for the Krishṇaswāmi temple, built by Kṛishṇadeva Rāya, in 1513 A.D. shows only the *garbhagriha*, the *sukhanāsi* and the *navaranga.*

Now the *pradakshiṇā* itself was not always empty. The *pradakshiṇā* of Viṭṭalaswāmi temple contains the beautiful stone-car, irresistibly reminding one of the car festival, which was obviously used as a shrine.

Over the *pradakshiṇā* rose the shrine. During Kṛishṇadeva Rāya's time, below the first element of the temple above the *pradakshiṇā* was introduced a new strip of space utilised not for the usual elephants of the Hoysaḷas or the Pāndyas, but for the Portuguese *fidalgos* and their horses! This was imitated by the feudatories, for instance, in Madura. Above this element came the *upānam* which, in the Viṭṭalaśwāmi temple, by far the finest specimen of Vijayanagara architecture, was adorned with scrolls of vines, flowers, birds and geometrical designs.

Now on the *upānam* was carved the *padmam,* the symbol of life in the Vedas, which is rarely absent in Vijayanagara architecture of these days. The lotus petals are closer, and though a little raised, they add not a little to the elegance of the temple.

Above the *padmam* came the *Kumudam,* ornamented with ridges from above and below with a band-space filled up with various designs. This was not always found suitable for it is absent in the Viṭṭhalaśwāmi temple at Vijayanagara.

Next was carved the *Kanṭham* which, in the Hazāra Rāma, Viṭṭhalaśwāmi, and Kṛishṇa temples at Vijayanagara, was meant for depicting phases of social life like dancing girls, wrestling matches, and similar incidents.

Now, as though to complete the lotus flower on the *Kanṭham,* was carved the *bodigai,* a more or less inverted *padmam.* These completed the ground plan of the Vijayanagara temple during Kṛishṇadeva Rāya's time.

Over all these ornamentations which comprised the ground floor of the typical Vijayanagara temple during Kṛishṇadeva Rāya's days, rose the pillars. Since architecture of this school had reached a high standard of development it is possible here to differentiate only the various pillars in a number of temples. Square rather than the round pillars were common during this period, and the latter type ceased to be used as a main pillar, but only served as a decorative pilaster of the *kumbhapanjaram.* This decoration can be seen in the Hazāra Rāma temple at Vijayanagara. The pedestal of this pilaster is square ; above it rose the *kumbham* which is only an adaptation of the *kumbham* of the pillar itself and it is likewise carved all round with a blank strip running above it. The rest of this pilaster had no other peculiarities, but it may be remarked that it was carved apparently for its symbolistic depth of associations, as it has been called 'The Vase of Plenty.'

The square pillar was always in vogue at this time. The pedestal or the *aśvapāda* was fully ornamented as in the Hazāra Rāma temple. The square is seen now in a double form, and in the *Kalyāṇa Maṇḍapa* of the Viṭṭalaśwāmi temple the double pillar was separated and to the extra pillars were attached, obviously for support if not for decoration, *caryatides*, in the shape *gajasimhas* or rather the soldiers seated over horses which are not very realistic. These can also be seen in the *Kalyāṇa Maṇḍapa* of the Vaikunṭha Perumāḷ temple at Vellore. It may here be observed that in the Viṭṭalaświmi temple, the extra pillar is not detached from the main pillar, but in the Kṛishṇa as well as in the corridor of the Viṭṭalā-śwāmi shrines the pillars are separate.

Other characteristics of this double pillar may also be noticed, for example, in the pillars on entering the Viṭṭalaśwāmi temple, the small double pillars have lions for their pedestals. Moreover, the images of the king and his three queens were sometimes carved as in the main pillar of the *Kalyāṇa Maṇḍapa*, of the Vaikunṭha Perumāḷ temple at Vellore, built by Kṛishṇadeva Rāya. This square pillar was also engrafted on *dīpamāles* or lamp pillars, for instance, in the Nārāyaṇa temple at Bhaṭkal, where the elegance of the whole work is striking.

The square pillar was further embellished. It was divided into *śadurams* or squares on which either mythical, religious or social subjects were carved. From the lower four ends of this square issued cup-like edges called *nāgabandhama*. On the top of this pillar was placed a closed lotus, the *munai*, from which during this period, as the lotus blossomed, the bud or the *pūmunai*, would issue forth, in glorious exuberance. During this age this *pūmunai* was generally small and not protruding as it came to be in Achyuta Rāya's days.

Over these pillars came the roof. This was elongated and gorgeously decorated and stamped many a time with the unforgettable and memorable *kīrtimukha* seen on the *aśvapāda* of pillars as well as on the walls of temples. Over this roof was carved a series of *kūḍus* or niches enshrining images of deities, which are quite visible, in the Viṭṭalaśwāmi temple, clearly showing that the whole temple must have been complete before 1530 A.D. The corners of these roofs, as in the case of this shrine, had rings to dangle chains enshrining lamps.

There was nothing particular about the door, and the entrance, apart from the *mukha maṇḍapa*, was graced either with elephants elaborately designed, or with *dvārapālas*, the door-protectors, armed with maces found in the Hazāra Rāma temple compound.

All these were crowned by the *vimāna*. This was sometimes erected over the *ardhamaṇḍapa* as in the Krishṇa temple at Vijayanagara, otherwise the *gopurams* were, as noted before, of brick work finished with stucco work. A visit to Vijayanagara even today shows the excellence of this craftsmanship which must be more seen than described especially since this stucco has been in ruins. This brick work, of course, was raised on a stone basement which was adorned with pillars, often single only, and between these, either the memorable *kīrtimukha* often made its appearance, or there was carved the *goṣṭapanjaram* pavilion. All this brickwork having crumbled, and it is regrettable that no more enduring substance was used,—a fuller description of the *vimāna* cannot be obtained.

III. SCULPTURE

On the walls of temples or of other buildings was displayed the sculpture of the Vijayanagara craftsmen. Probably in the whole range of South Indian sculpture it would be difficult to find a match to vie with the variety of Vijayanagara sculpture. In order to prove this one should go primarily to Vijayanagara not to mention Śrī-śailam, Vellore or Muḍabidri or even Bhaṭkal, where are unravelled in stone a social history in stone of this age. Take Vijayanagara, for example, and in it the House of Victory. Here can be seen prancing monkeys in unimaginable shapes, kings receiving embassies, queens as well as their husbands witnessing a dancing match, noblemen hunting in the forest either the wild deer or hogs or boars, along sometimes with women with bows, arrows and lances, at times on horseback or on foot, women looking in the mirror or dancing girls in action, captives brought before the king and a variety of other topics. They are drawn with a caricaturistic touch, pregnant with realism, vitality and power. The obvious heaviness of Hoysaḷa sculpture, especially of the horses, for instance, which one notices at Haḷebīḍ or at Dvārasamudra, is conspicuous by its absence in Vijayanagara sculpture of this period. The deer, the dogs, the prancing horses or the marching soldiers look alive instinct with life, vigour and freshness which are unforgettable.

Much cannot also be said about the imagery during this because few images have survived either the vandal or the wrath of time. But what examples survive bear witness to the excellence of Vijayanagara craftsmen. The *repoussé* images of Kṛishṇadeva Rāya and his queens are a triumph of skill and charm. The headless statues found in the Viṭṭhalaśwāmi temple, probably representing one of Kṛishṇadeva Rāya's queens, show great skill in carving and imagery. The imitation on stone of the genuine saree worn by women in those times is indeed a pleasant sight, and lingers long in one's memory.

IV. MUSIC

Krishṇadeva Rāya himself was also an accomplished musician like Rāma Rāya. In the Kṛishṇapura epigraphs he is specially eulogised as being unrivalled in music[8] This can be confirmed by external evidence. Paes tells that Christovao de Figueiredo presented this monarch certain musical instruments with which he was greatly delighted.[9] He also liked to hear music. In 1514 Barbosa states on what occasions Kṛishṇadeva Rāya used to delight in song. " They (the women of the palace) bathe every day in pools of water, and sing and play on their instruments, and in a thousand ways amuse the king."[10] During *Sati*, the *Sīḍī* rite, and when nobles went to see the monarch, music[11] was indulged in. As the sculptures show, the drum, the horn, the pipe, the *kōlāṭa*-stick, were all used in producing this music.

V. THE THEATRE

There is little doubt that the theatre existed in the times of Kṛishṇadeva Rāya. Dramas like " *Jāmbavati Kalyāṇam* " written by the emperor himself were staged in honour of the Spring Festival before a large audience.[12] This can be corroborated by internal evidence. In a play called " *Tāyikund Nāṭaka* " which was actually staged during this period, two persons one *Nāṭuva* Nāgayya, who as his name suggests was an actor, and a lady, '*a pātri*' evidently a dancing girl, took part, and such was their skill in acting that they were awarded gifts of land.[13] This clearly shows that mixed acting was in vogue during those days but at the present stage of research no further light can be thrown on the nature of the contemporary stage.

VI. DANCING

The dancing girls were proficient not only in acting but also in other respects. At the age of ten, Barbosa tells us, the parent of a maiden used to take her to " a monastery and the house of prayer of that idol, with great honour, and accompanied by her relations entertaining her like one that is going to be married."[14] Thus they

8. E. I. I. p. 401.
9. Sewell, *A Forgotten Empire*, p. 251.
10. Stanley, *Barbosa*, p. 88.
11. *Ibid*, pp. 92, 95, 89.
12. S. K. Aiyangar, *Sources*, p. 142.
13. 99 of 1916.
14. *Barbosa*, p. 96.

became the " *dēvadāsis,*" but the manner in which they were treated is surprising. Paes tells us that they were " not low in the estimation of the public, and that they were tolerated with great consideration." " These women " he continues " are of loose character and live in the best streets that are in the city; it is the same in all cities, their streets have the best rows of houses. They are very much esteemed, and are classed among those honoured ones who are the mistresses of their captains ; any respectable man may go to their houses without any blame attaching thereto. These women (are allowed) even to enter the presence of the wives of the king and they stay with them and eat betel with them, a thing which no other person may do no matter what his rank may be."[15] This only reveals the state of morality prevailing in that age. Only these were permitted to approach the staircase of the " House of Victory " during the *Mahānavami,* when their wrestling was witnessed and in fact a special match was arranged by Kṛishṇadeva Rāya himself.[16]

No wonder with all this patronage they became fabulously wealthy. " Who can fitly describe to you " says Paes the great riches these women carry on their persons ? . . . collars of gold with so many diamonds and rubies and pearls, bracelets, also on their arms and on their upper arms, girdles below and of necessity anklets on the feet."[17] They even owned lands, servants and many other things besides. Paes comments not that women of such a profession should obtain such wealth, but that there are women among them " who have lands that have been given to them and litters and so many maid servants that one cannot number all their things."[18] A number of carvings at Vijayanagara depict these dancers with numerous ornaments, for instance in the Hazāra Rama's temple as well as on the House of Victory.

These carvings show us different types of dancing girls. Some of them in the two edifices referred to above, wear *pyjāma* like trousers probably after the Muhammadan custom, and over them, the skirt. Generally they wore nothing above the waist except their crowded ornaments, as is done even to-day in Malabar or the Bali Islands. In other carvings there are dancing girls having only a skirt and no trousers at all ! Then on the top row of the outer wall of Hazāra Rāma's temple near the gateway, and in a few carvings or pillars of temples there are dancing girls absolutely nude.

15. Sewell, *Op. Cit.* p. 242.
16. *Ibid,* p. 270.
17. *Ibid.*
18. Sewell, *Op. Cit.,* p. 270.

These dancing girls kept alive the art of dancing. On all mornings of the Mahānavami when Kṛishṇadeva Rāya was in the chapel of the House of Victory,[19] during all car festivals,[20] on Saturdays before the images in the temples,[21] they had to dance, and in the afternoon of the festival they had to wrestle.[22] But though it is not now possible to know all the technicalities of dancing, still it must have been properly organized, for sculptures of this period show dancing girls and a master for instance on a bas-relief of the Viṭṭalaśwāmi and the House of Victory. This is confirmed by epigraphs. On 25th January, in 1518 A.D., Kṛishṇadeva Rāya gave two villages for the maintenance of a dancing master, in the temple of *Brahmīśvara*.[23] But it is not possible to know whether this master organized the *kolāṭa* dances so often seen on the House of Victory or the Hazāra Rāma temple. Probably such dances were organized, by a mutual understanding and practice, by the women themselves. It may here be noted that the carvings showing these dancers are among the most beautiful of the sculptures in Vijayanagara, for the litheness of form, faultlessness of expression and the beauty of execution. But still as these sculptures show, far more difficult and complicated dancing in varying postures and poses, were conducted before the admiring king and his queens.

VII. THE DANCING SALOON

Even the women of the palace danced in public after they had mastered this art in a regular school of dancing. How they were able to learn and correct their own faults can be realized after reviewing Paes's excellent account of this dancing hall. " This hall " he begins " is where the king sends his women to be taught to dance. It is a long hall and not very wide, all of stone sculpture on pillars which are at a distance of quite an arm's length from the wall. These pillars stand in that manner in all around the building ; they are half pillars made with other hollows (?) all gilt. In the supports (or pedestals) on the top are many great beasts like elephants and of other shapes ; it is open so that the interior is seen, and there are on the inner side of these beasts other images each placed according to its character ; there are also figures of men turned back to back and other beasts of different sorts. In each case from pillar to pillar is a crossbar (the architrave) which is like a panel and from pillar to pillar are many such panels ; there are images of old men, gilded

19. Sewell, *Op. Cit.*, p. 266.
20. *Ibid*, p. 262.
21. *Ibid*, pp. 241 and 379.
22. *Ibid*, p. 271.
23. Rangacharya, *Top List*, II, p. 1222.

and of the size of a cubit. Each of the panels has one placed in this way. These images are over all the building. And on the pillars are other images, smaller, with other images yet more subordinate, and other figures again, in such a way that I saw this work gradually diminishing the size from on these pillars with their designs, from pillar to pillar, and each time smaller by the size of a span as it went on becoming lost, the most beautiful dome I ever saw. Between these images and pillar runs a design of foliage, like plates (*a maneyra de lamines*) all gilt with reverses of the leaves in red and blue, the images that are on the pillars are stags and other animals, and they are painted in colours with the pink on their faces; but the other images seated on the elephants as well as on the panels, are all dancing women having little drums (tom-toms)

"The designs of these panels show the position at the ends of dances in such a way that on each panel there is a dancer in the proper position at the end of a dance; this is to teach the women, so that if they forget the position in which they have to remain when the dance is done they may look at one of the panels where is the end of that dance. By that they keep in mind what they have to do.

"At the end of this house on the other hand is a painted recess where the women cling on with their hands in order better to stretch and loosen their bodies and legs; there they teach them to make the whole body supple, in order to make their dancing more graceful. At the other end, on the right, is the place where the king places himself to watch them dancing, all the floors and walls where he sits are covered with gold and in the middle of the wall is a golden image of a woman of the size of a girl of twelve years, with her arms in the position which she occupies in the end of a dance."[24] No wonder the king took such a personal interest in this art which was taught in a hall where probably the whole of Bharata's Nāṭyaśāstra was illustrated in sculpture and imagery, and it is such a misfortune that this wonderful structure has not survived. But among the surviving buildings there exists a *maṇḍapa* opposite the *Kalyāṇa Maṇḍapa* of the Viṭṭalaśwāmi temple, on the northern side, but not as profusely decorated as the former. The throne platform which it contains, the rich frieze running down below its base representing various types of musicians, dancers, and drummers performing before an appreciating king probably Kṛishṇadeva Rāya, suggest that this *maṇḍapa* was very likely also used by the king to witness public exhibitions of dancing which must have reached a high standard of perfection in Vijayanagara times.

24. Sewell, *Op. Cit.*, pp. 288-9.

17

The Authorship and Importance of the Amuktamalyada as a source of History for the Reign of Sri Krishnadevaraya

By

Mr. V. S. Ramachandra Murty, B.A., (Hons.),
Teacher, P. R. College, Coconada.

'The date 27-1-1519 A.D., is one of the important dates in the History of the Vijayanagara Empire and also a landmark in the Development of the Telugu Literature (J. A. H. R. S., IX, part 4, last page). It was on that date that Krishṇadēvarāya while on his expedition against Kalinga, was at Vijayavati (Bezawada) and was worshipping Āndhra Madhusūdhana, and fasted for the *Ēkādaśi* there. It was on that famous night that the God appeared to him in a dream and bade him compose the story of Āṇḍāḷ, the daughter of Vishṇuchitta Periyāḷvār, one of the twelve Vaishṇava Saints, in Telugu, the best of the Dēśabhāshas, and dedicate it to God Venkaṭēśvara. So Krishṇadēvarāya began writing this monumental work which is a reliable and contemporary work for reconstructing the history of Krishṇadēvarāya's reign.

Tradition, as well as the writings of a few poets, and commentators, somehow attribute the authorship of this monumental work to Allasāni Peddanna, the author of Manucharitra and an important and much loved court poet of Krishṇadēvarāya. Briefly I enumerate below the arguments of those that say that Āmuktamālyada was written by Allasāni Peddanna. Mr. V. Prabhakara Sastry Garu of Madras wrote a fine article in which he adduced very strong arguments to prove that Āmuktamālyada was written by Allasāni Peddanna (*Andhra Patrikā,* Durmati, Māghamāsa, Pāḍyami). The following arguments are all taken from the Sanjīvini Vyākhya of Āmuktamālyada by M. M., V. V. Sastry.

1. In the introductory portion of Āmuktamālyada, the following Sanskrit works have been attributed to Krishṇadēvarāya :—

(*i*) Madālasā Charita, (*ii*) Satyāvadhūprīṇanam, (*iii*) Sūktinaipuṇīgânachintāmani, (*iv*) Sakalakathāsārasangraham, and (*v*) Rasamañjari.

But none of them have been till now found. None of them or even Āmuktamālyada, was claimed for Krishṇadēvarāya in the books written to extol his greatness like Krishṇarāyavijayam or Rāyavāchakam. They only claim him as a great warrior, and a great patron of literature and as a great donor. On the other hand, we know of a Sanskrit work called Rasamañjari in the name of one Bhānusūri. Recently, the authorities of the Madras Oriental Library, found a manuscript of a book named *Prapanchandarpaṇa*, in which it was stated that *Satyavadhūpariṇaya* and *Rasamañjari* were written by Peddanna. So it is argued that Āmuktamālyada was written by Peddanna himself, but in the name of his monarch. Secondly, it is argued that a monarch, who was mostly pre-occupied with military life, and whose mother-tongue was Kannaḍa and not Telugu, could not write such a monumental work. He might have had an absorbing interest in its study, as proved by his patronage of the Telugu poets, but to expect from him such an excellent work is rather unbelievable. Thirdly, a contemporary of both Peddanna and Krishṇadēvarāya, *i.e.*, Tenāli Rāmakrishna Kavi attributed this work to Peddanna, in his Paṇḍitārādhyacharita. The author of the Telugu prosody by name K. Appakavi, and Gudipati Venkatakavi and the author of Srīnivāsa-vyākhyā, also attribute the authorship to Peddanna. The introductory portion of the work was, with slight modifications copied from Manucharitra. These are the arguments of those that say that the author of Āmuktamālyada was Allasāni Peddanna.

But if the style of the book were to represent a man the style of Āmuktamālyada indicates an author quite different from the author of Manucharitra. The very conception, of the work, the composition, the material used, the style, and the medium through which it is expressed, the situations, and the plot, all show a different man than Peddanna. Peddanna was fond of exaggeration. The author of Āmuktamālyada was fond of realistic descriptions, and he was primarily a worshipper of Nature. There is an undertone of vanity in the poet to exhibit all that he learnt ; the work as a whole shows the author to be immature in the traditions of the Telugu language; the style of the work is not uniformly smooth going; it limps at certain places. The inappropriate and out-of-place similes and lack of good Telugu idiom, and the use of high-flown Sanskrit, give it a unique place in the Prabandha world. Besides the greatness of a Vaishṇava philosophy is extolled in this work. All these arguments go to prove that Āmuktamālyada must have been written by Śrīkrsihṇadēvarāya, himself, to whom the study of Telugu—the best of the *Dēśabhāṣhas*—was a hobby. The consensus of learned opinion also, is in favour of attributing this work to Krishṇadēvarāya. The opinion of such a learned scholar as Mahamahopadhyaya Vedam Venkatarāya Sastry, that it appears to be the work of Krishṇadēvarāya deserves weighty consideration. So we are of opinion that Āmuktamālyada might have been written by Krishṇadēvarāya himself.

Whatever that may be, Āmuktamālyada gives us valuable information about the campaigns of Krishṇadēvarāya. In the introductory portion of the book, the genealogy of the monarch is given from the moon. 'Of his own achievements which he gives us in the words of his court poets, he has a very long account. The fire of his valour which was kindled by his sword coming into contact with the rocks of Udayagiri, advanced to Koṇḍavīdu, and after defeating Kasavāpātra, crossed the Jammilōya and reduced successively the district of Vēgi (Vēngi), Kōna (the modern Godāvary Delta) and Koṭṭāmu, Kanakagiri, Poṭnūru, Māḍemulu, Oḍḍadi,' and burnt Cuttack so that the Gajapati fled from there. In verse 41 the Muhammadan soldiers of the cities of Gulburga and Sāgar killed in battle by Krishṇa, are said to be in heaven giving trouble to the Gods.

In the next verse he is said to have fought with the troops of Ādilkhān and having killed him in battle. Verse 43 describes his munificent benefactions. The six Colophons at the end of the six cantos give us the important particulars of his conquests. (Refer *Sources of Vijayanagar History*, p. 132.)

Colophon for chapter	I.	Capture of	Udayagiri.
Do.	II.	„ „	Koṇḍavīḍu.
Do.	III.	„	Koṇḍapalli.
Do.	IV.	„ „	Worship of God at Simhāchalam and the erection of a pillar of victory at Poṭnūru.
Do.	V.	„ „	Destruction of the fortification of Kembāvi.
Do.	VI.	„ „	Battle of Nairāmaṇa.

These are in brief the details that we get from the Āmuktamālyada. Some of the conquests mentioned above in the work, find no mention either in the Amarāvati inscription, Ahobilam inscription, or the Siṃhāchalam inscriptions. They are places on his way to Cuttack. They need identification. It is said that after conquering Udayagiri and Koṇḍavīḍu, Krishṇadēvarāya crossed Jammilōya and reduced successively Vēgi, Kōna, and Kōṭṭāmu, Kanakagiri, Poṭnūru, Māḍemulu, Oḍḍādi, and Cuttack. Udayagiri and Koṇḍavīḍu are too well known. Jammilōya is not possible for identification. Vēgi was the district or Vishaya of Vēngi, (and is identical with the modern Taluqs of Ellore, Ernagudem, and Bhimavaram, in the West Godavary District, till the sixth century A.D.). It was famous for a long time as a territorial unit because it was the bone of contention for many dynasties. It was under the Śālankāyanās, and the Vishṇukundins and the Eastern Chālukyan monarchs, and this Vishaya as a territorial unit was in existence as late as the 17th century A.D. The above description of Vēngī Vishaya holds good only till the sixth century of the Christian Era. But under Chālukyas it underwent considerable changes in extent. In the Āndhra Mahābhārata, Rajahmundry was included in the Vēngī Vishaya. Like Kalinga its boundaries were always changing along with the dynasties that ruled it.

Kona has been identified by Dr. S. Krishnaswamy Aiyangar, with the Godavary Delta (S. V. H., p. 133). But Kona is and I think was, not the whole of the Godavary Delta. It connôtes only the Amalapur and the Rajole Taluqs of the East Godavary District. We have epigraphic evidence to show that this Kona was under the Haihayas during the 12th and 13th century A.D. They had marital relations with the Chālukyas of Nidadavolu, who had in their turn marital relations with the Kakatiyas (S. I. I. V., Nos. 123, 124, 125, 127).

The next place was Koṭṭāmu. It may be identified with the modern Koṭṭāmu a village very near Tuni, and which is even now under a Zemindar who resides at Tuni, in the East Godavary District. I am not able to identify Kanakagiri. Next we had the mention about Poṭnūru. At this place Krishṇadēvarāya, erected a pillar of victory, denoting his conquest of the dominions of Gajapati. This fact is alluded to in two verses at the beginning and in the colophon for chapter IV of Āmuktamālyada. " This Poṭnūru is 12 miles from Bhimilipatam, on the bank of the Chittavalasa River. The pillar has now disappeared, but frequent discoveries at Poṭnūru of fragments of sculptured stones and gold coins bearing the bull upon them strengthen the traditions regarding its departed importance." Vizagapatam Gazetteer, p. 230. Now Māḍemulu and Oḍḍādi need identification. This Māḍemulu is made mention of Srīnādha, a famous Telugu poet of 14th century, A.D. He mentions in his Bhimēśvarapurāṇam, (Verse 29) and in his Kāsikhanḍam (Verse 34) the existence of seven Māḍemulu. They were called 'Sapta Māḍiyamulu' by Srīnādha. This word Māḍiyamulu must have changed into Māḍemulu by the time of Krishṇadēvarāya. These Māḍemulu represent the major portion of the Vizagapatam Agency, now under the Jeypore Zemindary. There is a village now by name Māḍugula or Māḍgōle, near Oḍḍādi, in the Vizagapatam District. From this place the agency area begins. This Māḍgōle was for a long time under the *Mannē* chiefs or 'Forest Lords.' Oḍḍādi was said to be under a dynasty of kings, who belonged to Matsya Vaṁśa. Cuttack is the same as the modern Cuttack, and was the capital of the Gajapati Kings of Orissa.

To a small extent we find corroboration, in Āmuktamālyada for the polity, very well described by the foreign travellers. A detailed study of the Vijayanagara polity is made by my learned friends, Mr. K. Iswara Dutt[1] and Dr. B. A. Saletore[2].

Mr. K. Iswara Dutt is of opinion that the colophons indicate the chronological order of the campaigns of Srī Krishṇadēvarāya. I entirely agree with that opinion, and join him in his statement 'that the Emperor-poet is also a great historian, who depicts his achievements with chronological precision.' 'In this respect the colophons of the cantos of his monumental work are veritable mines' (J.A.H.R.S., IX, iv, 43 ff.). The conquests of Udayagiri, Koṇḍavīdu, Konḍapalli, and his worshipping the God at Siṃhāchalam and erection of a pillar of victory, are things that are so often repeated in articles on Vijayanagara History, and they need no commentary here. But the colophons at the end of chapters V and VI, need some elucidation. The colophon at the end of chapter V, describes the destruction of the fortification at Kembhāvi. This Kembhāvi is to be identified with the modern Kembhāvi 12 miles south-west by south from Yēwūr, in the Nizams Dominions, in the Raichore-Doab. This name means the "Red well." (See Indian Atlas (1854) sheet 57 and also Hyderabad Survey sheet 79 (1885). This name occurs in Basavapurāṇa also. We have inscriptional evidence to show that this Kembhāvi was under the Western Cha-

1. Studies in Vijayanagar Polity., J.A.H.R.S.
2. Social and Political conditions of Vijayanagar. By Dr. B. A. Saletore.

lukyans, but was ruled by subordinate Haihaya princess, during the 11th and 12th century, A.D. (Ep. Ind. XII, 291, 292). This Kembhāvi expedition, mentioned by Krishṇadēvarāya in his colophon to chapter V of Āmuktamālyada might refer to the expedition to Gulbarga, which is referred to also in verse 41 (Āmuktamālyada) This might have been achieved just earlier than the battle of Raichore, or along with it. In verse 41, it is said, that Krishnadēvarāya killed the Muhammadan soldiers of Gulburga and Sagar. This Sagar is very near Kembhāvi and so the expedition referred to in the colophon at the end of canto V refers to the battle at Gulbarga.

The learned Editor of the *Sources of Vijayanagara History,* expressed his opinion that this battle might refer to the Battle of Raichore which found no mention in any of the inscriptions of Krishṇadēvarāya. This suggestion is not tenable because the battle of Raichore is referred to by Krishṇadēvarāya in his work at the end of canto VI. It is unfortunate that this colophon of canto VI, is omitted by the Editor in the *Sources of Vijayanagara History,* because he was not able to understand what Nairmamanam is. This colophon at the end of canto VI, describes the Capture of Nairamanam, from the Yavanas. "This Nairamanam is the modern Nairamanur, a small village now situated at 7 miles N. E. of Manvi, near the north bank of the Tungabhadra River, in the Raichore doab.' This place is very near Raichore and Kembhāvi is 70 or 80 miles away from Raichore. So I am of the opinion that the Raichore Battle is described at the end of Canto VI and the conquest of Gulbarga is alluded to in the colophon at the end of chapter V. (See also J.A.H.R.S., IX, part IV, 62, ff.)

Thus the work gives us the necessary literary evidence to corroborate the description of Nuniz. Its value is enhanced in the absence of any epigraphical evidence.

There is another bit of new information which is got from this work. In all the Telugu works of the time, and in the inscriptions as well we only find the names of Chinnadēvi, and Tirumaladēvi. But Āmuktamālyada gives us a new name, i.e., Annapūrṇādēvi.

Hence Āmuktamālyada, a work written by Krishṇadēvarāya with the help of his court poets, is as important a contemporary literary evidence for the reign of Krishṇadēvarāya.

18

Economic Conditions in the Time of Krishnadevaraya

BY

MR. G. S. DIXIT, M.A.,

Maharaja's College, Parlakimedi.

THE EXTENT OF THE VIJAYANAGARA EMPIRE

A LINE drawn from Ankōlā[1] on the West Coast to Raichur,[2] a few miles south of the river Krishṇa and continued along the Krishṇa river to its mouth,[3] would form the northern boundary of the Empire, in the days of Krishṇadēvarāya. The peninsula south of this line, with the exception of the Malabar coast,[4] formed the Empire.

The Empire can be divided into three well-defined natural divisions, *viz.*, the Canara coast between the western ghats and the Arabian Sea, the Deccan plateau between the western ghats and the eastern ghats, and the Coromandel coast.

POPULATION

All foreign travellers who visited the Empire are unanimous in declaring that it was very densely populated. Nicolo Conti in 1420 A.D., declared that the numbers of the people exceeded belief.[5] Abdur Razzāk, who wrote in about 1443 A.D., said, "It is

1. The Portuguese travellers usually begin the description of the empire from this port. See Paes. F.E., p. 236. But some territories north of Ankōlā and adjacent to Goa seem to have been in the empire. The towns in this part mentioned by Nuniz (F.E., p. 386) cannot be properly identified. Belgaum was in the kingdom of Bijapur, see (F.E., p. 340) and (Brigg's Firishta, Vol. III, p. 73). The principality of Bankāpur in the present Dhārwār district was in the empire (Nuniz F.E., p. 374). These facts must fix the line from Ankōlā to Raichur. The line will be very irregular.

2. The Raichur-Doab, including the fortresses of Raichur and Mudgal, was conquered by Krishṇa from Bijāpur. Briggs III, pp. 49-50.

3. Nuniz F.E., p. 320. The treaty between Pratāparudra Gajapati and Krishṇa fixed the Krishṇa as the boundary between the two empires. The Krishṇa must have formed the boundary between Gōlconda and Vijayanagara. No authority mentions anything about this boundary. But Śrīśailam a few miles south of the Krishṇa in this part of boundary was in the empire (V. R. II Kurnool 454, 455, and 578).

4. Kumbḷa was the last Vijayanagara port in this part. Barbōsa says "Here ends the kingdom of Narasymga" (Vol. I, p. 197 and footnote).

5. Major. p. 32.

so well populated that it is impossible to give an idea of it without entering into most extensive details."[6] Between Mangalore and Belour or Bidrūr he came across each day to some city or populous town.[7] The Canara coast was so thickly populated that it looked like a single town to Barbosa (1504-14 A.D.)[8] Paes in 1520 A.D., declared, " The whole country is thickly populated with cities, towns and villages."[9]

With the existing evidence it is not possible to calculate satisfactorily the exact population of the Empire. Mr. Moreland has calculated the population of the Deccan kingdoms and Vijayanagara Empire on the basis of the number of troops which fought at Rākshasa-Tangaḍi. He says " France had arranged before the year 1914 to mobilise one out of 31, and Germany one out of 32, so that if the recruiting organisation of Deccan and Vijayanagara was as efficient as that of modern France and Germany, their united strength of a million would imply a population of about 30 millions".[10] According to the same method of calculation (no other method seems to be possible) the population of the Vijayanagara Empire under Krishṇa would be 18 millions since his troops which fought at Raichur in 1520, numbered, according to Nuniz,[11] 600,000.

THE CITIES

The important towns on the West coast were Ankōlā, Mirjān, Honāwar, Bhatkal, Baindūru, Bārakūr, Basrūr, Mangalore and Kuṁbla.[12] In the central part of the Empire, Raichur, Ādavāni, Ānēgondi (Hastināvati), Vijayanagara, Penukonda, Śrīrangapaṭṭaṇa, Dwārasamudra, Ikkēri, and Bankāpura were important.[13] In the eastern part Śrīśailam,[14] Koṇḍavīḍu,[15] Udayagiri,[16] Kāla-

6. Major, p. 26.
7. *Ibid*, p. 20.
8. Barbosa I, p. 194.
9. F.E., p. 237.
10. India at the death of Akbar, p. 19.
11. F.E., p. 327.
12. Paes F.E., p. 236, Barbosa I, pp. 182 to 197.
13. Raichur, Briggs III, pp. 49-50, for Śrīrangapaṭṭaṇa and Ikkēri see Rāyavāchakamu, sources p. 111. For Bankāpura see F.E., p. 122 f.n., for the rest of the towns in the central part, see E.C.V. part I, Bl. 75.
14. V.R. II Kurnool 454.
15. E.I. VI., p. 230.
16. V.R. II Nellore 791.

hasti,[17] Tirupati,[18] Chandragiri,[19] Pulicāt,[20] Mailāpūr,[21] Kānchi, Chidambaram, Kumbhakōṇam, Tanjore, Madura, Śrīvilliputtūr, Tinnevelly, Ramēśwaram and Dhanuṣkoṭi.[22]

The greatest city of the time was Vijayanagara. For a detailed description of the city in its palmy days one must read the accounts of Abdūr Razzāk,[23] Barbosa,[24] and Paes.[25] The city, as it existed in the time of Krishṇa, could be divided into three parts, *viz.*, Hampi, the nucleus of the city, containing the Virūpāksha temple and the magnificent bazaar in its front;[26] the citadel containing the king's palace, the administrative offices, the Hazara Rama temple and the House of Victory, and Nāgalāpūr (modern Hospet) built by Krishṇa.[27] All these 3 parts had a plentiful supply of water. The Turuttu channel and the Tungabhadra supplied water to Hampi then as now.[28] The citadel being on a higher level than Hampi could not be supplied with water by this channel. Mr. Longhurst guesses that the citadel was supplied with water by wells.[29] Nāgalāpūr's water-supply was from the tank constructed by Krishṇa.[30] Paes says that there were 100,000 houses in the city.[31] This meant that the city had a population of 500,000.

AGRICULTURE

Barbosa, Paes, and Nuniz give an account of the fertility, crops, cattle and agricultural operations in the various parts of the Empire. The Canara coast was very fruitful and contained many farmsteads.[32] Much rice was grown here and exported to Malabar

17. V.R.I. Chittoor 135.
18. A.S.R. 1908-9, p. 176.
19. E.C. V, part I Bl. 75.
20. Barbosa II, p. 132.
21. *Ibid*, p. 126.
22. All the towns from Kāñchi to Dhanuṣkōṭi are mentioned in Rāyavāchakamu sources p. 117, with the exception of Tanjore for which see Nuniz F.E., pp. 384-5.
23. Major, p. 24.
24. Barbosa I, pp. 200-2.
25. F.E., pp. 253-58.
26. F.E., p. 260 Paes.
27. F.E., p. 246.
28. Longhurst Hampi Ruins, p. 51.
29. *Ibid*, p. 51.
30. F.E., p. 365.
31. *Ibid*, p. 290.
32. Barbosa I, p. 184.

and Ormuz.[33] The lands near Goa produced much wheat, grains, gingelly and cotton, and contained many goats and cattle.[34]

Paes[35] describes the route from Bhatkal to Vijayanagara (probably via Honāwar and Bankāpūr[36]) as well cultivated and very fertile and provided with quantities of cattle such as cows, buffalos and sheep. There was plenty of rice and Indian corn (Joḷa or Jawar), grains, beans and an infinity of cotton and plenty of good wheat. The region round Bankāpūr, the present Dhārwār district, is described by Nuniz[37] as very rich in seed-plots and cattle-breeding farms.

In the eastern parts the district of Pulicat grew no grains but produced abundance of rice.[38] The Coromandel coast is described by Barbosa[39] as very fruitful and abounding in rice, flesh-meat, wheat and all vegetables.

AGRICULTURAL OPERATIONS

The cultivation of rice is described by Barbosa,[40] thus, " All around they sow it in valleys and flats with water for it is sown and reaped in water; they plough the land as we do with oxen and buffaloes yoked in pairs, the plough-share has a hallow in it wherein the rice is carried when the land is flooded, and as the share ploughs the rice goes on settling down under water and earth. On dry land they sow by hand. And every year this land (in Majandur on the Canara coast) bears 2 crops."

IRRIGATION

Sir Thomas Munro[41] described the country which is situated round the capital, *viz.*, the Ceded districts or Rāyalasīma, in the beginning of the 19th century thus; " To attempt the construction of new tanks is perhaps a more hopeless experiment than the repair of those which have been filled up, for there is scarcely any place where a tank can be made that has not been applied to this purpose

33. *Ibid* I, pp. 185 and 188.
34. Nuniz F.E., p. 376.
35. F.E., p. 237.
36. F.E., p. 122 footnote.
37. *Ibid*, p. 386.
38. Varthema's Travels, p. 195.
39. Barbosa II, p. 125
40. *Ibid* I, p. 192.
41. Quoted in Gribble's History of Deccan, Vol. I, p. 188.

by the inhabitants. In a sub-division of the Cuddapah district there were in an area of 3,574 square miles no less than 4,194 tanks of various sizes."

This result was mainly due to the irrigation policy followed by the Vijayanagara Emperors. Krishṇa declared that "the State should create irrigation facilities by the construction of tanks and the excavation of canals; the land should be given on a favourable rate of assessment to poor ryots for cultivation which would of course bring in plenty of money to the treasury."[42]

Krishṇa constructed a huge tank near the southern entrance to Nāgalāpur or Hospet.[43] Nuniz[44] describes the usefulness of this tank and Krishṇa's interest in the welfare of his people thus, "By means of this water they made many improvements in the city and many channels by which they irrigated rice-fields and gardens and in order that they might improve their lands he (Krishṇa) gave the people the lands which are irrigated by this water free for 9 years, until they had made their improvements, so that the revenue already amounts to 20,000 pardaos." Besides this, Krishṇa constructed the great dam and channel at Korragāl and the Basavaṇṇa channel both of which are still in use and are of great value to the country.[45] His provincial governor Koṇḍamarasayya built in the Udayagiri province the Anantasāgaram and the Kāluvāyi tanks.[46]

Vyāsarāya, who was honoured by Krishṇa by many grants of lands[47] built the Vyāsarāya Samudra on the border between the Kolar and Cuddapah districts[48].

INDUSTRIAL PRODUCTION

With regard to the industrial position of India and Europe in the sixteenth century, Mr. Moreland says, "It is still to my mind indisputable that in the matter of industry, India was more advanced relatively to western Europe than she is to-day." [49] One important

42. Āmuktamālyada IV 26; See Mr. N. Venkataramaṇayya's Studies in the History of the II Dynasty of Vijayanagara, p. 186.

43. F.E., p. 364. The tank is called Rāyarakēre or king's tank, but it is now dry.

44. F.E., p. 365.

45. F.E., p. 162.

46. 336 of 1915.

47. 390 of 1919, 363-A. By V. R. I.

48. Q.J.M.S., October 1924. Somanātha's Vyāsayōgi Charithra

49. India at the death of Akbar, pp 155-56.

difference between the present and mediæval Indian industrial organization is the extreme dependence of the people of India on other countries for all their requirements except foodstuffs, at the present time. In mediæval times India was self-sufficient. She imported mostly horses for war and luxuries for the court. The lives of the common people were in no way affected by the foreign imports.

TEXTILES

We have very little information regarding the centres and methods of production. The foreign writers give us information mostly with regard to the foreign trade while the Indian writers took existing conditions for granted.

Kan-pa-mai, 167 miles from Calicut (which is identified with Coimbatore), was a great centre of cotton manufacture. In that place and around it a kind of cloth called chit-li (chih-li-pu) was made. It was sold there for 8 or 10 gold pieces. Raw silk, dyed in various colours was woven into flowered pattern goods and made up into pieces 4 to 5 feet wide and 12 to 13 feet long. Each length was sold for one hundred gold pieces.[50]

The next great centre of textile manufacture was Pulicat. Abundance of printed cotton cloths, worth much money in Malaca, Pegu, Sumatra, and Gujarat and Malabar, were manufactured.[51] Very fine cloth was made near Goa.[52]

MINING AND METALLURGY

Diamonds. Much of the diamond in Vijayanagara came from Vajrakurur about 20 miles south-west of Gooty. The Governor of Gooty was to give all diamonds which exceeded 20 mangelins in weight to the king.[53] Garcia de Orta, who came to India in 1534 says that there were 2 or 3 rocks in Vijayanagara which yielded many diamonds. He also located another diamond mine in the Deccan.[54] False diamonds, rubies, topazes and white sapphires were fabricated and were good imitations of the true ones.[55] Sapphires were found near Calicut.[56]

50. Mahaun. J.R.A.S. 1896, p. 345.
51. Barbosa II, p. 132.
52. Nuniz F.E., p. 386.
53. *Ibid*, pp. 388 and 389.
54. Barbosa I, p. 226, footnote by Dames.
55. *Ibid*, II. p. 221.
56. *Ibid* II, p. 223.

Metals. In Vijayanagara city both wrought and unwrought metals, copper in abundance and quicksilver were found.[57] Loads of iron were exported from Bhatkal.[58]

Metal work. Metal work consisted in making (*i*) Jewellery, (*ii*) Weapons of warfare and (*iii*) Household articles.

(*i*) Jewellery was required by (*a*) Temples, (*b*) Court, (*c*) Soldiers and (*d*) Common people.

(*a*) Krishṇa was lavish in presenting jewellery to the temples. An example will suffice. He gave to Kālahasthīśwara a necklace set with precious stones, worshipping paraphernalia, and a golden prabhāvaḷi set with precious gems.[58-a]

(*b*) The dancing girls attached to the Court were fabulously rich. They wore ornaments made of gold, emeralds, diamonds, rubies, and pearls from head to feet. After minutely describing every one of the ornaments Paes exclaims, " Who is he that could tell of the costliness and the value of what each of these women carries on her person."[59]

(*c*) The idea of decorating the persons was so strong that soldiers and even horses and elephants were decorated. The foreheads of horses and elephants were covered with silver or gold plates set with many huge precious stones. The armours of cavaliers were gilded both inside and out.[60]

(*d*) Men wore only ear-rings set with fine pearls. But women wore nose-rings (ముక్కెర), ear-rings, necklaces of gold and jewels and very fine coral beads and bracelets of gold and precious stones.[61]

(*ii*) *Weapons.* The weapons of the horsemen were swords, battle-axes, javelins and shafts. The Muslim soldiers in Krishṇa's army had javelins and Turkish bows, with many bombs, spears and fire missiles. The bows were plated with gold and silver and the arrows were very neat and feathered.[62] When we remember that his army was usually a million strong and could be in-

57. *Ibid* I, p. 203.
58. *Ibid* I, p. 189.
58-a. 150 of 1924 and 180 of 1922.
59. F.E., 273 and 274.
60. *Ibid.*, pp. 276 and 277.
61. Barbosa I, 205 ; 207-8.
62. F.E., pp. 276 and 277.

creased on occasions to two millions we can imagine the work it provided to the metal workers.[63]

(*iii*) *Household articles.* Metal vessels were used for cooking purposes. Barbosa says that much copper was used for cooking pots and other vessels by the country people.[64] Metal vessels were used in worshipping gods. Purandara Dasa of this period in his famous song " Udara vairāgyavidu " compares the worship kit of a pretentious Brahmin to a brass-ware shop.[65]

Perfumery. Of the minor industries the most important seems to have been the production of scents. The people of this period would appear to have had an insatiable love for perfumes and flowers. " The substances with which they are always anointed are these : white sandars-wood, aloes, musk and saffron, all ground fine and kneaded with rose water. With these they anoint themselves after bathing and so they are always highly scented."[66] Rose water, camphor, musk and scented materials were available in Vijayanagara.[67] Rose water could also be had in Pulicat.[68]

Wages. Barbosa says that it was the custom among the Muslims and Indians that when the workmen came to begin any work they gave them a certain quantity of rice to eat and when they departed at night they gave them a *fanam* each.[69] Nuniz confirms Barbosa with regard to the daily payment of wages. " He has 1,600 grooms who attend the horses, and has also 300 horse trainers and 2,000 artificers, namely, blacksmiths, masons and carpenters and washermen, who wash his clothes. These are the people he has and pays every day ; he gives them their allowance at the gate of the palace."[70]

COMMERCE

Foreign Trade of South India in the 15th century. The essential feature of the foreign trade of South India in the 15th century

63. *Ibid,* pp. 279 and 280.
64. Barbosa I, p. 191.
65. Purandara Dāsana Padagalu II, p. 26. He was the contemporary of Vyāsa Rāya. *Ibid* 214, 215, and 216, part I.
66. Barbosa I, p. 205.
67. *Ibid* I, p. 203.
68. *Ibid* II, p. 132.
69. *Ibid.* II, p. 99.
70. F.E., p. 381.

was the concentration of business on the west coast, particularly the Malabar ports, of which Calicut was the most important.[71] Merchants from South Africa, Abyssinia and Arabia brought articles to this port for distribution in India.[72] Ships from Pegu and Malacca on their way to the Red Sea halted at Calicut and took Indian goods for distribution in various directions. Thus Malabar was a great commercial centre. The whole of this trade was in the hands of the Muslims who had settled in all the important ports of the Indian Ocean from Madagascar to Malacca.[73] With the coming of the Portuguese towards the close of the fifteenth century this monopoly of the Muslims, of the carrying trade of India, was broken.

Foreign Trade in the 16th century. Barbosa's account written between 1504 and 1515 gives an account of how the foreign trade was passing from the hands of the Muslims to the hands of the Portuguese. "The Ormus ships come hither (Bhatkal) every year, bring horses in great numbers and many pearls, which they sell here to the kingdom of Narsynga, but now on account of our armies, they take them to Goa, with many other kinds of merchandise. A few ships belonging to the Moors venture to come to this spot (Bhatkal) to take in loads of spices, notwithstanding that by the rules and orders of our people they are forbidden so to do."[74]

Albuquerque's occupation of Goa[75] affected adversely the trade of the Malabar ports and placed Bijāpūr and Vijayanagara completely in the hands of the Portuguese for all their foreign requirements, especially horses from Arabia and Persia.

Articles of foreign trade. Exports. The articles of export were cloth, rice, iron, saltpetre, sugar and spices.[76] The Portuguese bought cloth from the Vijayanagara merchants either at Ankōla or Honāwar.[77] Pulicat exported a large quantity of printed cloth to Malacca, Pegu and Sumatra.[78] Rice (mostly of the coarse variety) was exported from Basrūr, Bārakūr, and Mangalore to Malabar, the Maldive Islands, Ormus and Aden.[79] Loads of iron were bought

71. Moreland, p. 199.
72. Abdur Razzak, p. 13.
73. Moreland, pp. 198-200.
74. Vol. I, p. 189.
75. Commentaries II, pp. 100-111.
76. Heras. Āravīḍu, pp. 62 and 63 and Barabosa I, pp. 189-198.
77. Heras, pp. 62 and 63.
78. Barbosa II, p. 132.
79. *Ibid.* I, pp. 189-198.

by the Malabar people from Bhatkal.[80] The Portuguese also bought iron from the Vijayanagara merchants.[81] Powdered sugar was exported to Ormus from Bhatkal.[82] Ships from Mecca came to Bhatkal for spices.[83]

Imports. The imports into the empire were horses, elephants, pearls, copper, coral, mercury, vermilion, china silks and velvet.

In 1515 Krishṇa proposed to Albuquerque to send him 1,000 horses annually for £20,000. The Portuguese viceroy refused the offer saying that such a privilege would destroy trade. Albuquerque cared more for the improvement of the Portuguese trade than for the friendship of Vijayanagara. Nevertheless, the relations between the Portuguese and Krishṇa continued to be friendly.[84] Elephants were imported from Ceylon.[85] Pearls came from Ormus.[86] The Portuguese merchants supplied copper, coral and vermilion to Vijayanagara.[87] China supplied silks through the Portuguese and spices and drugs through the Muslims.[88] Bengal and Malacca exported spices and drugs to Vijayanagara.[89] Velvets came from Mecca.[90]

Coasting and inland trade. Among the communities engaged in the coasting and inland trade the most prominent were the Muslims, the Malabares and Chettis or Śettis. The Muslims and the Malabares were more prominent in the coastal trade while the latter confined themselves mostly to internal trade.

The Muslims. Though their importance as a trading community received a set-back owing to the coming of the Portuguese at the time we are considering, the Muslims still controlled much of the Indian coastal trade. They were to be seen in every one of the important ports on the Indian coast. They were a prosperous com-

80. *Ibid.* I, p. 189.
81. Heras, pp. 61 and 62.
82. Barbosa I, p. 189.
83. *Ibid.* I, p. 188.
84. Heras, p. 59.
85. Barbosa II, p. 113.
86. *Ibid.* I, p. 189.
87. Heras, pp. 62 and 63.
88. Heras, pp. 62 and 63 and Barbosa II, p. 129.
89. Barbosa II, p. 125.
90. F.E., p. 276.

munity.[91] While the foreign trade on the west coast was fast passing out of their hands they were struggling to maintain their position on the eastern coast. They brought goods from China, Malacca and Bengal to Coromandel coast.[92]

The Malabares were very enterprising. They supplied their country's products, *viz.*, spices, cocoanut products, palm sugar and palm wine to the Canara coast and took back coarse rice and iron.[93]

The Śettis in the Kannaḍa and Telugu countries and Chettis in the Tamil countries carried on the internal trade of the Empire.[94] The Chettis in Tamil Nāḍ were men of high standing, dealing in abundance of precious stones and pearls.[95] They were noted for their cunning in every kind of traffic in goods.[96]

Articles of inland trade. The Koṇḍavīḍu inscription of Nādindḷa Gōpa gives a list of the articles of inland trade.[97] The list includes most food-stuffs (with the exception of rice) such as pulses, millets, wheat, vegetables, salt, tamarind, spices, cocoanut, ghee, jaggery, sugar, betel leaves and areca nut, dyes such as dammer and gallnuts, metals such as iron, lead, tin and copper, raw materials such as cotton and manufactures like steel chisels, cotton thread and gunny bags.

Means of communication and roads. Carts were known, but were not made much use of, probably due to the bad condition of the roads. Paes proves the existence of wheeled traffic when he says, " across this open space (in a part of the city of Vijayanagara) pass all the carts and conveyances carrying stores and everything else.[98] Pack animals and porters were the usual means of transport. The Koṇḍavīḍu inscription quoted above says that the means of transport were kāvaḍīs, headloads, pack-horses, pack-bullocks

91. E. and D. IV, p. 101.
92. Barbosa II, p. 125.
93. *Ibid.* I, pp. 186-197.
94. *Ibid.* II, 125, for Chettis, Lingāyats and Brahmins also took part in trade. See for the former Barbosa II, p. 125 and for the latter F.E., p. 390 Nuniz.
95. Barbosa II, p. 123.
96. *Ibid.* II, p. 126.
97. E.I. VI, pp. 230-239.
98. F.E., p. 254. See Appadorai Economic conditions in South India, where literary and inscriptional evidence is quoted for the existence of carts in S. India. Mr. Moreland's statement (p. 7) that in S. India carts were practically unknown has to be modified.

and asses.[99] Barbosa says that pepper was brought to Vijayanagara from Malabar on asses and pack-cattle.[100] Paes speaks of five or six thousand pack-oxen carrying merchandise from Vijayanagara to Bhatkal.[101] One conductor or driver was in charge of 20 or 30 oxen.[102]

Vijayanagara was the centre in South India. One road ran from Vijayanagara to Goa through Bankāpūr.[103] Another road seems to have run from Bankāpūr to Bhatkal via Honāwar.[104] Paes came from Bhatkal to Vijayanagara ; but none of the intermediate places can be satisfactorily identified. There seems to have been a road from Vijayanagara to Mailāpūr passing through Penugonda, Chandragiri, Tirupati and Pulicat.[105]

Krishṇa's military campaigns and religious tours may point to the existence of the following roads :

(1) Vijayanagara to Śivanasamudra and Śrīrangapaṭṭaṇa.[106]

(2) Do. to Ādavāni and Raichur.[107]

(3) Do. to Udayagiri, Koṇḍaviḍu, Kondapalli and along the coast to Simhāchalam and Śrī-kūrmam.[108]

(4) Tirupati and Kāḷahasti to Kānchi, Chidambaram, Madura, Rāmēśwaram and Dhanushkoṭi.[109]

CURRENCY AND PRICES

Vijayanagara had a gold standard with a gold currency. The standard coin was the *varāha.* Dr. M. H. Krishṇā[110] says that the rulers of Vijayanagara retained as their standard the weight they

99. E.I. VI, pp. 230-239.
100. I, p. 203.
101. F.E., p. 237.
102. Barbosa I, p. 163.
103. Barros says that Bankāpūr was on the road to Vijayanagara from Goa. See F.E., p. 122 footnote.
104. *Ibid.*
105. This was the route followed by Nicolo Conti. Major p. 7.
106. Sources, pp. 112 and 113.
107. F.E., p. 323.
108. F.E., pp. 316-319. Symandry is not Rajahmundry but Simhādri or Simhāchalam. For Śrīkūrmam see 56 of 1912.
109. Rāyavāchakamu. Sources, p. 116.
110. Deccan Numismatics in Mss.

had inherited from one of their predecessors the Kālachūrya, Murāri, namely about 52.5 to 53 grains, the average being generally 52.7 grains. The following coins existed in Krishṇa's time :[111]

Gold	(1)	Varāha
Do.	(2)	Half varāha (Pratāpa)
Do.	(3)	Quarter varāha
Do.	(4)	Haṇa (Fanam) 1/20th varāha
Silver	(5)	Tar 1/60th varāha
Copper	(6)	Jital 1/90th varāha

The Pardao or Pratāpa was current throughout the year, according to Paes.[112] Barbosa found it in use in Gujarat.[113]

There is abundant evidence to show that the prices were very low. Paes describes Vijayanagara as the best provided city in the world and stocked with provisions such as rice, wheat, grains, Indian corn (Jola or Jawar), and a certain amount of barley, beans, pulses, horse-gram and many other seeds which grow in the country. He says that these were very cheap. Fowls were sold at the rate of three for a Vintem (1.7d. or 1½ annas) inside the city and four for the same coin outside. One Vintem or 1½ annas sufficed for the purchase of 6 or 8 partridges or 12 to 14 doves.[114] Grapes sold at three bunches a fanam or Haṇa or 8 annas and pomegranates 10 for a fanam. In the city markets 12 live sheep could be had for a Pardao or Rs. 5 and in the hills 14 or 15 for the same coin.[115] In Vijayanagara a knight with a horse and a slave girl was expected to live on a monthly allowance of 4 or 5 parados, *i.e.* at Rs. 20 or Rs. 25.[116]

THE STANDARD OF LIFE

Upper Classes. We know more of the life of the upper classes than of the classes below them in the social scale. The fact was that the life in the court appeared so interesting to the foreigners that they have devoted more attention to this subject than to the life of the poor. We have some evidence of the amount of money that the members of this class could spend. We can imagine the

111. Deccan Numismatics in Mss.
112. F.E., p. 283.
113. Barbosa, first Vol., p. 156.
114. F.E., p. 258.
115. F.E., p. 375.
116. Barbosa I., p. 210.

money available for spending by the king when we are told that he was in the habit of saving 10,000,000 *Pratāps* every year.[117] But the nobles did not save. They knew only how to spend. Probably, the fear that their property might be confiscated by the king at any time, left them no option but to spend.[118] We hear of ministers and governors with revenues ranging from 1,100,000 *Pratāps* to 15,000 *Pratāps*. Out of this revenue the governors or ministers were expected to pay the king roughly about 1/3rd, and with the remainder they were also expected to maintain their quota of horses, elephants, and soldiers. We are told that the full quota was not usually maintained by the nobles. Thus, a large part of the income of the nobles was available for spending.[119]

Housing. The King of Vijayanagara according to Barbosa, " has great and fair palaces, with many enclosed courts and great houses very well built, within them are wild open spaces, with water tanks in great numbers. . . . . . In the city as well there are palaces after the same fashion wherein dwell the great lords and governors thereof."[120] Paes describes the street containing the nobles' houses near the king's palace thus:—" from here to the King's palace is all streets and rows of houses, very beautiful, and houses of Captains and other rich and honourable men; you will see rows of houses with many figures and decorations pleasing to look at."[121] The wide street in front of the Virūpāksha temple in Hampi is described by Paes as " a very beautiful street of very beautiful houses with balconies and arcades."[122] The houses in Nāgalāpūr or Modern Hospet were all one-storeyed, and flat-roofed. They had pillars and were all open with verandahs inside out, where they could accommodate their guests and they looked like houses belonging to the King.[123]

Clothing. The dress of the nobles in Vijayanagara is described by Barbosa thus—" their men wear certain clothes, a girdle below wound very tightly in many folds and short white shirts of cotton or silk or coarse brocade, which are gathered between the thighs

117. F.E., p. 282.
118. *Ibid.*, p. 385.
119. *Ibid.*, pp. 384 to 389.
120. Barbosa I., p. 203.
121. F.E., p. 254.
122. F.E., p. 260. The street still exists but the houses are in a ruined condition.
123. F.E., p. 246.

but open in front; on their heads, they carry small turbans, and some wear silk or brocade caps, they wear their rough shoes on their feet without stockings. They wear also other large garments thrown over their shoulders like capes."[124]

The dress of the women of the upper classes is described by Barbosa as follows : " the women wear white garments of very thin cotton, or silk of bright colours, five yards long: one part of which is girt round them below and the other part they throw over one shoulder and across their breasts in such a way that one arm and shoulder remains uncovered...... They wear leather shoes well-embroidered in silk ; their heads are uncovered and the hair is tightly gathered into a becoming knot on the top of the head."[125]

Food. Except the Brahmins, Vaiśyas, Lingāyats and Jainas, the rest ate meat and fish.[126] Nuniz's statement that the kings of Vijayanagara ate sparrows, rats, cats, and lizards, is hardly believable.[127] The Āmuktamālyada says that the dishes changed from season to season. The list of preparations it gives are all to be seen to-day.[128] The chewing of betel-leaves appeared peculiar to the foreign travellers and most of them have described the process in detail.[129]

Umbrellas made of finely-worked silk with many golden tassels and many precious stones were used by the nobles.[130] At night they used torches of oil—the torches ranging from 4 to 12 according to rank. The king, however, had 100 to 150 torches.[131]

The Middle Class. Next in rank to the upper classes came the merchants. We know very little about this class. The Muslims, who were mostly merchants, were prosperous as has already been told. They put on better dresses than the common people. They used furniture unlike the others.[132]

The common people. The picture that we get from the inscriptions about the life of the common people is in total contrast to the

124. Barbosa I., pp. 205 and 206.
125. *Ibid.*, pp. 207 and 208.
126. Barbosa I., pp. 217 and 218 and Paes F.E., p. 242. See Saletore II., p. 311 footnote.
127. F.E., p. 375.
128. I Canto verses 80-83.
129. Barbosa I., p. 169.
130. *Ibid.* I., pp. 206 and 207.
131. Nuniz F.E., p. 380.
132. Barbosa I., p. 147.

accounts of the travellers which mostly relate to the life of the upper classes. Heavy taxation oppressed the cultivators who, in one case at least refused to pay them,[133] but in most cases, migrated to other provinces, where taxation was probably lighter. In Ramnad, the farmers were so much harassed by heavy taxation that they migrated to another place in 1500 A.D.[134] In 1507 A.D. the people of the North Arcot district paid 33 taxes, 32 of which were levied by the temple and one by the crown.[135] Another inscription of 1512 A.D. states that Krishṇa remitted the taxes which were collected from the dēvādāya and brahmādāya lands.[136] An inscription of Śrīmushṇam in the Chidambaram taluk tells how heavy taxation led to the migration of farmers and how Sīnappa Nāyakar an officer of Krishṇa, enquired into the grievances of the ryots and reduced the taxation.[137] Another inscription states that the Sthānīkas of the temple of Perumāḷ-kariyavar went on a deputation to Krishṇa in Vijayanagara and complained of the injustice done by the authorities stationed at Dēviyakuricchi village belonging to the temple. The chief Amaram Timmaraśu introduced them to the king, and got their grievances redressed.[138] Two facts emerge from these inscriptions: (1) the provincial governors and officers oppressed the people with heavy taxation and (2) Krishṇa was determined to put down oppression whenever it was brought to his notice.

Occasionally the foreign travellers have something to say about the life of the common people. Barbosa says that their houses were thatched, "but none-the-less are very well-built and arranged according to occupations in long streets with many open places."[139] The foreign travellers were struck by the insufficient clothing of the people. One example will suffice. Abdur Razzāk says that the people were naked except for a *lankouṭah* from the navel to above the knee.[140] The other descriptions are similar.[141] It must be noted, however, that no traveller attributed the insufficiency of clothing to the poverty of the people.[142] Nicolo Conti says " they cannot wear

133. (92 of 1918).
134. (50 of 1916).
135. 353, 355, 396 of 1912.
136. 180 of 1913.
137. 246 of 1916.
138. 449 of 1913.
139. Barbosa I., p. 202.
140. E. and D. IV., pp. 100–101.
141. Nikitin. Major p. 12 and Barbosa I., p. 181.
142. See Appadorai Vol. II., pp. 759 and 760.

more clothing on account of the great heat and for the same reason they wear only sandals and not shoes."[143] Abdur Razzāk says that the costume of the beggar and the king was the same,[144] no doubt, on account of the climate. We have not much evidence with regard to the food of the common people. Jowar or Jola or Indian corn appears to have been the staple food of the common people in the central part of the Empire.[145]

BIBLIOGRAPHY

	Abbreviations.	Full Names.
1.	Appadorai.	Economic conditions in South India. (1000-1500 A.D. 2 Vols.)
2.	Barbosa.	The book of Duarte Barbosa 2 Vols. edited by L. Dames.
3.	Briggs.	Rise of the Muhammadan power in India by Firishta translated by Briggs.
4.	Commentaries.	Commentaries of Afonso D'albuquerque.
5.	E. & D.	Elliot and Dowson—History of India as told by its own historians.
6.	E. C.	Epigraphia Carnatica.
7.	E. I.	Epigraphia Indica.
8.	F. E.	Forgotten Empire by Sewell.
9.	Heras.	The Aravidu dynasty of Vijayanagara.
10.	J. R. A. S.	Journal of the Royal Asiatic Society.
11.	Major.	India in the 15th century. Ed. by Major.
12.	Moreland.	India at the death of Akbar.
13.	Q. J. M. S.	Quarterly Journal of the Mythic Society.
14.	Saletore.	Social and Political life in Vijayanagara.
15.	Sources.	Sources of Vijayanagara History—Ed. by Dr. S. K. Aiyangar.
16.	V. R.	V. Rangacharya—Inscriptions of the Madras Presidency. 3 Vols.
17.	336 of 1915.	Refers to inscriptions collected in that year, noted in the annual reports on South Indian Epigraphy.

143. Major, p. 22.
144. E. and D. IV., pp. 101-102.
145. F.E., pp. 237 and 333.

19

Krishnadevaraya and his Literary Circle

By

Mr. Nidhathavolu Venkat Rao, B.A.

Imperial Bank of India, Coconada.

The reign of Krishnadēvarāya is a glorious chapter in South Indian Literary History. The Imperial Court had representatives of Sanskrit, Telugu, Kanarese and Tamil poets, who contributed largely to their respective literatures. Krishnadēvarāya was not merely a patron of letters but was himself a scholar and a poet of rare merit. His accomplished poetical scholarship, mingled with that of religious toleration, his proverbial patronage of poets and his extraordinary grasp of human nature, made his Imperial Court "*Bhuvana Vijayam*," the resort of every wandering ministrel and the peripatetic poet. Krishnadēvarāya bestowed the highest praise on the Telugu language, and his reign is one of the brightest periods in Telugu literature as we shall see in this paper. Not only Telugu literature, but Sanskrit and other South Indian vernaculars received equal patronage and added lustre to the grandeur of a reign, the history of which is to be written in golden letters in the annals of South India. We shall first take up Sanskrit.

SANSKRIT

In the introduction to his Telugu work Āmuktamālyadā, Krishnadēvarāya states that he wrote the following works in Sanskrit:—

(1) Madālasā Charitra; (2) Satya Vadhū prēṇanamu; (3) Sakalakathā Sārasangrahamu; (4) Jñana Chintāmaṇi; and (5) Rasamanjari.[2]

1. Ahalya Raju Ramabhadra Kavi, one of the Court poets of Krishnadēvarāya wrote a Telugu Kāvya of the same name. The book is still unprinted but the introductory portion is now printed by the Telugu Academy of Coconada.

2. Should be distinguished from Rasamanjari, a famous work in Sanskrit poetics by Bhānukavi. The Telugu Academy possesses a copy of the Jāmbavatī Kalyāṇam, and I had an opportunity of going through the work. The academy it seems, wanted to bring out the work and published a portion of the first act in Samskrit Sahitya Parishad Patrika in Calcutta. The copy on hand is full of errors and the printing was stopped for want of a second copy. (Vide Samskrit Sahitya Parishad Patrika, *Vol. XVII,* No. 6, October 1934).

Though unfortunately all of the above are lost to us, yet we may infer from the verse describing the above that the first is noted for its rhetoric, the second for its suggestivity, the third for its *purāṇic* lore, the fourth for its expression, and the fifth for its melody. In a Sanskrit anthology known as 'Prapancha Darpaṇam,' the anthologist quoted some stanzas from Satyavadhuprēṇanamu and Rasamanjari, and attributed their authorship to Allasāni Peddanna, the poet Laureate of Krishnadēvarāya. He further attributed another work on poetics called "Alamkāra-sāra-sangraham" to Krishnadēvarāya, a work unknown to us till now. The quotations from 'Prapancha Darpaṇam' cannot be taken by us as correct. The anthologist is a modern, and of Āndhra Dēśa, where the tradition that Āmuktamālyadā was written by Peddanna is still current.

Another Sanskrit work of Krishnadēvarāya known to us is Jāmbavatī Kalyāṇam'. It is a drama in five acts and describes the marriage of Jāmbavatī, daughter of Jāmbavān, and one of the eight *Paṭṭa Mahishis* of Śrī-Krishna. From the prologue, we learn that the drama was enacted during the Chaitra (Spring-festival) of Virupāksha, the tutelary god of Karnāṭak Empire residing at Hēma-kūṭa, in the city of Vijayanagara. The style of the drama is excellent and I give from each act a verse to illustrate the point.

Jāmbavatī Kalyāṇam.

Act I. वेतण्डोच्चण्डगण्डस्रुतबहुलमदस्यन्दगन्धानुबन्ध-
भ्राम्यद्भृङ्गानुषङ्गप्रकटपदरवोदीर्णकर्णातिथेयाः ।
चञ्चत्संचारपञ्चाननिनदसभाभुग्नकुम्भीन्द्रदम्भा-
वन्यावन्या वि[पि]नागा विदधतिकुतुकं चारुविन्यासभाजः ॥

Act II. स्वभावशिशिरस्फुरन्मधुरिमस्रवन्तीजलं
तलाः प्रकृतिशीतलाः प्रतिपदं तरूणाममी ।
कलाञ्चलल्लशुकशारिकामुखविहङ्गवाग्भङ्गयो-
भरन्तिहृदयस्य मे रुचिरहर्म्यवासस्पृहाम् ॥

Act III. मम मनइव पद्मं म्लानिमभ्येति कान्ता-
विरहमहमिवायं याति हा चक्रवाकः ।
रविरपरपयोधेरन्तरे रूढरागः
पतति महति मोहे मामकीनो यथात्मा ॥

Act IV. माया यामवती सृजन्ति बहुशो माहेन्द्ररत्नप्रभं
शोणाश्मद्युतिरातनोति कुहनासन्ध्यासमुज्जृम्भते ।
मिथ्यातारकजालकं कलयते मुक्तामणीनां चयं
सान्द्रं(म्लाय)यते सुधांशु (ह) षदाभ्यासामृषाचन्द्रिका ॥

Act V स्फारोत्तारविलोचनामृतझरीपूरैस्समासिच्यमां
लज्जावेशवशात्पुरस्सहचरीगात्रेणसंभाविता ।
आकम्पादयथा यथाप्रसरया गत्या शनैरेयुषी
लक्ष्यालक्ष्यवपुर्लता विजयते लावण्यकल्लोलिनी ॥

राजाधिराजपरमेश्वरसकलकलाभोजराजविभवमूरुरायर
गण्ड श्रीमत्कृष्णरायमहारायविरचितं
जाम्बवतीकल्याणं नाम नाटकम् समाप्तम्

LOLLA LAKSHMĪDHARA AND DIVĀKARA

Lolla Lakshmīdhara and Divākara, are the two great Sanskrit poets who adorned the court of Krishnadēvarāya. These two were formerly at the court of Vīra Rudra Gajapati, King of Orissa, and after Krishnadēvarāya's conquest, they became court poets at Vijayanagara. Of these two Lakshmīdhara is the greatest, and wrote many works of *Samviti, Sāhitya, Āgama, Jyōtisha,* and Philosophy. In the Colophon[3] at the end of his commentary on

3. Colophon I. इतिश्रीलोल्लुकुलसंप्रदायप्रवर्तकभ्रमराम्बिकावरप्रसादसमुल्लसितमहासारस्वतभट्टलोल्लटादिग्रन्थविवरणकर्तृश्रीमहामहोपाध्यायाचार्यसप्तमेन साहित्यपारिजात स्मृतिकल्पतरुप्रबन्धप्रबन्धृलक्ष्मीधरार्यषष्ठेन भारतार्णवपाठाख्यसाहित्यमीमांसाग्रन्थद्वय प्रकटितविरिञ्चिमिश्रपञ्चमेन मीमांसाद्वयादिजीवातुनिर्मातृपुरुषोत्तममहोपाध्यायनत्प्रा प्रभाकरामृतवाहिनीप्रभावाखण्डनखण्डनाद्यनेकप्रबन्धसन्दर्भप्रवर्तकनिरुपममहोपाध्याय लक्ष्मणार्यपौत्रेण नयविवेकदीपिकाप्रबन्धसंविधातृमहोपाध्याय विद्वत्सार्वभौमनूतनव्यासाद्यनेकबिरुद्धाङ्कितश्रीविश्वनाथभट्टारकतनयेनपार्वतीगर्भशुक्तिमुक्तारत्नेन बहुकृतसुधीरत्नेन मन्त्रात्मविशेषेण निखिलयामकतन्त्रार्णवावगाहरुद्रेण आश्रदीकृतः गजपति वीररुद्रेण नीलगिरिसुन्दरचरणारविन्दचञ्चरीकेण वाणीसहचरीवे.ण वाचस्पतिविलासाद्यनेकस्मृति

Saundarya Lahari of Śrī Śankara, he gives the names of his ancestors for six generations, and also their literary productions and titles, as well as the names of his own other works. He is the author of Kondbindu and Khajo inscriptions[4] in Krishnadēvarāya's time. Divākara wrote a Mahākāvya known as Bhāratamitra, concerning the story of Mahā Bharata.

MINISTER TIMMARASU

The famous minister Timmarasu was also a great Sanskrit scholar and wrote a commentary called " Manoramā " on Agastya's[5] Bāla Bhāratamu. This book is still unprinted.

NĀDINḌLA GOPA

Nādinḍla Gopamantri, Governor of Konḍavīḍu, is the nephew of minister Timmarasu. He wrote the ' Chandrika ' commentary on Krishna-miśras famous allegorical drama ' Prabhodha-Chandrodaya ' (the rise of the moon of intellect). The commentary is the earliest and the most authoritative, and reveals the depth of the learning of the commentator. He is also the author of Krishṇārjuna Samvādam, a *Dvipada* work in Telugu.

YUSA DĒCHA

The minister of Nādinḍla is Yusa Dēcha, a disciple of Lolla Lakshmīdhara already referred to, and he wrote commentaries on Śiva Pancha-stava. They are :—

1. Mahimnam	by	Pushpadarita.
2. Malhanam	,,	Malhana Kavi.
3. Anamayam	,,	Danḍin.
4. Hatyuddham	,,	Hatyuddha.
5. Nilakanṭha-stava	,,	Purāṇic.

निबन्धनलक्ष्मीधारद्यनेकसाहित्यनिबन्धननयविवेक भूषणाद्यनेकगुरुमतनिबन्धनयोगदी-पिकाद्यनेक पातञ्जलनिबन्धनमानवधर्मशास्त्रदीपिकाकर्णावतंसाद्यनेककाव्यकल्पकेन आश्रितजनकल्पकेन निग्रहानुग्रहकौशिकेन श्रीमहोपाध्यायलक्ष्मीधरदेशिकेन कृतेयं लक्ष्मीधराख्या सौन्दर्यलहरीस्तुतिव्याख्या संपूर्णा ॥

The importance of such colophons to research scholars need hardly be emphasised.

4. As Vidyānātha of Pratāprudrīya fame Epi. Indica. Vol. VI., pp. 117, 223.

5. Agastya the author of Bāla-Bhāratamu and seventy-three other works is now identified by scholars as those of Vidyānātha, of Pratāprudrīya fame.

It is not possible in this article to discuss the authorship of the above works and their nature. They are in vogue in the Telugu country since the eleventh century, and Dēcha wrote commentaries as they were found in his time. The commentaries are unprinted. It is to this minister that Tenali Ramalinga has dedicated his earliest work 'Udbhaṭavadhya charitramu' in Telugu. Dēcha's son Śankara Kavi is a Telugu poet of considerable merit and wrote the work, 'Harischandrōpākhyānam,' in *Prabandha* style.

BANDAM LAKSHMINĀRAYAN

Bandam Lakshminārayan wrote a work on music in five chapters called "Sangīta Sūryōḍayam," and dedicated it to Krishnadēvarāya. The introductory portion of the work is useful to historians, as it gives some rare information regarding Krishnadēvarāya's early campaigns. He was the nāṭyāchārya of Krishnadēvarāya's court, and from this we learn that Krishnadēvarāya had a great taste for music and dancing. Bandam Lakshminārayan is a great writer of music for his times, and had the following titles:—

1. Abhinava Bharatāchārya.
2. Rāyabāyaka.
3. Toḍarmalla.
4. Sūkshma Bharatāchārya.

He was amply rewarded by his patron. Krishnadēvarāya presented him all the royal insignia, elephants, gold palanquin, two white pearled-umbrellas and Malahari Vādyas.

Lakshminārayan's "Gem in music" is one Bhāratam Vishṇubhaṭṭa. Lakshminārayan had a taste for Telugu literature, and one Bhānukavi translated Panchratnam into Telugu, and dedicated it to Lakshminārayan. Bhānukavi has mentioned that there were other scholars and poets at that time, i.e., Narasinham Krishna, but did not give any further information regarding them.

ĪŚVARA DĪKṢITA

Īśvara Dīkṣita wrote a big and a small commentary on Vālmiki Ramayaṇam at the instance of Śrī Krishnadēvarāya. He recited the seven *Kāṇḍas* of the Ramayana in sixty *Ghaṭikas,* and elicited the admiration of Krishnadēvarāya.

TUKKĀ DĒVI

Tukkā Dēvi is Krishnadēvarāya's wife, the Gajapati's daughter. To her, the well known Tukkā Panchakam is attributed. Scholars have differed in the opinion as to the authorship of these five Ślokas. Tukkā's father, the Gajapatī is a patron of Sanskrit poets, and she might have learned Sanskrit at her father's place.We cannot close this subject without a reference to her, as she is the only Sanskrit poetess known to us in Krishnadēvarāya's time.

TELUGU

The Telugu poets and their works in the reign of Krishnadēvarāya are too well known to scholars both because of their literary greatness and historical sense. But adhering to the subject, a list of authors and works of the reign will not be out of place.

1. *Allasāni Peddanna*—a Nandavarika Brahmin and a converted Vaishṇava. The greatest poet of the reign and won the title, Āndhra Kavitā Pitāmahā. His Manucharitram, is as well known as his Harikathāsāram which is irrecoverably lost.

2. *Nandi Timmanna*—Niyōgi Śaiva—disciple of Aghōra Śiva Āchārya, nephew of Nandi Mallaya one of the twin poets who translated the Varāha purāṇam and dedicated it to Narsa Nayaka, father of Krishṇadēvarāya. He wrote Pārijātāpaharaṇam, and Thristhalī Daṇḍakam. The latter is quoted by Appa Kavi twice in his prosody. His Vānīvilāsam is lost.

3. *Mādayyagari Mallana*—Niyōgi—Śaiva disciple of the above Aghōra Śiva Āchārya ; author of Rājaśēkhara Charitra, and dedicated to Nādindla Appa-mantri brother of Gopamantri, and nephew of minister Timmarasu.

4. *Dhūrjaṭi*—A pure Śaiva of Kāḷahasti wrote Kāḷahasti Māhātmyam and Kālahastīsvara Śatakam.

5. *Ayyalarāju Ramabhadra Kavi*—Niyōga Vaishṇava, disciple of Mummiḍi Varadarāya. Author of Sakalamathasāra Sangraham and Rāmābhyudayam. The first was written at the command of Krishnadēvarāya, and the second work was dedicated to a nephew and the son-in-law of Krishnadēvarāya.

6. *Pingali Sūranna* }
7. *Rāmarāja Bhūshana* } supposed to have been in Krishnadēvarāya's reign, but wrote long after his reign. Pingali Sūranna's Rāghava-Pāṇḍavīyam, Kalāpurushodayam and Prabhāvatī-Pradyumnam are well known. Rāma Rāja Bhūshaṇa's Vasucharitra became so famous even in the early days of its reception that it was

translated into Sanskrit from Telugu by Kāḷahasti Kavi, a disciple of the famous Appayya Dīkshita.

8. *Tenali Ramalingam Kavi*—Niyōgi Brahmin, a Śaiva by name Rama*linga*, and after a Vaishṇava, by name Rama *Krishna*. His earlier work Udbhaṭārādhya-charitram was dedicated to Yusu Dēcha mantri, minister of Nādinḍla Gopamantri at Koṇḍaviḍu, about 1530 A.D. He was then known as Kumāra Bhārathi. His later works Panḍurangamāhātmyam and Ghaṭikāchala māhātmyam were written between 1560-70 A.D. His Kandarpakētu Vilāsam is now known to us only by quotations from an anthology in Telugu written about 1600 A.D.

9. *Kandukūru Rudra Kavi*. A goldsmith by caste. He wrote Nirankuśōpākhyānam an excellent Prabhandha, Sugrīva Vijayam, a Yakshagāna and a Hari Śataka. Tradition avers that he lived for twelve years in Krishnadēvarāya's court.

10. *Tallapāka Pedda Tirumalayya* belongs to the Sankarshaṇāchārya family at Tirupati Dēvastānam. He wrote many a Sankīrtana in praise of god Śrī Venkaṭesvara, the deity of Krishṇadēvarāya. He wrote Harivaṁsam (Dvipada), a Sṛngāra Śataka and a commentary in Telugu on Bhagavat Gita. His *nīti-sīesa-padya śatakam*, in *seesa* metres of intrinsic value, was highly appreciated by Krishnadēvarāya. Besides these he wrote Venkaṭēśvaroddhāraṇam in Telugu ; and a work on prosody.

11. *Tallapaka Chinnanna*. He was the son of the above Pedda Tirumalayya, and his real name is Tinevēngaḷanātha. He is known for his Dvipada (couplet) style and one of the greatest Sankarshaṇāchāryas of his times. He wrote Paramayōgi-vilāsamu and Ashṭamahishi Kalyāṇam.

12. *Chintalapūḍi Yellakavi* hailed from the court of Medinira-navam of *Poṭnūru* whom Krishṇadēvarāya conquered and at whose capital erected a pillar of victory. Krishṇadēvarāya tested his poetry and conferred upon him the title of Rādhāmādhavam for his work Rādhāmādhavam. He lived after Krishṇadēvarāya and wrote Vishṇumaya-nāṭakam and Tāraka Brahmarājiyam. The last work was dedicated to Nanja-Timmarasu, writer of Military Accounts of Achyutadēvarāya, successor of Krishnadēvarāya. Krishnadēvarāya's Telugu work Āmuktamālyadā is the crowning work of the age as it emanated from the crown. Vallabhācharya otherwise known as Kavi Dēvēndra wrote Līlāvatī of Bhaskarāchārya in

Telugu, and dedicated it to Bommalata-Kāḷa, the confidant of Krishṇadēvarāya and afterwards Achyutadēvarāya. Kumāra Mallama, the famous Telugu poetess and authoress of Rāmāyaṇa, was honoured by Krishnadēvarāya—Yeḍapāṭṭi Yerranna wrote Kumāranaishadham, and Malhana Charitra, and Sankusala Narsinha Kavi, author of Kavi Karṇarasāyanam belong to Krishnarāya's reign though they were not directly patronized by him.

KANARESE

Kanarese literature received great impetus from Krishnadēvarāya, and the following are some of the greatest poets of the reigin.

1. *Timmanna,* son of Bhānukavi of Bhāradvāja *Gōtra,* known as Karnāṭa Kavi Sārvabhauma, overlord of Kanarese poets. He began the Kanarese Mahabhāratam, left unfinished by Kumāra Vyāsa Nāraṇappa, from the Śānti-parva and completed it, and dedicated it to Krishnadēvarāya.

2. *Vyāsarāya or Vyasatīrtha.* The great Madhav saint of Krishnadēvarāya's time, disciple of Śrīpādarāya and founder of the Vyāsarāya *mutt.* He wrote many works like, Tarka Tānḍavam and Nyāyamrita and Tātparya-sangraha in Sanskrit. He has written many *Kīrtans* in Kanarese, which are still sung and which are full of devotion in praise of Śrī Krishna. Krishnadēvarāya respected Vyāsatīrtha so much that he offered his own *gadi* to him.

3. *Purandaradāsa.* A disciple of Vyāsarāya, a writer and singer of great repute in the time of Krishnadēvarāya in Kanarese. He lived at Panḍhārpūr, wrote many songs which still holds the minds of the people to-day, and died in 1564.

4. *Kanakadāsa.* A contemporary of Purandaradāsa. He belongs to Kaginde in Dharwar district. He wrote Mohan-Tarangiṇi, Naḷacharitra, Hari-Bhakta-Sāra and Ramadhyana Charitra.

5. *Abhinava Vādi Vidyānanda* of Bhallāṭakipura (Gersoppa) compiled an anthology called Kāvya Sāra in 1533. He was a Jain and was at Vijayanagara at the time of Krishṇadēvarāya.

6. *Mallaṇārya of Gubbi.* Śaiva, and lived at the time of Krishnadēva Rāya. He is known chiefly for his two works Bhava-Chintā-Ratna in Kanarese (1513) and Vīraśaivāmṛta embodying the principles of Vīraśaiva religion (1530).

7. *Kumāra Vālmīki* (*Narahari*), it is said wrote Vālmīki Ramayana at this time. He is placed about 1500, and his date is not finally settled.

8. *Chāṭu Vithalanātha,* lived about 1530 in Krishṇarāya's and also in Atchyutadēva Rāya's time. He translated into Kanarese Bhāgavatapurāṇam.

TAMIL

1. *Kumāra Sarasvati* was a Tamil poet in the court of Krishṇadēva Rāya, and celebrated the marriage of Krishnadēva Rāya with Gajapati's daughter in Tamil verse.

2. *Mandalapurusha,* a Tamil Jain, and author of the Chuḍāmaṇi Dictionary in Tamil is said to have been in the court of Krishnadēva Rāya.

3. *Jñānaprakāśar* who belongs to Veḷḷaḷa vaṁśa was patronised by Krishnaḍēva Rāya. The author was a native of Tondamanḍalam, and wrote 'Manjarippā' in Tamil in praise of Krishṇadēva Rāya. His other work is Kacchikkalambakam.

4. *Tattvaprakāśa Kavi,* the *Archaka* of Tiruvārūr temple is a Śaiva, and wrote application in Tamil verses to Krishṇadēvarāya to put an end to the disorder in the *Pūja* of the deity. Krishna-Rāya made every possible arrangement for a better upkeep of the temple and the poet again sent Tamil verses praising Krishṇadēvarāya for his noble deed.

5. *Harihara-Dāsa* wrote Irusamaya-viḷakkam and he is a Śaiva. That this poet lived at the time of Krishṇadēvarāya is known from the introduction to the work, wherein it is stated that Krishṇadēvarāya conquered and erected a 'Pillar of Victory.' He also described the famous Simhāchala shrine.

20

The Historical Importance of Parijatapaharanam

By

Mr. Bandhakavi Kesava Rao, B.A.,
Innespet, Rajahmundry.

Parijatapaharanam which is a Prabhandam in five cantos, is one of the gems of Telugu Literature. The author is Nandi Timmanna, a great poet of rare merit. He belongs to Āndhra Niyogi Brahmin community. At the end of the canto V, the poet gives us some information about his own family. He was the son of Nandi Singāmātya and Tippāmba and was the nephew of Malayamārutakavi. Aghora Śivāchārya was his spiritual Guru.[1] This monumental work has been dedicated to Śrī Krishṇadēvarāya, and it gives us in a nutshell the conquests of his reign. As a contemporaneous work, its utility to the students of Vijayanagara History is inestimable. It is also said that he composed another work, *Tristhali Daṇḍaka.* The controversy, whether his name is Nandi Timmanna or Mukku Timmanna, is still a living one and the consideration of space does not permit me to go into the details. Timmanna mentions in this work that Krishṇadēvarāya was pleased with his poetic talent and diction, and he got munificent gift of "*Agrahāram*" from his patron. It is also mentioned that Krishṇadēvarāya was in the habit of celebrating "Vasantōstavam" just like Bhoja and used to invite poets from all parts of the country. After examining their poetic talent, he bestowed on them lavish gifts of gold. This can be illustrated from the verse 139 in canto I. It is said that Krishṇadēvarāya had special favour towards Nandi Timmanna and Allasāni Peddanna. In the last canto, Krishṇadēvarāya is said to have performed the gift of Tulāpurusha (*i.e.*) weighing himself in gold and precious stones which were distributed among the learned.

When Pārijātāpaharaṇam was written, as established by Mr. K. Īśwara Dutt of Cocanada in his fine article in J.A.H.R.S. Vol. IX, part 4 page 55. "Timmanna described the campaigns of the Emperor up to the capture of Koṇḍavīḍu and Koṇḍapalli and also stated that the Tulāpurushadānam was made by the king. These events were corroborated by the Amarāvati Record. He also adds, that the Emperor was eagerly expected to go against the

1. Sources of Vijayanagara History.

Gajapati. Therefore, we can unhesitatingly fix the date between 25-7-1515 and 21-12-1515 A.D.[2]"

The theme of Pārijātāpaharaṇam is a well known one. But there is a traditional story, given, for taking up this story, by Timmanna for his work. It is said that Krishṇadēvarāya was reticent with his wives to whom Timmanna was given as "*Araṇam*" (marriage gift). So they complained to Timmanna about the attitude of Krishṇadēvarāya. To please him and inform him indirectly that it is unjust for a monarch like Krishṇadēvarāya who is equal to Lord Krishna himself to be reticent with his consorts even if they behave somewhat imperiously towards him. It is said in a verse in Pārijātāpaharaṇam that one cannot expect proper behaviour with ladies when they are offended. But this tradition appears to be fictitious as we have evidence to show that it was purely written to exhibit his poetic talent and win the praise of his patron.

It is usual with the poets of yore to give an account of the family history and achievements of their patrons to whom the works were dedicated. Timmanna is not an exception to this. In the beginning of this Telugu poem, dedicated to Krishṇadēvarāya, the poet gives an account of the family of his patron. This portion of the introduction is important for an historian. From the introduction of the poem (verses 7 to 16) we can deduce the following genealogy:—

Turvasu (Lunar race)
|
Īśvara—Lakkāmba
|
Tippāmba —Narasa— Nāgāmba
| |
Vīranarasimha Krishṇarāya

In the family of Turvasu of the Lunar race, was born a king by name Īśvara, who excelled in virtues even God Śiva who is also called Īśvara. In the battle at Kandukūr which he fought with the cavalry of the Mohammadan Ruler of Bedar (Bendandakoṭa), he caused their blood to flow in many streams. Īśvara married Lakkāmba, and had a son, Narasa by her.[3] The *Varāhapurāṇam* also narrates the above facts.

2. *Campaigns of Krishṇarāya* in J. A. H. R. Vol. IX, part 4, page 55.
3. S. V. H., page 106.

With regard to Narasa's conquests, we are to know he was famous for his conquests and munificent gifts. He ascended the throne of Vijayanagara which was a mirror to the whole world. This can be instanced from the verse 12 in the introduction. When the lord of Kuntala country was in trouble he showed his prowess and captured the town of Vidyāpura. He killed the Persian (Mohammadan) ruler in the battle of Mānavadurga. He captured the town of Madurā killing the Chōla ruler and exhibited his swordsmanship to Hauna ruler of Seringapatnam. His exploits are also described in Achyutarāyābhyudayam. He laid a bridge across the Kāveri and captured the town of Seringapatnam. The Telugu poems *Jaiminibhāratam* and *Varāhapurāṇam* amply demonstrate the above facts. He celebrated the sixteen sacred gifts. These can be witnessed in the verse 13 of the introduction.

Narasa had two wives Tippāmba and Nāgāmba through whom he got Vīranarasimha and Krishṇarāya respectively (Verses 14, 15, 16). We do not hear any noteworthy achievements of Vīranarasimha except that he ruled over the extensive Empire (verse 15)

After the demise of Vīranarasimha, Krishṇarāya, son of Nāgāmba, ascended the throne of Vijayanagara. He is described as God Krishṇa born again into the world.

The later portion of the introduction throws much light on the conquests and campaigns of Krishnadevarāya. A battle was fought on the banks of the Kāveri near the Western Ghats, the water of which was made quite red with the blood of large number of enemies whom he killed. In the second canto in the verse 103 he is praised as having pulled the walls of Ummattūr and Śiva Samudram, the citadel of the Raja of Ummattūr. These fall under the southern conquests of Krishṇadēvarāya. The Ummattūr chiefs were turbulent and attempted to become independent at the time of the accession of Krishṇadēvarāya. Their capital was Śiva Samudram. Krishṇarāya was forced to wage war against them and defeated them at Śiva Samudram and gave pardon to the Raja. This is also confirmed by the Amarāvati inscription of Krishṇadēvarāya dated 8-7-1515 A.D. The conquest of Śiva Samudram is also portrayed in the Telugu works Rāyavachakam and Krishṇarāya Vijayam.[4] The conquests of Śiva Samudram and Ummattūr is thus established by the above identification.

4. S. V. H., pages 111, 130, 131.

It is stated in the introduction of the poem that he defeated Vīrabhadra, son of Pratāparudra, and having captured him, " Gave him back his life." Vīrabhadra was the Viceroy of Koṇḍavīdu. He was considered to be a powerful and valiant Ruler. We have to turn to the pages Nuniz, who gave a graphic account of the conquest of Koṇḍavīdu. The date of capture of Koṇḍavīdu is fixed as 23-1-1515 A.D.[5]

The introduction tells us during his triumphant march to the Gajapati territories, he captured—Udayagiri, Vinukoṇḍa, Koṇḍavīdu, Bellamkoṇḍa, Velupukoṇḍa, Jallipalli, Anantagiri and Kambhammeṭṭu. The Amarāvati inscription records that after the conquest of Udayagiri he captured the forts of Vinukoṇḍa and Bellamkoṇḍa and laid seige to Koṇḍavīdu and captured alive Vīrabhadra. The date of the Amarāvati inscription is 8-7-1515 A.D. In the Ahobilam inscription it is stated that, after the captures of Udayagiri, Vinukoṇḍa, etc., he went to Dharaṇikoṭa. Its date is 21-12-1515. We can therefore assume that he captured the above forts during the period 18-7-1515 and 21-12-1515. The conquests mentioned in the poem are corroborated by inscriptions.

Further in the beginning of the second canto the poet describes Krishṇarāya staying in a palace called Malayakūṭṭa. In the verse 139 at the end of first canto he is represented to have heard along with his queens the works composed by the poets assembled at his court for the spring festival every year. It is mentioned in Krishṇarāya Vijayam that Mādayagāri Mallana, Allasāni Peddana and Nandi Timmana followed the king to the battle field which was fought with Bijapur kings. He is praised in high flown verses.

The historical importance of the poem lies in its contemporaneity . The conquests of Krishṇarāya have been given in this work with chronological exactitude. In this respect Manucharitra and *Āmuktamālyaḍa* supplement this work. Krishṇadēvarāya himself describes conquests at the end of each canto in his famous work *Āmuktamālyada*. The evidence mentioned in this work is corroborated and borne out by inscriptions, testimony of foreign writers and other Telugu works like Jaiminibhāratam and Varāhapurāṇam. Hence the historical importance of the poem is unique in its authenticity.

5. Ep. Ind., VI. pages 109-133.

21

The Battle of Tālikōta—Before and After

(From Muslim Sources)[1]

By

Prof. K. K. Basu, M.A.,
T. N. J. College, Bhagalpur.

In area about four hundred leagues and full of cities and towns, the kingdom of Vijayanagar[2] was an extensive and well-cultivated country. Its *terra firma,* lying sandwich-wise between the mountains and the rivers were under cultivation. The dependencies of the empire were uncircumscribed in both length and breadth. There were no less than sixty harbours and about an equal number of strong and impregnable fortresses, and gold, diamond and emerald mines in the realm. The region could boast of many valuable produce and its return amounted to twenty crores of *hun.* The military strength of the state consisted of four *lacs* of cavalry and ten *lacs* of infantry.

At the time when the entire peninsular India acknowledged the supremacy of the Bahmani Dynasty the Muslims carried on holy wars against the people of Vijayanagar. In such campaigns the forces of Islam generally won victories over their adversaries, and at times, they also had a bad time of it. On the whole, the Muhammadans reigned supreme over the South. Subsequently, when the Bahmanis ran low, some five or six independent sovereignties cropped out. These principalities often pulled different ways and sailed under false colours. Each was intent on wickedness; one tried to cause evil to the other.

Thus compelled by circumstances, these states, oftener than not, implored help and protection from the ruler of Vijayanagar,

1. Translated from *Busutin-us-Salatin* of Mirza Ibrahim Zubuiri who prefers the account of Rafiuddin Shirazi to Qassim Ferishta. Rafiuddin was in the service of 'Ali 'Ādil Shāh of Bijapur, for twenty-one years and he joined the court five years before the battle of Tāḷikōṭa. As an important minister of the State and a taster of royal provisions Rafiuddin enjoyed the privileges of the Sultan's companionship and thus, he is surely more reliable than Ferishta, who came to Bijapur in 1589, some twenty-four years after the battle.

2. The writer spells Vijayanagara as Vijayanagar.

who in consequence displayed signs of rattishness and vanity. The Hindu army sent in aid of any of those Muslim states misconducted themselves, playing mischief with the masjids and the Holy Book. They would, on their return journey, put in confinment thousands of people from the countries they visited and would forcibly seize their possessions and confiscate them.

Now, at the time when, Ramraj,[3] in aid of ' Ali 'Ādil, (The Sultan of Bijapur) having trampled upon Ahmadnagar had put to waste the territory from Daultabad to Junnar and smote its inhabitants, his temper exceeded all moderation and he reverted to his former habits. He now turned out from the court those Muslim ambassadors, who had so long enjoyed his favours. With a view to showing his contempt for the Musalmans he began detaining their agents at the levees for a pretty long time. These foreign legates were also forbidden to ride on horses at the close of these receptions. Thus, on account of the impotency of the Muhammedans, Ramraj, whose head had been turned by the wine of vanity and egotism, now became freed from all suspense or danger and he assumed a lofty bearing.

Though closely related with Ramraj, 'Ali 'Ādil Shāh shrugged his shoulders at the Rāja's sauciness and impertinence. For worldly and religious point of view the suppression of the infidel was by him deemed essential. He held a council and sought the advice of his faithful officers on the matter. " Every Muslim in general," the Sultan addressed them, " And their rulers in particular lie under an obligation to carrying on holy wars against the vicious unbelievers. They should not shut their eyes to the merit that is attached to the act of subduing the refractory and evil-disposed non-Muslims who have drunk deep the wine of arrogance." " Every Muslim," the Sultan further advocated, "Should assume the offensive against them and spill the wine of vanity from the cup of their brain. If not, the safety of the Believers and the maintenance of order in the country would be at stake." "It is for this reason," the Sultan finally added, " that we should gird up our loins, and having placed our reliance on God, should wage holy wars against the unbelievers, who are liable to be massacred, and acquire fame thereby. If, by the Grace of God, victory is ours, Islam becomes resplendent and the Muslims are liberated from the persecution of the infidels. But if anything untoward happens we then attain the dig-

3. Rāmrāj was the minister of Sadāśiva Raya, the King of Vijayanagar, and the *de facto* ruler of the State.

nity of a martyr and also gain honour on the Day of Judgment. In both cases, victory or defeat, we become distinguished like the two great martyrs Ḥasan and Ḥussain."[4] "What piece of advice," the Sultan ultimately enquired, "Do you now offer ?"

Kishwar Khān Lāri and Abu Turāb Shirazi, the two trusted servants of the court, replied, "Ramraj is distinguished for wealth and power. With a big army and a full treasury he strikes terror into the heart of the people. Without the co-operation of all the Muslim powers any open rupture with him is liable to be inefficacious and also ruinous." "It is, therefore, advisable," they at last suggested, "that the Muhammedans should at first unite their efforts and ride full tilt against the Raja." The Sultan yielded his assent to the proposal.

Now, it so happened that, Qutb Shah, (the Sultan of Golconda) on account of his close proximity to the state of Vijayanagar, had fallen a victim to the persecutions of the infidels and was sorely pressed. He would, therefore, always pray to The Almighty so that He might seal the doom of the Raja. (Hussain) Nizām Shāh of Ahmadnagar, likewise, was at cross purposes with Ramraj. His repeated discomfitures at the hand of the Vijayanagar ruler, the destruction of his country and property at the Raja's hands and finally the loss that he had sustained in respect of elephants, horses, banners and other paraphernalia of royalty, had made Hussain Nizām Shāh distressed and aggrieved and he would always bite his thumb in resentment. He sought a remedy for all these and looked for a mature and considerate advice. He believed that the strength of 'Ali 'Ādil depended upon the support of Ramraj and so long as the latter was on the side of the former his object was unattainable. He, therefore, at first bestowed his consideration upon putting down Ramraj, for once 'Ali 'Ādil was deprived of the Raja's support, he (Nizām) would wreak his vengeance on the Bijapur ruler. Hussain Nizām Shāh was pretty certain that the annihilation of Ramraj was inconceivable unless an alliance was formed with Bijapur.

Thus, Nizām Shāh was constrained to make an agreement with 'Ali 'Ādil and to come to an understanding with him. In consultation with Qutb Shah, H. Nizām Shāh sent an embassy to 'Ali 'Ādil and made over to the latter the key of the Sholapur fortress that had so long formed an apple of discord between them. "We be-

4. Hasan and Hussain were the sons of Hazrat Ali Murtaza by Hazrat Fatima, daughter of the Apostle.

lieve," wrote Nizām in his letter to 'Ādil,, "In the oneness of the Great Creator, in the Prophethood and mission of Muhammad who acts as our advocate on the Day of Judgment, and in the leadership and guidance of The Twelve Imāms,[5] upon them be peace!" It now behoves us that we should set aside our jealousies and disputes in petty worldly affairs, and having purged our hearts be united with each other. In keeping with the saying in the Qurān that "*All true believers are brethren*" we ought to make a common cause against the Hindus, who are our enemies in matters temporal and spiritual, and having made them eat the humble pie rescue the faithful from their molestation. In reward of our action we would, in fact, gain fame in this world and remuneration hereafter. Further, this great and glorious achievement of ours would ever remain recorded in the pages of Time. God forbidding, if my suggestion, which bears a spiritual and worldly significance, does not meet with your approval and we revert to our old habits, let confusion seize us! Let alone the immediate losses that we sustain in matters of religious and temporal, the evil-minded unbelievers are sure to crush us under their iron heel. The insignia of rebellion and impiety will thus ever remain unfurled in the universe and there would be no peace and prosperity left to the Muslims in the South."

'Āli 'Ādil lent himself to the suggestion and came to terms with Nizām Shāh. In order to strengthen the alliance, 'Ādil wanted to establish a matrimonial alliance with the latter. It was now proposed that Chand Bibi Sultan, daughter of Hussain Nizām Shāh would be given in marriage to 'Ādil, and that Bibi Hadiya Sultan, sister of 'Ādil be coupled with Prince Murtaza, the son of H. Nizām Shāh. It was further settled that the marriage festivities being over, the contracting parties would march upon Vijayanagar.

The marriage festivities commenced soon. The cities of Bijapur and Ahmadnagar were adorned and decorated. The walls and doors of the houses, the streets and the market-places were all illuminated. Hither and thither, the young and the old, revelled and caroused, and took their pleasure. The doors of the treasury were kept unlocked, and a free and lavish distribution of jewels, robes of

5. The Shias, also known as the Imâmiyas, look upon the Imāms as the rightful heirs of the Prophet. The list of twelve Shia Imāms begins with Ali and ends with Muhammad Al-Askari. The Shias maintain that Ali was the first legitimate Imām, divinely illuminated and preserved from sin and they accordingly reject the first three Caliphs recognised by the Sunnis, Abu Bakr, Umar and Usmān.

honour and gems was made. From every street and every house there broke forth peals of merriment and revelry which reverberated the Heavens....... The pomp and grandeur of the festivities and the liberality in the presentation of rewards beggar all description. These rounds of pleasures at last came to an end, and then there followed social entertainments which lasted for nearly three months.......

Afterwards, Chand Bibi, (daughter of Nizām Shāh), the largest pearl in the royal diadem, led her august steps to Bijapur and thereby shed lustre to that seat of mirth. Likewise did the most exalted Hadiya Bibi (sister of 'Āli 'Ādil Shāh), the precious pearl of the casket of greatness and good fortune, brightened Ahmadnagar by her world illuminating radiance.

The marriage celebrations being now over, 'Ali 'Ādil and Nizām, in accordance with the pact that they had formed, prepared themselves for an encounter with Ramraj. They soon settled all preliminaries for the holy war. It was settled that 'Ali 'Ādil . . . should commence battle. Thus, 'Ādil sent a skilful ambassador to Ramraj demanding the surrender of—the fortresses, Raichur and Mudgal, which the Raja had forcibly taken possession of ....

The Raja, on the other hand, made a smile of contempt at the words of the Bijapur plenipotentiary and had him dismissed from the court. The agents of the other Muslim kings were treated likewise.

After the return of the legations, H. Nizām Shāh, Qutb Shah and 'Ali Barid (of Bidar) advanced against Vijayanagar with a big army and necessary provisions. On account of the grudge that he bore against H. Nizām, Burhan 'Imād-ul-Mulk (of Birár) kept himself aloof and took no part in the expedition.......

Reaching the vicinity of Tāḷikōta that was within the confines of Bijapur territory, the confederate forces pitched their tents. In conformity to his rank and dignity, 'Ali 'Ādil Shah entertained the allied army. He provided them with food and beverage of various sorts, delicious repast of every variety, fruits of every kind, sweets of different qualities, multiform dishes and sweet scented vegetables......The entertainment having come to an end, 'Ali 'Ādil, Nizām Shāh, Qutb Shah and 'Ali Barid met together and showed proper courtesy and right civility to one another. The parties entered into fresh pacts and treaties and promised to remain firm and indomitable at all hazards. They now marched against Vijayanagar.

Ramraj, on his part, having received the news about the confederacy and of their attack, remained undaunted. He began recruiting soldiers and collecting materials for war. At first, he sent out his brother with twenty-thousand cavalry, and one lac and five hundred big elephants to meet the enemies. For purposes of reinforcement, the Raja sent another brigade in charge of his second brother. He ordered his generals to block the fords of the Krishna and offer opposition to the advance of the adversaries. The Raja then personally set out with a huge army and marched through the Carnatic. It is said that, the three divisions of the Hindu forces numbered one *lac* of cavalry and five *lacs* of infantry.

The vanguard of the Hindu army placed big cannons and raised fortresses at the fords, and made the fortifications as strong as the Alexandrian Wall. Reaching the Krishna, the Muslims found their passage blocked. They now made arrangements for crossing the stream by some other way. The secret spies brought informations that they had discovered new passages towards the upper and downward course of the river. The divers explored the river and ascertained its depths. They reported that, the entire army with its bag and baggage, cannons, elephants and camels could safely pass over the stream at two or three (newly-discovered) spots.

'Ali 'Ādil took alarm; he summoned his officers and held a consultation with them. After a great deliberation the advisers thought out a remedy. "The solution," one of them said, " of this intricate problem depends on stratagem and dissimulation. Even the leader of the band of warriors, the Prince of the prophets and apostles has pronounced that, war is an organised hypocricy. We need play a double game now. We would make a show of making a passage through the unknown fords..... When we put ourselves in motion our opponents would abandon the known fords which they had strongly fortified; and as soon as they leave their posts we despatch a body of active and expert cavalry to get hold of our enemy's fortifications. Thus, when the ford comes into our possession we can force our way through the river, unopposed and undisturbed." " To us " the speaker finally concluded, " This seems to be the only artful procedure."

The Sultan nodded assent to the advice thus offered. A rumour was spread out that the Muslims contemplated forcing their passage by a different route. Then the entire confederate force edged its way along the river bank and made preparations for going across. When the Hindus came to know of the movements of their enemies, they thought it useless to tarry any more at the fords that they had fenced round. They made a simultaneous move.... Meanwhile, at midnight, a selected number of active and vigorous Muslim cavalry safely swam across the river and captured all the field-works of their opponents. Little did the Hindus think that their enemies would so easily cross the stream. They now repented for their folly, and a great disappointment prevailed in their rank and file.......

At the peep of day, the allies settled all preliminaries for the holy war and drew up their forces. Twelve banners were unfurled in the confederate army. These insignias were decorated with the names of the twelve distinguished Imāms and contained in bold letters the Qurānic verse, *"Help from Allah and victory near at hand."* 'Ali 'Ādil's presence at the right wing imparted to it firmness and solidity which were comparable to those of the Alwand mountain.[6] The left wing was equally rendered strong by Qutb Shah and 'Ali Barid, and the centre was graced by Hussain Nizām Shāh. Large field-pieces, one chained with the other, were arranged in the van of the army. The war elephants were placed overspread.

The Muslims . . . rushed at their opponents with great violence and impetuosity . . . . The Heaven was so much reverberated by the sound of the drums and trumpets, and the hubbub and din of the warriors that even the denizens of the forest and the fish in the rivers became perturbed and agitated.

Ramraj, on the other hand, out of excessive vanity and arrogance had made no effort in marshalling his forces. Having separated his family and baggage from the army, he flew at the Muslims with his promiscuous and unsystematic host. Howevermuch the councillors took objection to the Raja's taking his seat on the throne and advised him to ride on a horse, Ramraj took no notice of them. "Fie upon it," he cried out in disapprobation, "The war is unworthy of any notice. There is no earthly reason why we should be apprehensive!"

The army of Islam now rushed head-long upon the Hindus and a sanguinary conflict ensued. The soldiers of the belligerents became mixed up in the melee. At times the Muslim warriors put their enemies to death, at others the Hindus victimized their opponents.

Ramraj now found out that his hope had told him a flattering tale. Down he came from the throne on which he was seated and took

6. A high mountain in Hamadan, eighty leagues from Ispahan.

a golden chair. An umbrella, gold embroidered and made of velvet with pearls and golden chains embellished all round, was spread over his head. The Raja caused heaps of gold and silver coins, ornamented weapons and valuable jewelleries to be spread before him. " I will," Ramraj made a public declaration, " In case of success and victory, reward my soldiery not only with these gold and jewels but also by promoting him to higher rank and dignity." Such an animating proclamation no doubt spirited up his soldiers and they all presented a bold front. His unerring matchlockmen and his skilful archers with their faultless aim mowed down the enemies and played havoc upon them. . . . At last some fifty-thousand Hindus fully armed with swords and guns rushed foremost and having worsted the left wing of the Muslim forces drove them pell-mell.

Upon this, Nizām Shāh, Qutb Shah and 'Ali Barid made a combined attack upon their enemies. Discovering that the Hindus were carrying everything before them and that the defeat of the Muslims was imminent, Nizam ordered his men to set up his personal camp. The work of fixing up the royal tent in the thick of the action was, in the language of the South, called *Rahtanat* and it was usually resorted to in extreme cases. Nizām Shāh now resolved to hold out he would either win the battle or give up his life. With him there were hundred palanquins of his female-folk each in charge of one *Khwajah-sarah*, who, if the worst came to the worst, might put the ladies to the sword.

'Ali 'Ādil Shah, on the other hand, who gave battle to Tirmalraj, the elder brother of Ramraj, waded knee-deep in his opponent's blood. At last when Tirmalraj made a retreat towards Kanauj, 'Ali 'Ādil ran after the fugitive and smote him. The Bijapur Sultan then turned against Ramraj, who thought that, by running at him the Sultan was going to court death.

However, Ramraj was now simultaneously attacked and hemmed in by Nizām Shāh, and Qutb Shah in his front and by 'Ali 'Ādil in the rear. Meanwhile, Nizam had no information of 'Ali 'Ādil's victory over Tirmalraj or of the conflict in which the former was engaged with the enemies. So, when he found the right wing of the allied army missing he became white as a sheet. Rumi Khan, an officer-in-charge of Nizam's artillery soon made his appearance. "Where are the cannons ?" Nizam interrogated. In reply the Khan said, " They are in readiness and two of the heavy guns are at their posts." " Why don't you," Nizam again enquired, " set them to work ? What makes you tarry ?" Whereupon the field-pieces were manipulated and down fell the Hindu army like the leaves scattered by the pestilential wind of autumn.

Seated on an elephant Rumi Khan now made a forward movement. In his front were the artilleries that belched out deadly fire and the enemies dared not face him. Rumi thus came upon a number of soldiers that had assembled at one particular spot, and it so happened that Ramraj happened to be present in that crowd. The Hindu soldiery frightened to death at the vehemence of their assailants, tumbled down one upon the other. They took no account of their leader's safety and thought of deserting the battle-field. . . .

Having received a wound during the rush made by the retreating soldiers, Ramraj kept standing unattended. When Rumi drove his elephant against Ramraj, a personal attendant of the latter, placed himself in front of his master. Dilpat Rao Brahman, for such was the name of the valet, cried out, " Halt ! Don't you hurt the Raja ! " At the mention of the Raja's name Rumi ran his elephant against Ramraj and made it lift him up by its probocis.

Like a flash of lightning Rumi returned to his army and placed his captive before Nizam. The latter greatly rejoiced over the incident. He offered a seat to the prisoner and joined in a conversation with him. " How do you do ? " Nizam made a sarcastic enquiry. In reply, Ramraj touched his forehead which implied that whatever was destined had happened.

Hakim Qasim Beg Tabrezi, a trusted courtier of Nizam Shah, now came upon the stage. " God bless me ! " he cried in amazement, " What's good in having a tittle-tattle with the *detenu* ? It is expedient that he should be immediately put to death. Take time by the forelock, and wreak your vengeance, else 'Ali 'Ādil who is pressing the enemies hard would come and carry Ramraj off ! " So, Nizām Shāh ordered for the execution of Ramraj and commanded that the severed head was to be put on a spear and exposed to public view.

At the sight of the Raja's head, the Hindu soldiers ran for their lives. (In fact) such a battle in which millions of unbelievers ranged themselves against the Faithful was not within one's previous experience. Flushed with victory the army of Islam now followed up the fugitives and cut them to pieces. On every side there were the heaps of the dead. The whole land for miles together, became red as scarlet by the blood of the slain. The battle-field presented a tragic scene of the dead and the dying soldiers and animals, and of gold, jewels and other chattels lying interspersed. The victors received such a large booty of gold and jewels, horses and swords, helmet and cuirass, male and female slaves that they became well off. A proclamation was soon issued to the soldiery enjoining them to keep a sharp eye upon such spoils of war as elephants, cannons, flags and drums that belonged to the State only. But they were permitted to retain for their personal use cash, gold, jewels and ornaments. Thousands of elephants, a huge amount of cash and a prodigious quantity of articles were thus collected before the Sultans. The rank and file received gifts in cash and kind.

The whole space lying between *Āl-i-Kandi*, the place of battle, situated at a distance of twenty miles from Vijayanagar, and the latter city, was strewn over with the dead. Some twelve days were spent in calculating the number of the slain and the wounded. The total number of those that were victimized figured one million. This enquiry was carried on at the time of pursuing the fugitives.

After this momentous victory, the Sultans fell on their knees and offered their prayers to the Almighty. During the course of twenty days that they remained at the seat of war, the Sultans took their ease and nursed the wounded and the sick. Then they turned towards Vijayanagar where they razed the lofty buildings and temples to the ground. This work of destruction was carried out with a vengeance.

Vijayanagar was an extensive city, flourishing and well-populated. It had never experienced any foreign invasion for ages. The nobility, the wealthy, the soldiery, the peasants and the artisans all drove a roaring trade. During the confusion and disorder following the Muslim invasion, the citizens out of fear lurked in their houses, cellars, wells and reservoirs. Those that were well-to-do betook themselves to the neighbouring mountains and caverns with their families and chattels. . . . The Muslim army remained at Vijayanagar for about six months. To a distance of twenty leagues round the city everything was burnt and reduced to ashes.

Tirmalraj, the elder brother of Ramraj who escaped unhurt from the battle-field took refuge in the fort of Palconda. The son of Ramraj, with all his relations, also took shelter in a wide and deep cavern situated at a distance of three leagues from Anagondi.[7]

7. Anagondi situated on the Tungabhadra in Raichur district (Hydrabad).

22

The Nayakas of Keladi

By

Mr. N Lakshminarayan Rao, M.A.

Office of the Government Epigraphist for India, Ootacamund.

One of the most prominent feudatory families which rose to power under the Vijayanagara rulers and finally established as an independent state was that of the Nāyakas of Keḷadi. As a complete history of this family cannot be compressed into the short space available in this volume, I shall here content myself with fixing the chronology of the chiefs of this house and give a brief account of the dynasty as gathered from inscriptions and other sources.

The first member of the family who rose to eminence was Chauḍa-Gauḍa of Keḷadi, a village in the Shimoga District of the Mysore State. He was born of humble parents who were cultivators; his father was Basappa of Paḷḷivayal and his mother Basavamāmbe.[1] Though the exact process by which Chauḍappa came to the front cannot be ascertained, all accounts agree in attributing his rise to the hidden treasure which he unearthed one day while ploughing his field. By means of this treasure he and his younger brother Bhadrappa seem to have gathered round them a band of armed men with whose help they began to take possession of the neighbouring villages and probably tried to carve out a small principality for themselves. The date of this acquisition of power by the brothers cannot be determined with any exactitude with the material now available. The *Keḷadi-Nṛipa Vijaya* (*K. N. V.*) a Kannada work in *champū* style dealing at length with the history of this family states that the emperor of Vijayanagara who recognised the growing strength and influence of these brothers and invited them to his presence was the great Krishnarāya, though it places in A.D. 1499 Chauḍa's installation as the Nāyaka of Keḷadi, which according to this very source took place after the latter had returned from Vijayanagara.[2] This date, it should be noted, was full ten

1. *Śivatatvaratnākara*, (published by B. M. Nath & Co., Madras), *Kallōla* V, *Taraṅga* 2 and *K. N. V.*, p. 8.

A copper-plate inscription (*Mys. Arch. Rep.* for 1928, p. 66), which appears to be suspicious, carries back the pedigree of the house by two generations. According to this grant Dēvāgōṇḍa (-gauḍa) and Gōpa-Gauḍa were grandfather and father respectively of Basappa, whose name is given as Basa-Gauḍa.

2. Mysore University edition, pp. 29ff.

years before Krishṇarāya ascended the throne. The Śivatatvaratnākara *S. T. R.* an encyclopædia in Sanskrit, which also gives a history of the family, however, does not mention the name of the Vijayanagara king who sent for Chauḍappa. But this much is certain that Chauḍa was powerful enough to record on stone a grant of land in his own name in A.D. 1506,[3] without mentioning any paramount sovereign. It appears not unlikely that the adventurous career of Chauḍa began sometime in the reign of the Tuḷuva king Vīra-Narasiṁha who, according to Nuniz, " during the six years of his rule Busbalarao was always at war ; for, as soon as his father was dead, the whole land had revolted under its captains."[4] The brothers were promptly ordered by the sovereign to be seized and imprisoned at the capital.[5] It is worth noting that both the *S.T.R.* and the *K.N.V.*, the two chief literary sources for the history of this family are silent about this inglorious incident. An opportunity having presented itself to show their loyalty, the Keḷadi brothers offered their services to put down a rebellious chief ; and when they succeeded in their undertaking the king appointed Chauḍa as the chief of Keḷadi and other places that the brothers had captured.[6] Though both the *S.T.R.* and the *K.N.V.* inform us that the title of *Nāyaka* was conferred upon Chauḍa by the king of Vijayanagara, his inscription referred to above as well as a record of the time of his son[7] Śadāśiva-Nāyaka his name is presented only as Chauḍa-Gauḍa and in neither of them is the title of *Nāyaka* applied to him. That the title of *Nāyaka* is not coupled with his name even in the epigraph of the reign of his son would indicate that the Nayakship of Keḷadi was not founded during the time of Chauḍa. The change of the family's capital from Keḷadi to Ikkēri in the cyclic year Prajōtpatti (= A.D. 1511-12) is attributed to Chauḍa by *K.N.V.* Rice, however, places the event in about A.D. 1560[8] without citing any authority and Fr. Heras in the reign of Chikka Saṅkaṇṇa[9] on the authority of *S.T.R.* But according to this work the builder of Ikkēri was Veṅkaṭappa I.[10] The *K.N.V.* ascribes to him a rule of 14 years

3. *Mys. Arch. Rep.* 1930, p. 219, No. 65.
4. Sewell : *Forgotten Empire*, p. 314 f.
5. Rice : *Mysore*, Vol. II, p. 458.
6. *Ibid.*
7. Madras Epigraphical Collection No. 397 of 1928.
8. *Mysore and Coorg from Inscriptions*, p. 156.
9. *Āravīḍu Dynsaty*, p. 423.
10. *Kallōla VI, Taraṅga* 1, verses. Apparently Fr. Heras was led to this error by the *Sources of Vijayanagara History*, which attirbutes the construction of Ikkēri to Chikka-Saṅkaṇṇa.

from A.D. 1499 to 1513,[11] but the only epigraph of his, known so far, is dated Śaka 1429 (A.D. 1506).[12] In the inscription of Chauḍa-Gauḍa, just mentioned, the title of *Yāḍava-Murāri* is applied to him, though the *S.T.R.* states that the title was given to Sadāśiva-Nāyaka by Rāmarāja. Moreover the dates assigned in this literary work to the Keḷadi chiefs[13] up to the time of Veṅkaṭappa-Nāyaka I, do not tally with those that can be obtained for them from inscriptions and I have therefore adopted only the dates known for each member of the family from epigraphs. This and *Kōṭe-Kōlāhala* were characteristic *birudas* of the family borne by all the rulers from Sadāśiva-Nāyaka onwards. Chauḍa had two sons Sadāśiva and Bhadra. From the inscription of Sadāśiva noticed above we learn that the name of his mother was Virupamma.

There is no means of ascertaining the exact date of Sadāśiva-Nāyaka's accession. While the *K.N.V.* gives us to understand that he ruled from A.D. 1513 to A.D. 1545,[14] the earliest reliable date for him as recorded in an inscription at is the cyclic year Krōdhin corresponding to A.D. 1544-45.[15] And among his numerous inscriptions there are two which furnish for him the date Śaka 1487[16] (=A.D. 1565). It may be noted, however, that though these records are on stone and otherwise beyond suspicion, the details of date recorded in them do not work out correctly. But a stone inscription[17] at Hoysāḷa in South Kanara district, is dated Śaka 1486, Rudhirōdgarin, Bhādrapada, śu. 12, Sravana-dvadasi corresponding quite regularly to A.D. 1563 August 30. So we may safely conclude that he ruled at least up to A.D 1563 and probably upto A.D. 1565. In the *K.N.V.* we are told that Sadāśiva-Nāyaka met the emperor, who was pleased with his prowess and bestowed upon him the title of Immadi-Sadāśivēndra-Nāyaka.[18] But

11. Not found in the Mss.
12. *Mys. Arch. Rep.* 1930, p. 219.
13 Apparently Rice's dates for these Nāyakas are based on this work.
14. Not found in the Mss
15. *Ep. Carn.*, Vol. VII, Sk. 255. A copper-plate grant (*Mys. Arch. Rep.*, 1928, p. 66) dated Śaka 1431 (current), Vibhava, Kārthika, ba. 30 Ra[vivāra] solar eclipse, purports to belong to his reign. But the date cited in it is irregular. There was no eclipse in the month of Kārthika in the cyclic year Vibhava and though in the next year Śukla = Śaka 1432 current, a solar eclipse did occur in Kārthika the week day was Monday. Moreover the date appears to be too early for Sadāśiva as it would be improbable that he did not issue any records for 35 years after he began to rule. Further the editor of the Report had remarked that the record appears to be spurious (p. 119),
16. *Madras Epl. Collection* Nos. 292 and 301 of 1932.
17. *Ibid*, No. 283 of 1931-32.
18. See pp. 30 and 32.

according to the *S.T.R.*[19] the Vijayanagara king whom the Nayaka met was Rāmarāja, the *de facto* ruler of the kingdom during the reign of Sadāśivarāya. The statement of the *S.T.R.* is in perfect accord with the dates obtained for Sadāśiva-Nāyaka from inscriptions, all of which mention either Sadaśivarāya or (Aḷiya) Rāmarāja as his overlord. From the same work we learn that Rāmarāja placed him at the head of an army in a campaign against the rulers of Kalyāṇa and Kalburgi who were joined by the lord of Bijāpur. Sadāśiva-Nāyaka easily defeated the enemy and aided Rāmarāya in capturing the city of Kalyāṇa.[20] This battle is placed by Fr. Heras in about A.D. 1549.[21] In recognition of the services rendered on this occasion, Ramarāja besides bestowing upon Sadāśiva the titles of *Rāya-Nāyaka* and *Kōṭe-Kōlāhala* appointed him governor of Chandragutti, Bārakūru and Maṅgalūru. And it may be noted that in the earliest record of Sadāśiva-Nāyaka of A.D. 1544-45 noticed above, he is not mentioned as the governor of any district. But in an inscription[22] dated Śaka 1474 (A.D. 1550) he is for the first time, stated to have been ruling Āraga (18 *kampaṇas*). He was administering the district under the orders of Sadāśivarāya, who was reigning at Hampi. We do not, however, find him governing the districts below the ghats, i.e. Bārakūru, Maṅgalūru, etc., till A.D. 1554. It may be interesting to observe here that one[22-a] of the inscriptions of the reign of Sadāśivarāya states that it was the *Mahāmaṇḍalēśvara* Veṅkaṭādrirāja that had entrusted Sadāśiva-Nāyaka with the administration of Bārakūru.[23] This Veṅkaṭādri is no other than the brother of Aḷiya Rāmarāya and was wielding considerable influence. The next notable achievement of Sadāśiva-Nāyaka was his invasion of the country of Barīdu Pādushah, Sultān of Bidar, which was also undertaken at the bidding of Rāmarāya.[24] This must be one of the several encounters between the rulers of Vijayanagara and Bidar. He was then asked to put down the rebel chiefs of Tuḷu and Kēraḷa. It was probably with a view to keep these chiefs under control that Sadaśiva-Nāyaka was made the governor of Tuḷu-rājya which we find him ruling till A.D. 1565. Another chief that was taken captive by Sadāśiva-Nāyaka was Mādarasa of Baṅkāpura.[25] The extent of territory governed by Sadāśiva is stated in an inscription[26] of A.D. 1563 to be 56 *gāvudas* comprising Āraga, Gutti thirty-six *kampaṇas*, Tuḷu-rājya, Bārakūru and Maṅgaḷūru.

19. *Kallōla V, taraṅga* 5.
20. *Ibid.*
21. *Āraviḍu Dynasty*, pp. 79 ff.
22. *Ep. Carn.*, Vol. VIII, Nagar 77.
22a. *Mad. Ep. Coll.* No. 433 of 1928.
23. *S. I. I.*, Vol. VII, No. 366.
24. *S. T. R.*, *Kallōla V, taraṅga* 5.
25. *Ibid.*
26. *Mad. Ep. Coll.* No. 487 of 1928-29.

Inscriptions dated Śaka 1488[27] (A.D. 1566) i.e., one year later than the last known date of Sadāśiva-Nāyaka, refer themselves to the reign of Immaḍi-Sadāśiva-Nāyaka ; and A.D. 1566 is the only date available for him so far. It may therefore be surmised that he was the successor of Sadāśiva-Nāyaka. But none of the inscriptions of Immaḍi-Sadāśiva tell us whether this was his name or surname nor do they reveal the relationship that he bore to his predecessor. As has been stated above, Immaḍi-Sadāśivēndra was, according to the *K.N.V.*, the title bestowed on Sadāśiva-Nāyaka by Krishṇarāya, the emperor of Vijayanagara. The *S.T.R.*, however, tells us that under this name Sadāśiva-Nāyaka installed his younger brother, Bhadrappa, on the throne of Keḷadi just before his retirement.[28] A copper-plate inscription of A.D. 1592 about whose genuineness there is no room for suspicion, states that Sadāśiva-Nāyaka and Yimmaḍi-Sadāśiva were the grandfather and father respectively of Veṅkaṭappa-Nāyaka I,[29] thus indicating that Immaḍi-Sadāśiva-Nāyaka was the surname of Doḍḍa-Saṅkaṇṇa, whose son was Veṅkaṭappa I, according to all authorities. While we learn from the *K. N. V.* that the successor of Sadāśiva-Nāyaka was Doḍḍa-Saṅkaṇṇa-Nāyaka, the elder of his two sons, the *S.T.R.* gives us to understand that Sadāśiva was succeeded by Bhadrappa. Though the evidence regarding the identity of Immaḍi-Sadāśiva is conflicting, I am inclined to think that the epigraphical document which refers itself to the reign of the son of Immaḍi-Sadāśiva in A.D. 1592, barely six years after the only known date of the latter chief, is entitled to greater credence than the literary sources which are removed by centuries from his time. I would therefore identify Immaḍi-Sadāśiva-Nāyaka with Doḍḍa Saṅkaṇṇa, the father of Veṅkaṭappa and son of Sadāśiva-Nāyaka. Other evidence also seems to support this identification. Fr. Heras has stated on the authority of *Keḷadi-Arasu-Vaṁśāvali* that Doḍḍa-Saṅkaṇṇa was deposed.[30] There is perhaps a veiled allusion to this unfortunate incident in the statement of the *S.T.R.* that the emperor asked Doḍḍa-Saṅkaṇṇa to stay at the capital with his family, entrusting the administration of his territories to his younger brother.[31] This work further states that after ruling the kingdom for some time Doḍḍa-Saṅkaṇṇa went on a pilgrimage[32]—probably on account of

27. *Ep. Carn.*, Vol. VIII, Nagar 1 to 4 and *Mys. Arch. Rep.* 1923, p. 83, No. 73.
28. *Kallōla V, taṙnga* 5.
29. *Op. Cit.* p. 180.
30. *Mys. Arch. Rep.* for 1923, pp. 105ff.
31. *Kallōla V., taraṅga* 7.
32. *Ibid.*

his deposition. To this pilgrimage of Doḍḍa-Saṅkaṇṇa a large space is devoted in the *K.N.V.* The fact that the few inscriptions of Immaḍi-Sadāśiva are all dated in the same year viz., Śaka 1488, would indicate that his reign was short and uneventful.[33] Probably, it is this personage who is represented as fettered and manacled in a sculpture in the Aghōrēśvara temple, with the label Huchcha Saṅkaṇṇa-Nāyaka. All these taken together would lead us to the surmise that Doḍḍa-Saṅkaṇṇa was also known as Immaḍi-Sadāśiva. The only historical fact of his reign that is worth mentioning is his campaign against the Portuguese in company with Rāmarāya's cousin Viṭṭhala, which is recorded in the *S.T.R.*[34] This probably refers to Viṭṭhala's southern expedition in the course of which he came into conflict with the Portuguese on the Fishery Coast.[35] Though the lord of Goa is stated to have been captured, we have no means of verifying the correctness of this statement. If so, this victory must have been achieved when Doḍḍa-Saṅkaṇṇa was the Yuvarāja under his father for the last known date of Viṭṭhala is A.D. 1558.

All authorities are agreed that Chikka-Saṅkaṇṇa succeeded Doḍḍa-Saṅkaṇṇa and inscriptions which refer themselves to the reign of Saṅkaṇṇa-Nāyaka without the epithet Doḍḍa or Chikka have probably to be assigned to the younger of the two brothers. The earliest of these records[36] is dated Śaka 1492 (A.D. 1570) and the latest[37] Śaka 1503 (A.D. 1580). But we also find epigraphs of Rāmarāja-Nāyaka, the son of Doḍḍa-Saṅkaṇṇa ranging in date from Śaka 1493[38] (A.D. 1570) to Śaka 1508[39] (A.D. 1586). The explanation of this overlapping of dates is found in a lithic record from S. Kanara, dated Śaka 1500 (A.D. 1577), which states clearly that Saṅkaṇṇa-Nāyaka and Rāmarāja-Nāyaka were together ruling over Gutti, Āraga, Bārakūru and Maṅgaḷūru districts.[40] It may therefore be

33. One of these (*Mys. Arch. Rep.* 1923, p. 83) gives him the titles *Mahārājādhirāja* and *Paramēśvara*. As these *birudas* are not known to have been borne by any ruler of this family the application of them to Yimmaḍi-Sadāśiva is probably due to a mistake of the engraver who, on account of the similarity of the names of the overlord Sadāśivarāya and his feudatory, omitted the name of the former before that of the Nāyaka.

34. *Kallōla V, taraṅga* 7.

35. Heras, *Op. Cit.* pp. 158 ff.

36. *S. I. I.* Vol, VII, No. 389.

37. *Ibid.*, No. 375.

38. *Madras Epigraphical Collection* No. 574 of 1929-30.

39. *S. I. I.* Vol. VII, No. 321.

40. *Madras Epigraphical Collection* No. 267 of 1931-32. By mistake both the chiefs are stated, in the *Annual Report on S. I. Epigraphy* for the year, to be the sons of Sadāsiva-Nāyaka.

concluded that at least up to A.D., 1580 these two princes ruled their dominions jointly. Their loyalty to the paramount authority even after the staggering disaster of Rakkasa-Taṅgaḍi is noteworthy. Most of the records of these two chiefs mention the ruling Vijayanagara sovereigns Sadāśiva, Tirumala or Śrīraṅga.[41] One great achievement of Saṅkaṇṇa was the subjugation of Bhairādēvi of Gērusoppe.[42] He is also described as having defeated Maṁjulakhāna (Manzar Khān).[43] The *K.N.V.* makes Chikka-Saṅkaṇṇa the contemporary of Aḷiya Rāmarāja and relates that he took part in the battle of Rakkasa-Taṅgaḍi.[44] But this statement cannot be relied upon as the earliest date known for this Nāyaka is A.D. 1570, i.e., five years after the catastrophe of Rakkasa-Taṅgaḍi and one year before the only known date of Immaḍi-Sadāśiva (Doḍḍa Saṅkaṇṇa). As noted above the latest available date of Chikka-Saṅkaṇṇa is A.D. 1580; and we find inscriptions of his co-regent Rāmarāja-Nāyaka dated Śaka 1503 (A.D. 1582)[45] and Śaka 1508 (A.D. 1586).[46] There is however no means of ascertaining definitely whether both the uncle and nephew ruled conjointly till A.D. 1586 or Rāmarājayya ruled independently after A.D. 1580. No outstanding exploit is recorded about Rāmarājayya. But he was keeping intact his hereditary province. According to an inscription[47] dated Śaka 1495 (A.D. 1573), he was ruling, under the orders of Śrīraṅgarāya, the districts of Āraga, Gutti, Bārakūru, Maṅgaḷūru and other kingdoms 'devolved in succession.' It is necessary here to draw attention to a serious error of the *S.T.R.* which besides telling us that Chikka-Saṅkaṇṇa was succeeded by Veṅkaṭappa, makes Rāmarāja-Nāyaka the latter's younger brother and *Yuvarāja*.[48] But Veṅkaṭappa is known to have been the younger brother and successor of Rāmarājayya.

While the initial year of Veṅkaṭappa-Nāyaka's reign is placed in Śaka 1505 (A.D. 1588) by the *K.N.V.*,[49] the earliest known for him from epigraphic records is Śaka 1514 (A.D. 1592).[50] We find him acknowledging the suzerainty of the Vijayanagara king till A.D. 1613, in which year he is stated to have been ruling Tuḷu-rājya and Malerājya, as a subordinate of Veṅkaṭapatidēva Mahārāya I.[51] The Italian traveller Pietro della Valle who went to Ikkēri

41. See *e.g.*, *Madras Ep. Collection* No. 487 of 1928-29, *Ep. Carn.* Vol. VIII, Sorab 35 and *Ibid*, Tīrthaḷḷi 5.

42. *S. T. R.*, *Kallōla V*, *taraṅga* 15.

43. *Ibid.*

44. pp. 66f.

45. *Ep. Carn.*, Vol. VIII, Sb. 232.

46. *S. I. I.* Vol. VII, No. 321.

47. *Ep. Carn.*, Vol. VIII, Tl. 5.

48. *S. T. R. Kallōla V*, *taraṅgā* 16.

49. See p. 70.

50. *Mys. Arch. Rep.* 1923, pp. 105ff.

51. See *S. I. I.* Vol. VIII, No. 297.

with a Portuguese embassy states that "this prince Venkatappa Naicka was sometime vassal and one of the ministers of the great king of Vidia Nagar . . . but after the downfall of the king . . . Venkatappa Naicka remained absolute prince of the State of which he was governor, which also being a good soldier, he hath much enlarged."[52] In an inscription of his grandson and successor Vīrabhadra, he is described as a diamond elephant goad to the rutting elephants the bounding Tauḷava kings, a sun to the darkness the Kirātas, a boundary mountain to stop the great ocean of Mlēchchhas ever seeking to overflow the south in victorious expedition.[53] The *S.T.R.* and *K.N.V.* attribute to him numerous victories among which may be mentioned the repulsion of the Bijapur forces under Maṁjula-Khāna, which had come to help a certain Hanuma, who invaded his territory and the defeat and capture of Bhairādēvi of Gērusoppe, who was a feudatory of Bijapur. In commemoration of the first victory he erected a pillar at Hangal.[54] He acquired territory down to the borders of Malabar and even came into conflict with the Portuguese. So powerful was he that the Portuguese sent an embassy to him in A.D. 1623.[55] He greatly increased the power of his dynasty and largely extended his kingdom by his conquests. The latest date available for him from inscriptions is Śaka 1551[56] (A.D. 1629), which was also the last year of his reign according to *K.N.V.*[57] He married a daughter of Virupaṇṇa-Nāyaka,[58] whose name is not known, and had a son named Bhadrappa. This prince died during the lifetime of his father, leaving a son named Vīrabhadra. The latter was assisting his grandfather Veṅkaṭappa in the administration of the province, and in course of time succeeded him.

Vīrabhadra-Nāyaka's earliest date gathered from inscriptions is A.D. 1629,[59] which is also given as the first year of his reign in the *K.N.V.*[60] From this reign onwards the dates assigned in this work to the chiefs of this family may be regarded as fairly correct. In 1631, the Portuguese were able to obtain from the king of Ikkēri (i.e. Vīrabhadra) a treaty under which he agreed not only to cede the island of Kamboli and the fort of Barakālur but also allowed

52. Sewell, *Forgotten Empire*, p. 220n.
53. *Ep. Carn.*, Vol. VII, Sh. 2.
54. *S. T. R. Kallōla, VI, taraṅga* 13.
55. Rice, *Mysore and Coorg from Inscriptions*, p. 158.
56. *Ep. Carn.* Vol. VIII, Sb. 266.
57. See pages 90 and 92.
58. *Ep. Carn.*, Vol. VIII, Tl. 97.
59. *Mys. Arch. Rep.* 1923, p. 107.
60. p. 93.

them certain trading privileges.[61] He had to shift his capital in A.D. 1638 from Ikkēri to Bidanur on account of Ranadulla Khan's attack on, and devastations of the former place.[62] An inscription of A.D. 1641, however, describes him as 'having given protection to the southern kings alarmed by the great army of the Pātuśāha' (i.e., the Sultān of Bijāpur).[63] The same record also praises him as 'a long right arm to the *Rājādhirāja Paramēśvara* Veṅkaṭādri.' It is not possible to determine whether the sovereign referred to here was Veṅkaṭa II of Vijayanagara who reigned from A.D. 1630 to 1642 for, none of the epigraphic records of Vīrabhadra mentions any paramount ruler. If, on the other hand, the monarch meant was Veṅkaṭapatirāya I, who died in A.D. 1614, the services of Vīrabhadra must be considered to have been rendered when, as *Yuvarāja*, this Keḷadi prince was the lieutenant of his grandfather. It may be interesting to notice here a copper-plate grant[64] whose date falls into this reign. This record which bears the date Śaka 1553, Pramōda, Mārgaśira, śu. 5 (=A.D. 1630 November 28, Sunday; not verifiable) refers itself to the reign of Vīrappa-Nāyaka, son of Rāmarāja-Nāyaka. Though this prince is mentioned in the *K.N.V.*[65] under the name of Vīra-voḍeya, he is not known to have ever ascended the throne. If the grant is genuine we must surmise that he ruled for some time jointly with Vīrabhadra. Śaka 1567 expired or Śaka 1568 current (A.D. 1645) is the latest date recorded for him both in inscriptions and in the *K.N.V.*[66]

Vīrabhadra-Nāyaka had no sons and is, therefore, stated to have placed the administration of the kingdom in the hands of his uncles Śivappa-Nāyaka and Veṅkaṭappa-Nāyaka, having crowned the elder of them.[67] The *Chikkadēvarāyavaṁśāvaḷi*, however, informs us that Śivappa-Nāyaka murdered his chief Vīrabhadra-Nāyaka and ascended the throne and hence Chikka-dēvaraja the *Yuvarāja* of Mysore rejected the presents offered to him by such a traitor.[68] Though there is no apparent reason for doubting the veracity of this statement, no other evidence in support of it is available from any other source. The epigraphs of Śivappa-Nāyaka, who

61. Not found in the Mss.
62. *K. N. V.*, p. 98.
63. *Ep. Carn.* Vol. VII, Sh. 2.
64. *Ibid.* Tl. 51.
65. p. 71.
66. *Ep. Carn.*, Vol. VIII, Tl. 40 and *K. N. V.*, p. 106.
67. *S. T. R., Kallōla VI, taraṅga* 27.
68. Ramanuja Iyengar's edition .

was one of the most distinguished members of his house, range in date from A.D. 1652 to 1659. According to the *K.N.V.*[69] he ruled from A.D. 1645 to 1660 and as the latest known date of his predecessor is 1645, there does not seem to be any objection to accept the date assigned to him by the Kannaḍa work. Among his military achievements, the one that had far reaching consequences was the recapture of Vēlāpura (Vellore), from the enemy who had taken possession of it after driving out the emperor Śrīraṅgarāya. Hearing of the victory of Śivappa-Nāyaka Śrīranga who was wandering without a home came back to Vellore and gave him many titles and honours.[70] The incident narrated here seems to refer to the siege of Vellore by the combined forces of Bijapur and Golconda and the consequent flight of Śrīraṅga.[71] Śivappa who was a great warrior and who, according to Leonard Paes 'possessed enormous wealth and maintained a standing army of forty to fifty thousand men,' could easily achieve the victory claimed for him in the *S.T.R.* 'In 1653, the Bednur chief, with the help of the Dutch, drove the Portuguese out of the Honavar fort';[72] he also recovered from them other forts such as Ikkēri, Sorab and Udagaṇi, etc.[73] and built many forts in the Kērāḷa country.[74] In 1657 he recaptured from the Portuguese the forts of Kundapur, Gangolli and Mangalore.[75] He was constantly at war with the Oḍeyars of Mysore and at one time laid siege to the fort of Paṭṭaṇa (Śrirangapaṭṭaṇa)[76] which was their capital. An inscription describes him as ruling over Āraga, Gutti, Bārakūru, Maṅgāḷūru and other places, his kingdom stretching to the western ocean.[77] According to Leonardo Paes his possessions extended from the Tudry river to Kasargod or Nileśvar.[78] Thus the testimony of literature and inscriptions agree with that of foreigners in describing him as a successful warrior who confirmed the stability of his kingdom. He also introduced the land assessment known as Śivappa-Nāyaka's *shist*[79] which was in prevalence for a considerable time after him.

69. p. 116.
70. *S. T. R. Kallōla VII, taraṅga* 14.
71. pp. 2370 of the *Mys. Gaz.* by Mr. Hayavadana Rao.
72. *North Kanara Gazetteer*, p.
73. *K. N. V.*, p. 110.
74. *S. T. R., Kallōla VII, taraṅga* 14.
75. Not found in the Mss.
76. *K. N. V.*, p. 115.
77. *Ep. Carn.* VI, Sg. 11.
78. Rice: *Mysore and Coorg from Inscriptions*, p. 159.
79. *Ibid.*, p. 158.

I have very little to add to what has been already written about the successors of Śivappa by Rice and other scholars. So, I do not consider it necessary in this short paper to treat individually the reign of every ruler that followed Śivappa. The order of their succession and dates will be found in the pedigree of the dynasty given at the end of this article. Here I shall only make a few observations concerning three of them. The last date of Sōmaśēkhara-Nāyaka I was A.D. 1671 both according to Rice and the *K.N.V.* but there are two inscriptions which furnish for him the dates Śaka 1596 (A.D. 1674)[80] and Śaka 1599 (A.D. 1677).[81] It has therefore to be surmised that he lived up to A.D. 1677, though the administration of the kingdom was being carried on in the name of her husband by his wife Chennammāji, the heroic Keḷadi queen, who defeated the army of Aurangazeb which was pursuing Rājārāma. son of Śivāji, and gave him shelter. Another important fact disclosed by a third record[82] is that Chennammāji the initial year of whose reign is given by the *K.N.V.* and Rice as A.D. 1671, had as early as Śaka 1583 (A.D. 1661) issued independently, an order granting a piece of land. This date, it must be noted, falls into the reign of Bhadrappa-Nāyaka, who was the elder brother of Sōmaśēkhara-Nāyaka I and for whom inscriptions supply us with the dates A.D. 1661 to 1663. How could Chennammāji, the lawful wife (*dharmapatnī*) of Sōmaśēkhara I, make a grant under her own authority in the reign of Bhadrappa ? It is difficult to solve this problem unless we suppose that, Sōmaśēkhara also began to rule in A.D. 1661 and was co-regent with his elder brother up to 1663 which is the earliest date yet discovered for Sōmaśēkhara from inscriptions,[83] and that Chennammāji was associated with her husband in the government of the country from the very commencement of his reign. The third chief whose life has to be touched upon here is Sōmaśēkhara III, the last of the Nāyakas that exercised ruling powers. According to Rice, he died unmarried in Poona, whither he was taken by the Marathas.[84] But in the publisher's preface to the *S.T.R.* we are told that "on hearing that Hyder was contemplating an invasion of the Maratha country, he (Sōmaśēkhara) was kept under the protection of the Desai of Nargund," that he married a daughter of Basappa-Śeṭṭi at Nargund, where his descendants are still living.

A few words may now be said about the monuments of the Keḷadi chiefs, their coinage and religious and literary activities.

80. *Ep. Carn.* Vol. VIII, Tl. 188.
81. *Ibid.* Tl. 77.
82. *Mys. Arch. Rep.* 1927, p. 145, No. 170.
83. *Ep. Carn.*, Vol. VII, Sk. 27. 84. *Op. Cit.*, p. 161.

Chaudappa is stated to have built the temple of Rāmēśvara at Keḷadi, his grandson Doḍḍa-Saṅkaṇṇa installed the image of Vīrabhadra in a building by the side of the temple of Rāmēśvara and erected at Ikkēri the Aghōrēśvara temple.[85] These structures which are still preserved in a good condition have been fully described in the *Mysore Archaeological Report,* for 1932,[86] from which I give an extract :—" The Rāmēśvara temple is a medium sized structure built completely of greenish grey stone in the mixed Hoysaḷa-Dravidian style which was prevalent under the Ikkēri Nāyakas. The Vīrabhadra temple is nearly similar in form to the Rāmēśvara temple. The Aghōreśvara temple at Ikkēri is a remarkable piece of work specially because it is the largest and finest example of the Ikkēri school of architecture which appears to have flourished in the Malnāḍ during the Vijayanagara period. It reminds us of several characteristic features of Hoysaḷa architecture. It combines Hoysaḷa with Dravidian features and suggests that the architecture of Malnāḍ unlike that of Maidān was not overwhelmed by the Southern or Dravidian style but retained numerous features of Hoysaḷa style ". In the temple of Aghōrēśvara are to be seen three prostrating figures, in low relief, bearing the labels Sadāśiva-Nāyaka, Bhadra-Nāyaka and Huchcha Saṅkaṇṇa-Nāyaka.[87] Other noteworthy monuments of the Keḷadi rulers is the Champakasarasī-*maṭha* at Ānandāpura, and the tank in it called Champakasaras, both stated to have been built by Veṅkaṭappa-Nāyaka.[88] About these Rice says that this *maṭha* " must also probably have been a superior building. There still remain some fine stone elephants and a splendid tank belonging to it built round with steps of laterite ".[89] A fine specimen of the sculpture of this period is the exquisite figure of the fabulous bird *gaṇḍabhēruṇḍa* in the ceiling of the Vīrabhadra temple at Keḷadi.[90] Town planning had also reached a high level of excellence during this period. The city of Ikkēri which was visited by Pietro Dela Valle is described by him as follows :—" It was in a beautiful plain with three fortified gates and three ditches . . . The town was very large . . . and was laid out in broad shady streets and there were many pools of water and a few groves."[91]

85. *S. T. R., Kallōla V, taraṅga* 4, 9, and 10.
86. pp. 40ff.
87. *Mys. Arch. Rep.* for 1911, p. 21.
88. *S. T. R., Kallōla VI, taraṅga* 13.
89. *Ep. Carn.* Vol. VIII, Introduction, p. 16.
90. *Mys. Arch. Rep.* 1928, plate XI.
91. *Della Valle,* Travels III, 220.

The Keḷadi Nāyakas issued their own gold coins which are well known by the name of Ikkēri-*varāhas*. The gold coins of Sadāśiva-Nāyaka, which were probably restruck from time to time till the end of the dynasty, have been described by the veteran scholar MM. Rao Bahadur R. Narasiṁhacharya. He says :—"They bear on the obverse the figure of Śiva holding the trident in the right hand and the antelope in the left with Pārvatī seated on his left thigh, while on the reverse there is the legend *Śrī-Sadāśiva* in two or three horizontal lines in Nāgarī characters. This obverse which was derived from the coins of Harihara, Dēvarāya and Sadāśiva of Vijayanagara was also adopted subsequently by Hyder and Kṛishṇa-rāja Oḍeyar III of Mysore. It is of some antiquity being found in the Tinnevelly coins of the Koṛkai king Karikāla, who ruled in the early part of the 12th century. That these coins do not belong to Sadāśivarāya of Vijayanagara is clear from the absence of the epithet *Pratāpa* on the reverse."[92]

Virasaivism appears to be the faith to which the Nāyakas adhered but their catholicity and toleration are amply borne out by inscriptions and literature. They were great devotees of the Advaita *maṭha* at Śringeri to which institution they made several grants; and the *biruda viśuddha-vaidik-ādvaita-siddhānta-pratishṭhāpana* was borne by them. An inscription at Śriṅgēri dated Śaka 1542 (A.D. 1621) states that Veṅkaṭappa-Nāyaka I re-established Śriṅ-gēri.[93] Another of the same place[94] records the restoration of the endowment of the Śriṅgēri *maṭha* by Śivappa-Nāyaka. Sach-chidānanda-Svāmin, the Advaita *guru* of Muḷabāgilu (in the Shimoga District) who was also a recipient of many gifts from this family granted the village Bhadrasamudra in Śaka 1588 for the increase of the glory of Sōmaśēkhara-Nāyaka.[95] They also gave liberal patronage to the Dvaita *maṭhas* at Uḍipi and Kūḍali. Rāma-rāja-Nāyaka made a grant of land in Śaka 1493 (A.D. 1571) to the celebrated *Dvaita* teacher and scholar Vādirājatīrtha for worship in the temple of god Kṛishṇa[96] at Uḍipi. It is interesting to observe that this gift was made in order that Sadāśiva-Nāyaka may obtain reunion with Śiva. At the time of the reinstallation (*punah-pratishṭhā*) of god Kṛishṇa at Uḍipi by Vēdavēdyatīrtha, disciple of Vādirājatīrtha, in Śaka 1536 (A.D. 1613) Veṅkaṭappa-Nāyaka granted to the temple the village of Hūvinakere in Bārakūru-rājya.[97]

92. *Mys. Arch. Rep.* 1909.
93. *Ep. Carn.* Vol. VI, Sg. 5
94. *Ibid.*, Sg. 11.
95. *Ep. Carn.* Vol. VIII, Tl. 156.
96. *Ibid.*, Sb. 35.
97. *S. I. I.*, Vol. VII, No. 297.

Sōmaśēkhara-Nāyaka III made a grant of the village Sāvagoṇḍanahaḷḷi to Raghurājatīrtha of the Kūḍali-*maṭha*.[98] They made endowments not only to Hindu institutions but also to mosques. As an instance of this may be mentioned a grant of land made in Śaka 1550 (A.D. 1627) by Veṅkaṭappa-Nāyaka I to a mosque built by him at Bhuvanagiridurga.[99] Though no gift is known to have been made to any Christian institution, " there were more than thirty thousand Christians among the subjects of Śivappa-Nāyaka."[100]

As regards literature, Veṅkaṭappa-Nāyaka I wrote a commentary in Sanskrit on *Śivagita*[101] and got a Kannaḍa work of the same name as well as another entitled *Śivāshṭagīte* written by Tirumalabhaṭṭa.[102] During the same reign the poet Raṅganātha Dīkshita wrote a commentary on the Āgamic work *Tantrasāra*. Aśvapaṇḍita, another scholar in his court, wrote a treatise on horses known as *Mānapriya*. Rāmānuja-Śriṅgin, a great Viśishṭādvaita teacher, was greatly respected and supported by this Nāyaka.[103] The patronage afforded by this ruler to the Mādhva scholars Vādirājatīrtha and his disciple Vēdavēdyatīrtha has already been mentioned. Basavappa-Nāyaka I, the adopted son of Chennammāji, wrote the *Śivatatvaratnākara*[104] in A.D. 1708. He was also the author of another Sanskrit work named *Subhāshita-suradruma* and the Kannaḍa work *Sūktisudhākara*.[105] Appayya of Bhaṭakaḷa, who composed many songs in Kannaḍa and to whom MM. R. Narasimhacharya assigns the date *circa* A.D. 1705, seems to have been a protegé of this ruler.[106] Nirvāṇayya, a minister of Sōmaśēkhara II, wrote the *Śivapūjāvidhāna* in Kannaḍa.[107] Thus the Nāyakas of Keḷadi were not only scholars well versed both in Sanskrit and Kannaḍa but were also patrons of many learned men and poets.

98. *Ep. Carn.* Vol. VII, Sh. 98.
99. *Ibid.*, Vol. VIII, Tl. 38.
100. Rice : *Mysore and Coorg from Inscriptions*, p. 159.
101. Sources of Vijayanagara History, p. 345, n.
102. *K. N. V.*, p. 88.
103. *Ibid.*
104. *S. T. R.* p. 434.
105. *K. N. V.*, p. 175.
106. *Lives of Kannaḍa Poets*, Vol. II, pp. 1-2.
107. *Ibid.* p. 28.

Pedigree of the Nāyakas of Keḷadi.

- Chauḍa-Gauḍa, A.D. 1506.
  - Sadāśiva-Nāyaka, A.D. 1544-45 to 1565.
    - Doḍḍa Saṅkaṇṇa-Nāyaka *alias* (?) Immaḍi Sadāśiva-Nāyaka, A.D. 1566.
      - Rāmarāja-Nāyaka, A.D. 1570 to 1586 (co-regent with his uncle).
        - Vīrappa-Nāyaka, A.D. 1630.
      - Veṅkaṭappa-Nāyaka I, A.D. 1592 to 1629.
        - Bhadrappa.
          - Vīrabhadra-Nāyaka, A.D. 1629 to 1645.
    - Chikka Saṅkaṇṇa-Nāyaka, A.D. 1570 to 1580.
      - Siddappa.
        - Śivappa-Nāyaka, A.D. 1652, 1659 (1645 - 1660).[108]
          - Bhadrappa-Nāyaka, A.D. 1661 to 1663 (1661 - 63).
          - Sōmaśēkhara-Nāyaka, A.D. 1663 to 1677 (1663 - 71) *married* Chennammāji, A.D. 1661 to 1697 (1671 - 97).
            - (adopted) Basappa-Nāyaka I, A.D. 1702 to 1714 (1697 - 1714).
              - Sōmaśēkhara-Nāyaka II, A.D. 1722 to 1737 (1714 - 39).
              - Vīrabhadra.
                - Basappa-Nāyaka II, A.D. 1740, 1752 (1739 - 54) *married* Virammāji[109] (1757 - 63).
                  - (adopted) Chenna-Basappa-Nāyaka, A.D. 1755 (1754 - 57).
                  - (adopted) Sōmaśēkhara-Nāyaka III,[110] A.D. 1758.
        - Veṅkaṭappa-Nāyaka, A.D. 1660 (1660 - 61).
  - Bhadrappa

108. The dates inside brackets are those given by the *K. N. V.* and Rice; others are those found in inscriptions.

109. No epigraph of this queen's reign has yet come to light.

110. No date is assigned to this ruler in the *K. N. V.*

23

An Interesting Chapter in the History of Vijayanagara

By

Mr. N. K. Venkatesam Pantulu, M.A., L.T.,
Retired Lecturer, Anantapur.

The rise and fall of the kingdom of Vijayanagara was not a mere historical accident. It was a very significant event in the age-long history of India. The Fourteenth Century was an age of literary and art Renaissance in Europe. Italy took the lead in this Renaissance, as it was in Italy that the Græco-Roman Culture had still the embers in a latent condition. The great Vedantic Culture established in India by Śrī Śankarāchārya and kept a living force in the Karnāṭaka Country through the Mutt at Śringeri, founded by the Jagadguru, was gradually losing its hold on the people. The Mahomedan invasions were threatening not merely the political atmosphere of the country, but their advent was becoming a menace even to the social and religious welfare of the people during the fourteenth century. The culture and the civilisation of the people were threatened with a set-back. It was then that the Sage of Virūpāksha, Śrī Vidyāraṇya Svāmi, the renowned commentator of the Vedas, hailed from the Mutt of Śrī Śankarāchārya of the Kāmakoṭi Pītha of Kānchipuram and heralded a spiritual and political Renaissance in the Karnāṭaka country. A new life was given to the Mutt at Śringeri and as many as eight Mutts were founded in the Karnāṭaka country, to serve as spiritual beacon-lights for the country. The Sage who founded his own Vīrūpāksha Pīṭha at Pampa, now known as Hampi, helped his own disciples Harihara and Bukka to inaugurate a political sovereignty at Hampi, the seat of Śrī Vīrūpākshēśvara and Śrī Bhuvanēśvari. This kingdom which was established in 1336, reached its high-water mark during the celebrated reign of Śrī Krishṇadēva Rāya, but owing to political and historical circumstances, the kingdom grew weak, after the sovereignty of the Saṅgama and the Sāḷuva Dynasties (1336 to 1505). During the reign of Krishṇadēva Rāya, the kingdom extended over the reign covered by the present " Presidency of Madras, with the addition of Mysore and the other native States in the Peninsula." Though the Empire actually broke up after the historic battle of Tālikōta (1565), it may be said that the glory of the Empire began to wane even during the sovereignty of Achyuta Rāya, the brother of Krishṇadeva Rāya. History has recorded the events leading up to the battle of Tāḷikōṭa, the breaking up of the Empire, the dispersal of the powerful and power-loving chieftains of the ruling dynasty, only to wander out to Penukonda, Chandragiri, Mysore, etc., making efforts to continue the cultural and political activities of the Vijayanagar Kings for some length of time, until a new order replaced the old order of things.

This interesting chapter, however, has reference to the passing of the cultural and political sovereignty of a section of the House of the Vijayanagar Kings to a distant and different scene. Tirumalamma, the Queen of Achyutadeva Rāya had a sister by name Mūrtimāmba. She was given in marriage to an officer of the king's household, a shrewd and intelligent dependent of the king, and a gifted and loved disciple of the court-astrologer and Pandit, Govinda Dīkshita, who was later to play a prominent part in the cultural and political atmosphere of the region covered by the Delta of the Cauvery known as the Tanjore Samasthāna in the Chōla Dēśa. The period covered by these rulers, known as the Nāyaka Kings of Tanjore extended from the middle of the sixteenth century to the middle of the seventeenth century. The sovereignty during the period was held by Chevvappa, the husband of Mūrtimāmba, who obtained the Principality of Tanjore as his dowry, Achyutappa and Raghunātha Nāyaka, a great patron of letters and a distinguished author. This last sovereign of Tanjore was to the Tanjore Principality what Krishṇadēva Rāya was to Vijayanagar. Govinda Dīkshita was the minister of these three Nāyak Kings, and with the co-operation of the king and the gifted minister, the region was made a very flourishing and cultured colony of the kingdom of Vijayanagar. Govinda Dīkshita's son Yāgñanārāyana Dīkshita, the Court-Poet, says in his work Sāhitya Ratnākara that Govinda Dīkshita was given Ardhāsana by the king Raghunātha Nāyaka and that the king learnt the art of government from the great scholar, philosopher and statesman, Govinda Dīkshita.

The literary and historical works of the period and the inscriptions of the period bear testimony to the magnitude of the good work done by the Nāyaka Kings in Tanjore. For one thing the present Sarasvati Mahāl Library attached to the palace at Tanjore reveals the extent to which Āndhra Literature and culture permeated the Chōla Dēśa, which is now claimed as a Tamil country. The network of Pāṭhasālās even now persisting in that region shows the spirit in which the work of literary and educational reconstruction was handled by this section of the rulers of Vijayanagar who had the headship of Tanjore in their hands for over a century. The irrigation system of the Cauvery, which even to this day leaves very little water to be delivered to the Sea-God Varuna, shows the perfection with which the works of national well-being were undertaken by the Nāyaka Kings of Tanjore.

The fine state of the country during the rule of the Nayak Kings is shown in the beautiful description of the region given by Kaḷālē Vīrārāju, the commander-in-chief of the Mysore kings, who passed in that century through the region, during his expedition to the south. He thus describes the region in Chapter 34 of the Sabhā Parva in his *Āndhra Vachana Bhārata* (p. 101) :—

సహదేవుండు కావేరీదర్శనంబు గావించుటయును, నయ్యెడంగల రాజులనిర్జించుటయును, సవిస్తరంబుగ నా నతీయవలయునని నతండు జనమేజయునుద్దేశించి, సహదేవుండు గావించిన సాహసంబు నీకెఱింగించెద. ఆకర్ణింపుము. అట్లుకాననద్వీప నివాసుల నోర్చి చోళరాజ్యంబు ప్రవేశించి యయ్యెడ సాలమోధ, యర్జున బిల్వంబులును జంబూశాలశిలీకింశుకంబులును, సప్తపర్ణ కాశ్మరశ్యామల కన్యగ్రోధ ప్లక్షోదుంబర శమీపలాశంబులును, నశ్వత్థఖదిర బదర్యశ్వకర్ణ ఖరంజితింత్రిణీతాల శిరీషకుటజంబులును, నింబమధూకపున్నాగ క్షీరకనకుళకుంద చంపక ప్రియాళుశోకతిలకంబులును, నతిముక్తకర్ణికార నాగకేతక కురవక జాతీకందళయూధికాంకోల కరవీరంబులును, బాటలక్రముక నారికేళ పనసామ్రచూత పుండ్రక కదళ్యాడకనీప వేతసంబులును, మొదలగు మహీరుహంబులచే దనరారెడు నుభయతీరంబులవలనను, హంసకారండవ కురరసారస శుకచక్రవాక ప్లవజల వాయస సముద్రకాకక్రౌంచ జలకుక్కుట ప్రముఖంబులను జలవిహంగ సందోహంబులవలనను, వేదవేదాంగ పారగులగు మహీసురులవలనను పుణ్యాశ్రమస్థానంబులవలనను, జైత్యవృక్షంబులవలనను, నభిరామంబగుచు నుభయతటంబులగనుపట్టుతరుశ్రేణులవలనను, బ్రసూనమాలికా అలంకృతయగు బాలిక చందంబునం బ్రకాశమానయగుచు నానాపుష్పమన్వితంబులగు లతానికుంజంబులవలన నవరత్నభూషణాలంకృతయగు కాంతాలలామంబుకైవడిం దోంచుచుంగమలోత్పలకల్వార ప్రముఖ పుష్పరజోగణంబులవలనం జందనపరాగ శోభితయగు చంచరాపితెరగు నంగీకరింపుచు హృద్యంబును, నప్సరోగణసేవితంబును, పరమపావనతీర్థ సమేతంబును, ద్రిజగత్పావనంబును, కలుషరహితంబును, సకలజనాధారంబును, నతివిస్తారంబును పైకతద్వీపశోభితంబును, స్వాదూదకపరిపూర్ణంబును, బుణ్యస్వరూపంబును, గలకావేరింగనుంగొని ప్రహృష్టాంతరంగుండగుచు, మనరాజ్యంబు నంగంగానది చందంబున నీరాష్ట్రంబునం గావేరిప్రకాశింపుచున్నయది, అనియనుచరులతోడ నన్నదీ మహత్వంబుపలుదెఱంగులంగొని యాడెను.

If the Kingdom of Vijayanagar has disappeared now under the stress of historical cataclysms, if the Tanjore Nāyak Kings have long left the scene of their activities, there is still much which has been left behind by them, to impress us with the magnitude of their effort in the onward march of Indian Culture and Civilisation. The historic ruins of Hampi give us an insight into the ancient, mediaeval and modern history of Pampā Kshētra and the Glory of the Vijayanagar Empire. The Āndhra Literature in the Tanjore Sarasvati Mahāl Library, the smiling fields and the network of irrigation works, the cultural centres in the region watered by the Cauvery are all proofs positive of the great truth of life, that what passes away is what is not worth remaining, and what remains is the work of man, as the instrument of God, that holds aloft the Light of Divine Wisdom in this Eternal World of His. We, His Agents of a Season pass, but our work remains for all time. For life is evanescent, but work is permanent. That is the lesson left on the pages of Indian History by the brief episodes of the Empire of Vijayanagar and the Kingdom of the Tanjore Nāyaka Kings, from the fourth decade of the fourteenth century to the middle of the seventeenth century.

BIBLIOGRAPHY

1. *Govinda Dīkshita, the Minister of the Tanjore Nayak Kings*, by N. K. Venkatesam Pantulu, (originally published in the Quarterly Journal of the *Andhra Historical Research Society*, Rajahmundry. Vol. II. Parts 3 and 4, 1928).

2. *Govinda Dīkshita and His Literary Successors*, by N. K. Venkatesam Pantulu. (Paper read at the Seventh Indian Oriental Conference at Baroda, in December 1933, as the Delegate to the Conference deputed by His Holiness Sri Sankaracharya Svāmiji of Kāmakōṭi Piṭha and published in the Quarterly Journal of the *Andhra Historical Research Society*, Rajahmundry, Vol. IX, Part I, July 1934.)

3. Summary of the above paper, under the original heading, "The Contribution of the Karnāṭaka Families to Sanskrit Literature in the Tamil Country." (Proceedings of the Seventh Indian Oriental Conference held at Baroda, December 1933. pp. 37 to 42).

4. *The Ruins of Hampi*, by N. K. Venkatesam Pantulu. (Price As. 4.).

5. Kaḷale Vīrarāja's *Andhra Vachana Bhāratamu*, Sabha Parvamu, (Price Re. 1-8-0).

24

Rule of Vijayanagara over Kongu Country

By

Rao Sahib C. M. Ramachandra Chettiar, B.A., B.L.,
President, District Educational Council, Coimbatore.

INTRODUCTION

Limits of Kongu—its features. "Kongu" country is a geographical unit in the Tamil-speaking tracts of South India. In physical features it has the shape of a cup surrounded by mountain ranges on all its sides excepting the south-east, where there is a gap sloping towards the Chōla country. The sacred river Kāveri divides the country into two parts running from north to south and then south-eastwards and finally emptying itself through the gap on the fertile Chōla plains. On the north the country is bounded by Toppūr, Barugūr and Talamalai ranges, on the west by the Nīlagiri and Veḷḷingiri ranges, on the south by the Ānamalai and Palni hills and on the east by Kollimalais, Javvādis and Shervaroys.[1] There are a number of gaps or passes between these ranges which afford railway and road communications with the neighbouring countries. Kongu-nāḍu is comprised of the present district of Coimbatore, a major portion of Salem and few taluks of Trichi and Madura districts. From time immemorial this part of South India had been regarded as a separate territory for all purposes including political, even while it was under the sway of other mighty powers. This country has developed a civilisation and a peculiarity of its own and has kept them up in spite of inroads from universalism, catholicity and outside influence.

Earlier Account. Tamil literature from the earliest days has assigned a separate existence for this country and the inscriptions of the mediæval days confirm the veracity of the statement. The country was known as Kongu and the people were called "The Kongar". Some of the names of the kings who ruled over the country have also been recorded. During the *Śangam-age,* "The Kongar" were a virile and fighting race and a number of military feats wherein the Kongar and their kings have taken part, have been recorded in the poems of Puṛa Nānūṛu. *Śilappadhikāram,*

1. There is an old Tamil Stanza which gives the boundaries of Kongu-Nāḍu.

an ancient Tamil classic, mentions the name of the Kongu kings of its days as Kongu Iḷaṁ-Kośar and states that they performed a festival of sacrifice in honour of the Pattinikaḍavul, Kaṉṉaki, who wreaked vengeance by seeking justice from the Pāṇḍya king for the unjust execution of her husband at his inadvertant orders. In the early days, the country had strong fortresses scattered through the length and breadth of the land, from which strong-holds war-loving chiefs known as *Vēḷirs* ruled the surrounding country. An important chief among them was Adigamān of Tagaḍūr, the modern Dharmapuri. The later day inscriptions styled him even as the Kongu king. The chieftains were often at war with their neighbours and kept the military spirit unquenched. From the 2nd century to the 9th century the Ganga dynasty ruled over the country from their capital at Talakkāḍ situated on the northern bank of the Kāveri. Under their rule the country seems to have enjoyed peace and plenty. They have been classed as Kongu chiefs by the local chronicle "Kongudēśa Rājākkaḷ". The Ganga line was overthrown by the rising Chōla Empire of Tanjore in the 9th century. Rājēndra Chōla captured their capital Talakkāḍ and annexed the Kongu country. The Chōla viceroys perhaps selected from the royal line, ruled over the Kongu country. In course of time, when the central power became weak, the viceroys asserted their independence. Even a dynasty seems to have been set up. They are named "Kongu Chōlas" by the historians. This line seems to have lasted for 2½ centuries and the epigraphical records show that much progress had been effected during their days. The Hoysalas of Halebīḍ (Dvārasamudra) put an end to their independence and occupied the major portion of the country. They were in their turn overthrown by the end of the 13th century and the beginning of the 14th century by the Afghan invasions from Delhi of Ala-ud-din Khilji and his generals. The Muhammadan occupation was neither long nor effective. Probably they never occupied any portion of, or had they any effective control over, Kongu country. After the overthrow of the Hoysalas a few minor chieftains appear to have held sway over the land till they were subdued by the rising power of Vijayanagara. From the 14th to the 17th century, the country was under Vijayanagara rule and was influenced to a considerable extent by the new Karnāṭak civilisation. It is the purport of this paper to deal with that chapter in Kongu history.

Sources of information. Information for a study of this period have to be culled out from the number of sources. The epigraphical records chiselled on the walls of the numerous temples and slabs in the country afford a good supply of material from which we could construct a political account of the country. The existence of various Telugu and Kanarese communities in the midst of a purely Tamil population, an account of their inflow into such a country and a comparative ethnological survey of their customs and manners, would make an interesting study in the social progress and architectural works found in the temples show us the high degree of the attainment in the development of art during those days. The establishment of temples, and the grants and endowments for worship in their favour, manifest the extent of the religious upheaval in that period. The migration into the country and colonisation of the same by artisans and trading communities show how the rulers wanted to develop the country economically. The buildings of anicuts over rivers and the digging of irrigation tanks prove the interest of the rulers in the welfare of the rural population by developing their agricultural facilities. From a study of the period through the above said sources of information, we could understand the problems and their details with a certain amount of accuracy and precision and could construct a narrative dealing with all aspects of activities of the then existing society.

Political aspects. At the instance of the greedy and relentless Ala-ud-din Khilji, his general Malik Kafur invaded South India and overthrew Halebīḍ, the capital of the Hoysalas in the year 1310 A.D. With the idea of subjugating all other southern states, he proceeded further south and extinguished the Pāṇḍya dynasty at Madura. A short lived sultanate was established there. Whether Malik Kafur actually passed through Kongu country during his southern raid is doubtful, as there are no direct records to that effect. But there is proof in an inscription recording the destruction of a temple during a Muhammadan raid. Though Halebīḍ fell, the Hoysala house was not destroyed at once, for we find the records of Vīra Baḷḷāḷa III till 1341 A.D. We have his last record at Daṉāyakankoṭṭai in the Kongu country of the year 1338 A.D. Hence it is clear that Vīra Baḷḷāḷa survived the attack of the Muhammadans and continued his administration long after Malik Kafur's invasion.

The Vijayanagara Empire was established by the enterprising brothers Bukka and Harihara in the early 14th century. They founded the capital Vijayanagar in the year 1336.[2] They slowly extended their rule towards the neighbouring tracts. On the north the enterprising Muhammadan state of the Bahmanis rose at Kul-

2. Now there is difference of opinion as regards the date.

burga and arrested their progress. On the south the field was open and their efforts were successful. The disorganised south gave an advantage to the new rising Empire and within a short period the whole South India came under their control. The Kongu country shared the fate with her sister territories of the South. The first Vijayanagara inscription in the Coimbatore district is found at Modalli and is dated 1368 A.D. It is a record of the reign of Kampaṇṇa Udaiyār II, and proves directly the entry of Vijayanagara into this land. The latest record of the Vijayanagara kings is dated 1667 and it was during the reign of Śrīrangarāya. Hence we can define the period of the rule of Vijayanagara over Kongu country as having lasted from 1368 to 1667 for full 3 centuries.

A careful study of the inscriptions of this period throws light upon the question how the Vijayanagara kings slowly entered the Kongu country, what time they took to occupy the entire state, how they lost influence by the traitorous activities of their viceroys who set themselves up as independent chiefs for a time, how Krishṇadēvarāya recovered the lost power, how the rule continued for a century more and how the rising dynasties of Mysore and Madura snatched the power for themselves. We will deal hereafter in detail with the evidence afforded about these points from the inscriptions and other sources.

SANGAMA OR DYNASTY I

Kampaṇṇa Udaiyār II (Son of Bukka I) A.D. 1368. Three inscriptions of this sovereign have been deciphered in the Coimbatore district, one at Modalli[3] and two at Sadayampāḷayam[4]. The earliest among them is dated 1368 which has been shown above as the date of the commencement of Vijayanagar entry into this country. A very important political fact is related by the Sadayampāḷayam inscriptions of this period. They say that Kūraiyūr temples which were desecrated and defiled by the Muhammadans were renovated and rebuilt subsequently by Avudayarāja. The temples were Nāgēśvaram Uḍaiyār and Vaḍugu Piḷḷaiyār. The destruction of the temples would have been done during the sweeping invasion

3. Madalli :—Ep. Rt. 246 of 1913.
4. Sadayampāḷayam :—135 and 136 of 1920.

"In 1365-66, Bukka I turned his attention to the south, and sent his son, Kampaṇṇa Uḍaiyār, or Kampa II, to overthrow the Muhammadan Sultanate of Madura."—*Salem District Gazetteer.*

The above quoted Sadayampāḷayam inscription might be after this campaign.

of the Muhammadans either of Malik Kāfur or of the subsequent incursions, during the short lived Sultanate at Madura. Evidently, the Muhammadans were driven out, or would have gone away without settling themselves permanently, and a subsequent ruler renovated the temple. This has been done during the first Vijayanagara sovereign, who entered Kongu. This act is an example of real Vijayanagara spirit. Thence Kongu country began to feel the true Vijayanagara influence.

Vīra Arayappadēva (Harihara II) A.D. 1386-97. There are three inscriptions of this king at Eragandhaḷḷi[5] and Singanallur.[6 and 7] all in Koḷḷegāl. They are dated 1386, 1390 and 1397 respectively. The inscription of 1386 is a record on a Vīrakkal which was installed to perpetuate the heroic death of a Gowḍa in fighting with the robbers after killing some with an axe. It might be noted in this connection that there are a good number of Vīrakkals in Kongu Nāḍu similar to those found in Kannaḍa (Karnatic) territories. Vīrakkals are memorial stones of heroic men who die for their country on battle fields, in fighting with wild beasts to protect crops and human beings, and with robbers, who waylay high roads. Very rarely such memorial stones bear the names of the heroes and their dates. We are fortunate here to have these details engraved in the above said Vīrakkal.

Vīra Dēvarāya I (Son of Harihara II) A.D. 1408. There is only one inscription of this king in this country. It is dated 1408 and is found in Singanallūr.[8] We have to note that the power of Vijayanagara was not felt much in the Kongu country during the reigns of this ruler as well as that of his father the previous ruler. We find that the inscriptions of their reigns are confined to the Koḷḷegāl taluk more or less on the borders of Kongu country. Hence we have to conclude that the effective occupation had not yet been achieved during these two reigns.

Vīra Harihararāya III (Son of Dēvarāya I) A.D. 1400-1412. Two inscriptions of this king have been discovered one at Vijaya-

5. Eragandhaḷḷi :—Ep. Rt. 179/1910.

6 & 7. Singanallūr :—18/1910. This mentions 500 merchants of Ayyavale. "Some time prior to 1384, Hari Hara II sent his son Virūpāksha on an expedition to the south, and this prince claims victories over the kings of Tonḍai-Manḍalam, the Chōla, the Pandyas and Ceylon. One or other these campaigns must have brought the Salem district under the sway of Vijayanagara." p.—*Salem District Gazetteer.*

8. Singanallūr :—Ep. Rt. 19/1910, mentions Mahāpradāna Nāgama Nāyaka.

mangalam[9] dated 1412, and the other at Komaralingam[10] dated 1400. Vijayamangalam is the famous Jaina centre situated almost in the centre of Kongu country. It is on the main trunk road between Coimbatore and Erode. Komaralingam is an important *Agrahāram* situated on the northern bank of Amrāvati in South Kongu. The existence of these two in the centre and the South Kongu testify that Vijayanagara rule had already extended over the entire Kongu Nāḍu.

Dēvarāya II (son of Vīra Vijaya Rāya), A.D. 1419-1451. There are two inscriptions of this king dated 1440 and 1441. (in Coimbatore District). Both of them are found at Kolinjivāḍi, now a suburb of Dhārāpuram on the southern bank of the Amrāvati.[11] Kolinjivāḍi is in South Kongu far east of Komaralingam. The former is in Dhārāpuram taluk, while the latter is in Udamalpet taluk. The existence of Kolinjivādi inscriptions confirm the entire occupation by Vijayanagara of the Kongu country during the earlier reign itself. There are four other inscriptions at Palni (Madura),[12] Trichī and Salem districts.

The above said sovereigns belong to the first Vijayanagara dynasty, *viz.*, Sangama dynasty. After Devarāya II there were a few other sovereigns of this dynasty. We do not find their inscriptions in this territory. They were weak rulers as is evidenced by the usurpation of the 2nd or Sāḷuva dynasty. Moreover they were short lived. Hence it is quite natural that no inscriptions of their reigns are found in this distant territory. All the same, it is clear that the entire Kongu country came under the Vijayanagara rule even during the days of Harihara III.

SĀLUVA OR DYNASTY II

There is a complete gap in the inscriptional evidence for nearly three-fourths of a century between the days of Devarāya II of the first dynasty and the famous Krishṇa Dēvarāya of the third dynasty. The absence of inscriptions during this period is accounted for in detail hereafter. Though there are no inscriptions of the second or

9. Vijayamangalam :—Ep. Rt. 596/1905 in Chandranātha (Jain) temple.

10. Kumaralingam :—Ep. Rt. 132/1909, the name of the village is given as Kumaranga-Bhīma-Chaturvēdimangalam.

11. Kolinjivāḍi :—Ep. Rt. 581/1893 and 583/1893. (511, 5-257-59).

12. Palni :—Ep. Rt. 610/94, 740/09, 193/10 and 196/10.

Note.—Kolinjivāḍi Inscriptions 583/93 records the destruction of the temple of Śokkanātha of the village in the Muhammadan raid and the subsequent renovation by the Tarangaya Manṛāḍiyār.

Sāḷuva dynasty, yet a mention has been made in a Telugu poem dedicated to the Emperor Sāḷuva Narasimha, the founder of the second dynasty about his conquest of a number of forts including Dhārāpuri in Kongu country. The poem is " Jaimini Bharathamu " written by Piḷḷalamarri Pina Vīrabhadra. The relevant lines from the poem are : —

Jinayōpāya Vihāra Bōnagiri henjī Kongu Dhārāpurī
Penukoṇḍāya khilaika durgaharaṇa prēnkhatpratāpodayā.

These lines reveal the conquest by Sāḷuva Narasimha of the forts of Bonagir, (Bhuvanagiri), Ginji, Kongu Dhārāpuri and Penukoṇḍa. Dhārāpuri of Kongu cannot be other than Dhārāpuram on the river Amrāvati. We have already mentioned about the existence of two inscriptions of Devārāya II dated 1440 and 1441 at Kolinjivāḍi, now a suburb of Dhārāpuram. Hence it is clear that the fort of Dhārāpuram (Dhārāpuram has a ruined fort even now) had been brought under control even during the reign of Devarāya. Hence to say that Sāḷuva Narasimha conquered Dhārāpuram is only a poetical exaggeration of a continued occupation which itself was considered to be a victorious conquest, which is a common usage in poetical imagination among the poets who sing the praise of their patron kings. After the reign of Devarāya, the control over Kongu seems to have been loose as will be explained in the following section.

UMMATTŪR AND TERKKANĀMBI INTERREGNUM[13]

Whenever the central power weakens, the viceroys and petty chiefs throw off the yoke and set up independence leading to the downfall of their masters. This is the bane of Indian politics. History has repeated itself any number of times and it had done so in this period as well. After Devarāya II, his successors were weak and dissensions arose regarding succession. The control of distant territories became ineffective. Kongu country was far away. It was under a viceroy who ruled at Ummattūr. These chieftains grew powerful, and, as the sovereign of Vijayanagara became weak, they began to exercise acts of independence. They issued edicts in their own names as if they were sovereigns. Accession of territories

13. During the interregnum mentioned above, a few inscriptions of the reigns of Bhujabalarāya Immaḍi Narasa), 1492, Vīra Narasa 1506, Mallikārjuna 1476, have been found. But they are all on the borders of Kongu country only.

and wars with their neighbours were common. These overt acts of independence are common in such cases. The causes for such acts are the recognition of viceroys as smaller kings rather than mere officers with delegated powers. Military and Revenue affairs were never controlled by the central power. Hereditary system of succession is a bane to effective control. These causes led the Ummattūr chiefs to hold their own in defiance of the central power. We now give an account of the rulers who acted practically as independent sovereigns in this interregnum.

Vira Nañja Rāya Uḍaiyar.[14] About 10 inscriptions of this chief are found in this country of which 9 are in the Coimbatore district and one is at Palni in Madura district. Some of the dates are 1489, 1497 and 1499. They correspond with the confused period after Devarāya II, and that of the early part of the Sāḷuva dynasty. The inscriptions in the Coimbatore district show that they are scattered throughout the length and breadth of the Kongu country. The very fact that this chieftain's name has been used in all the edicts goes to show that he had tried to assert his independence in spite of his suzerain. At Periyapāḷayam, 9 miles east of Tirupur railway station, there is an old temple, with the major portion now in ruins, containing an inscription of his. This place was known in the 9th century as Kurakkuttaḷī, and has got the sanctity of being mentioned in the sacred Tēvāram of Śrī Sundaramūrti Nāyanār (825 A.D.). Near this place there is a big irrigation tank still in use. It is known as Nanjarāyaṅkuḷam after this Ummattūr chieftain. Nanjarāya is known to have been an enlightened prince who interested himself in the agricultural uplift of the country.

Vīra Chikkarāya Uḍaiyār.[15] This prince is the son of Vīra Nanjarāya. Three inscriptions of his are found and they are dated 1508 and 1512. As they are found at Avanāśi, Kunnatur and Kuntur, the extent of his rule seem to have been the same as that of his father. With this chief the hereditary line seems to have disappeared.

14. Nanjā Rāya's Inscriptions are found at Avanāśī—198/09, 200/09.

15. Chikkarāya:—Avanāśi 199/09, gift by a merchant.
Kunnatur—Inscriptions S. Dists. No. 6, gift of a tank.
Kuntur—23/10, gift of tascas for providing food and clothing to 50 Voḍeyars of Śivāchār seat of *Śānta Dēvara Simhāsana,* in Hadināḍu.

Vīra Nanjaṇṇa Uḍaiyār.[16] This prince is the son of Dhēppana Uḍaiyār. It is not known how he is connected with the former chiefs. There are four inscriptions of his ranging from 1507 to 1517. They are scattered throughout the country, as they are found at Nambiyūr, Paṭṭaṇam, Palni and Dhārāpuram. Another name Nanjamma Uḍayār, son of Pratāpa Harihararāya is also mentioned in the last inscription.

Terkkanāmbi Mādayya. There is a fine symmetrical masonry tank built of chiselled stones in front of the Pērūr temple. On its 16 sides there are Tamil and Kannaḍa inscriptions to the effect "*Terkkanāmbi Śankaraiyana maga-Mādayyana sēva.*" The tank had been constructed by this chief, when he ruled over the country. But the dates are not given. He constructed a Śiva temple on the eastern bank of the tank and named it after himself as Mādavīsvaram. Probably he was a viceroy of Vijayanagara during this interregnum.

TUḶUVA OR DYNASTY III—KRISHṆA DĒVA RĀYA (1509-1530)

The Sāḷuva dynasty was succeeded by the Tuḷuva dynasty of which Krishṇadeva Rāya was the most brilliant monarch. He was a man of action and considerable ability, and he determined to extend the empire by bringing all the vassals under his control. Vijayanagara rose to its height under this illustrious monarch. The battle of Raichur drove away the Muhammadans beyond the Krishṇa. His eastern campaign added the Northern Sircars to his territories. His southern progress as far as Rāmēśvaram, as depicted in the brilliant account in Telugu Rāyavāchakamu and in the poem Krishṇarājavijayamu by Kumāradūrjati, was responsible for bringing all the southern States as far as Rāmēśvaram and the Cape under his control. Soon after Krishṇadēva ascended the throne he found that the viceroys in the south had become disobedient during the prior weak regimes. One of such viceroys was the Ummattūr chief under whose control Kongu country was. Krishṇadevarāya proceeded against him and reduced the fort of Śvasamudram in a single day's fight. The Raja was driven out and another viceroy Parvatarāhuta by name was installed. This campaign would have

16. Vira Nanjamma Uḍayar—Nambiyur. 202/09.
Paṭṭanam—210/09 ; six merchants rebuilt the village and called it Śrīnāthapaṭṭaṇa.
Kattangani (Dhārāpuram), 278/1920. The father's name is given as Hari Hara Rāya.

taken place in 1510, the very next year after Krishṇadēvarāya's accession to the throne, for we find an inscription at Erode of the date 1510-11 mentioning Parvatarāhuta as the viceroy of Krishṇadēvarāya.[17] This viceroy unlike the prior Ummattūr viceroys seems to have been a loyal one, for we find thereafter that Krishṇadēvarāya had been recognised as the real sovereign throughout the Kongu country. About 7 inscriptions have been found scattered in Coimbatore, Salem and Madura districts. They range from 1518 to 1528. The inscription of 1518 found at Kokkarāyapet,[18] Salem district, describes Krishṇadēvarāya as "Rājākkaḷ Tambirān" meaning king of kings. It shows that Krishṇadevarāya was wielding real sovereign power. The other inscriptions in the Salem district are one at Indore[19] (Dharmapuri taluk) and the other at Trichengoḍ.[20] The latter is dated 1528. It deals with the endowment of market tolls to celebrate certain festivals. In the Coimbatore district there is an inscription dated 1545 found at Sēvūr in the centre of the district.[21] In Madura district there is one at Palni dated 1520.[22] According to it an officer Koṇḍaiyadēva makes a gift to the temple. In the Dindigal taluk there is an inscription at Agaram[23] and another at Taḍikombu,[24] both dated 1522. According to the latter 24 houses had been built and endowed. This incident reveals a colonization scheme. We find therefore inscriptions supporting the literary evidence mentioned above in confirming the control of Krishṇadeva over Kongu.

ACHYUTARĀYA 1530-1542[25]

About 11 inscriptions have been discovered of this sovereign ranging from 1530 to 1540. They are found in Coimbatore, Salem and Madura districts. The Dindigal fort shrine has an inscription of the year 1538. Atamankoṭṭai inscription dated 1530 makes gifts of taxes.

17. Erode—169/10. Parvata Rāhuta.
18. Kokkarayapet—466/13. 25th January, 1518.
19. Indore—13/1900.
20. Trichengoḍ—651/05.
21. Sēvūr—S. Dists.—27.
22. Palni—612/93.
23. Agaram—4/94.
24. Taḍikombu—S. Dists. No. 3, p. 47.
25. Achyuta's—Avanāśi, Eraganahalli, Kuntur, Modalli, Dindigal, Atmankoṭṭai, Tāramangalam and Kokkarāyanpet.

SADĀŚIVARĀYA 1540-1567[26]

About 8 inscriptions have been found ranging from 1544 to 1565. This prince was almost a prisoner. But his suzerainty was acknowledged throughout the empire till the fall of Vijayanagara at the battle of Rākshas-Tangadi in 1565. We know that Aḷiya Rāmarāja was the real ruler. During this reign a southern campaign seems to have been projected under the command of Timmaraja in the year 1545. This campaign is echoed in the inscription at Ratnagiri, Trichinopoly district, which says that Rāmarāja Chinna Timmayya made a gift to the temple. This person is a prince of Āravīti family. Timmarāja is mentioned in two other inscriptions at the same place. The name of Aḷiya Rāmarāja who was the real ruler is mentioned in an inscription dated 1556 at Kārimangalam (Salem district). After the capture of Madura by Nāgaṇṇa and his son Viśvanātha and the establishment of a hereditary viceroyalty, the Madura feudatory Nāyaks began to throw off the yoke of Vijayanagara. The central power having become weaker since the death of Krishṇadēva, Madura Nāyaks had begun to raise their heads even as the Uḍaiyārs of Śrīrangapaṭam. With Sadāśivarāya, the Tuḷuva dynasty became extinct.

ĀRAVĪṬI OR DYNASTY IV

After the defeat of Vijayanagara in 1565, the princes of the Āraviti dynasty became the ruling ones. But their rule was very weak and nominal. Very few inscriptions of these sovereigns are found. Vīravenkaṭapati I (1586-1614) is represented by three inscriptions in Erode and Śivasamudram bearing the dates 1588 and 1604. Śrīranga is represented at Dharmapuri by one inscription dated 1619. Rama IV is represented by an inscription dated 1629 at Taḍikombu. Śrirangarāya is represented by four inscriptions in Coimbatore district dating from 1655 to 1667. With him the names of Vijayanagara kings disappeared from Kongu country. Even these sovereigns of Āravīṭi dynasty were merely nominal heads, for as mentioned above, Madura and Mysore had begun to encroach upon the Kongu country. A few copper-plates of the Nāyaka kings Tirumal Nāyaka and Chockanātha bearing the dates 1655, 1665 and 1667 really show that they had assumed full sovereign power, though they owed theoretical allegiance to Śrīrangarāya.[27] Tirumal Nāyaka of Madura was actually in possession

26. Sadāśiva—Kollegal, Śingaṇattūr, Ratnagiri, Kārimangalam 5/1900 and Tāramangalam.

27. C. P. of Nāyāks—Sewell's History—186, 190. Ind. Ant. 1916

of the whole of south Kongu and a relative[27-a] of his, Aḷagadri Nāyaka, built the famous Kanaka Sabha at Pērūr which possesses some of the most exquisite sculptural pillars in South India. The Mysore kings rose to power and vied with Madura for the possession of the Kongu country. The earliest Mysore record is that of Krishṇaraja dated 1557 found at Kāramaḍai.[28] But Mysore really came to the scene during the reign of Kaṇṭīrava Narasarāja 1638 to 1659. The inscription at Erode of the year Manmatha, records the triumph of Mysore over Madura at the famous battle of Erode.[29] This battle decided the fate of Kongu, for from that time onward the whole of Kongu Nāḍu came under the control of Mysore Voḍeyars. The above brief sketch of the political history will show that Kongu country was under Vijayanagara nominally for three centuries from 1368 to 1667 but effectively for 1½ centuries from the reign of Devarāya I *viz.*, 1400 till the fall of Vijayanagara 1565. Even during this period there was an interregnum of the recalcitrant viceroys of Ummattūr. But all the same the influence of Vijayanagara was felt in this territory throughout the three centuries in social, religious and economic spheres. After all, the civilization of the successors of Vijayanagara was also the same as that of Vijayanagara.

Social aspect. Before the advent of Vijayanagara, Kongu Nāḍu was purely a Tamil country. The Hoysaḷas would have been responsible for the settlement of a small percentage of Kannaḍa population. The Kannaḍa families would have crossed the ghats by the Nīlgiris or Hasanūr passes. They generally favoured the foot of the hills and settled mostly on dry lands. Even now their villages are found all along the foot of the ghats. The taluk of Koḷḷegal has a purely Kannaḍa population even from the early days. The advent of Vijayanagara was responsible for much of Telugu immigration. The campaigns of Vijayanagara brought large numbers of Telugu soldiers into the south, and many of them settled here. The principal officers who administered the country were mostly of Telugu or Kannaḍa extraction. Naturally along with them several families followed. Trade and industry brought a large population. The State aided such enterprises. As a result of such a colonization, we find to-day in Kongu Nāḍu a good percentage of Telugu and Kannaḍa population. The following figures taken from the census report of 1931 are instructive :—

27-a. Half brother (S.K.).
28. Kāramaḍai—record—Ins. S. Dists., p. 32, No. 11.
29. Erode Ins.—170/1910. (Dalavayi Hampayya and Madura).
Salem Dists. Gazetteer, pp. 69 to 71.

Portions of districts in Kongu Nāḍu.	Telugu percentage.	Kanarese percentage.	Tamil percentage.
Coimbatore East	14.6	...	85.4
Coimbatore West	27.0	11.9	61.1
Salem North	16.9	8.8	74.3
Salem South	15.6	...	84.4
Madura North	22.7	9.8	67.5
Trichy West	16.3	...	83.7

A study of these figures will illustrate how far Telugu and Kanarese tongues have penetrated into purely Tamil area. Along with the languages the customs and manners of the people have come in. Till a few decades ago there were even Telugu schools in many of the villages and there existed even a few poets among the Telugus. In certain taluks there are pure Kannaḍa and Telugu speaking villages without any admixture of other tongues. In many of the villages the village headmen and the priests are found to be either a Kannaḍa or a Telugu man. Under such circumstances the influence exercised by Vijayanagara over the country would have been considerable even in social matters. There are a few inscriptional records to testify social legislation as well. Caste troubles have been decided by the assemblies of villagers which were guided by village officers appointed by the State. It is curious to note that the Telugu and Kannaḍa communities who settled in Kongu Nāḍu have kept up their customs and manners intact even till to-day. Some of the traditional accounts about their immigration are very interesting and noteworthy. Stories of faith, folklore, folk-songs, games and amusements have been preserved by them in spite of the mingling effect in their adopted country. Caste customs have never been altered. Though such unmingling and separate tendencies exist, yet Hindu society has tolerated such differences and for all outward purposes everything in the land seemed to be sailing smooth.

Religious aspect. During the regime of Vijayanagara old temples have been renovated and fine sculptures have been added to the temples. Nāyaka viceroys were also particular in beautifying the temples so also the Ummattūr chiefs. Pērūr owes its grandeur to the Nāyaka chief, Aḷagādri, while Avanāśi to the Terkkanāmbi Śankariah, several temples in the Salem and Madura portions owe their renovation to Vijayanagara.

The village priests who officiate even to the Tamilian communities are often found to be Telugu prohits. Grants and endowments for worship in temples have been liberally made during the Vijayanagara regime. With the construction of Maṇḍapams in the temples, fine art had been patronized and sculptors have been imported into the country. The superb architecture of Pērūr, Periyapāḷayam, Tāramangalam and Taḍikombu has become proverbial. Chains in single granite, huge lotuses hanging from the canopy with revolving rings round the lotus buds, irremovable stone balls in the mouths of chimerical beasts are some of the wonders in stone wrought by the Vijayanagara sculptors.

Economical aspect. It would be curious to note that most of the artisan communities in Kongu Nāḍu are Telugu or Kannaḍa people. Among the weavers Telugu and Kannaḍa Devāngas are prominent. They are in huge numbers not only in villages but also in cities like Coimbatore and Salem. They look for their central religious headship to the mutt on the Hēmakūṭa hill near the Pampāpati temple at Hampi (Vijayanagara). The tradition current among them show that they came towards the south during Vijayanagara regime. Goldsmiths, washermen, petty trading communities like Kempatties, Turaiyas, are all of Kannaḍa or Telugu extraction. Among the agricultural classes, the Kannaḍa *Okkiliga*, Telugu *Kāpu*, Telugu *Kamma* are very prominent. The last among them have become prominent in cotton cultivation, ginning and spinning. Not only among these higher classes but even among the depressed communities there are Kanarese and Telugu *Chakkiliars*, and Kanarese *Holeyas* found everywhere. Most of the villages have *Chakkiliar natams* whose inhabitants form the bulwark of agriculture in the land. From these facts it would be plain how far Vijayanagara had helped Kongu country in the development of industry and agriculture. There is the evidence of inscriptions to prove that the state took active steps in importing artisans, especially weavers, and colonising them in specific areas. To improve agriculture, rivers have been dammed, irrigation tanks have been dug. We have already given one example of an irrigation tank by the name of Nanjarāyaṅkuḷam. These are in brief some of the improvements made in the Kongu country by the enlightened monarchs of Vijayanagara

25

The Vidyasankara Temple, Sringeri

An example of early Vijayanagara Architecture

BY

DR. M. H. KRISHNA, M.A., D.LITT. (LOND.),
Professor of History, Mysore University and Director of Archæology, Mysore State.

ARCHITECTURAL history and the diffusion of artistic traditions has its own story to tell about the cultural connections of the Vijayanagara empire. A detailed study and analysis of a typical structure of the early Vijayanagara period may be of much interest.

CONSERVATION WORK

Before we proceed to study the details of the Vidyāśankara temple, it may just be mentioned that this monument only marks the commencement of a great series of architectural contributions made by the rulers of that empire. Most of their work is in the nature of additions to or renovations of more ancient monuments inherited from the days of the Cholas, the Hoysalas, the Chāḷukyas, etc., for the Vijayanagara kings believed in a motto which they have published at the conclusion of a large number of their inscriptions that it is more meritorious to restore and uphold the charity of previous generations than to make fresh constructions. The early Vijayanagara rulers followed this policy and wherever their kingdoms spread they studied the needs of all the ancient monuments to whatever creed or sect they might belong and made all possible attempts at conserving them. There are very few temples in South India where their handiwork is not seen. For example the service they did for the famous temple of Belur may be described. By the days of Bukka the beautiful Keśava temple of Belur had become rather damaged both by time and by action of foreign armies. Where the beams and corner-stones had been broken as in the beautiful Śukanāsi of the Belur temple, massive granite pillars were given as props to uphold the roof and the tower over it. The main gate-way which had been damaged by Gangu Salar was rebuilt with a granite base and a masonry tower by Guṇḍappa Danāyaka a general of Vijayanagara. Similar conservation work was done at Tirupati, Kanchi, Śrīrangam, Madhura and other places.

ORIGINAL TEMPLES

This does not mean that the Vijayanagara people neglected to build pretty temples of their own. A detailed study of the architecture of South India would reveal how much of original construction also we owe to Vijayanagara. By way of example may be mentioned the famous temples of Hazara Rāma and Viṭṭala at Vijayanagara and the temple Vīrabhadra at Lepakshi each one of which is an architectural gem. But the purpose of the present article is to describe the earliest of these new structures exclusively designed and constructed during the Vijayanagara epoch. The Śringeri temple would easily take its place as one of the very best architectural pieces of the period though not as one of the biggest.

FOUNDERS OF ŚRINGERI

Among the numerous records existing in Śringeri and its Mutt, two of the most important historical documents are those published by Mr. B. L. Rice in the *Epigraphia Carnatica* as Śringeri No. 1 and in the *Mysore Archæological Report for 1933* as No. 2. In the former we learn of a gift made to the Śringeri Guru Bhāratitīrtha by the five brothers Hariyappa, Kampaṇṇa, Bukkaṇṇa, Muddappa and Mārappa and Ballappa Daṇaika the 'son-in-law.' The inscription starts with an invocation "*Vidyātīrthāya guravē parasmai tējasē namah*" which means "Obeisance to Vidyātīrtha who is the divine lustre." It is probable that the brothers visited Śringeri in order to pay homage to Vidyātīrtha but actually met only Bhāratitīrtha his disciple.

VIDYĀTĪRTHA

After the death of Harihara I, Bukka I came to the throne and in 1356 visited Śringeri for a second time. He appears to have met Vidyātīrtha himself. Very soon after, Vidyātīrtha appears to have passed away leaving Bhāratitīrtha as the sole head of the Mutt. Vidyātīrtha who was also called Vidyāśankara appears to have been held by his contemporaries in great reverence, and in his memory was constructed a large stone temple which is unique in many respects. In fact it is one of the finest pieces of architecture constructed during the three and odd centuries of Vijayanagara rule in South India.

MIXED COMPOSITION

It is a well known fact that the Chāḷukyan style of architecture flourished and attained its greatness under the Hoysala rulers. In the early part of the 14th century it was this Chāḷukyan tradition that was existing in the Kanarese districts of the Vijayanagara empire. But already the traditions of the Tamil country had commenced to have their influence and we see in the Vidyāśankara temple a remarkable example at a synthesis of some of the prominent features of the two styles.

POSITION

The situation of the temple is one of the most picturesque in Karnāṭaka comparable in some respects with the position of the Taj at Agra. The Tungā rushing down from the hills makes a loop here flowing first towards the west, then towards the north and then turning east. Just where the last turn is taken its left bank is steep and high ; and on this high ground within 50 yards of the river this beautiful temple has been built facing east and thus parallel to the river. A very fine view is obtained from the opposite bank.

GENERAL APPEARANCE

A general glance at the temple gives the impression that it is somewhat like the famous Hoysala monuments. It is built on a platform with a high basement. The upper portion of its walls has rows of turrets under which stand large sculptured images. Above a set of double caves rises a tower whose general look is like a stepped pyramid. The temple is built entirely of granite of which there appears to be a quarry in Śringeri.

PECULIAR PLAN

The plan of the temple is extraordinarily interesting and peculiar. Two semi-circles or apses form its eastern and western ends ; and they are connected by an oblong block so that the whole shape is roughly that of an oval with the middle of the sides straight. The building has a *garbhagriha*, a wide *sukanāsī*, with which is connected a semi-circular *pradakshiṇā*, and a *navaranga* with a large central square. It reminds us of the Buddhist Chaitya, the Vishṇu temple at Aihole and perhaps of the palaces of the Achæmenian emperors. But there is little doubt that the architect has taken its cue from the round-backed Hoysala temples and introduced numerous importations from the Chola temples of South India The result is an attractive and highly interesting composition in which are mixed up several features of the Chāḷukyan and the Draviḍian styles.

HIGH BASE

The platform which follows the contour of the main temple is a strongly built structure with a number of cornices one of which bears small *kīrtimukhas* on its dentil projections. Since the temple has six doorways, the platform has six sets of steps each of which is flanked by a pair of elephants. The animals have no individuality and are not comparable to Hoysala elephants in similar positions.

The temple is raised upon a basement more than 5' in height which with another set of cornices reaches up to a height of about 8' The basement has nearly half a dozen cornices and about five sculptured bands making, in all nine noticeable rows. The bands and cornices offer a pleasing contrast of light and shade which is in imitation of similar Hoysala work.

WALL FRIEZES

At the bottom come a row of horses with accoutrements and their riders sometimes leading them. The second band has a row of elephants accoutred and in various interesting postures. The third band is a cornice with a rope design. A lion frieze appears on the fourth, while the fifth is in the shape of eaves with drops at the bottom and a row of lion headed *kirtimukhas* on the face.

LEGENDARY FRIEZE

The sixth band is perhaps the most interesting of all since it contains hundreds of little panels illustrating the *purāṇas,* traditions, etc. The chief subjects dealt with are those, commencing from the east and running clockwise :

1. The life history of Śri Śankarāchārya which is specially interesting because even the Śankaravijaya appears to have been written a little after this date.

2. The fight of Arjuna with Śiva as the Kirāta. This is very finely depicted.

3. Śankarāchārya teaching his disciples.

4. Yogis in various attitudes.

The seventh and eighth bands contain a cornice and a row of Yakshas.

WALL IMAGES

Above the bands there is a long row of large granite images carved in relief which show that the 14th century Karnāṭaka artists were capable of translating into granite a good deal of the beauty of Hoysala soap-stone work. There are sixty-one groups in all. A detailed note on these would be out of place here since the temple is almost a sculptural museum. Among them may be noted the great *purāṇic* Gods, the ten *Avatāras* of Vishṇu, various forms of Śiva and of Śakti, Venkaṭeśa, Vyāsa, Sankarāchārya, Gaṇeśa, etc. These larger figures are generally placed under some kind of arch and the more important of them are enshrined in niches with ornamental towers or *toraṇas*.

The tower is a remarkable architectural piece with the projection in front decorated by a *Kīrtimukha*.

The building has six door-ways symmetrically placed, three on the east and three on the west.

INTERIOR

The temple is peculiar in not having either a Mukhamanṭapa or a porch. The Navaranga which is a structure having twelve highly ornate pillars of the Draviḍian type. On the back side each pillar has an ornamental pilaster raising out of a Kalaśa and bearing one of the twelve signs of the Zodiac. It is said that the sunlight falls upon the Ram pillar during the month of Aires and on the Bull pillar in the month of Taurus. The central ceiling of the Navaranga is above 16 ft. high and this result is achieved by a corbelled construction the weight being poised upon the very heavy brackets. The central ceiling has a very fine design with a padma in its dome and a large pendent on which perch beautiful birds. At the back of the Navaranga is the Pradaksiṇa a narrow passage which goes around the Śukanāsi and the Garbhagriha and contains the shrines of Ganeśa, Brahma, Vishṇu, Maheśvara and Durga. In the sanctum stands a large pedestal with a high Linga known as the Vidyāśankaralinga.

HOYSALA ELEMENTS

The Chāḷukyan or perhaps more appropriately the Hoysala elements in the Vidyāśankara temple appear to be the following: The apsidal ends, the rows of cornices, the absence of the Mukhamanṭapa the plinth platform outside the temple, the friezes of horses, elephants, lions, etc., carved on the basement, the pilasters, niches and large images on the upper wall, the double roof, the stepped pyramid tower with its frontal projection and the general impression of the whole structure.

DRAVIDIAN ELEMENTS

The Draviḍian features of the temple are :—The inner covered pradaksiṇa, the designs on the balustrades supporting the steps, the rope shaped cornice, the three stories of the tower, the metallic finial on the top, the drapery of the images, the great pillars of the Navaranga, the use of granite instead of soap-stone and the general absence of the characteristic round pillars of the Hoysalas.

MIXED STYLE

Perhaps it would be right to say that the external aspect of the building is more Chāḷukyan, and the internal aspect more Draviḍian. The Vidyāśankara temple shows that except where they restored or copied earlier forms the early Vijayanagara architects and sculptors continued the traditions of the Hoysalas though they were much influenced by the Draviḍian style. There cannot be much doubt that the Vijayanagara Empire inherited the art of Hoysalas and tried to build stronger the more spacious and more permanent structures by the use of granite and some of the features of the Draviḍian style. This tendency to retain some of the Hoysala features and combine them with the Draviḍian forms is visible also in the Viṭṭalasvāmi temple at Hampi and elsewhere.

26

Development of Sanskrit Literature under Vijayanagara

By

Mr. S. Srikantha Sastri, M.A.
Lecturer, Maharaja's College, Mysore.

The culture of India has been throughout the ages dominated by the testing idea of a continual process of actualization and animation of the beautiful as a space-thought and time sequence is of importance only as indication of a specific Beauty in the universal rythm. As a civilisation however, India represented the notion of *Karmic* process suffused not with the soul but with the intellect, and thus evolved a particular structure unique in its form of language symbolism. In polity the city state, in fine arts—denomination and conservation, in philosophy sensualism and entrophy, in religion the Become, in the sciences rationalistic phenomenalism, characterise all civilisations. In the history of Vijayanagara we see this process of a culture becoming a civilisation. Though there is no antithesis between form and the Memory, the synthesis of the two become evident only in certain special symbols of which Vijayanagara Sanskrit literature furnishes the best example.

The Vijayanagara epoch was as it were the last spiritual crisis involving the conflict between the tyranny of reason as expressed in dialectic demonstration, and the feeling against emotional liberation in the infinite as expressed in the Bhakti literature. In the earliest period of Vijayanagara literature, the reverence for the past and the passion for conservation was balanced equally with fore-thought. This is nowhere more evident than in the monumental commentary on the Vedas. Sāyaṇa acknowledges his indebtedness to previous Āchāryas and contemporaries like Hastāmalaka, Gomati, Dhanuṣka Yajvan, Ātmānanda, Rāvaṇa Bhaṭṭa Bhāskara, Hariswāmin, Skandaswāmin, Bhavasvāmin, Haradatta, Venkata-Mādhava, Govinda Svāmin, Udgīthāchārya, Bharata Svāmin, Mahisha, Nārāyaṇa, Kaparda Svāmin, Uvaṭa, but this is in no way lessens the greatness of Sāyaṇa Bhāshya. Sāyaṇa was assisted by Panchāgni Mādhava, son of Nārāyaṇa, Narahari Sōmayāgi, Nārāyaṇa Vājapēyi, Paṇḍari Dikshita, Nāgābharana, Vāmanabhaṭṭa and others. This co-operative spirit and the high authority of the various authors who were content to subordinate their own identity for the sake o' knowledge, reveal the greatness of their spiritual attainment.[1] The foundation for this had been firmly laid in the last years of Vīra Baḷḷala when great philosophers like Vidyātīrtha, (of the Rudrapraśna Bhāshya, etc.) Śankarānanda (of Dīpikā on māṇḍukya, Brihadāraṇyaka, etc. and of Vivēkasāra), Śrīkanṭha Nātha had produced their works. The Advaitic writers in the Vidyāraṇya epoch are represented in the following table :

Ananyānubhava
|
Svayam Prabha = Svaprakaśānubhava
a Prakāśatman Nārāyaṇa-jyotisha

Ānandānubhav or (Ānandātman) Ānandāgiri I | Kaivalyānanda | Anubhavānanda
Lakshmidhar | Śankarānanda, Suddhānanda | Sārngpāṇi
Bōdhagiri Svayamprakaśa I | Śaivagña Vishṇu Vidyā Śamkara
or Ānanda Jñāna | Mahādēva Sarsvati | Vidyāraṇya, Sāyaṇa, Bhoganāth

Nṛsinha
|
Gauda Jñānottama-Satyānanda
Vigñānātman | Chitsukha
Ānandagiri | Sukhaprakāśa or Ānandasaila
Akhanḍānubhūti or Akhanḍānubhava
|
Akhanaḍananda
Chitsukha II

Among the Vīra Śaiva philosophers in the proto-Vijayanagara period, Pālkuriki Somanātha was the outstanding figure. In the

1 गंगायां निवसन्ति ये मुनिवराः श्रीसायणार्य प्रभो ।
तेपि त्वत्क सभास्तरैः विदधते स्पर्धां न पुण्याधिकैः ।
एते ते द्विजपुंगवास्त्रिचतुरान्वेदान् षडंगान्वितान् ।
व्याख्यातुं प्रभवः पृथक् पृथगितो वेदान्तविद्या अपि ॥

court of Vīra Pratāpa Rudra II he wrote in Sanskrit Somanātha bhāshya (Basavarājīya), Rudra Bhāshya, Ashṭaka, Panchaka, Namaskāra *gadya,* Aksharānka *gadya,* Panchaprārthana *gadya,* Basa vōdāharaṇa, Chaturvēda tātparya Samgraha. He mentions his teachers and contemporaries Chennarama Karasthaḷi Sōma Renṭāla Mallinātha, Gobburu Sangana, Pālkuriki Sūranna, Karasthaḷi Viś-vanātha, Guru Lingārya, Kaṭṭukkurki Pōtidēva. The Pāśupata Śaivas of the Goḷāki Maṭha wielded immense power and the contemporary of Rudramāmba and Pratapa Rudra was Viśvēśvara Śambhu who is perhaps identical with Viśvēśvara Śiva who is said to have been responsible for division of Vīra Śaivas into Vīra Bhadras and Vīra Mushṭis.

विश्वेश्वरशिवाचार्यो धीमान्राजगुरुस्स्वयम् ।
एवमाज्ञापयद्वीरः शैवाचार्यशतैर्वृतः ॥
बीजछेद शिरछेद कुक्षिछेदादिकर्मभिः ।
वीरभद्र समाख्याता दशग्रामस्यरक्षकाः ॥
भद्रास्स्युरपरे भक्ताः विंशतिर्वीरमुष्टयः ।

Another centre of Kālāmukha Śaivism was the Huli Maṭha presided in the last quarter of the 13th century by Jñānaśakti and Sāmba Śakti. The Pushpagiri Maṭha at Śrīsaila was also under the Kāḷā-mukhas in 1292 presided over by Soma Śiva. Baḷagamve—the foremost centre of Kāḷāmukha Śaivism in the 12th century was now losing its importance; but at the same time Mūvara Kōne Santati Parvatāvaḷi line is found at Mungavalli and Ālampūr. The name Kriyāśakti occurs frequently in the records of the Yādavas of Dēva-giri and the Kriyāśaktis who were the *Kula-gurus* of the Vijaya-nagara dynasty were therefore Kāḷāmukhas and not Kashmir Saivas of the Pratyabhijña school as usually assumed. In Ś. 964 Gonabhūpa made a grant to Kriyāśakti paṇḍita, the disciple of Vādirudra. In Ś. 1174 Virōdhi, is mentioned Lakuḷāgama Samaya Samuddhara Somēśvara the disciple of Kriyāśakti. It is probable that Lakuḷāgama came later to be identified with Śuddha Śaivāgama as distinguished from Viśishṭādvaitic tenets of Vīra Śaivism.

The Vaishṇava Dvaita philosophy had as its exponents in the last quarter of the 13th century Nārāyaṇa Paṇḍita to whom Sumadhva-vijaya, Aṇumadhvavijaya, Sangraha Rāmāyaṇa, Māṇi-manjari, Advaita Kālānala, Naya Chandrikā, Madhvamantrā-rtha-Manjari are attributed. Padmanābha-tīrtha the immediate successor of Ānand-tīrtha is said to have written Ānandmālā, Sannyāya-ratnāvaḷi, Sattarka-ratnāvali, etc. Narahari-tīrtha is said to have written commentaries on Yamaka Bhārata, and on the Upanishad and Sūtra *bhāshyas* of Ānand-tīrtha. Mādhav-tīrtha is said to have commented on the Rig, Yajus and Sāma Vedas.

The Vaishṇava Viśishṭādvaita tradition from the time of Bhagavad Rāmānuja continued to be handed down in five *paramparas*—(1) Mantra paramparā, (2) Mantrārtha gurù paramparā, (3) Śrī Bashya guru parampara, (4) Āśrayaṇa guru parampara and, (5) Grantha paramparā. The succession list up to Vēdānta Dēśika and Piḷḷailoka is as follows : —

Rāmānuja

(1)	(2)	(3)	(4)	(5)
Paṭṭāvalis of Parakāla and Ahōbila Maṭhas	Kiḍambi Ācchan	Piḷḷān	Embār	Piḷḷān
	Kiḍambi Ramanuja Appuḷḷār	Vishṇu Chitta	Pārāśara	Embār
	Kiḍāmbi Srīrangarāja	Nādādūr Ammaḷ	Nanjīyar	Aḷavān
	Kiḍāmbi Appuḷḷār	Appuḷḷār	Nampillāi	Bhaṭṭar
	Vēdānta Dēśika	Vēdānta Dēśika	Śrī Krishṇa	Naṁjīyar
	Brahma-tantra Svāmi	Nainār	Piḷḷai Loka	Nampillāi
			Maṇavāḷa	Śrī Krishṇa
			(8 Maṭhas).	pāda
				Īyaṇṇi
				Mādhava

The greatest figures were Dēśika and Piḷḷai Lōkāchārya responsible for the distinctions between Vaḍagalais and Tengalais. Vēḍānta Dēśika was born at Tiruvēndīpuram[1] in 1269 A.D. and lived up to 1371 A.D. (J.B.B.O.R.S., 1915-16), and wrote more than a hundred works. The Ānandaranga Vijaya Champu of Śrīnivāsa goes so far as to assert that a *Gopa*[2] founded the empire of Vijayanagara by the grace of Vēdānta Dēśika.

1. Tūppil, near Conjīvaram and not Tiruvendipuram was his birth place.
2. This is the Gōpana or Gopaṇārya who played a prominent part in southern conquests of Kampaṇa.

The Jaina scholars also were prominent in the first quarter of the 14th century. Among those mentioned in inscriptions are :—

Dēśi-gaṇa
Māghanandi

- Nēmi-chandra
- Abhaya-chandra
  - Bāla-Chandra (who wrote a commentary on Sāra Chatushṭaya).
    - Abhayachandra
      - Śruta Muni
        - Prabhendu
          - Śruta Kīrti 1384 A.D.
    - Ramachandra Maladhāri (author of Guru Pancha Smṛiti 1300 A.D.)
      - Śubhachandra.
        - Padmanandin.

Śrēyāṁśa
Bhaṭṭanatha 1280 A.D.

- Bahubali Maladhāri
  - Padmanandi 1303 A.D.

Sēna-gaṇa.
Padma Sēna
Lakshmī Sēna.
Chandra Sēna.
Munibhadra 1388 A.D.

In Sāhitya the patronage of Pratāparudra was responsible for the output of many Kāvyas, dramas and works on rhetoric like Pratāparudra Yaśobhushaṇa of Vidyānātha Ēkāmranātha. Kolāchala Mallinātha, the grandfather of the famous commentator, was bathed in gold by Vīra Rudra.

कोलाचलान्वयाब्धीन्दुः मल्लिनाथो महायशः ।
शतावधानविख्यातो वीररुद्राभिवर्षितः ।
मल्लिनाथात्मजः श्रीमान् कपर्दिः मन्त्रकोविदः ।
अखिलश्रौतकल्पस्य कारिकावृत्तिमातनोत् ॥

Kapardin, the son of Mallinātha I, wrote a Kārikā Vṛtti on all Śruta Kalpas.

II. THE VIDYĀRAṆYA EPOCH, 1336-1386

The principal motive in the foundation of the Vijayanagara empire had been the restoration of Sanātana Dharma which had suffered grievously at the hands of the Muslim invaders.

श्रुतिरस्तमिता नयःप्रलीनो विरता धर्मकथा च्युतं चरित्रम् ।
सुकृतं गतमाभिजात्यमस्तं किमिवान्यत्कलिरेकधन्यः ॥

Therefore it was not in a spirit of contempt towards the vernaculars that greater importance was attached to Sanskrit literature which was the source of all knowledge worth having. But Vidyāraṇya and his contemporaries did not deny the right of women and Sūdras a knowledge of the scriptures, for that knowledge is also to be found in Purāṇas, etc. and in the vernaculars.[3]

ननु--एवं सति स्त्रीशूद्रसहिताः सर्वेऽधिकारिणः स्युः--इष्टं मे भवत्वनिष्टं मेमाभूदित्याशिषः सर्वजनीनत्वात् । मैवं...अनुपनीतयोस्तयोर्वेदाध्ययनमनिष्ट-प्राप्तिहेतुः । कथं तर्हि तयोस्तदुपायावगमः । पुराणादिभिरिति ब्रूमः—अत एवोक्तम्:—

स्त्रीशूद्रद्विजबंधूनां त्रयी न श्रुतिगोचरा ।
इति भारतमाख्यानं कृपया मुनिनाकृतम् ॥

Similarly in his Sūta Samhitā Vyākhyāna, Mādhava Mantrin says: येषां तु हीनजातीनां पुराणेप्यनधिकारः तेषामपि स्वदेशभाषयैव तत्त्व-विद्यायामधिकारः ।

In this period we witness the process of re-statement and systematisation of all branches of learning. Vidyāraṇya and his associates took all knowledge for their province. The attempt to prove that Mādhavāchārya is not Vidyāraṇya (*Indian Historical Quarterly* VI and VII) has no proper basis. The identity has been accepted by Mr. R. Narasimhachar and Dr. S. K. Aiyangar. The latter on the authority of Chaunḍappa says that "the very terms in which Chaunḍappa refers to Vidyāraṇya unmistakably indicate Mādhavāchārya, the brother of Sāyaṇa to be the Vidyāraṇya of tradition."[4] The works attributed to Mādhava Vidyāraṇya are Vyavahāra Mādhavīya, Vivaraṇa Pramēya Samgraha, Brahma-vidāśīrvāda Paddhati, Jīvanmuktivivēka, Manu Smriti Vyākhyā, Panchadasi, Kalāmādhavīya, Āyurvedanidana (?) Śamkara Vijaya (?) Kālanirṇaya, etc. The works of Sāyaṇa are Dhātu-Vriti, Subhāshita Sudhānīdhi, Puru-

3. This is an old idea for which much earlier authorities can be quoted.
4. Introduction to Sources of Vijayanagara History p. 4.

sharta Sudhānidhi, Ayurvēda Sudhānidhi, commentary on the Vedas, commentaries on the Śatapatha and Taittarēya, Alaṁkāra Sudhānidhi, Prāyaschita Sudhānidhi, Yagña tantra Sudhānidhi. In the commentary on Sama Veda one Panchāgni Mādhava, son of Nārāyaṇa is mentioned. In the Dhātuvriti, Yagña Nārāyaṇa and Kunḍinārya are mentioned. The work on Āyurvēda is said to have been really the work of Ēkāmranātha, whose grandson Śrīśailanātha wrote a medical work Praśnottara-ratnamālā.

एकाम्रनाथो यत्तातः सायणामात्यचोदितः ।
समग्रहोत्सुबोधार्थमायुर्वेदसुधानिधिम् ॥

In the production of Alaṁkāra Sudhānidhi, Bhoganātha and Gōpālasvāmin had their share. In the commentary on the Vedas, Mādhavaś Jaiminīya Nyāyamālāvistāra is quoted as his own. Similarly Vidyāraṇya in his Kālanirṇaya quotes from Bhāratitīrtha's Vayyāsika Nyāyamālā Vistāra." Therefore, it is clear that there was no literary piracy ; but in the interest of learning, egotism was subordinated to the general good. The works of Bhognātha-Bhāratitīrtha are Ramōllāsa, Tripuravijaya, Udāharaṇamāl , Mahā-Gaṇapatistava, Śringāramanjari, Gaurināthāshṭaka, Dṛgdṛ yavivēka, and a portion of Panchadaśi. The son of Sāyanāchāry , Mādhava is the author of Sarvadarśana Sangraha composed in the time of Jayatīrtha.

The Dvaita tradition was represented by Akshōbhyatīrtha and Jaya-tīrtha. Akshōbhya is said to have written Mādhava Tattvasāra-samgraha, and defeated Vidyāraṇya in dispute when Vēdānta Dēśika was the arbitrator and set up a pillar of victory at Mulubagal.

असिनाऽतत्त्वमसिना परजीवप्रभेदिना ।
विद्यारण्यमहारण्यमक्षोभ्यमुनिरच्छिनत् ॥

But Advaitins claim that it was Vidyāraṇya who proved to be the victor.

अक्षोभ्यं क्षोभयमास विद्यारण्यमतिः ॥

Akshōbhya's disciple Jayatīrtha ṭikāchārya was a prolific writer, and, according to tradition, he obtained the permission of Vidyāraṇya for the publishing of his works. Jayatīrtha is said to have been the author of 23 works. Tatvaprakāśikā Sudhā, Nyāyavivaraṇa, Pramēya dīpikā, Nyāya dīpikā, Pramāṇa Paddhati, Vādāvaḷi, Adhyātmāmrita-tarangiṇi, Śatāparādha Stotra, Padyamālā, and

Ṭippaṇis. A Vyāsatīrtha, the disciple of Jayatīrtha, is the author of Jayatīrthavijaya and Ṭikas of several Upanishads.[5]

Vedānta Dēśika died in 1370 A.D. In 1366 A.D., the leader of the Śrivaishṇavas of the 18 nāḍus was Śrī Tirumalai Tātayya who made a compact with the Jainas at the direction of the emperor Bukka. Brahmo-tantra or Naināār Śri Śailēśa, Aṇṇan or Prativādi-bhyankara continued the Viśiṣṭādvaitic tradition.

The Śuddha Śaivāgama flourished under the direction of the Kriyāśaktis. Kāśivilasa was the guru of Mādhavamantrin, the author of Śaivāmnāyasāra and Sūta Samhitā Vyākhyā. The successor of Kāśī-vilāsa was Triyambaka Kriyāśakti the teacher of Gangādēvi and Deparāja (of Sobagina Śōne). The successor of Triyambaka was Chandrabhūshaṇā who arbitrated in the dispute between Śrīnātha and Gauḍa Dinḍimabhaṭṭa.

The Jaina scholars of the time were Paṇḍitarāya Śrutamuni Sinhanandin, Pushpasēna, Maghanandin the disciple of Amara Kīrtyā chārya of Balātkāragaṇa. Their disciple was Irugappa Daṇḍa-nātha who continued to serve from the time of Harihara II to Dēvarāya II. He was the author of Nānārtha-Ratnamālā. The epitaphs at Śravaṇa Beḷgola recording the deaths of Harihara II and Dēvarāya II show that this important centre as well as Tiruparuttu Kuṅṛam received royal patronage.

The expounding of Smriti texts continued. Tarka also claimed the attention of scholars like Chennubhaṭṭa,[6] the son of Sahaja Sarvajña Vishṇu Dēvārādhya and the author of a Ṭīkā on Kēśava-miśra's work; the Tarka-bhāshā-vivarana of Mādhava-bhaṭṭa, the Tarka-bhāshā-ṭīkā of Balabhadra, the Tarka-bhāshā-prakāśa of Nārāyaṇa-bhaṭṭa and Tarka Prakāśa of Murāri-bhaṭṭa.

In fine arts and exact sciences there was also a great output of literature. Gangādēvi, the wife of Kampa, and the authoress of Kamparāja-vijayam was an outstanding figure. Narahari, a disciple of Vidyāraṇya, commented upon the Kāvya-prakāśa and wrote the Naishadha-dīpikā.

5. There is also a Jayatīrtha Vijaya by Saṁkarshaṇāchārya (*Cat. Skt. Mss.* of Madras, 1882-3).

6. One Chennubhaṭṭa received a grant in 1390 A.D. when Ramachandra, son of Dēvarāya I was ruling Udayagiri. The grant was composed by the court poet, Dēvarājamiśra.

यं प्रासूत त्रिलिंगक्षितिपतिसततारावितान्घ्रिः स्वयंभू ।
पातिव्रत्यैकसीमा सुकृतिनरहरिं नीलिमा यं प्रसूता ।
यं विद्यारण्ययोगी कलयति कृपया तत्कृतौ दीपिकायाम् ।
स्वैरं नीराजितोभूदललितपदो (?) दिग्मितो सर्ग एषः ॥

(India Office Catalogue, Pt. VII. 3832).

Vidyā-Mādhava seems to have been the name of several individuals. One was the author of a commentary on Kumārasambhava and on the Kirātārjunīya.

कुमारसंभवस्यास्य व्याख्याने गुणवानयम् ।
षष्ठः सर्गः समाप्तोभूत् विद्यामाधवनिर्मिते ॥
वेदव्याकरणास्पदं कविमहाराजः स तर्कः स्मृति ।
छंदो लक्षण काव्यजाटक कलाविज्ञान संपन्निधिः ॥
ज्योतिश्शास्त्राविदग्ध्रमाभिजनिता दुर्गर्वसर्वंकषो ।
विद्यामाधवपंडितो विजयते विद्वद्विभूषामणिः ॥

श्रीमद्गुणवती ग्रामविशिष्ट नीलालय (?) स्थानसंभूतैरखिलविद्यानिवासै विद्यामाधवपंडितैर्विरचितं विद्यामाधवनामधेयं व्याख्यानं समाप्तम्—

He seems to be identical with the astronomer Vidyāmādhava Sūri, the author of Muhūrta Darśana or Vidyā-Mādhavīya. His son, Vishnū Sūri, commented upon his father's work in Muhūrta dīpikā, and was a contemporary of Mallappa Oḍeya, the son of Bukka.

श्रीमान्मल्लप्पभूपः सजयति जगतीभूषणीभूतधामा ।
पारावारावगाढक्षितिधरशिखरप्रस्फुरत्कीर्तिपूरः ॥
किं ब्रूमोऽस्यप्रतापं नरपतिचरितादीन्द्ररक्षातिदक्षः ।
श्रीभर्तुर्वासुभूमिर्वितरति जलधिर्यस्यरत्नानि नित्यम् ॥
वीरश्रीथरबुक्कभूपतिमहासाम्राज्य लक्ष्मीकरा
लंबोदारचरित्रविक्रमरसस्त्यैं वकालम्बनः ॥
शिवागमाचार विशुद्धचक्षुः तदात्मविद्यापरिरब्धकंधरः ।
समस्तसंपत्कर संश्रियोऽयं भूपः क्षितिंरक्षति रामसृष्टाम् ॥

A Vidyāmādhava, the author of Pārvati-Rukmanīya was the court poet of a Chāḷukya Somadeva of Rajyadurga(?), and was well versed in astronomy.

जगत्यजय्यो जगतीपतीनां पर्तितिःप्रतिष्ठातिव सद्गुणानाम् ।
चालुक्यवंशप्रभवः प्रभावान् पृथुप्रभावो भुवि सोमराजः ॥
महाकवीशोन्नतभद्ररुद्रो वादींद्रराजाधिप जामदग्न्यः ।
ज्योतिर्गतिज्ञान चतुर्मुखश्च विद्यामहामाधवपंडिताख्यः ॥
इह सुमहित काव्ये पार्वतीरुक्मिणीये।
शुभमवसितराजत्संपदानंदचिह्नम् ॥
नवमनवमार्थं सर्गमाधत्तसश्री ।
पदनखमिति विद्यामाधवः पंडितेंद्रः ॥

Under the patronage of Bukka II, Lakshmaṇa Paṇḍita wrote a medical work, Vaidyarāja Vallabha.

III. THE LATER SANGAMA DYNASTY, 1386-1486

In this epoch the court of Sarvagña Singaṇa[7] and of Dēvarāya II were the two most important centres of learning. According to the Kuluvachēru grant, after the return and death of Pratāpa Rudra II, Prolayanāyaka won back Warangal from the Muhammadans. After him there was a Kāpayanāyaka who was served by 75 chiefs who became independent later. Vēma was one of them. Kāpayanāyaka is perhaps Kaṇhya Naik of Ferishta. Ekāmranātha mentions a Vīrabhadradēva, son of Pratāpa Rudra who abandoned Warangal for Koṇḍavīḍu. A son of Pratāpa Rudra is mentioned as ruling in Kadapa district in 1314 A.D. (Pramādicha).

THE REDDIS OF KONḌAVĪḌU AND RĀJAMANḌRI

- Komaṭi Prola-Annamā
  - Mācha
    - Reḍḍi Pota
    - Nāga.
      - Pedda Komaṭi
        - Komaṭi Vēma (1410 A.D.)
          - Rācha Vēma (1420-1424)
        - Mācha
  - Vēma I (1320-50).
    - Pina-Komaṭi
    - Anapota (1350-62)
      - Kumāragiri (1383-1400)
      - Mallāmbika-Kāṭaya (1391).
    - Ana Vēma (1362-83)
    - Doḍḍāmba
    - Vēma Sāni
  - Anna
  - Mallareḍḍi.

- Vēma of Rājamanḍri (1386-1419)
  - Kāṭa (son-in-law of Harihara II).
  - Kanitalli
  - Kumāragiri Reḍḍi 1414. Vīra-Bhadra.

THE PADMA NĀYAKAS

- Rēcharla Singama (at Rāchakonḍa).
  - Ana Pota 1344-1380.
  - Singaya
    - Ārana Mādanāyaka
    - Sarvagña Śingama.
  - Mādanāyaka 1396.

Ana Vēma of Konḍavīḍu is styled Karpūra Vasantarāya, and was the patron of Trilochanāchārya. In several eulogistic verses he is praised as a great lover and patron of scholars.[8] Kumāragiri was the patron of Śrīnatha and the contemporary of Harihara II and Firozshah. Pedda Kōmaṭi was not only a poet, but a patron of poets like Śrīnātha (who was his Vidyāthikāri) and of Abhinava Bhaṭṭa Bāṇa Vāmana Bhaṭṭa. He is the author of Amaruka Vyākhyā, called Śringāra dīpika.

8. आन वेम महीपाल स्वस्त्यस्तु तव बाहवे ।
आहवे रिपु दोर्दण्ड चंद्रमण्डल राहवे ॥

राज्यम् वेमः सुचिरमकरोत् प्राज्यहेमाद्रिदानो
भूमीदेवैर्भुवमरुम्यो मुक्तशेषामभुङ्क्त ।
श्रीशैलाग्रात्प्रभवति पथि प्राप्त पाताळ....
सोपानानि प्रथमपदवीमारुरुक्षुश्चकार ॥
माचक्षोणिपतिर्महेन्द्रमहिमा वेमक्षितीशाग्रजः ।
हेमाद्रेः सदृशो बभूव सगुणैः तस्यत्रयो नन्दनाः ॥
कीर्त्या जाग्रति रेड्डिपोतनृपतिः श्रीकोमठोन्द्रस्ततो ।
नागक्ष्मापतिरित्युपात्तवपुषो धर्मार्थकामा इव ॥
वेमाधिपो माचविभुश्च नंदनौ श्रीकोमटीन्द्रस्य गुणैकसंश्रयौ ।
भूलोकमेकोदर जन्मवान्छया भूयोवतीर्णाविव रामलक्ष्मणौ ॥
सवेमभूपः सकलासुविद्यास्वतिप्रगल्भो जगनोब्बगण्डः ।
कदाचिदास्थानगतः कवीनां काव्यामृतास्वादपरः प्रसंगात् ॥

इति श्रीवीरनारायण सकलविद्याविशारद पेद्दकोमटी वेमभूपालविरचिता शृंगारदीपिका समाप्ता——

Vāmana Bhaṭṭa Bāṇa dedicated his Vipranārāyaṇa Charitra or Vēma Bhupālīyam to Vēma. Vāmana seems to have resided at Vijayanagara also for some time where he composed his *Bhāva Sṛnagārbhūshana.*

सूत्रधारः—मारिष ! अद्यखलु चराचरगुरोरुत्तुंगतुंगभद्रातरंगताळवृता-पनीयमानसंध्याताण्डवपरिश्रमस्य हेमगिरिकूटश्रीळाकरहेमकूटशृंगविहितमंगलायतनस्य कामागमनिधिवामभागस्य शेखरीभूतशीतभानुशकलस्य भगवतोविरूपाक्षस्य चैत्रयात्रामहोत्सवे

रतितन्त्रदेशिकानां रतिपतिनिगमान्तवावदूकानाम् ।
वैदग्ध्यभूषणानामेषा परिषत्समागता विदुषाम् ॥

Perhaps the real author of Amarukha Vyakhyā was Vāmana himself. One Viśvēśvarabhaṭṭa is mentioned as the donee in a grant of Pedda Kōmaṭi. (E. I. XI, p. 315). He may perhaps be identical with Viśvēśvara Kavi who wrote Chamatkāra Chandrikā under the patronage of Sarvagña Singa. Pedda Kōmaṭi was also the author of a work on music Sangīta Chintāmaṇi.

Sarvagña Singama was perhaps the greatest literature of the period. Several works are attributed to him. In his *Nāṭaka Paribhāshā*, he says :

अथ रूपकनिर्माणपरिज्ञानोपयोगिनी ।
श्रीशिंगघरणीशेन परिभाषा निरूप्यते ॥

In his *Sangīta Sudhākara*, the colophon is

इति श्रीसिंहभूपालविरचितायां संगीतरत्नाकरटीकायां संगीतसुधाकराख्यायाम्

In his *Rasārṇava Sudhākara* :

इति श्रीमदान्ध्रमण्डलाधीश्वर प्रतिगण्डभैरव श्री अनपोतनरेंद्रनंदनभुजबल भीम श्री सिंगभूपालविरचितायाम्—

इति श्रीमण्डलाधीश्वर श्री अनपोतनरेंद्रनंदन बलभुज बलभव (?) श्रीशिंगभूपालविरचिते रसार्णवसुधाकर नाम्नि नाट्यलंकार शास्त्रे

Under his patronage eminent scholars like Peddabhaṭṭa, Kālāchala Mallinātha, Bommala Kaṇṭi Appalāchārya, Śrīnātha, Viśvēśvara flourished. About Mallinātha we get this information from Pada Yojana a commentary on Champu Rāmayana by Nārāyaṇa Paṇḍita.

कपर्दि तनयो धीमान् मल्लिनाथोऽग्रजः स्मृतः ।
द्वितीयस्तनयो धीमान् पेद्दभट्टोमहोदयः ।
महोपाध्याय आख्यातः सर्वदेशेषु सर्वतः ।
मातुलेयकतौदिव्ये सर्वज्ञेनाभिवर्षितः ॥
गणाधिप प्रसादेन प्रोचे मन्त्र वरान् बहून् ।
नैषधज्योतिषादीनां व्याख्याताभूज्जगद्गुरुः ॥
पेद्दभट्टसुतः श्रीमान् कुमारस्वामिसंज्ञकः ।
प्रतापरुद्रीयाख्यानं व्याख्याता विद्वदग्रिमः ॥

Mallinātha besides his commentaries wrote also Vaiśya Vaṁśa Sudhārṇava.

Viśvēśvara Bhaṭṭa in his Chamatkāra Chandrikā says:

कृतिरभिमतकृतिचतुरा यदि चतुरोदात्तनयगुणोदारा ।
इति लक्षणकृतिरलं रचये सिंगनृपगुणोदाहरणम् ॥

इति सरससाहित्य चातुरीधुरीधुरीण विश्वेश्वरकविचन्द्रप्रणीतायाम् श्रीसिंह-भूपालकीर्तिसुधासारशीतलायाम् ।

One Viśvēśvarāchārya (probably of the Bhikshāmaṭha) is the author of a commentary on the Naishadha called Padavākyārtha-panchikā which is quoted by Mallinātha. Another Viśvēśvara-pandita is the author of Śamkara Vākhyāvṛitti.

Bommala Kanṭi Appalāchārya wrote his commentary on Amara under Singama's patronage.

कुमारसिंगभूपेन लक्ष्यलक्षणवेदिना ।
शोधितश्चेदयं ग्रंथः किंशोध्यश्शोधनांतरैः ॥
कुमारसिंगभूपेन यः कदापि नशोधितः ।
यः ग्रंथश्शोधितस्याप्यन्यैः किंबुधैर्व्यवहृयते ॥
काव्यालंकारनानार्थतत्त्वभावितमानसः ।
कुमारसिंगभूपाल एक एवास्ति नापरः ॥
कुमारसिंगभूपाल कृतयस्तस्य नित्यशः ।
एधयंति मुदं दृष्ट्वा दृष्टां कृतिनः परम् ॥

Another poet in the court of Singama was Sākalya Malla who was defeated by Nainār Varadāchārya, the son of Vēdānta Dēśika.

Kātaya Vēma, the brother-in-law of Kumāragiri, was made the ruler of Rājamanḍri and defeated Pedda Kōmaṭi of Konḍavīḍu. Pedda Kōmaṭi's minister, Singana, is the author of Soma-Siddhānta-Vyākhyā.

पेद्दकोमटिदेवेन्द्रमन्त्रिणा तेन धीमता ।
ज्योतिर्विद्यानिराघाट सरस्वत्पारदृश्वना ।
शिंगयामात्यरत्नेन भुविलोकहितैषिणा ।
क्रियते सोमसिद्धान्तव्याख्या गूढार्थदीपिका

इति सकलसिद्धान्त मतानुसारिणा मामिडिशिंगणाचार्येण विरचितायां सोमसिद्धान्त टीकायां गूढार्थदीपकायां—

Kāṭaya Vēma had commented upon Śakuntala and other works of Kālidasa. Besides he wrote Vasantarājīyam in the name of his brother-in-law, also called Kumaragiri Vijayam (E. I. IV, p. 325).

मुनीनां भरतादीनां भोजादीनां च भूभुजाम् ।
शास्त्राणिसम्यागलोच्य नाट्यवेदार्थवेदिनाम् ।
प्रोक्तं वसंतराजेन कुमारगिरिभूभुजा ।
नाम्ना वसंतराजीयं नाट्यशास्त्रं यदुत्तमम् ।
तत्रोक्तिनैव मार्गेण दर्शिताऽशेषलक्षणाम् ।
कवीनामाश्रयो मन्त्रि काटभूप तनूभवः ॥
सोऽयं वेमविभुः कुमारगिरिणा राज्ञा नियुक्तः कृतो
नाट्यानां त्रितयं कृतं कृतधिया श्रीकाळिदासेन यत् ।
तस्योद्दीर्णरसार्णवस्य रसिकः शाकुन्तलादेः स्वयम्
व्याख्यानं कुरुते कुमारगिरिराजीयाख्यमस्मै हितम् ॥

In about 1443 A.D. Dēvarāya II destroyed the power of the Reḍḍis of Konḍavīḍu and Rajamanḍri, and conquered Kalinga. His court was the meeting place of Jaina, Vaishṇava, Śrivaishṇava, and Vīra Saiva scholars. Virūpāksha is the author of the Sanskrit drama, Nārāyaṇī Vilāsam. Under Vīra Bhūpati who is styled Rāja Vyāsa-Vālmīki, Chaunḍapāchārya wrote Prayōgaratnamālā. Dēva Rāya II is spoken of as Vīra-Śaivāgama-Sampanna, in a record of Ś. 1340, Viḷambi. Vīra Śaivism was re-promulgated by ministers of Dēva Rāya like Lakkaṇṇa, Jakkaṇṇa, Chāmarasa, etc. Mostly this literature was in the vernaculars. But Sanskrit scholars were no less prominent. Sāḷuva Gopa Tippa, the viceroy at Muḷubāgal wrote on music, dancing, tāla, and on Alankāra. Two of his works are Kāmadhēnu, a commentary on Vāmana's Kāvyālankara, and Talla dīpika. But the leading court poet was Gauḍa Dinḍimā-bhaṭṭa who was defeated by Śrīnātha.

Śoṇādri Contemporary of Harihara and Bukka.
Aruṇagiri (Dēvarāya II)
Yōgānanda Prahasana ; commentary on Saundaryalahari, Vibhāgaratnamālā.
Rājanātha (Sāḷvanarasimha)—Sāluvābhyudavam.
Śoṇādri or Aruṇagiri (Rāmābhyudayam Vīrabhadra Vijayam) Virabhadra Vijayam)
Rājanātha (Achyuta) Achyutarāyābhyudayam
Bhāgavata-Champu.

In the *Yogānanda Prahasana*, Aruṇagiri styles himself,

श्रीडिंडिम कवि सार्वभौम इति प्रथित बिरुदांक नामधेयः सरस्वती प्रसादलब्ध कवितासनाथः श्रीमानरुणगिरिनाथः......

He also seems to have had the titles Abhinava Bhavabhūti, Ashṭabhāshā Paramēśvara, Chēra-Choḷa-Pāṇḍya-Prathamārādhya, Kavimalla-galla-tādana pāṭu. Kavimalla is probably the author of Udāra Rāghava. There was also a poet Rājaśēkhara who composed the Śrīrangam plates of Dēvarāya.

The Śrīvaishṇava scholars of the time were Mukunda Reḍḍi, or Kandāḷa Appalāchārya said to have been defeated in dispute by the Vīra Śaivas, Jakkaṇṇa, and Channarasa. Eṛṛāpragaḍa, the author of Harivaṁśam, Narasimha-purāṇamu and Araṇyaparva of the Telugu Bhārata was under Ānapota (c. 1360), and he mentions Śrivaishṇava teachers previous to this Mukunda Peḍḍi.

Vēdānta Dēśika.

Nainār, or Varadāchārya.
- Kiḍāmbi
  - Maṇavāḷa
- Ghaṭikaśatakam Ammāl,
  - Ādi Vaṇ Śatagōpa of Ahobilam
    - Tōlappāchārya (of Smriti-ratnākara).

Peddinṭi Singarāchārya.
- Tirumala Tirumalāchārya (the disciple of Kandale Paradesika Appālāchārya, and the *guru* of Eṛṛāpragada).

The Jaina scholar, Nemichandra, is said to have defeated all opponents at the court of Dēva Rāya II, and obtained a certificate of victory.

Among Vīra Śaiva Sanskrit scholars, Māyidēva Vibhū or Mageyya Māyadēva wrote Anubhava Sūtra, and Viśēsharthaprakaśika at Ipuri or Iholē. Ivvaṭūri Somārādhya, a descendant of Paṇḍitārādhya was the *guru* of Bānūra Pōtanna.

Dēvanna Bhaṭṭa wrote his Smriti Chandrika, and a work on music Sangīta Muktāvāḷi. In a grant of 1424 one Sampat Kumāra Paṇḍita is mentioned.

Some Advaitic scholars also figure in literature and inscriptions.

Ānanda Sarasvati.

Aṃrtēndratīrtha | Amṛta prajña | Nārāyaṇagiri (1416 A.D.).

Sadānanda Vyāsa, the author of Vēdānta Sāra should be assigned, to this period, Chitsukha II of Tattvapradīpikā, and of the commentaries on Khaṇḍangrantha and on Nyāyamakaranda is perhaps of this period as he has been criticised by Vyāsarāya.

Vidyāraṇya

Ātmarāma

Narasimha

Nārāyana of Bhāgvat Samhitārtha (in Kannaḍa)

Another Advaitic teacher was Vidyāśrama the *guru* of Paramjyoti yati.

Malikārjuna Immaḍi Dēva Rāya is perhaps the real author of Mahanaṭaka Sudhānidhi. He also seems to be the real author of Ratiratnapradipikā, the colophon of which runs thus :—

इति श्रीप्रौढदेवरायविरचि तायां-रतिरत्नप्रदीपिकायां.

One Kannaḍa poet, Kallarasa, wrote his Janavaśya or Mallikārjuna Vijaya or Mādanatilaka basing it on the information which Mallikārjuna imparted to his wife. Gangādhara, the author of Gangādāsapratāpa-vilāsam was patronised by Mallikārjuna. A poet, Kāḷamēgha, is mentioned in an inscription of 1468 A.D. Mallikārjuna is said to have made a grant to Rāghavēśvara Bhārati of Gōkarṇa-maṭha. Virūpāksha had as his guru Ānandatīrtha in Āragarājya (1475 A.D.). But according to Prapannāmṛitam he was at first a Vīra Śaiva, and was converted by Eṭṭūr Narasimhachārya and Śrīrangāchārya, the descendants of Śri Śailapūrṇa. Kallarasa or

Kallāmātya wrote his commentary on Sangīta Ratnākara of Śārṅgadēva.

IV. THE SĀḶUVAS AND TUḶUVAS (1486-1556)

The revival of Vaishṇavism in its Dvaitic and Viśishṭādvaitic forms is the cardinal point of interest in this period and this is reflected in the literature. Sāḷuva Narsiṁha believed himself to have been born by the grace of Narasiṁha of Ahōbilam who is called *Kula Daivata* in Rāmābhyudayam. Pillala Maṟṟi Pina Vīrabhadra says he was also a devotee of Vēnkaṭādrinātha. His general, Tuḷuva Narasiṁha or Narasā Nāyaka, was also a devotee of Vēnkaṭādripati. Rāmābhyudayam is really the work of Śoṇādri, the son of Rājānātha. Śoṇādri also wrote the Sāḷuvābhyudayam.

The Mādhavāchāryas of this period were men of high learning and spiritual attainments.

Raghūttama wrote commentaries called Bhāvabodha. Śrīpādarāja was the contemporary of Vīra Narasiṁha whose sin of Brahmincide is said to have been removed by the grace of Śrīpāda.

श्रीमद्वीर नृसिंहराय नृपतेः भूदेवहत्याऽव्यथाम् ।
दूरीकृत्य तदर्पितोज्ज्वलमहासिंहासने संस्थितः ।
श्रीमत्पूर्वकवाटनायकपुरे सर्वेष्टसिद्धिप्रदः ।
श्री श्रीपादयतींद्र शेखरमणिः भूयात्सनःश्रेयसे ॥

Śrīpāda is said to have written only one Sanskrit work Vāgvajra.

यद्वाग्वज्राभिघोच्च प्रबल तम महाभ्रन्थ वज्रेण हृष्य ।
दुर्वादिक्ष्माधराणां यतिवरसुरपःछेदयामास पक्षान् ॥

Vyāsarāja was the leading Dvaita philosopher in the days of Krishṇadēvarāya. He was the son of Rāmāchārya and Sītāmbā, and born on 2nd April, 1447. He became a Sannyāsin in 1455 A.D. and studied under Brahmaṇya-tīrtha and Śrīpāda-rāja. He died in 1539 A.D. His contemporaries were Pakshadhara Miśra, Basava Bhaṭṭa of Kalinga, Vidyādhara, Chaitanya and Vallabhāchārya. The works attributed to him are Tarka-Tāṇḍava, Nyāyāmṛta, Bhedōjjīvana, commentaries on Māyāvāda-Khaṇḍana, Prapancha-mithyātvānumāna-Khaṇḍana and Tattvōdyota, Mandara-Manjari or Upādhi Khaṇḍana and Chandrika on Tattvaprākāśa. The Chandrikā is said to have been left incomplete and was completed by his tenth successor. About the same time Vijayadhvaja wrote his commentary on the Bhāgavata.

The Śrīvaishṇava scholars of the time were :

Sriraṇga-Dēśika
|
Ahobila
|
Venkaṭatātaraya
(A.D. 1522)

Allasāni Peddana was the disciple of Śaṭha-Gōpa-Yati. Krishna Deva is the author of Madālasa Charitra, Satyāvadhū prīṇana, Sakalakathā-sāra-samgraha, Sūktinaipuṇi Jñanachintāmaṇi, and Rasamanjari in Sanskrit, and of Āmuktamālyadā in Telugu. The Jāmabavatī Kalyāṇam was enacted on the occasion of Chaitra festival of Virūpāksha the protecting deity of Karṇāṭaka (Karnāṭa Rājyarakshāmaṇi). We learn that Krishna had the title Sakalakalā-Bhojarāja or Abhinava-Bhoja. Evidently this drama was was written before the king definitely leaned towards Vaishṇavism. Vyāsarāja is said to have occupied the throne on the occasion of *Kuhu Yoga* and made many grants. The Vaishṇavism of Vallabha, as the form of Śuddhādvaita, was also patronised. Vallabha, requested by the king, defeated all opponents of Vaishṇavism, and was bathed in gold by the king. In this Vallabha is said to have been assisted by Vyāsarāja.

But though personally the king leaned towards Śrīvaishṇavism, Śaivism was equally patronised. The Tamil Nāvala-charitai mentions the irregularities in Tiruvālūr temple, set right by the orders of Krishṇadēvarāya. The foremost scholar was however Lolla Lakshmidhara who was equally powerful in Orissa. In the colophon of commentary on Saundaryalahari, he gives a brief account of his ancestors and of his own achievements.

श्री लोल्लकुलसांप्रदायप्रवर्तकभ्रमरांबिकावरप्रसादसमुल्लसितसारस्वतभट्टलोल्लपतिग्रंथविवरणकर्तृश्रीमहामहोपाध्यायमहादेवाचार्यसप्तमेन साहित्यपारिजातस्मृतिकल्पतरुप्रबन्धप्रबंधृलक्ष्मीधरार्यषष्ठेन भरतार्णवपोताख्यसाहित्यमीमांसाग्रंथद्वयप्रणेतृविरंचिमिश्रपञ्चमेन मीमांसाद्वयजीवातुनिर्मातृपुरुषोत्तममहोपाध्यायनप्त्रा प्राभाकरामृतवाहिनीप्रभावळीखण्डनाद्यनेकप्रबंधसंदर्भप्रवर्तकबिरुदपदमहोपाध्यायलक्ष्मणार्यपौत्रेण नयवि

वेकदीपिकाप्रबंधसंविधातृमहोपाध्याय विद्वत्सार्वभौमनूतनव्यासाद्यनेकबिरुदांकितश्रीवि
श्वनाथभट्टारकतनयेन अधीत दशशतनयेन पार्वतीगर्भशुक्तिमुक्तारत्नेन बहूकृतकृतधी
चिरत्नेन लोल्लकुलकलशांबुसुधांशुना यशःप्रांशुना हरितगोत्र कल्पशाखिनाआपस्तंब
शाखिना षड्दर्शिनीपारदृश्वना प्रतिपक्षवृक्षझंझामातरिश्वना भ्रमरांबिकाप्रसादसमासा
दितप्रतिभाविशेषेणभुविशेषेण निखिलयामकतन्त्रार्णवावगाहिनारुद्रेण आश्रयीकृतगज
पतिवीररुद्रेण नीलगिरिसुंदरचरणारविंदचञ्चरीकेणवाणीसहचरीकेण सरस्वतीविलासा
द्यनेकस्मृतिनिबन्धन लक्ष्मीधराद्यनेक साहित्यनिबन्धननयविवेकभूषणाद्यनेकगुरुमतनिब
न्धनयोगदीपिकाद्यनेक पातञ्जलमतनिबन्धमहानिबंधनाख्यमानवधर्मशास्त्रटीकाकर्णाव
तंसबर्हावतंसाद्यनेककाव्यकल्पकेन आश्रितजनकल्पकेन निग्रहानुग्रहकौशिकेन श्रीमहो
पाध्यायलक्ष्मीधरदेशिकेन कृतेयं लक्ष्मीधराख्या सौंदर्यलहरीस्तुतिव्याख्या ॥

The Sarasvatīvilāsa written by Lakshmīdhara in the name of Pratāpa-Rudra has this colophon :

इति श्रीगजपतिगौडेश्वरनवकोटिकर्णाटकलुबुरगेश्वरशरणागतजमुनापुराधीश्वर
हुषान् साहिब् सुरत्राणशरणरक्षणश्रीदुर्गावरपुत्रपरमपवित्रचरित्रराजाधिराजराजपरमेश्वर
वीरप्रतापदेवमहाराजविरचिते सरस्वतीविलासे—

Evidently before Krishna conquered Orissa Lakshmīdhara resided in Pratāpa-Rudra's court, and when Krishna married the daughter of Pratāpa-Rudra the scholar seems to have gone to Vijayanagara. In the beginning of the Sarsvatīvilāsa there is a verse mentioning Vīrabhadra :

श्रीवीरभद्र नृपतिः श्रियमातनोतु नीलाद्रिराज निजपाद सरोजयामम् ।
यद्योगिभिर्हृदयपंकजमध्यभाग संरोधनादि वसमुद्धतरक्तभागम् ॥

This Vīrabhadra is probably the son of Pratāpa-Rudra, defeated by Krishṇa at Koṇḍavīḍu.

Lakshmīdhara thus praised Krishna in a *chātu* verse.

श्रीकृष्णक्षितिपालदत्तमणिभिः विद्वत्कवीनां गृहा
नानारत्नविचित्रकुट्टिमभुवो रत्नाकरत्वं गताः ।

अब्धिः केवलवारिपूरनिलयः संभाष्यते सज्जनैः
अंबोधिर्जलधिः पयोधिरुदधिः वारांनिधिर्वारिधिः ।

Several inscriptions at Koṇḍavīḍu mention Lakshmīdhara (E.I. VI, p. 230 A.D. 1520).

The pupil of Lakshmīdhara was Dēśayāmātya the secretary of Nādinḍla Gopa, the viceroy of Koṇḍavīḍu. Dēśayāmātyā wrote a Panchikā on Mahimna Stava by the graee of Lakshmīdhara. The pontiffs of Bhikshā-maṭha Īśāna Śiva and Aghora Śiva (1501-1541) figure also prominently. Aghora Śiva wrote a commentary on the Mṛgēndrāgama, and was the *guru* of Mādayyagāri Mallanna who wrote Rājaśēkhara Charitra in Telugu. The Jaina teacher Abhinava Vadividyānanda is said to have defeated opponents, in the court of Krishṇadēva.

In the realm of the fine arts Nādinḍḷa Gopa wrote a commentary on the Prabodha Chandrōdaya Nāṭaka and his uncle the famous Sāḷuva Timmarasa a commentary on Bāla Bhārata, called Manōhara. Krishnarāya is said to have learnt to play on the Vina under one Krishṇa, an ancestor of Raghavendra-tīrtha.

Under Achyuta the centre of literature shifts to Tanjore and Madhura. Kumara Tātāchārya was the preceptor (1542) of Bommalāṭa Kāḷa. Rājānātha Dinḍīma wrote Achyutarāyabhyudayam and Bhāgvata Champu, and Tirumalāmbā wrote Varadāmbikaparinayam. Achyuta, in his later years, was completely in the hands of his brothers-in-law—who were overthrown by Rāma Rāya, Tirumala and Venkatadri. Rāma Rāya caused Svara-mēla-kalānidhi to be written by Rāmayāmātya Toḍaramalla, who had the titles Abhinava Bharatāchārya Vāggēyakāra Toḍaramalla, and who had been made the governor of Koṇḍavīḍu.

The composers of the official records belonged to the family of Abhirama Kavi and were no ordinary poets.

Abhirāma.
- Sabhāpati (1512-1541).
  - Svayambhū (1540-71)
    - Rājānātha 1595
  - Kāmakōṭi 1580
    - Krishṇa Kavi 1588
    - Rāma Kavi 1634-1636.
  - Gaṇapārya 1575.
    - Kāmayya
      - Somanātha 1644-1647.

V. ĀRAVĪḌU DYNASTY (1570-1670)

Sadāśiva Dēva-rāya was merely the nominal ruler up to C. 1570 A.D., but the real power was in the hands of Rāma Rāya and his brothers. Tirumala can be said to have been the first of the Āravīḍu chiefs to assume imperial titles, even though inscriptions continue to mention the name of Sadāśiva-rāya. Tirumala (1568-1572), Śrī Ranga I (1572-1585), Venkaṭa I (1585-1614), Śrī Ranga II (1614-1615), Venkaṭa II (1630-42), Śrī Ranga III (1642-64) are the kings whose power became less and less as the Pāḷayagārs and Nāyaks of Tanjore and Madhura became more and more independent, though nominally acknowledging the suzerainty of the Vijayanagara emperors.

This was a period of great literary activity for the controversies among Advaitis, Dvaitis and Viśishṭādvaitis resulted in a vast output of philosophical works. It was not merely a barren scholasticism, but imbued with deep piety and devotion. Among the Dvaita scholars, the two disciples of Vyāsa-rāja, Vādi-rāja and Vijayīndra stood out pre-eminent. Vāḍī-rāja of Soddemāṭha was also the pupil of Vāgīśatīrtha. Vādi-rāja's pupil Veda Vedya received a grant from Venkaṭappa Nāyaka of Keḷadi in 1614 A.D. Among the numerous Sanskrit works of Vādi-rāja are :—

Gurvartha Dīpika
Pramēya Samgraha
Guru-rājīya
Tātparya Prakāśika
Iśā-bhāshya ṭīkā.
Tantrasāra ṭīkā.
Lakshābharaṇa
Sarasa Bhārati vilāsa
Rukminīśa Vijaya
Yuktimallikā.
Pāshanḍa-mala Khanḍana.
Nyāya Ratnāvaḷi
Bhūgōḷavivaraṇa.
Chakra-mīmāṁsa.
Haribhakta-sāra.
Kalpa-latā.
Gītā Vyākhyāna Vivaraṇa.
Śruti-tāla Prakāśaka.
Ēkadēśinirṇaya.
Samkalpa Paddhati.
Vāyu-stuti-purāscharana-vidhāna.
Stōtras and stutis.
on Raupya-pīṭha Krishṇa.
Chakra, Ashṭamahishī,
Krishṇa, Daśāvatāra,
Vāyu, Udupi Krishna,
Nṛsimha, Varāha, Hayagrīva,
Trivikrama Vishṇu,
Ramēśa Venkaṭēśa, Navagraha,
Kēśavādi Chatur-Vimsa-mūrtis, etc.

Vādirāja's younger contemporary Vishṇu-tīrtha Vijayīndra was the disciple of Vyāsarāja and Surēndra. Vijayīndra wrote 104 works in opposing Appayya Dīkshita. The more important of them are :—

Ṛg, prasthāna	Naya Manjarī
Bhēda Vidyāvilāsa,	Āmōdā
Nayamukura.	Nārayaṇa Śabdārtha-Vachana.
Mīmāmsānyāyamāla	Brahma Sutrārtha Samgraha.
Nyāya-mauktikamalā.	Kaṇṭakōddhāra
Adhikaraṇamālā.	Chakramīmāmsā
Naya-Champaka-mālā.	Madhavatantra Bhūshaṇa
Paratattva prakāśikā.	Upasaṁhāra-vijaya.
Appaya Kapola Chāpeṭikā	Ṭīkā on Pramāṇa Paddhati
Ṭīkā on Pramēyadīpikā	Ṭīkā on Nyāya Dīpikā.
Ṭīkā on Upanishad-prasthāna	Ṭīkā on Māyāvāda Khan-ḍana.

Vidyādhīśa of Uttarādi Maṭha (1619 A.D.) wrote commentaries on Vishṇu-tattva-nirṇaya, Ēkādaśi-nirṇaya, Vishṇu panchkōpavāsa-nirṇaya, Vākyārtha Chandrikā on the Sudhā, Dvaita-Vādārtha, Talvakāra Khanḍārtha, Oṁkāra Vādārtha, Tithi-traya-nirṇaya.

Venkaṇṇa Bhaṭṭa—Rāghavēndra-tīrtha was the disciple of Sudhīndra successor of Vijayīndra. Rāghavēndra was the contemporary of Yajñanārāyaṇa Dīkshita. Bhallava-puri Bhairavabhaṭṭa and Vīrabhadra-Panḍita. Rāghavēndra is said to have written a commentary on the four Vedas and forty two other works. The more important are :—

Parimaḷa.	Vādāvati-ṭippaṇa
Prakāśa on the Chandrikā.	Tarka-tānḍava-ṭippaṇi.
Nyāyamuktāvaḷi in Tantra Dīpikā.	Pratassamkalpa-gadya
Tattva Manjari.	Purusha-Sūkta-ṭikā
Bhāva Dīpikā	Ambhiriṇi-Śukta-ṭīkā
Daśa prakaraṇa tīkā	Hiraṇya-garbha-ṭīkā.
Daśopanishad-Khanḍārtha.	Mantrārtha Samgraha.
Tantra dīpikā	Bhaṭṭa Sangrahmīmāmsā.
Aṇubhāshya-ṭika.	Trivēda-vivṛtti.
Īśāvāsya-vivṛtti.	Bhāva Samgraha
Atharva vivṛti.	Rāma-Krishṇa-charitra-manjari.
Bhēda-bodhini.	

Varadarājāchārya of Ādya family, a contemporary of Vyāsarāja and Raghunātha wrote Varadarājīya on the Mahābhārata-tātparya-nīrnaya of Ānanda tīrtha. His son Narahari is the author of Ṭippaṇis on Bhāgvata tātparya-nirṇaya and on Vishṇu-purāṇa and also of Smriti Kaustubha. Yādavārya is the author of Karāvalambana stotra and of Ṭippaṇis on Bhāgvata tātparya, Sudhā, Yamakabhārata and Tattva-Sanikhyāna. His nephew Bidurahalli Śrinivāsatīrtha, a contemporary of Rāghavēndra wrote twenty-three tippaṇis a commentary on the 11th Skandha of the Bhāgavata, on the Vāyustuti, Adhikaraṇārtha Samgraha, Vikshipta-Khaṇḍārtha Samgraha, Purushasūktārtha, Āhnika Kaustubha, etc. Another contemporary of Yādavārya was Pāṇḍurangi-Ānanda-bhaṭṭa, the author of Kanṭakoddhāra and other works. His son Kēśava-Guru-rāja wrote 13 ṭippaṇis, Śēshavākyārtha, Chandrikā on the Sudha, Vakhyārthamanjarī, Guru and Laghu Chandrikā Vyākhyāna. Another contemporary was Śingeri Śrīnivāsa whose works are Tattvavāda Kanṭhā-bharaṇa, Baudha-dhikkāra, Smriti-Muktāvaḷi, Chakramīmāmsā, Rukminīharaṇa, Asaucha-nirṇaya, Padārtha Samgraha, and tippaṇis on Bhāgvata, Bhārata, Maṇi-Manjari, etc. His son, Vyāsāchārya, wrote Vṛndāvana Vyakhyāna Chatvāri Śēsha and also wrote commentaries on Aṇubhāshya, Tantrasāra Vyākhyāna, Shaṭpraśna, Vāyustuti, Pramāṇa Chandrikā, Tattva Samkhyāna, Mādhava Vijaya, etc. His son Narasimha wrote on Shaṭpraśna Īśa and Āhnika-taranginī.

The foremost exponents of the Vishishṭādvaita philosophy were, the Tātāchāryas and Mahāchārya.

Tirumala Tāta (Car of Krishnadēva).
|
Sudarśana.
|
Singarāchārya.

Tirumala Tōlappa (1550-80)

Śrīnivāsa (1550)
|
Lakshmī Kumār-Tātārya. (contemporary of Ramarāya and Venkaṭa I and author of Sāttvika Brahma Vidyā vilāsa and Panchāmatabhanjana.)

Other Sri Vaishṇava scholars are :—

Mahāchārya, or Doḍḍaiya, author of Chaṇḍa Māruta.
- Śrī Parānakuśa.
- Śrī Van-Śatagōpa (1584 A.D.) of Ahobila.
- Kandaḷe Śrīranga,
- Appaḷāchārya.
- Bhaṭṭaru Chikkāchārya.
- Pāraśara-Bhaṭṭar.

The Advaita philosophy was expounded and vindicated by a large number of scholars. Nṛsinhasvāmi, the disciple of Krishṇānanda Avimukta-kshētra wrote Advaita-Dīpikā Vivaraṇa-Bhāvaprakāśikā-Subōdhini on Vēdānta Sāra, Tattvavivēka, Ratna-Kōśaprakāśika and Advaita Dīpikā. The last work has been erroneously attributed to Appaya by the author of Prapannāmṛtam. Sadāśiva Brahmēndra Sarasvati is the author of Gururatnamālikā, Vṛitti on the Brahma Sūtras, and numerous songs and *stutis*. He was the contemporary of Ātmabōdhēndra of Kānchī. In the reign of Śriranga-rāya (1563-76) Bhairavavoḍeya made a grant to Śringeri Nṛsimha-bhārati and Mādhava Sarasvati of Harihara-pura Maṭha. He is perhaps a different individual from Mādhava Sarsvati who, with Viśvēśvara Sarsvati, taught Madhusūdana Sarsvati at Benares. One Mādhava Sarsvati, perhaps of the Hariharapura Maṭha was a native of Gōrāshṭra and devotee of Gokarṇa Mahabalēshvar and the author of a commentary on Sivāditya's Sapta Padārthi. The chronological sequence of the Advaitāchāryas of the period can be shown thus (I.A., 1904).

I Krishnānda Sarsvati
- Nṛsimhasvāmi
  - Venkatanātha of Vellunguḍi.
    - Dharmarājādhvari
      - Rama-Krishna.
  - Bhaṭṭoji Dīkshita
  - Rangōji.

II Viśvēśvarsarsvati
- Nārāyaṇabhaṭṭa
- Mādhava Sarsvati.
  - Madhusūdana Sarasvati.
    - Nārāyaṇa Sarsvati.
      - Gauḍa-Brahmānanda.

III Āchārya Dīkshtia

- Ranga-rāja makhin
  - Appaya (1554-1626).
    - Nīlakanṭha (?).
      - Venkaṭādhvarin.
  - Āchādīkshita
    - Nārāyaṇa.
      - Aruṇagiri (?)
      - Nīlakanṭha (1637 A.D.).

IV Ahōbala

- Lakshmaṇabhaṭṭa.
  - Tippa
    - Chokkanātha.

V. Govindadīkshita.

- Yagñanārāyaṇa Dīkshita.

VI. Bhuminalla

- Aśvathanārāyaṇā
  - Nallā
    - Nārāyaṇa
      - Ranganātha
  - Appa
    - Piḷḷai
      - Kunjallā
        - Venkaṭeśvara
          - Dakshṇāmūrti
            - Venkatēśvara
  - Chaturvēda
    - Nallā
      - Yagñarama
        - Nallā
          - Yagñarama
            - Rāmabhadra
              - Vaidyanātha

VII. Nārāyaṇa Dīkshita

- Chokkanātha

VIII. Bāvāji

- Gangādhara
  - Nṛsimha
    - Ānandarāya c. 1720
  - Tryambaka
    - Gangādhvarin
      - Nārayāṇa
  - Bhagavantarāya

IX. Mahādēvādhvarin

- Viśvēśvara
  - Mahādēvā
    - Viśvēśvara
      - Subrahmaṇya
        - Bāla Dīkshita
    - Vāsudēva
  - Nārāyaṇa

X. Chauṇḍāji Bālāji

- Mahādēva
  - Chidambara-yatin
  - Ghanashyāma
    - Chandra Śēkhara
    - Gōvardhana
  - Śākambhari

Nṛsinhāśvami's disciples, Bhaṭṭōji and Rangōji, were the contemporaries of Appaya and Jagannātha Paṇḍita. Bhaṭṭōji, apart from his grammatical work Manōramā and Sidhānta Kaumadi is the author of an *advaitic* work Dvaita Kaustubha Khanḍana; Jagannātha Paṇḍita is the author of Manōramā Kuchamardhana, Rasa-Gangādhara, Chitra-mīmāmsā Khanḍana, etc., and sought Moghul patronage. Appaya's father, Rangarāja, is perhaps the author of Advaita Mukura. Appaya was the contemporary of the three rulers Venkaṭapati (1585-1614), Chinna Bomma (1549-78—1601), and Chinna Timma. In his native place Aḍiyapalem, Appaya constructed the Kalakanṭhēśvara temple where an inscription of 1582 (Chitrabhānu) mentions Nīlakanṭha Dīkshita as his eldest son. According to the Viśvaguṇādarśachampu Tātā-Chārya is Appaya's maternal uncle.

कांचीमण्डल मण्डनस्य भविनः कर्णाट भूभृद्गुरोः ।
तातार्यस्य दिगन्तकान्तयशसोऽयं भागिनेयं विदुः ॥

Appaya's sister's son was Samara Pungava Dīkshita[9] whose Yātrā Prabandha refers to Appaya's Kanakābhishēka. Ratna Khēṭa Dīkshita lived in about the same period. Appaya wrote more than 100 works including Kuvalayānanda, Chitra-mīmāmsā, Vidhi-rasāyana, Śivārkamaṇidīpika, Śrīkanṭhabhāshyaṭīkā, Madhva-Śringa-bhanga, Śivatatvavivēka, Nigrahāshṭaka, Nyāyarakshāmaṇi, Kalpataru Parimaḷa, Pūrvottara-mīmāmsā-Vādaratnamālā, Hari-vamśasāra-Charitra-vyākhyāna, Siddhāntalēśa Samgraha and numerous Stōtras including the Dēvyaparādha Stōtra (erroneously attributed to Vidyāraṇya or Śamkara himself).

In Northern India the great Madhusūdana Sarasvati (1540-1647) was the author of Advaita-Siddhi, Siddhānta-bindu, Advaita-ratna Rakshaṇa, Vēdānta-Kalpalatikā, Samkshēpa Śāriraka Samgraha, Gūḍhārthadīpika, Bhagavadbhakti-rasāyana, Iśvarapratipatti-prakāra, etc. This profound learning has been admired in the mnemonic verse.

मधुसूदनसरस्वत्याः पारं वेत्ति सरस्वति ।
वेत्ति पारं सरस्वत्या मधुसूदनसरस्वती ॥

Another contemporary of Appaya in the South was Dharma Rājādhvari of Veḷḷānguḍi who wrote Vēdānta-Paribhāshā and Tattvachūḍāmaṇi on Gangeśa's Tattva Chintāmaṇi. The famous Govinda Dīkshita and his son Yagñanārāyaṇa were younger contemporaries of Appayya. Govinda seems to have had also a hand in some of Appaya's works. Appaya being an *Advaitin* had little animus against individuals unlike his opponents who too often indulge in personal abuse. His catholicity is shown by the fact that he has written a commentary on Vēdānta Dēśika's Yādavabhyudaya, and he assisted in the restoration of the Govindarāja image in its

9. A Samara Pungava Dīkshita figures in grants of 1502-1503 A.D. and was the teacher of Mahāchārya, the opponent of Appaya.

original place in Chidambaram, whatever the Prapannāmritam might say to the contrary. In one memorable Stōtra he pays equal homage and sees no distinction between Naṭarāja and Govindarāja.

मारमणमुमारमणं फणितल्पं फणाधाराकल्पम् ।
मुरमथनं पुरमथनं वंदे बाणारिमयुगबाणारिम् ॥

Under the patronage of Rāma Rāya and Venkaṭādri, Rāmayāmātya Toḍarmalla wrote Svaramēla-Kalānidhi. Tirumala is nominally the author of Śrutiranjiṇi on the Gīta Govinda ; and the real author seems to be Cherukura Lakshmīdhara who also wrote Abhīshṭārthadāyini on Prasanna-Rāghava and Shaḍbhāsha-chandrikā. Another writer on the fine arts was Punḍarīka Viṭṭhala a native of Sāvanadurga in the Bangalore district who migrated to North India and wrote Nartaka Nirṇaya, etc., and was patronised by Akbar and seems to have influenced Tānsen.

Some other Advaitāchāryas seem to have flourished in this period. Svayamprakāśa, the disciple of Kaivalyānanda and Śuddhānanda wrote commentaries on Advaita-Makaranda, Harimīdē-Stava, etc. His disciples seem to have been Māhādēva Sarsvati (the author of Tattvānusandhāna, and of Akhanḍa Yati, the author of Ṛjuprakāśikā). Akhanḍayati, in his previous *āśrama* was known as Ranganātha, and his parents were Kāḷahastyadhvari and Yagñāmbā. This Kāḷahastyadhvari is probably the author of Ratna-Kośa-Prakāśikā. Akhanḍayati wrote Ṛjuprakāśikā at the request of Immaḍi Jagadēkarāya. Immaḍi Jagadēka is probably the son of Pedda Jagadēkarāya of Chennapatṇa who claims to have driven away the Muhammadans from Penukonḍa in 1577 A.D. (E.C.I p. 28).

श्रीमान् श्रीनलगंतु वंश जनितः श्रीकाळहस्त्यध्वरी ।
यज्ञांबाच यमात्मजं प्रसुषुवे श्रीरङ्गनाथाभिधम् ।
सोऽयं सम्प्रति साधनोज्ज्वलमनाः प्राग्जन्मपुण्योदयात् ।
प्राप्याखण्डयतीशतामनुभवत्यारादखण्डं मुदम् ॥
सोऽयमखण्डो यतिराडिम्मडि जगदेकराय भूपेन ।
संप्रार्थितोस्ति सम्यग्वाचस्पत्यस्य कुर्वति व्याख्यानम् ॥

The centres of literary activity shifted to Tanjore, Madhura, Travancore, Keḷadi and Mysore.

THE MAHĀRĀSHṬRA RAJAS OF TANJORE UP TO 1700 A.D.

- Śāhaji.
  - Sambhāji
  - Śivāji
  - Venkōji 1676 A.D.
    - Sāhaji (1684).
    - Sarabhōji 1711.
    - Tukōji Tuljāji 1729 A.D.

KEḶADI CHIEFS.

- Chaunḍa
  - Sadāśiva
    - Doḍḍa Sankaṇṇa
      - Venkaṭappa I
      - Rāmarāja
    - Chikka Sankaṇṇa.
      - Siddappa.
        - Śivappa
        - Venkaṭappa.
  - Bhadra.
- Bhadrappa

NĀYAKAS OF TANJORE.

Achyūtadēva—queen—Mūrtiyambā-Chinna Chevva.

- Achyūta-Mūrtiyambā.
  - Raghunātha-Kaḷāvati.
    - Vijaya-Rāghava
    - Rāmabhadra.

Lingappa

- **Muttu Krishna. 1602-09.**
  - **Madhura Tirumala Nāyaka.**
  - **Muttu Vīra 1609-23.**

MADURA CHIEFS.

- Nāgama.
  - Viśvanāth (cont. of Krishṇa Dēva.)
    - Kumāra Krishṇa.
      - Vīrappa
        - Viśvanātha III
        - Kumāra Krishna II (1602 A.D.).
      - Viśvanātha II.
    - Chokkanātha
    - Cont. of Venkoji-Ekoji.

MYSORE WOḌEYARS.

- Timma Rāja II 1552-1571.
  (Boḷa) Chāmarāja IV 1571-1576.
  - Dēvarāja Woḍeyar m-Amṛtamma
    - Doḍḍa Dēvarāja (1659-72).
    - Chikka Dēvarāja (1671-1704).
  - (Bettada) Chāmarāja V 1576-1578.
    - Kanthirava Narsa. (1638-1659).
  - Rāja Woḍeyar (1578-1617).
    - Rāja Woḍeyar II
    - Chāmarāja VI, (1617-1637).

Under the patronage of the Tanjore chiefs the following scholars flourished. (1 A. 1904).

1. Rama Krishna the son of Dharmarājādhvari, and the author of Vēdānta Śikhāmaṇi and Nyāya Śikhāmaṇi.
2. Vaidyanātha Dīkshita—Smṛtimuktāphala and Rāmāyaṇa Dīpikā.
3. Śivarāma, son of Vaidyanātha, wrote Āhnika on the Smṛtimuktāphala.
4. Chokkanātha, the teacher of Rāmabhadra, and the author of Śabda-Kaumudi and Bhāshya Ratnāvaḷi.
5. Rangnātha of Manjari Makaranda.

6. Nalladiikshita wrote Subhadrā-pariṇaya, Śringārasarvasvābharaṇa, Advaitarasamanjari with his own commentary Parimaḷa.

7. Śrīnivāsa or Ikkīri Appā Śāstrin (Pūrnānanda-Yati) the pupil of Brahmānanda Sarasvati and the author of Prāyaschitta-dīpika and Upagrantha-dīpika.

8. Nīlakaṇṭha Dīkshita wrote Nīlakaṇṭha-Vijaya-Champu, Kalividambana, Naḷa-Charitranāṭaka, Gangāvataraṇa Kāvya.

9. Balakrishna Bhagvatpāda.

10. Yagñanārāyana Dīkshita, the son of Govinda Dīkshita and author of Sāhityaratnākara.

11. Ramabhadra Dīkshita whose works are : —

    Jānakipariṇaya—a nāṭaka.
    Śṛngāra Tilaka—a bhāṇa.
    Paribhāsha vṛīti-Vyākhyāna.
    Shaḍdarśana Siddhānta Samgraha
    Patanjali-charitra—a Kāvya.
    Āchāryastavarājabhūshana.
    Rāmastava Karṇa-rasāyana.
    Viśvagarbha-stava.
    Prasāda-stava.
    Tūṇīra-stava.
    Chāpa-stava.
    Bāṇa-stava.
    Ashṭaprāsa.

12. Rāmanātha Makhin.

13. Narahariyadhvarin.

14. Periyappa Kavi of Śringāra Manjari Sāharājiya.

15. Śrīvenkaṭēsa.

16. Yagnēśvara dīkshita.

17. Śrīnivāsa Makhin.

18. Bhāskara Dīkshita, author of Ratnatūlikā on the Siddhānta Siddhānjana of Krishṇānanda Sarasvati.

19. Venkaṭa Krishna, of Naṭēsa Vijaya Kāvya, Śrī Rama Chandrōdaya Kāvya, Uttara Champu, Kuśa-Lava Vijaya Nāṭaka.

20. Vēdā Kavi of Jīvānanda Nātaka and Vaidya Pariṇaya Nāṭaka.

21. Ānandarāya Makhin Āśvalāyana Gṛhya Sūtra Vṛtti.

22. Mahādēva Kavi, of Adbhuta-darpaṇa Naṭaka and Śuka Samdēśa.

23. Mahādēva Vājapēyin, of the Subodhini Boudhāyana Śranta Sūtra.

24. Sudhāra Venkaṭēśa, or Ayyā vāḷ the author of Sohendra Vilasa Kavya.

Śivabhakti Kalpalatikā.
Śivabhaktalakshaṇa.
Dayā Śataka.
Mātṛbhūta Śaṭaka.
Stuti-paddhati.
Ākhya Śasthṭi.
Tārāvaḷi Stotra.
Ārtihara Stotra.
Dōḷārṇava-ratnamālikā.
Kulirāṣṭaka.

25. Sāmavēda Venkaṭa Śāstrin, author of Upagrantha bhāshya.

26. Appādhvarin of Māyavaram wrote Ācharanavanīta, Madanabhūshaṇabhāṇa, Gaurī māyūra-champu.

27. Śrīnivāsadīkshita wrote Svarasiddhānta Chandrikā.

28. Venkaṭēśvara Kavi wrote Uṇādi-nighanṭu.

29. Bhūminātha wrote Dharma-Vijaya-Champu.

30. Vaidyanātha, author of Paribhāshārtha Samgraha.

Raghunātha of Tanjore was a great scholar and is said to be the author of Pārijātaharānam, Vālmīki Charitram, Achyutēndrābhyudaya, Gajēndramoksha, Naḷacharitra, Rukminī-Krishṇa-vivāha, Yakshagāna. He was proficient in music and wrote the Samgītasudhā where he says he invented new *ragas* like Jayantasena, Jayamangaḷa, Simhalalitā, and Tāḷas, Ratilīlā, Turangalīlā, Rangābharaṇa, Anangaparikramaṇa, Nandalīlā, Abhinandana, Nandanandana, Abhimāla. Rāmananda Rāmabhadrāmba wrote Raghunāthābhyudayam. Govinda Dīkshita wrote Sāhitya Sudhā, and his son Yagñanārayana Sahityaratnākara. Vijaya-Rāghava the son of Raghunātha was also an author in Telugu and wrote

Ragunāthābhyudayam. Madhuravāṇi was another poetess in the Court of Raghunātha.

On Advaita philosophy, Krishṇānanda Sarasvati wrote Siddhānta Siddhānjana. Gōvindānanda Sarasvati or Rāmānanda Svāmi wrote Bhāshyaratnaprabhā. He was the disciple of Gōpālānanda Sarasvati, the disciple of Śivarāmarāya of Kānchi. In his previous Āśrama he was known as Dharmābhaṭṭa the author of a Sāhityaratnākara, Brahmāmṛtavarshini, Krishṇa-stava and Narakāsēna-vyāyōga. His disciple is probably Brhmānanda Bhārati who calls himself a disciple of Rāmānanda Bhārati, the author of Vākyasudhā-ṭika, a commentary on Dṛg-dṛshya-viveka. Rāmānandasvāmi was the contemporary of Achyutasvāmi and of his disciple. Brahmānanda Bhārati is the same as Brahmānanda Sarsvati ; Rāmānanda should have been the contemporary of Krishṇānanda also.

This is only a meagre sketch of the immense mass of literature in Samskrit produced in the course of four hundred years of Vijayanagara rule. The importance of it cannot be gainsaid for the culture-history of our country, if not for the world. This cultural tradition was carried on untarnished under the Peshwas, the Woḍeyars of Mysore and the rulers of Tanjore and Madhura. This glorious heritage is ours to be cherished as a source of constant inspiration and instruction.

इति शम् .

27

Geographical Notes on the Chief Capitals of the Vijayanagara Empire

BY

MR. N. SUBRAHMANYAM, M.A., L.T., F.R.G.S.,

Lecturer in Geography, Teachers' College, Saidapet.

THE following are some of the purely *Geographical* notes on the chief Capitals of the Vijayanagara empire, which have been prepared from large-scale topographical maps. They may serve to throw useful sidelight on the history of the empire.

I. VIJAYANAGARA

The location of Vijayanagara, the capital of the empire, is something very remarkable, whatever doubts there may be as regards the exact historical origin of it. Its situation on the southern bank of the Tungabhadrā, after the river has swerved eastwards must have been the result of deliberate choice, as the river itself affords protection on the north, the direction from which the natural enemies of the empire were expected to invade.

As a matter of fact the Tungabhadrā was expected to be only a second line of defence, the first line of defence being further North, in the shape of the Krishnā river which fell within the boundaries of the empire, even in its inception. It, however, really turned out that the Raichur-Doab was often the bone of contention and as often the cock-pit between the contending powers of the north and the south. A closer examination of the one-inch ordinance survey map reveals the wisdom in the choice of the particular site for the Capital City, far north of Anagundi, on the other bank and south of Hampi are situated hills which practically served the purpose of fortifications.

Another interesting factor to be noted in connection with the location of the site is the existence of a gap leading to the coastal region along with the valley of the Dharmā, a westerly tributary of the Tungabhadra and through gaps in the ghats, beyond. This route has been of commercial importance to the Vijayanagara rulers in their relations with the Portuguese power at Goa.

When the empire extended southwards and eastwards and stretched from sea to sea and its hold over the Raichur-Doab became slippery, the Capital appeared to occupy a marginal rather than a central location, like Belgrade in Servia, before it became Jugo-Slavia. And this might appear to be the dynamic effect of the close proximity of the foe. But in the early period of the empire the capital did not occupy such a marginal location, but was rather central in the small kingdom that it then was, as stated above.

II. PENUKOṆḌA

Penukonda whereto the dynasty had to move after Tāḷikōṭa, was not merely an after-thought, but had served as an important watch tower guarding the Penner valley route to the south. No doubt in the early days, before Penukonda was chosen the lower hill of Gooty which commanded the more open country had served the same purpose. But the bigger hill, (Penukonda) was deliberately chosen later as it commanded a larger part of the country along the Chitrāvati and Penner routes to the south, the height of the peak being over 3,000 feet, the hill rising to a height of 1,200 feet, from the surrounding country. The one-inch map shows its location on a transverse gap in the ridge that separates the Chitrāvati and Penner valleys, which it commands. It is not far away from the Dharmavaram-Kadiri-Damalcheruvu route which leads to the Carnatic from the Deccan plateau. Hence it could guard the south-eastern plain also, which was a richer and a far more important country than the dry infertile and sparsely populated region in which the second capital was situated. Compared to Hampi which was on a river bank the transfer to Penukoṇḍa was in itself a calamity as there is not even drinking water available in the latter place.

III. CHANDRAGIRI

Chandragiri, the final capital of the empire in its last days, forms an important out-post in the Swarṇamukhi valley—opposite to the Tirupati hills. It commands several routes which join together either in this valley or in its neighbourhood. These are well brought out in the physical map. First of all there is the north to south coastal route which leads to the fertile plains and river valleys. The interior route from the north leading through Damalcheruvu to Chittoor, Vellore and the inland parts of the Carnatic, is reached from Chandragiri through a short narrow gap which is now taken by the railway from this place to Pakala. This gap and the Swarṇamukhi river form a sort of a transverse link between the coastal and the interior north to south routes referred to above.

Lord Śrīnivasa of Tirumalai hills on the opposite side of the valley was one of the titulary deities of the Vijayanagara emperors who used to visit the shrine and pay their homage as often as they could. The great Krishṇa Dēva Rāya, in his campaigns of victory, did not forget this important shrine. Can religious motive be one of the factors that influenced the choice of this third Capital ?

It is, however, significant that the capital should be steadily moving further and further south, showing the steady shrinkage of the empire. The choice of Chandragiri further shows that the richer coastal plain was better worth preserving when it came to a question of necessity, than the comparatively dry, infertile, thinly populated hilly tracts of the plateau.

28

Sri Vidyaranya and Music

By

Mr. P. S. Sundaram Iyer, B.A., L.T.,
Tanjore.

The world of Sanskrit Literature in general, and the music-knowing world in particular, will be glad to know that the *Holy Vidyāraṇya* was famed not only for his intense erudition in the Vedas and their exposition as exhibited through the various *granthas* of immortal fame in the shape of the Bhāshyas bequeathed to us ; but, he was also a musician that left his mark by recording his definite ideas in the science of music, which he stored up in his work *Sangīta-Sāra*—a treatise on Music. Even though the existence of this work is beyond any doubt, the scholars engaged in the collection of Sanskrit Mss. have not yet been able to recover the work in the original which, nevertheless, must exist in some private or public library in India. In the absence of the original work, the information regarding its existence was first gathered from a passage in *Sangīta-Sudhā*—a work written by the illustrious royal author, Raghunātha Nāyaka of Tanjore. The following plain words are found in the second chapter of the *Rāgadhyāya* of his work :—

संगीतसारं समवेक्ष्य विद्यारण्याभिध श्रीचरणप्रणीतम् । (संगीतसुधा)

which means "after consulting *Sangīta-Sāra* written by the *Holy Vidyāraṇya*". As for *Sangīta-Sudhā*, it is considered to be a work written by *Govinda Dīkṣita*, the minister of Raghunātha Nāyaka, but published in the name of the King,—from the fact that there is a passage in *Chatur-Daṇḍi-Prakāśikā*, a work on music written by *Vēnkaṭamakhin*, the son of *Govinda Dīkṣita*. The text of the passage runs thus :—

तल्लक्षणं तु संगीतसुधानिधिसमीरिते । अस्मत्तातकृते ग्रन्थे रघुनाथ नृपाङ्किते ॥ (चतुर्दण्डीप्रकाशिका)

which means :—"It has been explained in that work written by my father which bears the title *Sangīta-Sudhā* and whose authorship goes under the name of King Raghunātha." The *Sudhā* extends over seven *adhyāyas* on the model of Śārṅga-Dēva's *Sangīta-Ratnākara*. The second *adhyāya* and the third, the

Rāgādhyāya and the Prakīrṇakādhyāya refer to several statements as being found in *Sangīta-Sāra* of *Śrī Vidyāraṇya.* Let us note what the great author has to say on 'Rāgas' and other matters.

In the world of music there is of late, frequent talk regarding the principles to be followed in the elaboration of a Rāga or Ālāpa (Alapana or Alapti). Of course, there are technicalities such as Eḍúpu, Muktāyi, Karaṇa, Makariṇi and other terms, used by the musicians with reference to Rāga-singing. *Sangīta-Sudhā* has first fully written about Matanga's Rāga-classification and then depicts in detail the method of Ālāpa, and defines these very things and states that these have been *directly taken from Sangīta-Sāra* of *Śrī Vidyāraṇya* in the *Rāgādhyāya.*

Two Mss. of the *Sudhā,* the one in the Tanjore Palace Library and the other, in the Adayar Library, were examined; and they are found to contain only the first four chapters, the remaining chapters being yet to be discovered. The *Sudhā* was prepared by me for publication, in parts, in the Madras Music Academy Journal. A part, *viz.*, chapter I and part of chapter II, has appeared in print. Owing to the stoppage of the journal on account of financial difficulties, the publication of the remaining portion has been postponed. But the remaining portion is ready for the press, and could be published by any enterprising publisher who might offer to do so at his own cost.

Without any digression, let me quote in detail the passage in the *Sudhā* about the views of *Sangīta-Sāra* on *Rāga-Ālāpa* :

EXTRACT I.

॥ श्रीविद्यारण्यमतम् ॥

कर्णाटसिंहासनभाग्यविद्यारण्याभिधश्रीचरणाग्रणीभ्यः ।
आरभ्य रागान्प्रचुरप्रयोगान्पञ्चाशतं चाकलये षडङ्गान् ॥ ४१३ ॥
रागास्तु पञ्चाशदिहोपदिष्टा नट्टादयः सर्वजगत्प्रसिद्धाः ।

॥ मेलाः ॥

तेषां मताः पञ्चदशैव मेलाः क्रमात्तदुद्देशमिहामनामः ॥ ४१४ ॥
मेलेषु तेषु प्रथमोऽथ नट्टामेलस्ततो गुर्जरिकाख्यमेलः ।
मेलस्तृतीयस्तु वराटिकायाः श्रीरागमेलस्तु भवेच्चतुर्थः ॥ ४१५ ॥
स्यात्पञ्चमो भैरविकाख्यमेलोऽन्यः शङ्कराद्याभरणस्य मेलः ।
स्यात्सप्तमस्त्वाहरिकाख्यमेलो वसन्तभैरव्यभिधस्य मेलः ॥ ४१६॥

स्यादष्टमो गायकबोधहेतुः सामन्तमेलो नवमो निरुक्तः ।
काम्बोदिकाया दशमस्तु मेलस्त्वेकादशश्चापि मुखारिकायाः ॥ ४१७ ॥
मेलो भवेद् द्वादश एव शुद्धरामक्रियायास्तदनन्तरं स्यात् ।
केदारगौडस्य च मेल एको हीजुज्जिकायास्त्वपरोऽत्र मेलः ॥ ४१८ ॥
देशाक्षिकामेल इहान्तिमः स्यान्मेलाः क्रमात्पञ्चदशोपदिष्टाः ।
रागांस्तु मेलप्रभवांश्च तत्तद्रागप्रसङ्गेऽपि निरूपयामः ॥ ४१९ ॥

* * * *

॥ नट्टारागः ॥

द्वे धैवतीमार्षभिकां च हित्वा याः पञ्च शुद्धा इह जातयः स्युः ।
ता ग्रामरागे प्रकृतित्वमाप्ता हिन्दोलनाम्नोत्यवधारणीयम् ॥ ॥ ४५३ ॥
हिन्दोलरागात्प्रबभूव भाषा पिञ्जर्यभिख्यानवती किलेयम् ।
नट्टा तु तज्जान्यतयोपदिष्टा वक्ष्यामि तस्याः किल मेलमादौ॥४५४॥
षड्जस्तथा मध्यमपञ्चमौ च शुद्धाः स्वराः षट्छ्रुतिभिः समेतः ।
सधैवतः स्यादृषभोऽन्तरश्च गान्धारकः काकलिको निषादः ॥४५५॥
एतैः स्वरैः सप्तभिरत्र नट्टामेलो युतो गायकसंप्रदायात् ।
एवं निरुक्ते खलु साधु नट्टामेले ततोऽस्याः किल लक्ष्म वक्ष्ये ॥४५६॥
न्यासो ग्रहोंऽशः पुनरत्र षड्जः स एव वादी किल पञ्चमोऽसौ ।
संवादिभावं भजते विवादी गान्धारकश्चापि निषादकश्च ॥ ४५७ ॥
सधैवतः स्यादृषभोऽनुवादी नट्टागतं लक्षणमित्थमुक्तम् ।

॥ रागसामान्यलक्षणम् ॥

अनुक्तमन्यद्यदिहास्ति किंचिदानीय तत्तत्प्रकृतिभ्य एव ॥ ४५८ ॥
तस्य प्रयोगं प्रतिपादयामो यथाक्रमं गायकबोधहेतोः ।
आक्षिप्तिकादीनि निरूपयामो रागाङ्गभूतानि निरुक्तिपूर्वम् ॥ ४५९ ॥

॥ आक्षिप्तिको ॥

आक्षिप्यते स्म प्रथमं हि रागैराक्षिप्तिका नाम तदस्य युक्तम् ।
सैवोदितायित्तपदेन लोकैराक्षिप्तिकेयं तदिहादिमाङ्गम् ॥ ४६० ॥*

॥ रागवर्धनी ॥

आक्षिप्रिकायां स्फुरतां गतस्य रागस्य वृद्धिः क्रियतेऽनयेति ।
सा रागवर्धन्युदिता द्वितीयमङ्गं च लोका यडुपाख्यमाहुः ॥
तद्रागवर्धन्यधुनाभिधानमङ्गं तु केचित्करणं वदन्ति ।

*(Continued in Mss). This much appeared in the Journal of the Academy.

॥ विदारी ॥

या रागवर्धन्यभिधाङ्गयुग्मविभाजकोपाश्रिरसौ विदारी ॥
यड्डुपुमुक्तायिगिरा विदार्यो भाषानुरोधेन भणन्ति लोकाः ।

॥ स्थायी ॥

आदौगृहीतस्वर एव तान गणस्थितिः स्थायिपदाभिधानम् ॥
तच्छास्त्रलोकव्यवहाररीत्या लभेत रागस्य चतुर्थमङ्गम् ।

॥ वर्तनी ॥

नानास्वराणामिहतानवर्गो यद्वर्तते तेन तु वर्तनीयम् ॥
एषैव लोके मकरिण्यभिख्यामाप्नोति लक्ष्यप्रवणप्रयोगे ।

॥ न्यासः ॥

यन्न्यस्यते राग इहैव रागन्यासाह्वयं तेन तु षष्ठमङ्गम् ॥
अस्यापि लक्ष्यज्ञजनाः प्रयोगे मुक्तायि संज्ञां मुहुराद्रियन्ते ।
गोशब्दपर्याय तथैव गावी गोणीति गोपातलिकेति भिन्नाः ॥
तथैव नानाविधदेशभेदा भवन्ति शब्दा व्यवहारकाले ।
आयित्तिकाद्या अपि तद्वदेवाक्षिप्तादि पर्यायतया भवेयुः ॥
शास्त्रस्थितानामपिलौकिकानामतो न दोषो व्यवहारकाले ।

॥ आक्षिप्तिका ॥

आक्षिप्तिकायाः प्रथमं प्रयोगं वक्ष्यामहे गायकबोधहेतोः ॥
आरभ्य तारस्थितषड्जमादौ मध्यर्षभाख्यावधि चावरुह्य ।
आरभ्य तस्मादपितारषड्जपर्यन्तमप्यत्र यथाक्रमेण ॥
गौला च तानान्कति चिद्यथेष्टं न्यस्येत्पुनस्तारगषड्ज एव ।

॥ रागवर्धनी ॥

तां रागवर्धन्यभिधां प्रवक्ष्ये त्वारभ्य मध्यस्थितपञ्चमं तु ॥
आरुह्य तारस्थितपञ्चमान्तमामध्यषड्जँत्ववरुह्य तानान् ।
गीत्वाच कांश्चित्पुनरत्र मध्य षड्जस्तथान्यास इहोपदिष्टः ॥

॥ विदारी ॥

तस्या विदारीमथ लक्षयामो लक्ष्यप्रबोधाय यथा क्रमेण ।
आरभ्य मध्यस्थितमध्यमान्तं तारर्षभावध्यधिरुह्य पश्चात् ॥
मध्यर्षभावध्यवरुह्य तानान्न्यसेत्तु गीत्वा पुनरत्रषड्जे ।
मुक्तायिसंज्ञास्य तु रागवर्धन्यन्तस्थितैषा हि विदारिकायाम् ॥

॥ रागवर्धनी ॥

तां रागवर्धन्यभिधां द्वितीयां वक्ष्यामहे गायकबोधहेतोः ।
आरभ्य तारस्थितमध्यमान्तमारुह्य चातारनिषादमादौ ॥
आमध्यषड्जादवरुह्य चापि स्वैरं विचित्रान्द्रुतमानयुक्तान् ।
क्रमेण तानान्कतिचिच्च गीत्वा न्यसेत्पुनर्मध्यम एव षड्जे ॥

॥ विदारी ॥

अस्या विदारीमधुनाविदध्याच्च मध्यस्थितमध्यमात्तु ।
आरुह्य चातारगतर्षभं च मध्यर्षभान्तं च ततोऽवरोहेत् ॥
गीत्वा विचित्रान्पुनरुक्ततानान्न्सेत्पुनस्तारगषड्ज एव ।

॥ षड्जस्थायी ॥

षड्जान्तिमस्थायिनमत्र वक्ष्याम्यारभ्यतारस्थितषड्जमादौ ॥
क्रमेणचातारनिषादकान्तं षड्जर्षभौ मध्यमपञ्चमौ च ।
निषादकश्चेति च पञ्चमेस्युः प्रत्येकमेकं हि च तानमेषाम् ॥
स्वपूर्वपूर्वस्वरयोजनात्स्वोत्तरोत्तरेणापि विवर्जनेन ।
आरोहणेनाप्यवरोहणेन तानान्विचित्रान्दश साधु गीत्वा ॥
न्यसेत्पुनस्तारगषड्ज एव षड्जादिमस्थाय्युदितः किलैवम् ।

॥ पञ्चमस्थायी ॥

तं पञ्चमस्थायिनमामनामस्त्वारभ्य मध्यस्थितपञ्चमं तम् ॥
यथाक्रमं तारगपञ्चमान्तं स पञ्चमः किंचनिषादषड्जौ ।
तथर्षभौमध्यमपञ्चमौ चेदेषां स्वराणां क्रमशस्तु षण्णाम् ॥
प्रत्येकमेकैककतानमेषां, स्वपूर्वपूर्वस्वरयोजनेन ।
तथोत्तरेषामपिवर्जनेन त्वारोहणेनाप्यवरोहणेन ॥
गीत्वाक्रमाद् द्वादश तानभेदान्न्यसेत्पुनर्मध्यमपञ्चमेऽस्मिन् ।

॥ मध्यस्थायी ॥

स्थाय्युच्यते मध्यममध्यमस्य त्वारभ्य मध्यस्थितमध्यमं तम् ॥
समध्यमः पञ्चमकोनिषादः षडर्षभौ मध्यम इत्यमीषाम् ।
प्रत्येकमेकैककतानमेषां स्वपूर्वपूर्वस्वरयोजनेन ॥
तथोत्तरेषामपि वर्जनेन त्वारोहणेनाप्यवरोहणेन ।
गीत्वाक्रमादद्वादश तानभेदान्न्यसेत्पुनर्मध्यममध्यमेऽस्मिन् ॥

॥ रिषभस्थायी ॥

मध्यर्षभस्थायिनमत्र वक्ष्याम्यारभ्य मध्यर्षभमेव चादौ ।
आचर्षभात्तारगतात्क्रमेण स चर्षभो मध्यमपञ्चमौ च ॥
निषादषड्जावृषभः षडेते प्रत्येकमेकैककतानमेषाम् ।
स्वपूर्वपूर्व स्वरवर्जनात्स्वोत्तरोत्तरेणापि च वर्जनेन ॥
आरोहणेनाप्यवरोहणेन तानान्क्रमाद् द्वादशसाधु गीत्वा ।
न्यसेत्पुनर्मध्यगतर्षभेऽस्मिन्मध्यर्षभस्थायिनमेनमाहुः ॥

॥ षड्जस्थायी ॥

स्थाय्युच्यते मध्यमषड्जकस्य चारभ्यमध्यस्थितषड्जमादौ॥
तारस्थषड्जावधि च क्रमेण षड्जर्षभौ मध्यमपञ्चमौ च ॥
निषादषड्जाविति षट् स्वराणां प्रत्येकमेकैककतानमेषाम् ।
स्वपूर्वपूर्व स्वरयोजनात्स्वोत्तरोत्तरेणापि च वर्जनेन ॥
आरोहणेनाप्यवरोहणेन तानान्क्रमाद् द्वादश साधु गीत्वा ।
न्यसेत्पुनर्मध्यगषड्ज एव षड्जादिमस्थायिनमेतमाहुः ॥

॥ वर्तनो ॥

पश्चाप्यमून्स्थायिन एव गीत्वा गायेत्ततो वर्त्तनिकां क्रमेण ।
आरभ्य मध्यस्थितषड्जमादावारुह्य चातारनिषादमत्र ॥
आरभ्य षड्जं त्ववरुह्य तस्मात्तानांश्च कांश्चित्क्रमशोऽथ गीत्वा ।
न्यसेत्पुनर्मध्यगषड्ज एवं वर्तन्युदीता मकरिण्यभिख्या ॥

॥ न्यासः ॥

रागादिमन्यासमथाभिधास्ये त्वारभ्य तारर्षभमेव पूर्वम् ॥
मध्यर्षभान्तं त्ववरुहय भूयस्त्वारुह्य चातारगषड्जमेव ।
तानांश्च कांश्चित्क्रमशोऽथ गीत्वा न्यसेत्पुनस्तारगषड्ज एव ।
न्यासस्तु रागस्य निरूपितोऽयं सायाह्नगानेऽस्य च शक्तिलाभः ॥
श्रेयोविशेषश्च भवेज्जनानामिति स्फुटं संकथितात्र नष्ठा ।

(२) ॥ अथ गुर्जरी रागः ॥

संपूर्णरागःखलु गुर्जरो तन्मेलं तु रागप्रकृतिं वदन्ति ॥
गौडस्यमेले परिकल्प्यमाने संपूर्णरागा न भवन्ति तस्मात् ।
त्यक्त्वा ततः संप्रति गौडमेलं ग्राह्यो भवेद्गुर्जरिकाख्यमेलः ॥
नैतत्सहन्ते कतिचिन्नवोनाः संपूर्णभावः कथमस्यवेति ।

आरोहणे पञ्चमवर्जनेन सा गुर्जरी षाडव एव रागः ॥
अथोऽस्य मेलो न च कल्पनीयः क्लृप्ते पुनर्मालव गौडमेले ।
नैतद्विचारक्षममेभिरुक्तं पूर्णो यतो गुर्जरिकाप्यरागः ॥
यत्पञ्चमश्चाप्यवरोहमार्गेत्वथाप्ययं स्वीकृत एव पक्षः ।
भवेदनेनैव निदर्शनेन त्वारोहणे पञ्चम एव तस्मिन् ॥
कल्प्यस्त्वया मालवगौडमेलः प्रसिद्धभावादिह गायनानाम् ।
सा गुर्जरी सर्वजनप्रसिद्धा संपूर्णभावेन समन्वितेति ॥
पञ्चोत्तराण्णां प्रकृतिर्दशानां रागान्तराणामत एष मेलः ।
तं गुर्जरीमेलमथाभिधास्ये षड्जर्षभौ मध्ययपञ्चमौ च ॥
सधैवतश्चेति भवन्ति शुद्धा गान्धारकश्चान्तरनामधेयः ।
तथा भवेत्काकलिको निषादः स्याद्गुर्जरीमेल उदीरितोऽयम् ॥
न्यासो ग्रहोंऽशस्त्वृषभस्तु वेद्यः संपूर्णरागः कथितः प्रवीणैः ।
आरोहणे तस्य च केचिदङ्गीकुर्वन्ति वर्ज्यं किल पञ्चमं च ॥

॥ आक्षिप्तिका ॥

आक्षिप्तिकास्या अपि लक्ष्यतेऽत्र प्रारभ्यतारर्षभमेव पूर्वम् ।
मध्यर्षभान्तं च ततोऽवरुह्यारुह्यापि चातारगतान्निषदात् ॥
गीत्वा च तानान्कतिचिद्विचित्रान्न्यस्येत तारस्थितषड्ज एव ।

॥ रागवर्धनी ॥

तद्रागवर्धन्यथ तारवर्ती गान्धारगस्तारगधैवतान्तम् ॥
आरुह्य चामध्यगषड्जमत्रावरुह्य तानानभिधाय कांश्चित् ।
न्यस्येत तारस्थितिभाजि षड्जे विदारिकास्या अधिवर्ण्यतेऽथ ॥

॥ विदारी ॥

आरभ्य मध्यस्थितधैवतं प्राङ्मध्यर्षभान्तं त्ववरुह्य पश्चात् ।
आरुह्य तत्तारगतर्षभान्तं गीत्वा च तानान्कतिचिद्विचित्रान् ॥
न्यस्येत तारस्थितिभाजि षड्जे तद्रागवर्धन्यभिधीयतेऽस्य ।

॥ रागवर्धनो ॥

आरभ्यतारर्षभमा च तारनिषादतः स्यादधिरोहणं च ॥
आमध्यषड्जं त्ववरुह्य तानान्गीत्वा त्यजेन्मध्यगषड्ज एव ।

|| विदारी ||

अस्या विदारी त्वथ तारषड्जमारभ्य तस्मादवरुह्य पश्चात् ।
मध्यर्षभान्तं त्ववरुह्य पश्चात्तारर्षभान्तं त्वधिरुह्यकांश्चित् ।
तानान्विचित्रान्क्रमशोऽथ गीत्वा न्यस्येत तारस्थित षड्ज एव ॥

|| षड्जस्थायी ।

अथोच्यते संप्रति तारषड्जस्थायी समारभ्य तु तारषड्जम् ।
यत्र स्वरास्तारनिषादकान्तास्ते (तु) स्वरा मध्यमवर्जनेन ॥
प्रत्येकमेकैककतानमेषां स्वपूर्वपूर्वस्वरयोजनेन ।
अथोत्तरेषामपिवर्जनेन चारोहणेनाप्यवरोहणेन ॥
तानांस्त्वथो द्वादश साधु गीत्वा न्यसेत्तु तारस्थितषड्ज एव।

|| पञ्चमस्थायी ||

स्थाय्युच्यते मध्यगपञ्चमस्य त्वारभ्यमध्यस्थित पञ्चमं तम् ।
यत्र स्वरास्तारगपञ्चमान्ताः सप्तैव ते मध्यमवर्जनेन ।
प्रत्येक मेकैककतानमेषां पूर्वोक्तरीत्या च चतुर्दशैव ॥
गीत्वा च तानान्क्रमशो विचित्रान्न्यस्येत मध्यस्थित पञ्चमेऽस्मिन् ।

|| रिषभस्थायी ||

अथोच्यते मध्यगतर्षभस्य स्थायी तु मध्यर्षभमेव चादौ ॥
तारर्षभान्तं खलु सप्त ये स्युः स्वरा मता मध्यमवर्जनेन ।
प्रत्येकमेकैककतान मेषां पूर्वोक्तरीत्या तु चतुर्दशैव ॥
गीत्वा च तानान्क्रमशो विचित्रान्न्यस्येत्पुनर्मध्यगतर्षभेऽस्मिन् ।

|| षड्जस्थायी ||

संलक्ष्यते संप्रति मध्यषड्जस्थायी समारभ्यतु मध्यषड्जम् ॥
आतारषड्जं पुनरत्र सप्त स्वरास्तथा मध्यमवर्जनेन ।
प्रत्येकमेकैककतानमेषां पूर्वोक्तरीत्या तु चतुर्दशैव ॥
गीत्वा च तानान्क्रमशो विचित्रान्न्यस्येत मध्यस्थित षड्ज एव ।

|| वर्तनी ||

अथोच्यते वर्तनिका च मध्यषड्जं समारभ्य यथाक्रमेण ॥
आरुह्य चातारनिषादमस्मादामध्यषड्जं त्ववरुह्य कांश्चित् ।
तानान्विचित्रान्कतिचिच्च गीत्वा न्यस्येत मध्यस्तितषड्ज एव ॥

|| न्यासः ||

न्यासस्तु रागस्य भवेत्पुरोक्तविदारिकावत्पुनरुक्तिवर्जम् ।
प्रगे प्रगेया खलु गुर्जरीयमुक्ताञ्जनेयस्य मतानुरोघात् ॥

(संगीतसुधा-रागाध्याये)

The pretty long extract quoted above is expressing in its own clear style *Śrī Vidyāraṇya's* broad principles enunciated in *Sangīta-Sāra* as underlying Rāga-Ālāpana. The six particular *Rāga-Ālāpa-Angas* have been noted and clearly defined, *viz.*, (1) Ākshiptika (or Ayittam), (2) Rāga-Vardhini, (3) Vidāri, (4) Sthāyi, (5) Varttani (or Makarini) and (6) Nyāsā. Items 2, 3, and 4 comprise that part of Ālāpa commonly known as *Eḍupu* ; and item 5 is known as Tānam (or Madhyakāla) ; and the last portion is termed *Muktāyi* in the ordinary parlance. The description of the Rāgas, Natta and Gurjari, has been produced and that of the other 48 Rāgas are omitted for want of space in this special article appearing in a Commemoration Volume.

Śrī Vidyāraṇya's talent in the science of music is best exhibited here. It is to be noted that he mentions *15 mēḷas* in connection with these *rāgas*, and he mentions *Janya rāgas* in relation with them—*a point that has to be noted in the development of the classification of the rāgas in South India.*

EXTRACT II.

The *Prakīrṇakādhyāya* refers to the critical aspect of *Śrī Vidyāraṇya* with reference to the music performance. The requisite qualifications in a musician, both as regards the theory and practice are mentioned in his name in the following extract :—

दोषांश्च तेषां प्रवदामि विद्यारण्याभिध श्रीचरणोपदिष्टान् ।
ग्राम्योक्तिरेकोऽप्यपशब्द एकोऽप्यप्रस्तुत प्रस्तवनं तथा च ॥
पदे च जाडयं गमके तथैव प्रबन्धविज्ञानविहीनता च ।
तत्तद्रसानामनुकूलरागविवेकहीनत्वमचातुरीच ॥
गतिक्रियानिर्वहणाद्यभावो न्यूनाधिकाज्ञत्वमपि क्रियादौ ।
मन्द्रैकभावोऽपि तथास्वरेषु गृहीतगीतस्य तथा विभङ्गः ॥
संकेतितस्थायिपरिच्युतिश्च गानादिकालस्य विवर्जनं च ।
दोषैरशेषैः कथितैः समेतो वाग्गेयकारः स तु गर्हणीयः ॥
वाग्गेयकारस्य निरूप्य दोषान्लक्ष्मोच्यते केवलगायकस्य ।

मनोज्ञशारीरयुतोऽतिहृद्यशब्दश्च गीतग्रहमोक्षदक्षः ॥
रागाङ्गभाषाङ्गघनक्रियाङ्गोपाङ्गादिरागेषु विचक्षणश्च ।
एलाप्रबन्धादिषु तानभेदे नानाविधालप्तिषु तत्ववेदी ॥
मन्द्रादिमस्थानसमुद्भवेषु विना प्रयासं गमकेषु दक्षः ।
स्वाधीनकण्ठोऽपि च सूडमुख्य तालप्रभेदाकलनप्रवीणः ॥
स्वरश्रुतीनां परिमाणवेदी बहुप्रबन्धेषु जितश्रमश्च ।
प्रबन्धभेदेषु पटुश्च शुद्धच्छायालगाख्येषु च काकुभेदे ॥
स्थायीषु नानाविधतां गतेषु सञ्चारदक्षः प्रथितश्च गीत्या ॥
क्रियापराख्यस्य विशेषणस्य निरूपितं श्रीचरणं स्वरूपम् ॥

(संगीतसुधा-प्रकीर्णकाध्याये)

There are some other passages in *Sangīta-Sudhā* referring to *Sangīta-Sāra*. The absence of the original work is, of course, a great handicap for the verification of these facts. It is hoped that the scholars engaged in ransacking Sanskrit libraries will, ere long, unearth this precious work, publish it and lay the music world under a deep debt of gratitude.

Om Namo Narayanaya.

29

Lines of Future Research in Vijayanagara History

By

Rājacharitavishārada RAOSAHIB C. HAYAVADANARAO, B.A., B.L., F.R.ECON. S., M.L.C.,

Fellow of the Mysore University.

THE origin of the first dynasty is still enveloped in mystery. The earliest inscriptions relating to it are to be found in the North and West of Mysore State. More search is required here. A great deal has been written of the connection of certain of the Sringēri *Gurus* with the origin of this dynasty. There is still scope for research on this head, especially for one who can handle the works of these *Gurus*. Next we should like to know more about the fight for the throne which occurred after the death of Harihara II, between Bukka II, Virūpāksha II and Dēva Rāya I. We may find more inscriptions of Virūpāksha II in the *Araga* area of Shimoga District. We should like to know more of the identity of the person who tried to assassinate Dēvarāya II. Was he his brother Śrīgirī ? If so, the search for more inscriptional records of Srīgiri in the Maratakanagara (N. Arcot) area is necessary. Mallikārjuna's year of death is yet to be found out. Of the double revolution that occurred during his reign we want more information. Search for it in the present districts of Mysore, Kolar, Tumkur, Anantapur and Chickmagalur is necessary.

Of Krishna-Dēvarāya's time we have several hundreds of inscriptions and many literary works. Apart from the former, attention deserves to be concentrated on the latter. Among these, there are those written by himself or ascribed to him. Of these *Āmuktamālyada* in Telugu stands easily first. There is much work here for a good student. Among his Sanskrit works *Jāmbavati Kalyāṇa,* a drama, deserves attention. We learn from its prologue that it was actually enacted before those assembled to witness the *Chaitra* festival of god Virūpāksha during Krishna-Dēvarāya's own life-time. Of Peddana's great work the *Manucharitra,* already a great deal has been written. But it will still bear further examination, especially from the point of view of the social life of the people, of the Court life of the day and finally of the domestic life of his great Sovereign. More grants should have been made to him beyond the four known now, and a further search should be made for inscriptional records relating to grants made to or by him. Then, again, we know Peddana was at Bezawada evidently with the king—and made the gifts mentioned in the Kokatam grant of 1518 A.D. We know Krishna-Rāya's third expedition to the East Coast in 1516-17 A.D., when he visited Ahobalam in the Karnool District and encamped at Bezawada and remitted taxes amounting to 10,000 *Varāhas* in favour of Siva and Vishnu temples in the Chōḷa country. Did Peddana accompany him in the whole campaign, as tradition says he did, as a constant companion of the king ? As the Kokatam grant bears the date of 1518 A.D., it is possible he returned with the king of Vijayanagara at the end of the campaign and then went on his own personal business. Peddana's only other known work is *Harikathāsāramu,* stray verses from which are known. For a great poet, his output—if these are his only works—is very little. But what he lacks in quantity, he has amply made up in quality. A closer search for his *Harikathāsāramu* seems necessary to-day, as it might help to envisage the Vaishnavite fervour of Krishna-Rāya's day so well known to us already. Of Peddana's Guru Satakōpa-Yati, we know as yet very little. If more grants of Peddana can be found, probably a little more may be known of his *Guru.* One inscription dated in 1560 A.D. which mentions the *Matha* of Parānkusa Sri Satakōpa jiyangam, yields for him the titles of *Sarvatantrasvatantra* and *Ubhayavēdāntāchārya.* I have elsewhere ventured to identify the Satakōpa jiyangam of this record with the Satakōpa-Yati of the *Manucharitra.* If this identification is correct, then he should have been a great and important religious teacher of the time, seeing that Governors of Provinces and a great poet like Peddana were among his disciples. Of the works of the other poets of Krishna-Rāya's reign, much remains yet to be done. What is required is that a number of trained students should be induced to set to work on them and explore them from different points of view. Among these are Nandi Timmaiya, Sāluva Timma, Nādindla Gōpa, etc. The Kannada poet, Timmanna Kavi, who dedicated his *Bhārata* to Krishna-Dēva requires equal attention. He is said to have written the work at the instance of the king. Of philosophers, Vyāsa-Yati, the Madhva religious teacher, was a notable personage of Krishna-Rāya's time. His works have been published but students of history have yet to work out from them the state of religion and philosophy as current in Krishna-Rāya's time. Here is material ready to hand for such a work. Several inscriptions show the respect in which Vyāsa-Yati was held by Krishnā-Rāya. It is time that a keener search was made for Krishnā-Rāya's other works, especially in Sanskrit. The works which he has named in his Telugu work *Āmuktamālyada* cannot all have been lost to us. He has named at least five of these and the discovery of these works would add to our knowledge of not only his literary greatness but also to the conditions of the time that gave opportunities to so busy a king as Krishna-Rāya to indulge in literary work on the scale he appears to have done. Young scholars should undertake regular prose translations of the more important of these different works of Krishna-Rāya's reign and after, including his own. Such translations would prove of incalculable help to scholars of the period, Indian and European, who may not be acquainted with the languages used by the poets concerned.

The events connected with the internal dissensions and the triangular fight for the throne at the beginning of Achyuta-Dēvarāya's reign require clearing up to some extent. What is known of it is mainly from sources other than inscriptional. Inscriptional evidence is the one wanting on these events. But so far we have been unable to secure any such evidence. A closer looking into Achyuta's known inscriptions and a more careful scrutiny for more inscriptions of his reign would perhaps yield some valuable results. The 'Hoje' Tirumala episode deserves to be studied with even greater care than has been done so far, if the old mistakes are not to be repeated again and again as has been recently done. The fights for the throne at the beginning of the reign of Achyuta and after his death should be distinguished, if we are to determine the persons involved in each of them. In the one case the supercession was of the infant son of Krishnā-Rāya and in the other of the son of Achyuta. The latter is testified to by literary and inscriptional records; while the former is not reflected in inscriptions though we have references to it in Nuniz and Ferishta. Direct evidence from inscriptions is still lacking as to the date and place of death of king Sadāsiva Rāya, who survived Rāma-Rāja and the battle of Raksas-Tagdi. The manner of his death too is not known from the inscriptions. Perhaps the discovery of further epigraphic records may help to elucidate these still doubtful points. Beyond surmises and inferences, we have as yet no information of a reliable kind other than travellers' tales on any of these points. Penukonda, Chandragiri, and Srīrangam are still possible places for inscriptional finds about him.

The period of Tirumala I is well illustrated by literary works. His period of reign wrongly described, as I have shown elsewhere, as a short one, deserves to be better studied with the aid of these works. Some of the greatest known Telugu works belong to his reign. What more would be required for a picture of the conditions of the times—social, religious, etc.,—after the great battle of Raksas-Tagdi ? Here is work ready to the hands of a well chosen band of scholars. Easily first among these is the *Vasucharitra* of Bhattumūrti *alias* Rāmarājabhūshana. Bhattumūrti's other works and Pingali Surana's works all remain to be dealt with by students of history, especially from the point of view of the post-Raksas-Tagdi period. The continuity of social and religious life is reflected in them in no uncertain manner. For the reign of Srī-Ranga II and his contemporary Ibrahim Kutb Shah, we have Telugu poems well worth closer examination. Ibrahim Kutb was a patron of Telugu poets and writers.

For the Civil War that followed the death of Venkata I, we have a fairly good account made out from different sources. These sources are set out in detail in another place but what is now required is that we should work up the literary sources more carefully. Among these are Venkayya's *Rāmarājīyamu.* Vijayarāghava's *Raghunāthābhyudayam,* Yagnanārāyana's *Sāhitya-ratnākara,* Rāmabhadramba's *Raghunāthābhyudayam,* and Dāmarala Vēngala Bhupala's *Bahulāsva Charitramu.* Some of these fully confirm Father Barradas' account, so well known in this connection. Where Barradas fails us is as to what became of the opposing armies after they met on the plains of Trichinopoly. These authorities furnish us the details of the sequel. There is work here, on these volumes, for a good sized volume devoted to the Civil War.

For the post-civil war period, we have a great paucity of authentic material, as the usual inscriptions fail us. The literary authorities bearing on the period deserve accordingly the fullest attention here. The *Rāmarājīyamu* dedicated to Kōdandarāma (Rāmarāja V) comes in useful here. The period after Srī-Ranga VI—1681 A.D.—is the poorest at present in regard to details. Mysore, Keladi and Madura loom large on the same. Foreign traders settle down in India ; the kingdoms of Bijapur and Golconda disappear about 1688. Shāji and Sivāji came down South and Mysore rises to power and its kings fight Sivaji's successors for the overlordship of the South. With this, we enter on a new phase of history. Literary works and records of the foreign traders assume importance as sources and they remain yet to be exploited to the extent required.

30

Kannada Literature under Vijayanagara

(1336-1565 A.D.)

By

MR. D. L. NARASIMHA CHAR, M.A.,

Kannaḍa Pandit, Maharaja's College, Mysore.

THE early decades of the 14th century A.D. form an eventful period in the history of the Deccan in general and Karṇāṭaka in particular. It was then that an organised effort was made to safeguard Hindu culture from being swamped by an alien one, which was already firmly established in the north of India. The custodians of that culture, the followers of the religion of Mahamud (Peace be on them), belonged to a race of adventurers who poured into India in search of fresh fields. They were more courageous, hardy, and vigorous than the Hindus who confronted them. A better sense of communal solidarity prevailed amongst them. Success crowned their efforts in carving out kingdoms of their own and a considerable part of Northern India passed into their hands. They were now casting their ambitious looks, across the Vindhyas towards the South. The political condition of the Deccan at that period was far from satisfactory. The Yādavas and the Hoysalas, the two principal royal dynasties were antagonistic to each other and the country was insecure. This state of affairs encouraged Allauddin Khilji to send out his general Mallikafur to subdue the Deccan. First the Yādavas of Devagiri succumbed and within a short time the Hoysalas also were conquered. Leaders of thought like Vidyāraṇya foresaw the danger and with the aid of Hukka and Bukka, the two enterprising ex-officers of the Court of Warangal, established a small principality on the banks of the Tungabhadra and provided an ideal standard for the people to muster around. It must have been a period of great enthusiasm and incessant activity. Gradually the small kingdom went on expanding and became the glorious Vijayanagara empire. It succeeded in stemming the rush of foreign aggression, political as well as cultural and held the ground for about two and a half centuries. But for this supreme endeavour on the part of the leaders and the people concerned, Hinduism would have suffered severely. The foundation of Vijayanagara was a timely one, the result of the will and the need of the people. It is significant by its being so opportune.

But 'what has all this to do with literature', it may be asked. It is a truism in literary criticism that the literature of an age is the very criticism, that the literature of an age is the very reflection, sometimes idealised and intensified, of the life and thought of the people from whom it bodies forth. If this is so obvious, then, an intimate study of the literature of the Vijayanagara period must enable any one to see for himself, or at least to get glimpses of the condition of the times. The writings produced within this period are so large in number and so different in quality that it is not possible to envisage them in the space of an article. Though it is necessary to correlate the facts deduced from the study of one literature with those obtained from an investigation into others such as Telugu Tamil and Sanskrit, which have an enormous quantity of works belonging to this period, I have to confine my attention here only to the literature in Kannaḍa of the duration under consideration. Without presuming on my part any thorough acquaintance with all the works, I may attempt in this essay, to give an outline of the literary activity in Karnāṭaka and show how far it touches the life of the times. It is impossible for any body writing about Kannaḍa literature, to refrain from acknowledging his obligations to the three volumes of the Karnāṭaka Kavicharite, a work which has entailed thirty years of hard labour on the part of its author, Mahāmahōpadhyāya, Rao Bahadur R. Narasimhāchārya, M.A., etc.

RETROSPECT

Kannaḍa literature, by the time it came under the influence of Vijayanagara, had already witnessed two strong movements which left a permanent stamp on its tone and character. The first was the Jaina movement which had its origin sometime shortly after Nṛpatunga and culminated by about the end of the 12th century. During this time Jainism gained a favourite place in the life of the people. Literature was used as a medium for religious propaganda. The old *dēsi* style of writing gave place to the *mārgi* style of the Jaina poets, who were very great scholars in Sanskrit and Prakrit. The poets imitated their originals to such an extent that the language was generally Sanskritic with Kannada terminations. Indigenous metres were pushed to the background and Sanskrit metres were adapted to express their ideas. Now and then they looked back and wrote a stanza or two in the homely metres, as a matter of courtesy. Some poets like Pampa tried to blend the two styles and had a very keen eye for the idiom and raciness of the language. The 10th century was a period of intense creative activity and independent thinking. The works produced then do still remain as classics and have enormous power. Pampa and Ranna, the two stars of the century, did not find it difficult to express any subtle ideas through their language, because they had mastered the secret of it. Slowly the outburst of creative activity subsided and the writers succeeding, fell into a groove. Freshness was lost and pedantry drove away simplicity and grace. Some poets, like Nayasena, protested strongly on the undue importance given to Sanskrit words and phrases but they were not heeded. Moreover Jainism also fell into bad days and its influence was on the decline. Conditions were such that a second movement was necessary and like a hurricane, the Vîrasaiva movement swept over the country in the wake of Basava, the great reformer.

The *dēsi* style came into prominence. Basava forged a new style and almost a new language, to express himself. Old Kannaḍa of the *champu kāvyas* had become bookish and artificial by that time. The speech of the common folk had grown while the language of the books stagnated and petrified. Now it was time to discord the worn-out medium and take up the language of the masses. Basava did this with considerable dash and insight. His language is simple, terse and vigorous and fraught with his characteristic fervour and personality. People of all sorts and all grades of society were his followers. In their writings, they took the model of their master and produced a vast literature, mainly religious in nature, in a kind of poetic prose called " Vachana," which forms an unique feature of Kannaḍa. Some of the native metres like the *tripadi, sāngatya, ragaḷe,* and popular songs were revived and became the vehicles of the new religion. New metres like the *shaṭpadis,* destined to play a very great part in the times to come, were discovered, perhaps invented. The old *champu* style of writing fell into disuse, though scholarly poets like Harihara, were anxious to show themselves off in that style also. While the previous Jaina literature emphasised the aspect of Vairāgya and the transitoriness of the present world, the then new Vîrasaiva literature laid stress on the aspect of Bhakti with a personal god. Social equality, well-being, solidarity and self-sufficiency among the Vîrasaivas were the new doctrines of Basava, which attracted and galvanised the masses. The literature of the period reflects this new spirit both in form and in consent.

This went on for some time. But as soon as the master was removed from the scene of action in Kalyāṇ by Time, the Vîrasaiva movement got a severe shock. The loss of the unifying personality gave rise to inner dissensions. The community was split asunder. Kalyāṇ was destroyed by about 1200 A.D. The Vîrasaivas had to scatter in all directions, and spread themselves throughout Karnāṭaka. Their fervour had ebbed away. Degeneration had set in. The ideals of Basava were lost sight of and meaningless rituals dominated. In addition, the political conditions were growing from bad to worse. Alien aggressions caused a panic and by the time the 13th century came to a close, the Vîrasaiva religion was a spent force. There was also slowly evolving the counter movement of the Vaishṇavas, who also emphasised Bhakti.

THE BHAKTI MOVEMENT

The desire for a personal god who could be prayed to and worshipped instead of the Advaitic Brahman was so strongly felt by the masses that two kinds of Bhakti religions came to the forefront. One was Saiva Bhakti of Tamil Saivism and the other was Vaishṇava Bhakti which was preached by Rāmānuja early in the 12th century and by Madhvāchārya in the 13th century. As a result of this the epic heroes like Rāma and Kṛshṇa, who had by this time gained the status of *avatars,* were looked upon by the people as supreme gods, whose will controlled the destiny of the whole creation. The duty that man had to do in accordance with this theistic attitude was to strive to obtain the grace of the supreme deity by prayer and fasting and various modes of worship. So that the temple became the centre of social and religious life and even the Vīrasaivas who did not encourage the building of temples and worshipping of deities in preference to the *Ishṭalingam* did not refrain from erecting their own shrines to the various gods of the Saiva pantheon. Preaching and propaganda of these Bhakti cults went on unceasingly. The Vīrasaivas as well as the Vaishṇavas including the Jainas also, composed songs in the popular metres to be sung in accompaniment with musical instruments. Wandering bards travelled through the whole of Karṇāṭaka singing these devotional hymns and awakening the mind of the masses. It was not difficult with such vigorous propaganda for the Bhakti movement to percolate into every nook and corner of the country. Its philosophy was fatalistic subjecting the action of man to the will of a Supreme Being. Man had to watch with hungry eyes to the shower of Divine Grace. He had to work with this idea in him. But early in the days of Vijayanagara this could not have been the general outlook on life dominating the masses, because no great achievement could have been won with this attitude by human effort. The very fact that a vast empire was built up is a testimony to the heroic activity of the period. After a certain time the Bhakti movement must have degenerated into an effeminate, fatalistic philosophy as is evident from the spirit of the hymns sung by the later *dāsas* or devotees.

The earlier phase of the movement was characterised by intense activity and the later was the one emphasising passivity. It is easy to see the iron grip of the movement in every department of literary activity.

CLASSIFICATION

It is customary among historians of Kannaḍa literature to classify the content of it on the basis of the three principal religions—Jainism, Vīrasaivism and Brahminism. This has got its own advantages but for the purposes of this paper, it is better to attempt at a classification based on subject-matter. The principal sources from which poets gathered their several themes were the Jaina epics and stories, the lives of the sixty-three Saiva saints of Tamil Saivism, the *siva-purāṇas* and the Brahminic epics, *purāṇas* and other legends. Almost all the literature falls under these three main groups.

That no poet belonging to any one of these three communities did ever attempt to write of anything that did not concern his own religion, with the exception of some technical, secular works is noteworthy. Chāmarasa and Suranga, the two chief Vīrasaiva champions of the period under review, have expressed their attitude in very incisive words; Suranga told that he had sold his tongue to sing the glories of Siva only; while Chāmarasa maintained that stories other than those of the *Siva Saraṇas* were all tales of *dead men* writhing with the disease of birth and death and groping their weary way in the darkness of *Karma* and that such narratives were only meant for bad men who could not spend their time worthily. This attitude when viewed at this distance of time is remarkable for two healthy influences; it prevented Vīrasaiva writers to handle Brahminic epics and incidents and thus, while avoiding the dreary duplications of the same tales told and retold, to our endless disgust, conduced towards variety in subject matter; it forced them, since their stories were rather limited in range, to narrate the lives of contemporary saints and the *nutanas* or moderns in addition to those of the *puratanas* or ancients, thus giving the reader fresh material for study.

Besides the works belonging to the three groups noted above we have some literature bearing on the secular sciences, commentaries and semi-historical compositions.

We may proceed to describe them in their proper chronological order.

I. THE LIVES OF THE TĪRTHANKARAS

(*a*) The usual practice of the early Jaina poets in Kannaḍa was to compose a poem on the life of a Tīrthankara whom they particularly liked. Pampa, by writing his *Ādipurāṇa* had placed before them an excellent model. Soon after the establishment of Vijayanagara we find Bāhubali (1352 A.D.) and Madhura (1385), each writing in the traditional *Champu* style, a poem on the life of Dharmanātha the 15th Tīrthankara. Both of them were learned men, skilled in the use of Sanskrit and Kannaḍa, the last representatives of the *Mārgi* style of the Jainas. The story of the Jaina saint, narrated by very earlier poets in Sanskrit and Apabhramsa, was expanded by these authors in a leisurely way, with lengthy and numerous descriptions of the eighteen topics characteristic of a *mahā-kāvya*. Only one leaf of a manuscript of the poem by Bāhubali was available till now, but it is pleasing to note that a complete copy of it has come to light recently. Madhura was patronised by Mudda Dandēsa who was a minister of king Harihara, son of Bukkarāja and was a Court poet. Only four chapters of his work are found till now and they are enough to form an estimate of his talents. His introductory verses, wherein he praises himself and his poetry, are easily the very best of the stanzas in the whole book, as is usually the case with a large number of Kannaḍa poets. Of contemporary life and manners we get very little, as there could be no room for such things in a religious narrative. But occasionally it is a relief to come across some fine stanzas describing natural scenery in picturesque language. It is not possible to indicate the nature of the story as the work is incomplete, but one can rest satisfied that it cannot be totally different from the life-story of other Tīrthankaras. The same writer composed an inscription near the Kṛshṇa temple at Hampe in 1410 A.D. when his patron was Lakshmidhara, minister of Devaraya.

The story of Nemināthа was a favourite theme with many Kannaḍa poets but till the time of Mangarasa (1508) it was not sung in a popular metre. To his credit stand a good number of works. He has an easy flowing style and on many an occasion, he can make good use of it. Doddiah of Periyāpatṇa, near Mysore, wrote a poem on the life of Chandraprabha Jina in about 1550 and Padmakair composed a work on Vardhamāna. There is also a *Santināthacharite* in the *sāngatya* metre written in 1519 A.D. by Sāntikīrti.

But the greatest Jaina poem of the Vijayanagara period was yet to come. In about 1557 A.D. Bharatēsa Vaibhava was written by Ratnākara Varṇi. It is a huge poem containing ten thousand stanzas and the poet was able to complete it in nine months. One wonders at his ease and spontaneity. He narrates the story of Bharata, son of Ādinātha, the first Jaina. After the *nirvāṇa* of his father, Bharata wanted to become the sole monarch of the world and almost achieved his ambition by conquering all the kings of his time except his own brother Bāhubali. Thereupon ensued a fight between the brothers and Bāhubali, out of disgust for the joys of the present world and human vanity, renounced everything and became a *Sanyāsin.* After subduing all the passions, he became a *Kēvalin.* He has been immortalised by Chāvuṇḍarāya in the colossal statue of Ganmata, a poem in granite. Ratnākara represents the same sculpture in words. Both are equally vast and dignified. The poet in this work has tried to blend *Bhōga* and *Yōga* and has successfully shown that *Yōga,* coming after a full life of worldly happiness, is more permanent and significant. The poem contains many peaks of poetic excellence such as the colourful and almost sensuous descriptions of dancing, the delight of music, pictures of domestic life and the happiness that the present world has to offer. The style is easy, graceful and polished and almost enchanting like distant music. The work has lately been printed and has acquired considerable popularity, which it certainly deserves.

In passing the Bhārata of Sāḷva (C. 1550) may be mentioned. It is a Jaina version of the Mahā-Bhārata, whose story has been interwoven with that of Nēmi Jina by Jaina writers, from very early times.

(*b*) *Stories* : Since the days of Nayasēna in 1112 A.D., Jaina writers, in Kannaḍa, indulged in story-telling for the edification of their co-religionists. The stories were merely illustrative in character; any particular doctrine of Jainism such as non-injury or non-stealing, when followed strictly, would certainly be meritorious and lift man to a high level. The inculcation of these morals was the primary object of these stories, but some of them betray also fine literary merit. The *Jīvandhara-charite* is such a story. In the space of about half a century from 1424-1500 we see three poets handling this story. The subject itself is very old being narrated by many Sanskrit and Tamil poets. The *Jīvandhara-charite* of Bhāskara, written in 1424 A.D., is a fine specimen of this type of literature. The story narrates the romantic adventures of Jīvandhara, son of King Satyandhara and Queen Vijaya of Rājapura. The character of Kashṭāngāraka, the villain of the story, has been impressively delineated. The painful circumstances under which the hero was born, the way in which he overcame all the obstacles in

45

his way, the result of his meritorious deeds in a previous birth thrusting him forward in spite of himself and the evil machinations of his enemies, his many adventures and numerous marriages and finally the overthrow of his enemy Kashṭāngāraka—all these are vividly described. But there is nothing like an organised, well-knit plot here, save that all the adventures concern the same hero. Hence the book is episodic in character but all the same interesting. The style also is peculiar and does not betray any pedantry. It has distinct traces of the influence of Kumāra Vyāsa. The *Jīvandhara Sāngatya* of Bommarasa of Tera Kaṇāmbi, assigned to C. 1485 and the *Jīvandhara-shaṭpadi* of Kotisvara (C. 1500) treat of the same story.

Of the remaining tales the *Jnāna-chandrābhyudaya* of Kalyāṇa Kīrti (1439) and the story of Kāma are noteworthy ; those of Sanat-Kumāra by Bommarasa mentioned above, and Nāga Kumāra of Bāhubali (C. 1560) have older models to follow and are not so interesting, viewed as stories, as that of Jīvandhara Mangarasa already referred to, has narrated four different stories, two in *shaṭpadi* and two in *sāngatya*. The story of Vijaya Kumāri by Srutakīrti (C. 1567) marks the close of this type of literature. In all these, the poets had greater freedom to make their own changes, and as such a detailed study may reveal some valuable points of contemporary, social and religious life.

(c) *Commentaries* : Commentatorial literature could be said to have been rather scarce in Kannaḍa as compared with the vast volume of it available in Sanskrit or Tamil. Though there was a great need for such works and glosses on Kannaḍa classics, the few of them that are extant are on Sanskrit or Prākṛt works. This is inexplicable unless we assume, that the study of the classics fell into disuse and was not widely cared for and that no attempt was made to popularise them. Whatever might have been the reason, the fact remains a standing want in Kannaḍa literature. Some of the few commentaries available belong to the early years of Vijayanagara. In 1359 A.D., Kēsava-varni wrote explanatory glosses on the *Gommaṭasāra,* perhaps by Nemichandra in Prākṛt, and on *Srāvakāchāra* of Amitagati. Abhinava-Sruta-Muni (C. 1365) is said to have written a commentary in Kannaḍa on the *Sajjana-chitta-Vallabha,* by the poet Mallishēṇa. In 1455, Vidyānanda wrote a commnetary on his own Sanskrit work *Prāyaschitta.* Mention might be made of Yasah-Kīrti who wrote a gloss of Dharmasarmābhyudaya in C. 1500.

(d) *Miscellaneous* : Under this section come all those works, which having no definite narrative value, merely indulge in expounding some doctrines and moral codes of Jainism and also some prayers addressed to their saints. The *Sataka* literature will be dealt with in a separate section.

Āyata Varma, in his *Ratna-karaṇḍaka* written in about 1400, deals with *triratna* (three jewels) doctrine of Jainism, in the *champu* style. He seems to have based his work on a Sanskrit book of the same name attributed to Samanta Bhadra. Chandra Kirti (1400) composed his *Paramāgamasara* in 132 stanzas, in which he deals with the transitoriness of worldly life and the ideal of a better one to be achieved by all human beings. The two *Anuprēkshas* of Kalyāṇa Kīrti and Vijayaṇṇa deal with the 'twelve recollections of Jainism' while the Jnāna-Bhāskara Charite of Nēmaṇṇa (1559) seems to deal with the concept of knowledge and the way of acquiring it by reading the *sāstras* and meditation. The *stōtra* or prayer containing eight stanzas addressed to Gummaṭa by Madhura is devotional in nature as well as the Jaina-*stuti* of Kalyāṇa Kīrti.

II. VIRASAIVA PURĀṆAS

We have already seen that after the destruction of Kalyāṇ, the Virasaivas who had formerly congregated there, migrated into other parts of Karṇāṭaka. After the establishment of Vijayanagara we find two centres of Virasaiva activity in Southern Karṇāṭaka. One was established at Vidyānagara itself under the patronage of some generals like Jakkaṅārya and Lakkaṇṇa Dandēsa and another near Kuṇigal, on the banks of the Nāgini river, under the spiritual guidance of Tōnṭada Siddhalinga Yati. Both these centres were authoritarian and exerted a powerful influence on the Vīrasaiva community. Both undertook to train men and send them to other places to spread the religion, so that many minor *maṭhas* were established all over Karṇātak. The community was striving to retrieve the losses it had sustained and gain a firm hold on the masses once again. Thus a second movement of the Vīrasaivas came into being. This was not so remarkable or revolutionary as the first one, but all the same, it was a revival. Collection, codification and preservation of older communal literature, went on rapidly; scattered fragments were stringed together; commentaries were written on difficult texts; the *Vachana* experienced a temporary revival; anthologies of *Vachanas* were undertaken—in short the community kept very busy. The impress of this activity is to be seen in the vast body of literature produced between 1336-1565 A.D.

The purāṇic literature of the Vīrasaivas can be classified into five main groups (*a*) stories taken from the Saiva purāṇas, (*b*) stories describing the spiritual achievements of the 63 Saiva saints or called Purātanas, (*c*) stories of the Nūtana-Purātanas or neo-ancients as Basava and his contemporaries were called, (*d*) stories of Nūtanas or modern saints, (*e*) compendiums consisting of all and sundry tales of Virasaivism. We may now proceed to make a few observations on them, taken in the order indicated.

(*i*) (*a*) Episodes and stories from the *Siva purāṇas* were isolated and treated independently, emphasising wherever necessary, the *Saivite* atmosphere already found in them. Of such stories the most popular one is that of Harischandra. Rāghavānka had already vigorously narrated the same story and his work was a model of all later writers. We have Oduva Giriya (C. 1525) and Bombeya Lakka (1538) each telling the story in *Sāngatya,* the most popular song-metre of the day. Both of them follow Rāghavānka very closely, the latter reproducing in many places, the very phrases and ideas of the original. Next in the order of time comes the story of Sānanda Ganesha whose author was Oduva Giriya mentioned above. The story is found in the *Skānda purana* and in Kannaḍa it was formerly told by Kumāra Padmarasa (C. 1180). It extols the greatness of the 'Panchākshari Mantra' and Sānanda, the hero, is seen passing through hell rescuing the wretched sufferers there by the help of the incantation. It describes, in an exaggerated fashion, all the tortures of hell. *Vīrabhadra-Vijaya,* whose author was Virabhadrarāja (C. 1530) presents the story of the disasters consequent on the sacrifice of Daksha. Its poetic ideal is ambitious but the execution is mediocre. In *Bhikshātana Charitre* of Gurulinga Vibhu (C. 1550) there is better poetry. The story is one of the 25 *līlas* (sports) of Siva where he is represented to have been filled with remorse for cutting off one of the superfluous heads of Brahma and as wandering, with the skull in his hands, over the earth till he met Krishna in Dwāraka. It is a tiny but clever piece. Mention may be made of *svētana-sāngatya* by Mallikārjuna (1485), the hero of which appears to be a *purāṇic* character, who by his devotions obtained the grace of Siva. The story had been previously narrated in the *Basava-purāṇa.*

(*b*) Of the lives of the 63 saints the most interesting is the story of Sundara Nambi. It was first told in Kannaḍa by Harihara, with a light and delicate humour. Bommarasa composed it anew in C. 1430 and called it *Soundara purāṇa.* It abounds in many lovely stanzas and the descriptions are not unfrequently luscious. Suranga (C. 1500) whom we had occasion to mention early, and a poet imitating the *champu* style of Harihara, has narrated the stories of all the 63 saints. He seems to have taken them from the *Lingapurāṇa.*

He displays, in his description of hunting, the talents of a good poet, with his eye on his object. But he has not become popular even in scholarly circles, though the book was printed and made available. some years ago. He deserves better study. *Bhāva-chintāratna* and *Chōḷa-rāja Sāngatya*, respectively composed by Mallaṇārya of Gubbi (C. 1513) and Linga (C. 1550) are two poems treating of the same theme. The former gets its inspiration from a Tamil source. The story is mainly intended to show the greatness of 'Panchākshari.' It tells the legend of king Satyēndra chola, who condemned his son to death for the sin of, even unintentionally killing a lad, who was a devotee of Siva. After he was beheaded, it so happened that seven other heads had to be cut off and finally the king got back all the dead persons to life and ascended to Kailasa with them. The poem, though crude and grotesque, is not devoid of literary excellence and later on, it was the source of inspiration for a most popular work called *Rājasēkhara-Vilāsa,* by Shadakshari. Viruparāja (1519) and Cheramānka (1526) each narrated the story of Cherama, one of the 63 saints.

(c) The works on the life of Basava form an important group of this section. Among the Virasaiva authors writing of Basava, during the period under consideration, there seem to be two distinct schools. Both differ in essential matters. The leader of the first is Bhīmakavi (1369), author of the *Basava-purāṇa.* It is almost a literal translation of the Telugu *Basava-purāṇa* by Pālkuṛike Sōma. Besides the life of Basava the poem is full of many stories of the Saiva devotees, ancient as well as contemporary with Basava. Though its poetic quality is not of a high order, it still maintains its place among the Vīra-saivas as a granary of their legendary lore. Of the second school, the leader was probably Lakkaṇṇa Dandēsa (1428) in whose work, among many other things, is also found a version of the life of Basava. He finds his great follower in Singirāja (C. 1500), author of the Mala-Basava-chāritra which, after giving the biography of Basava, goes on to describe some of the 88 miracles that were performed by the hero. A comparative study of these two schools, in addition to others, is worth while to clear some misconceptions about Basava and his doings.

Kereya Padmarasa, Allama Prabhu, and Pālkuṛike Sōma have each a biography written by Padmaṇānka (C. 1385), Chāmarasa (C. 1430) and Virakta Tōnṭadārya (C. 1560) respectively. The first one called *Padmarāja-Purāṇa* describes the events in the life of its hero, who was a minister according to the story, under Narasimha Ballāḷa. He performed a miracle and revealed a tank where there was nothing before and hence the epithet Kereya attached to his name ; he defeated in debate a Vaishṇava controversialist, by name Tribhuvana Tātā and made him a Virasaiva. Padmaṇānka writes in a learned style, though he has employed the *Shaṭpadi* metre. The '*Prabhulinga Lîle*' of chāmarasa is a remarkable book in Virasaiva literature. It tells the story of Allama *alias* Prabhu Deva, an intellectual mystic and the brain of the Virasaiva movement. The character of the hero has been nobly conceived and his spiritual greatness unfolds itself before our eyes. The style too is in keeping with the theme and few works of the Virasaivas come up to this level. Pālkuṛike Sōma was a prolific writer in Telugu, Sanskrit, and Kannaḍa but it was his misfortune not to have found a good biographer in Virakta Tōnṭadārya, author of *Pālkuṛike Sōmēśwara Purāṇa.* The incidents in the life of the hero are described after long intervals of unnecessary and dreary episodes of other people. It is a patch-work of hundreds of stories which have nothing to do with one another—a conglomerate of heterogeneous elements. As a thesaurus of Virasaiva stories it is valuable.

It is hard to decide whether Revana Siddheswara was a *purātana* or *nūtana-purātana.* The more orthodox section of the Virasaivas, otherwise called the Arādhyas, claim a high antiquity for him while the followers of Basava make him an older contemporary of their 'master.' The earliest story that we have of Rēvanasiddha, is by Harihara.* Mallaṇa (1413) and Chaturmukha Bommarasa (C. 1500) continue the same traditional story. The *Ārādhya Charitra* of Nilakantha Sivachārya (C. 1485) describing the exploits of Panditārādhya, one of the five Virasaiva āchāryas deserves a passing mention here for its polemical quality.

Mahādevi Akka is one of the most celebrated names in Virasaiva literature. Her biographers are many from Harihara onwards. Of them the *Mahadevi-Akkana-Purāṇa of* Channa Basavānka (1550) is the most voluminous and is not without poetic merit. It is written in various *dēsi* metres and the pious character of the heroine and all the tribulations of her life have been clearly brought out. The story of Chikkaya, a contemporary of Basava and a writer of *Vachanas* also, has been narrated by the poet Basava (C. 1550)

* There is a work called Rēṇuka Vijaya in Sanskrit by Siddhanātha Sivāchārya composed in 1016 of the Vikrama Era, i.e., 959 A.D. But in the body of the work there is a reference to King Bijjaḷa (1156-1167 A.D.) which shows that the work has been purposefully ante-dated.

in the *Sāngatya* metre. The hero, who was a professional burglar in his attempt to kill Basava, was transformed into a great devotee of Siva. The *Udbhaṭa Dēva charite* of Basavānka (C. 1550) may be referred to here.

(*d*) Few *nūtana-purātanas* have the fortune of being commemorated by a biography. Tōnṭada Siddhalinga Yati mentioned before has two *purāṇas* celebrating his exploits. One entitled *Siddhēsvara purāṇa* was written by Virakta Tōnṭadārya (C. 1560) and the other called *Tōnṭada Siddēśvara purāṇa* was composed by Sāntēsa in 1561. Both these works, after giving some particulars of the hero, dwell at great length on the miracles performed by him and the incidents that happened during his sojourn in many places on a tour he undertook. His spiritual preceptor was Gosāla Channabasava of Haradana haḷḷi on the banks of the Kapila. Recently a copper-plate was discovered, going back to the last years of the Hoysaḷa Ballāḷas, in which a few facts concerning the *guru* have been mentioned but unfortunately the record appears to be a forgery.

(*e*) There are a few works which can be looked upon as compilations of Virasaiva mythology. Chief of them, after Lakkaṇṇa Dandêsa's *Siva Tatva Chintāmaṇi* (1428) is the *Vīrasaivāmṛta purāṇa* of Mallaṇārya of Gubbi (1513). It is a massive work containing more than 7,000 stanzas in the largest *shaṭpadi* metre and has drawn upon many earlier sources for its material of legends and stories. Kumara Channabasava's work (C. 1550) recounts in greater detail the stories already contained in the *Basava purāṇa* while that of Arādhya Nanjunḍa of Kikkêri, (C. 1550) of more modest extent and limited range, narrates a few other stories.

Any competent scholar taking upon himself the duty of studying all the works mentioned hitherto and of compiling a dictionary of Vīrasaiva mythology, will be doing the greatest service to students of Kannaḍa literature.

(*ii*) *Vachanas*: A revival of the Virasaiva movement must not be without its characteristic literature of *Vachanas*. It falls under two distinct classes—original and collected. Of original writers Tônṭada Siddhalinga, (C. 1470) the nucleus of the movement, is easily the best. But his *Vachanas* are cold and didactic and seldom give the glow of literature. When compared with the writings of Basava and his followers, his is a miserable performance. With him may be mentioned Jakkaṇāchārya (C. 1430), Swatantra

Siddhalinga (C. 1480) and Siddhalinga of Gummaḷāpur (C. 1480). Anthologies from the works of previous writers, arranged with a definite plan and purpose and commented upon whenever necessary, are many. The 'Sūnya Sompādane' is the best and most interesting of all. The others are unimportant.

(*iii*) *Commentaries* : A dozen commentaries, major and minor put together, are extant and it is interesting to note that some Kannaḍa works are also commented upon. We will here notice only a few of them which have some significance. The earliest of them are those of Gurudēva (C. 1350) on half-a-dozen Sanskrit *stotras*. Gurunanja's (C. 1500) commentary in Kannaḍa on the *Yajurvēda Bhāshya* of Bhaṭṭa Bhāskara, is said to be very learned. The commentaries of Channavira (C. 1500) on the Sāraswata Vyākaraṇa and others are erudite ; his *Kāsa Kṛtsna Dhātū Vyākhya* which is being printed, is remarkable from a linguistic point of view. Srīdharāñka (C. 1550) and Sānanda Siva Yōgi (C. 1480), both authors of voluminous commentaries, deserve mention. Virakta Tônṭadārya (C. 1560) has written a gloss on the three Satakas in Kannaḍa of Maggeya Māyi-deva.

(*iv*) *Miscellaneous* : There is much that is interesting in the material that comes under this section. We have here two poets professing royal connections in the service of literature. One is Dêpārāja (C. 1410) belonging to the ruling family of Vijayanagara and author of two works called *Sobagina Sône* and *Amaruka*. The first one is a cluster of stories of a romantic character while the second, being a translation of the famous *sataka* (centum) in Sanskrit by the poet Amaru, is the only one of its kind in Kannaḍa literature. The second poet is Rāmêndra (C. 1550), Chief of Kārkaḷa and author of *Soundarya Kathāratna* composed mainly in the *tripadi* metre. He has based his work on Kshêmêndra and narrates the thirty-two doll-stories noted in Indian literature. The individuality of this book consists in making use of the *tripadi* metre for narrative purposes. The poet Chandra (C. 1430) has written a work describing the audience hall of the god Virūpaksha of the temple at Hampe in classical style affording a fine and enjoyable reading. His stanzas have been quoted in an anthology of old Kannaḍa poetry, called *Kāvya Sāra*, by Abhinava Vâdi Vidyānanda (1533) and it is sufficient recognition for the poet. Of a similar purpose are the two works of Prabhuga (C. 1500) called respectively *chūdanāsthāna* and *vaibhōga-rājāsthāna* but praising the glory of god Siva in *Kailasa* and in the same classical language. Of the remaining works we may mention the *Rāmanātha vilāsa* of Sadāsiva Yōgi (1554) and the

Rajēndra Vijaya of Murige Desikêndra (C. 1560) for their *champu* style which was rarely effectively employed during their times.

III. THE BRAHMINIC EPICS

The Vaishṇava movement, which seems to have begun very early and whose impress on literature is to be perceived in the work of Rudra Bhaṭṭa (C. 1180) and in the songs of Narahari Tirtha (1281), gathered great strength under the aegis of Vijayanagara. It was the most flourishing movement of the times and had enormous influence over the masses. Brahmin writers, who till now had not taken in large numbers, seriously to cultivate the vernacular literature in preference to that of Sanskrit, rushed forward to throw open all the knowledge contained in their sacred writings, for the betterment of all people irrespective of caste or creed. Some of them engaged themselves in rendering the great epics of India into the language of the country, while others having renounced all their belongings, wandered from place to place preaching the philosophy of the Upaniṣads in homely language set to musical tunes. What the poets taught through their epics, the bards or *dāsas* preached through their songs. The feverish earnestness of these people appealed to the masses and everywhere in the country, we see evidences of a higher culture and a nobler ideal in the innumerable acts of charity and piety recorded in the inscriptions of this period.

(*i*) (*a*) We may now pass on to a critical appraisement of the adaptations of the three epics—Mahā-Bhārata, Rāmāyaṇa and Bhāgavata. The Mahā-Bhārata, so far as we know, was the first to capture the hearts of the Kannaḍa poets. Pampa, the father of Kannaḍa poetry, gave a dignified and spirited account of it in the 10th century but he was able to appeal to the cultured few only. It was left to Kumāra Vyāsa (C. 1430) to move and inspire and energise the masses through his adaptation, popularly known as 'Gadugina Bhārata.' It is not a translation of the original but a free and independent rendering. The object of the poet or Naraṇappa as he is called, was to glorify Krishna as the Supreme God and sing his praises, for His was the Spirit moving through the Bhārata, making and unmaking the lives of so many heroes. He was an inspired poet and poetry gushed out of him at his bidding through the grace of God Vīranārāyaṇa at Gadag. It is no exaggeration to say that, with the exception of Pampa, he is the greatest poet that Karṇāṭaka has ever seen. His luxuriant imagination and rich experience, clear, vigorous and beautiful style, dash and daring, fervour, earnestness and devotion, picturesque conceptions of character and situations, fresh and unexpected similes and metaphors—all these make his poetry sublime and everlasting. His is a glory never to be forgotten or bedimmed.

(*b*) Kumāra Vyāsa did not care to narrate the story of the last eight books of the Mahā-Bhārata. Timmaṇṇa, under the orders of Krishna Deva Raya, inefficiently rendered the rest into Kannaḍa. There is another rendering of the epic by Sukumāra Bhārati (C. 1550) otherwise called Chāyaṇa, but fortunately for the poet, the complete work is not available, save for two chapters of it contained in a dilapidated manuscript of the Madras Mss. Library.

(*c*) Of the versions of the Rāmāyaṇa that of Kumāra Valmîki (C. 1500) is the most popular, though unsatisfactory. He tried to imitate Kumāra Vyāsa in expression but could not achieve what he did. The Rāmāyaṇa of Battalêswara, a Virasaiva by religion, is a notable exception to the general observation made above. A manuscript of the work has been recently acquired by the Oriental Library, Mysore and a glance at it is enough to show its strong Saivite atmosphere and its many divergences from Vālmîki Rāmāyaṇa.

(*d*) Bhāgavata has been rendered twice into Kannaḍa, in the period under description. Nārāyaṇa Kavi (C. 1450) seems to have paraphrased it in prose, but the work is not found completely. It might have prepared the way for another version to succeed and displace it. In C. 1530 Sadānanda Yogi, known also as Nityātma-Suka, is alleged to have finished a rendering of the work into poetry. But there are scholars who have perceived five different hands at work to complete it. Be this as it may, it can be said that some episodes like that of Kuchêla have found a favourite place in the hearts of the masses, which fact is a testimony to the poetic quality of the work.

(*ii*) *Stories*: Brahmin poets of this period wanted to achieve gigantic things like the sculptors of Vijayanagara and chose extensive canvasses to display their poetic abilities; but Kanaka Dāsa, a household name in Karnāṭak and spiritually more than noble Brahmin, chose pretty stories from the epics and retold them elegantly. His *Naḷa-Charitre* is so popular that every school-boy knows it by heart. Simplicity, grace, delicate humour and rapid narrative make it a lovely work. The *Môhana-tarangiṇi* is a story by the same author, devoted to narrate the life of Krishna and though not so popular, has the characteristic imprint of the writer's personality. His *Rāmā-dhānya charitre* is a very curious story, probably invented by the poet himself, extolling the greatness of *Rāmadhānya* or Rāgi—the staple food-grain of the lower classes.

There seem to be much sarcasm and humour in the work but it is a pity that the only manuscripts available to the author of the Kavicharite, has now disappeared from its resting-place—the Oriental Library, Mysore. Another writer named Rāmarasa Virūpāksha (1538) author of *Harischandra Sāṅgatya* may be noticed.

IV. DEVOTIONAL SONGS

There is a vast body of lyrical literature popularly called *Dāsara padagaḷu.* Much of it has not yet come into print and its extent is not definitely known. Many songs are floating amongst the populace like fallen flowers on a quiet lake. Attempts are now being made to collect and print as much of them as possible. An authority in such matters and himself a Hari-dāsa, has informed the present writer that he has a collection of 25,000 songs. As such any study of this literature is found to be perfunctory. But enough is known to understand its spirit and purpose. Some of them are regular songs or *kîrtanas* with definite musical tunes while others called *suḷādis* are composed in a kind of rhythmic prose not without any musical value. The songs to whatever community they belong, all breathe the spirit of devotion and renunciation. The names of the deities invoked may vary but everything else is quite common to all. It is with this idea that Jaina and Virasaiva songs are also included under this section.

Of the Vaishṇva singers coming within the scope of this survey we find three great masters of their art—Srîpāda Rāya (C. 1500), Purandara Dāsa (C. 1540) and Kanaka Dāsa (C. 1550). Srîpāda Rāya was the pontiff of a Madhva *mutt* in Muḷabāgil and had some influence with the Vijayanagara kings of his time. The number of songs that he composed is not known but they can be easily distinguished from others by his signature 'Ranga Viṭhala' found at the end of his songs. Nothing need be said of Purandara or Kanaka as their songs are being sung and broadcasted through the radio and the gramaphone on every day in Karṇāṭak.

The output of songs among the Virasaivas and Jainas is rather meagre when compared with that of the Vaishṇavas. Guru Basava (C. 1430) and Nijaguṇa Sivayōgi (C. 1500) among the Saivas are known to have composed some, while Ratnākara, (1557) a Jaina, has done that service to his community. But there must be many more of them which have not yet reached the professional scholar.

V. SATAKAS

The *Sataka* literature of this period is rather prolific. There are about fifteen of them written by more than half a dozen poets.

The object of every writer was to inculcate some moral truths according to his own bent of mind. Every one of them has poured out his heart on the helplessness of man and the all-pervading power of God, invoking him to come to his rescue and alleviate his sufferings. The spirit of all the *Satakas* is that of pessimism and prayer. Devotion, knowledge and renunciation are the chief categories expounded in all except in that of Ratnākara (1557) called the *Trilōka Sataka* which describes the cosmogony of the Jainas. Maggeya Māyideva (C. 1430) is the opening writer of this group and has contributed three *Satakas* of considerable moving power, while Chandra (C. 1430), Gummaṭārya (C. 1500), Sirināmadhēya (C. 1550) and Channa Mallikārjuna (C. 1560) has each left a legacy of one *Sataka* which can touch and move the emotions. In this respect the *Aparājitēswara Sataka* of Ratnākara may be said to be the greatest. Vira-Bhadrarāja (C. 1530) has written five *Satakas* of unequal quality.

VI. SECULAR SCIENCES

A detailed study of the scientific literature of the period, though it does not strictly deserve the epithet with its modern connotations, will be interesting and useful. Under this section come all those works which treat of medicine, both human and veterinary, poetics, lexicography, astrology, erotics and cookery.

Of these the most widely cultivated is the science and practice of medicine. We have six works pertaining to this science. The *Vaidyāmṛta* of Srīdharadēva (C. 1500) and *Vaidya Sāngatya* of Sāḷva (C. 1550) give some recipes for human ailments while the *Khagēndramaṇi Darpaṇa* of Mangarāja (C. 1360), written under the patronage of King Harihara, is a masterly treatise on the various kinds of poisons, their effects and antidotes. Abhinava Chandra (C. 1400) and Bācharasa (C. 1500) have each composed a work descriptive of the various kinds of horses, their illnesses and medicaments.

We have only three writers who have taken to the study of the poetics. The most famous of them is Sāḷva (C. 1550), author of *Rasaratnākara* and *Sāradāvilasa,* which respectively expound the *rasa* theory and the concept of *dhvani* in literature, with numerous illustrative stanzas from older works. Though the author has not contributed anything of his own to the investigation of previous writers on the subjects, his works have still their own value. Iswarakavi (C. 1500) of *Kavi-Jihwā-Bandhana* is a curious writer. In the small work of four chapters he makes a few observations on prosody, grammar and the dialects of the Kannaḍa language. It has no particular object in view and the remarks on prosody and grammar have nothing fresh in them, while the statement that there were 1,200 dialectal varieties in Kannaḍa is staggering. The *Mādhavālankāra* of Mādhava (C. 1500) is a literal translation of Dandi's *Kāvyādarsa.*

Of lexicography there is a meagre story to tell. The earliest writer is Abhinava Mangarāja (1398) author of *Mangābhidhāna.* The *chaturāsya Nighanṭu* of Bommarasa (C. 1450), the *Kabbigara kaipiḍi* of Linga mantri (C. 1530) are less bulky and more popular while the *Karnāṭaka-Sabda-manjari* of Virakta Tōnṭadārya (C. 1560) eclipses them. When compared with the vast number of lexicons obtaining, for example, in Tamil literature, this output in Kannaḍa is thoroughly inadequate. Perhaps, Kannaḍa scholarship of a high order, comparable with that of Kesirāja, for example, was at a discount during the centuries concerned.

On astrology and prognostication we have four works. The *Narapengaḷi* of Subhachandra, the *Sakuna-sāra* of Lakshmaṇānka and the *Sakuna-prapañcha* of Chākarāja, all assigned to C. 1500 treat of birds, animals and objects of bad and good omen while the *Raṭṭana-Jātaka* of Gangādhara (C. 1550) deals with astrology and horoscopy. All these reveal some contemporary superstitions on which the actions of even the Kings depended.

Erotics and cookery are represented each by one work. The *Janavaṣya* of Kallarasa (C. 1450), written for the delectation of King Mallikārjuna, deals with erotics and aphrodisiacs. The *Sūpa-Sastra* of Mangaraja III (1508) is enjoyable by some men of good digestion. For a history of eatables, this book is indispensable.

SEMI-HISTORICAL WORKS

Though Kannaḍa literature did not care much for history as a distinct branch of study and for its own sake, there are numerous *bakhairs, kaifiyats* and local records which have not been explored and systematically studied. Some of them may belong to the period herein described. In literature there is a solitary example of this kind. The *Kumāra-Rāmana-Kathe* of Nanjunḍa (C. 1525) is history mixed with fiction and romance. One or two historians have analysed the work and deduced some historical facts. As poetry the work is not wholly negligible. It was an inspiration to another work of the same sort by Panchaḷa Ganga, a description of which is not genuine to this survey.

ACHIEVEMENT

From the above review of the literary activity of about two and a half centuries it is clear that in poetry there are a few summits of excellence. Kumāra-Vyāsa is easily the highest and the fullest expression of Vijayanagara culture and art. Among the Jainas there is none to contest the supremacy of Ratnākara, while among the Virasaivas though Chāmarasa's claim to superiority is powerful, it is not voluntarily conceded by Bommarasa of *Soundarapurāṇa* and Gurulinga Vibhu. The prodigious activity of the Vaishṇava dāsas has earned for them the gratitude of all and they succeeded in establishing a school of music, called the Karnāṭak School, justly praised in many parts of India.

31

Music under the Vijayanagara Empire

BY

Kinnari Vidwan HULUGUR KRISHNACHARYA,
Hubli.

MUSIC as a fine art is subject to evolution owing to economic, social and other causes. To describe the main features of music as it prevailed under the Vijayanagara Empire one must know the history and condition of the art during the preceding period. There is a tradition to the effect that Indian music is derived from the Sāma Veda. "सामवेदादिदं गीतं संजग्राह पितामहः" (*Sangīta Ratnākara*). Before the compilation of Nātya Śastra by Bharata there existed an independent Dravidian culture in the Deccan. Music, sculpture, painting and other fine arts were already highly developed. There is evidence of this in the Rāmāyaṇa of Vālmiki. Since the time of Sugrīva the Dravidian king who ruled the Deccan from his capital Kishkindā, the present Hampi, both the Dravidian and Aryan cultures interacted on each other. The final issue of this interaction was what is since known as Bhāratīya Sanskriti in which the cultures are so subtly blended as to make it almost impossible to separate its two strands. The credit of this cultural fusion is due to the constant past efforts of Karnāṭaka artists in all branches of culture. As regards music Bharata himself has admitted—तत्र दाक्षिणात्या भवेत् बहुगीतनृत्यवाद्या कैशिकीप्राया चतुरमधुरललितांगाभिनया and he has mentioned the region where this system prevailed—

दक्षिणस्यसमुद्रस्य तथा विंध्यस्यचांतरे।
ये देशास्तेषु युञ्जीत दाक्षिणात्यां तु नित्यशः।

As Bharata is supposed to be the first writer on Indian music it is plain that long before Bharata the combination of Dravidian culture was complete and assumed the form of -दाक्षिणात्य (पद्धति) संस्कृति the origin of which even Bharata was unable to trace.

During the period from 100 B.C. to 1450 A.D. Bharata's system was steadily developing until it reached its zenith in the time of Immaḍi Devarāya of Vijayanagara whose patronage to Chatura Kallinātha, the Āsthāna Panḍita encouraged him to write a commentary on the *Sangītā Ratnākara* of Śārngadeva. During this period of fifteen centuries many works on music were written by various authors a list of whose names may be seen on pp. 5 and 6 of *Sangītā Ratnākara* (Ānandāśrama Edition). Besides these independent works, many commentaries were written on Bharata's Nāṭya Śāstra. None of them has been very helpful in understanding the musical theory of Bharata except that of Kallinatha who alone was correctly able to interpret it. His work is exhaustive and incorporates all the views of and several quotations from previous authors down to his own time. It may thus almost be styled an encyclopædia of music in an abridged form. But for the commentary of Kallinatha it would have been immensely difficult to understand the text of *Sangītā Ratnākara* which is a work on Bharatamata embodying all the latter developments of it up to his own time. A couple of passages may here be quoted to give the reader an idea of the nature of the commentary without going deep into the technical aspects of the subject. While commenting on the verse

योक्ताऽस्माभिः कलासंख्या या दक्षिणपथि स्थिता p. 137 सं. र.

Kallinātha says— **अस्माभिर्भरतमतानुसारिभिरस्मदादिभिश्चेति** which means that he was a faithful exponent of Bharata's theory. In another place while commenting on the **लक्षण** of a Tāla mentioned by Śārngadeva on page 434 (**सं. र.**) Kallinātha regards the inclusion of **विराम** as a **तालांग** as a piece of error calculated to mislead ignorant people. It is a mistake which even some musicians of to-day are not free from. It was committed by Venkaṭamakhi (two centuries later than Kallinatha) in his Chaturdaṇḍi prakāśa (Vide his description of the **अंग**'s of Jhampa tāla). We feel Kallinatha to be quite right as this feature of **विराम** is not **रक्तिदायक** and besides is an exception to the general principle on which Tālās are constituted. On this topic Kallinatha says—

अत्र केचिदिदानीतना भरतं मन्या विरामस्यापि तालावयवत्वमंङ्गीकृत्य प्रस्तारादिषु तालप्रत्ययेषु तस्यापि समावेशंकृत्वा स्ववैदुष्यं प्रकाशयंतोऽज्ञान्प्रतारयंति। तैःस्वकीयमेव शास्त्रापरिज्ञानं प्रकाशितमिति प्रकाशयताऽभिनवभरताचार्येण सर्वज्ञेन चतुरेण कल्लिनाथविदुषां विरामस्य तालावयवत्वाभावे चतुरो हेतूनुपन्यस्य संग्रहश्लोकः कृतः।

and then he gives three verses composed by him arguing on the topic in a most logical manner. In this way several passages could be quoted to show how he has succeeded in maintaining the correct tradition of Bharata-mata against all unintelligent departures from it.

An important development of the 14th century is the rise of the Ugābhoga style of music. This had its roots in the theory of Sangīta Ratnākara of Sārngadeva (1210 A.D.). It was taken to North India by the great talented Karnāṭaka Vāggeyakāra Gopāla Nāyaka patronised by Sultan Ala-ud-din Khilji of Delhi. Although the style began to be cultivated as early as the beginning of the 14th century it underwent gradual evolution during the following centuries down to the 18th successively assuming the forms, the Dhruva style and the Khyāl style. The compositions in this style in Hindustani music which are available to us to-day almost all belong to the 18th century and some even to the 19th. But in Karnāṭaka the style had a distinguished career in the time of the Vijayanagara Empire and later. The commentary of Kallinātha discloses that the style was prominent in his time, all existing compositions being adapted to it. At about the same time hundreds of new compositions were composed in Kannaḍa known as Ugābhogas, a corrupt form of the word Udgrāha-Ābhoga explained in संगीतरत्नाकर. All Ugābhogas available to us to-day belong to Kallinātha's period. The Karnāṭaka style of music owes its name to the immense popularity of Ugābhogas at the time.

Kallinātha was the originator of the new mode of classifying Rāgas called the Mēlapaddhati now in vogue in the whole country in its different forms. He has enunciated rules for the development of these melas. All the features of the ancient system of classification known as the Grama-Murchana-Jāti-Rāga system were preserved intact by the new device and were now understood and appreciated by a wider range of the populace.

Our music is built upon three main elements, viz., स्वर, लय and वर्ण of which स्वर is developed into Rāgas, लय is developed into Tālas and वर्ण is developed into compositions (प्रबंध) including those having words with meaning (काव्य) those having mere syllables without poetry or meaning (बिरुद or रट) and those of a purely symbolic nature (वर्णात्मक or solpha syllables).

We have said something regarding स्वर, मेल and राग already—all of which comes under स्वरविवेक as styled by ancient writers. A few important facts will now be mentioned as regards लयविवेक.

47

In Sangītā Ratnākara Tālas, have been classified into three groups viz., मार्गताल देशीताल and प्रस्तारोक्तताल's. The last variety has been worked out mathematically and in great detail by Kallinātha in his commentary on संगीतरत्नाकर besides doing justice to the first two classes.

The वर्णविवेक has also been handled by him with great skill. He has shown how poetic compositions which were not originally written for music could nevertheless be set to music and he has enunciated the dictum— नास्तिकिंचिद्वृत्तं तु पदं गानसमाश्रयम् ।. He has described at great length compositions with meaningless syllables or numerous repetitions of syllables of words having meaning in the first instance. This, it should be remembered, furnishes the essential framework of both vocal and instrumental music and is calculated to enrich its beauty and variety in लय Music and the allied art of poetry make no doubt a highly pleasing combination with a great appeal. But it should be remembered that music by itself is capable of stirring the deepest emotions of the human heart. In music the meaning of words is secondary and is a sort of concrete commentary to the ineffable appeal of the harmony of sounds. The absence of poetry with meaning in music will not in the least harm the melody or detract from the aesthetic pleasure of music which is independently effected by the trinity of स्वर, लय and वर्ण or in other words राग, ताल and पद or बिरुद (articulate sound necessarily having any meaning). If this were not so we should feel that something was wanting when we were listening to instrumental music. But this has never been our experience. On the other hand if it is good instrumental music we seem to enjoy it all the more when it is unencumbered with any external content. Hear what Kallinātha says on this point :

अत्र पदावृत्त्या पुनरुक्तिदोषं पदार्थभागेनानर्थकत्वं वाऽऽशंक्य मतङ्गेन परिहृतम् । यथा सामवेदे गीतप्रधान आवृत्तिष्वर्थानाऽऽद्रियंते—इति । .... । अतः सामवेदप्रकृतिके सङ्गीते गानवशात्कचित्पदानां पुनरुक्तिरर्धोक्तिश्च न दोषायेति मन्तव्यम् । सं. र. p. 146.

A great change in the style of music took place, as has previously been described, during the time of Kallināthа. Before Kallinātha all melodic types were divided into two *grāmas*, but during Kallinātha's time the melodies of Madhyama grāma were with some alterations being assimilated to the Shadjagrāma. In this way some important melody-types were in danger of being lost to our system. These and other melodic types new to the system Kallinātha tried to place on a scientific footing. He used a new terminology for this purpose which is found in his Mela Prastāra Paddhati. Kallinātha has not mentioned a Mela Prastāra of his own but has provided a set of rules for a possible one, has indicated clearly the number of melodic types and has suggested an arrangement not found in any previous writer.

As has already been said, the theory of Bharata, though worked out by Śarngadeva in his Sangīta Ratnākara received no light until Kallinātha wrote his commentary on it. As one important aspect after another of the scientific theory of music of Bharata and Śarngadeva began to be understood in the light of this commentary later writers took to expanding on the theory with the help of previous writers. In so doing many blunders were committed on account partly of their own insufficient knowledge and of insufficient explanation of old texts. Apart from the theory the art of music was rapidly developing so that within a few decades after the period of Kallinātha it became an integral part of daily household life. Between 1500 A.D. and 1550 A.D. there appeared many authors who attempted to construct a new theory and link the prevailing art of their time to it. Among these Punḍarīka Viṭṭhala was the first to construct a Mela Prastāra after the manner suggested by Kallinātha. He was a pure Karnāṭaka Panḍita with an admirable talent and ambition to boot. He was a native of the Mysore Province which was at that time (about 1510 A.D.) a tributary State of the Vijayanagara Empire. The able ruler of the Province, about 1510, Beṭṭada Chāmarāja, for the first time made Mysore his capital and fortified it. At this time Punḍarīka Viṭṭhala wrote his Mela Prastāra which raised him to fame even outside the Vijayanagara Empire—a noteworthy fact. The period was a critical one. The Hindus under the Vijayanagara Empire were concentrating to face the foreign power, the Muhammadans and these latter were attempting to unite and planning an anti-Hindu campaign. In these troublous times Punḍarīka Viṭṭhala was patronized by Sultan Burhān Khān of the Faruki family ruling Khandesh from the capital of Ahmadnagar formerly known by the name of Ananda Vaḷḷi. It is a curious circumstance that a true Karnāṭaka Panḍita of such an extraordinary talent was not patronized by the emperor of Vijayanagara and that an orthodox Hindu who boldly presents himself to the Muhammadan sultan as a Karnāṭaka Panḍita was placed by him as a Durbar musician and encouraged to write a treatise on music.

To solve this mysterious question it is necessary to take into account the administration of the Empire which extended throughout the Deccan south of the river Krishṇā. The empire was divided into different Sāmanta Manḍalas for administrative purposes. The advisory body of prime ministers in the capital was selected from the different provinces governed by the representatives of the emperor. The true Karnāṭaka representatives in the assembly did not interfere in minor matters unless large political questions were involved in order to keep the sympathy of the large number of representatives from the different parts of the vast empire. Rāmarāja of Andhra and ruler of Śriranga raised himself successively to the highest post of representative of the emperor in the capital, married the daughter of Krishnadevarāya and thus became a nearest relative of the emperor and loved by him on account of his bravery and statesmanship. Through the relationship of Aḷiya Rāmarāja, Krishnadevarāya was obliged to satisfy what was desired by his son-in-law. In this way people from outside Karnāṭaka, mainly from Andhra had much influence in the assembly of the emperor. Rāmarāja was, as historians say, proud of his province and his people and it was he through whom Andhra influence steadily spread over Karnāṭaka of which there is a good example for us in the history of music. After Krishṇadevarāya's death Rāmarāja practically became the ruler of the empire and the successive nominal emperors were only puppets in his hands. During this period in 1550 A.D. Rāmarāja encouraged a Telugu chieftain named Rāmāmātya (who was a chief of the Konḍaviḍu estate near the east coast) to write a work on music. The work written by him is named as Swara-Mela-Kalānidhi (which name is not proper unless the work mentions the prastāra of melas). Rāmāmātya states in his work that he was a grandson of Kallinātha. He also gives the date of his work as 1550 A.D. Now the date of Punḍarīka Viṭṭhala ranges from 1510 A.D. to 1560 A.D., he having written four works one after the other viz., *Sadrāgachandrodaya, Rāga-manjarī, Rāga-mālā* and *Nartana-nirṇaya.* It is clear that Rāmāmātya and Punḍarīka were contemporaries. The first work of Punḍarīka was written between 1510 and 1525 as he mentions his patron Burhaṇkhān of Ahmadshāhi whose date must be the date of his work. The second work of his was written between 1525 and 1540; the third between 1540 and 1555 and the last between 1555 and 1565. In the first work Punḍarīka has fully discussed the Mela Prastāra; in the second he only touches the topic of Prastāra but gives his conclusions. In the third of his works, for the purposes of classification of Rāgas, he has adopted the system of परिवारराग's—an approximate grouping of the Rāgas on the principle of the melodic features which they exhibit in common. Scholars are of opinion that Puṇḍarīka's system of arranging the groups is more sensible than all other similar systems or मत's. The mention of Puṇḍarīka's system here is to show that he was the father of the system of Melas and Janya rāgas. Some who have evidently not studied the works of puṇḍarīka assume that Rāmāmātya was the first to describe Rāgas by the system of मेळ's or generic scales. This is not true as is clear from the very dates of the works of the respective authors. Puṇḍarīka's terminology is quite appropriate for the purposes of the Mela Paddhati, which Rāmāmātya hastened to adopt in his work. Although he did not understand the terminology completely and made many mistakes he tried his best to popularize it. But the system became hopelessly error-ridden in the hands of Venkaṭamakhi. Venkaṭamakhi has criticized Rāmāmātya on the Rāga lakshaṇas but himself lived in the proverbial glass house when he threw stones at others. Rāmāmātya's calling 4th śruti रि and 4th sruti ध as Shuddha Gandhāra and Śuddha Nishāda as well as his calling 4th śruti रि and 4th śruti ध as 5th śruti रि and 5th śruti ध was itself an error. Venkaṭamakhi unhesitatingly adopted this without any consideration of its correctness. So his work is not scientifically accurate in many respects. Puṇḍarīka's terminology has been deliberately coined by him to explain the process of obtaining the melas; he has given reasons calling one note by the name of another. This was not appreciated by or understood by Rāmāmātya and Venkaṭamakhi. Rāmāmātya gave wrong names to Śuddha रि, ग, ध and नि and tried in vain to fit the names to Śarngadeva's definitions without justifying his procedure by reference to any authority. His demonstration of śrutis on the playing Veena has become farcical and has no sort of connection with the systems of Bharata, Śarngadeva or Chatura Kallinātha. The same error was repeated by Venkaṭamakhi of Tanjore in constructing his system of 72 melas. He too has not given any reason for changing the proper names of Bharata's śrutis.. He has committed a blunder in stating that on the Śuddhamela-veeṇā with स, प, स, म strings as mentioned by Rāmāmātya the demonstration of śrutis is impossible and that it is only on the Madhya-mela-veeṇā that such a demonstration is possible. This shows that Venkaṭamakhi did not understand the correct method of obtaining the 22 śrutis of Bharata nor was he familiar with the technical process of changing the śuddha swara sthānas to one śruti below the actual places of śuddha रि, ग, ध, नि

swaras for purposes of demonstration. He did not know the proper use of grama and murchanas either. Hence the number of his melas came to 72 while the original Prastāra of Puṇḍarīka Viṭṭhala comes to 90 melas. Yet Puṇḍarīka had doubts about the finality of the number 90 as he was dimly aware of the possible existence of many more melody types. So he says **केचिद्विलुप्ताः कति चिद्विरक्ताः** etc., while Venkaṭamakhi was so arrogant of mastery over the Prastāra that he says :

> यदिकश्चिन्मदुन्नीतमेलेभ्यस्तुद्विसप्ततेः ।
> न्यूनं वाप्यधिकं वापि प्रसिद्धैर्द्वादशस्वरैः ॥
> कल्पयेन्मेलने तर्हि ममायासो वृथा भवेत् ।
> न हि तत्कल्पने भाललोचनोपि प्रगल्भते ॥ etc,

through his ignorance of the subject. He did not know that on the very hypothesis on which he started his Mela Prastāra the number would come up to 108 by substituting Vikṛtā Panchama in place of Śuddha Panchama in his 36 Pūrva melas. Now it would not be inappropriate if I take the opportunity of announcing on this auspicious occasion of the Sexcentenary celebrations of the Karnāṭaka Empire of Vijayanagara that the true Karnāṭaka Mela-Prastāra generally stated by Śarngadeva about 1220 A.D., made more explicit by Kallinātha about 1420 A.D., elaborated by Puṇḍarīka Viṭṭhala about 1520 A.D. up to the number 90 is now complete and that the total number of melas really comes up to 162.* It will be seen from the

*If Venkaṭamakhi had ever dreamt of the past and the future he would never have dared to speak as in the above quoted verses of his ; if his imagination had run over the mythical age he might have seen that though Bhālalochana (Shankara) being unable to take an avatāra in Kaliyuga was unable to alter his No. 72, yet Puṇḍarīka, the founder of Mela-Prastāra and the devotee of Viṭṭhala, an incarnation of Chaturbhuja Yādava Krishna, might again be born in Karnātaka to carry out his work and complete the Prastāra which had been left at the number 90 during his previous birth about 1500 A.D. If Venkatamakhi had any skill in guessing the future he might have known that an incarnation of Chaturbhuja Yādava Krishṇa would take place at the end of the 19th century or at least he would send his Representative Nālwadi Yādava Krishṇa after a long continental journey to set right the musical culture of Karnāṭaka by holding at Mahishapura his council of wise and worthy persons as Bhagavān Krishṇa assembled at Dwārāvatī on his return after Digvijaya from remote lands his council of Vibudhas, Vidyādharas, Apsaras, Yakshas, Gandharvas and Kinnaras.

preceding paragraphs that there was a great change in the science of music during the Vijayanagara Empire between 1450 and 1550. So far the theoretical and historical aspects of the subject have been considered. A few words will now be said about the practical aspect of Karnāṭaka music of the times.

About the time of Kallinātha music served as a happy medium to elevate the social, religious and philosophical ideas of the mass. Shri Shripādarāyaswāmi, a Mādhwa sannyāsi was the first to carry on this mission, which was initiated by Narahari-tīrtha the successor and disciple of Shri Madhvācharya. Shripādarayaswāmi was the *guru* of the emperor Sāluva Narasimha, over whom he had considerable influence partly owing to a miracle, it is said, he performed but chiefly owing to his piety and learning and the valuable work he was carrying on in social and religious spheres. He himself composed hundreds of scientific musical compositions like the Ugābhoga, Suḷāḍi, Gīta, Prabandha, etc., and made provision for the inculcation of higher thoughts to the mass of the Kannaḍa people who either could not understand the Sanskrit language or had no necessity for it. Śhri Vyāsarayaswāmi, the disciple of Shripadarāya succeeded his master and carried on the mission opened by his *guru* in addition to the writing of valuable works on the Oriental Sciences of Philosophy, Logic, etc. Shri Vyāsarāyaswāmi lived in Vijayanagara which was very dear to him and carried his Rāja-gurutwa to four successive emperors, including the great Krishṇadevarāya and took his samādhi about the year 1529 at the age of 92 years. He had three distinguished disciples, viz., Shri Vādirājaswāmi Purandaradāsa and Kanakadasa. All these three were living with their *guru* till his death and then set out for the different parts of Karnaṭaka where they popularized the Dāsakūta and Karnāṭaka music. Purandaradāsa almost attached himself to Pandharāpura (North Karnāṭaka) Kanakadāsa attached himself to Central Karnāṭaka at his pet village Kāginele and Vādirajaswāmi to the southern part of Karnāṭaka at Udipi. The composers of the Dāsakūta Parampara composed mainly two classes of songs, गीत's and प्रबध's on the one hand which were mostly लय-ताल प्रधान (in Kallinātha's words) and Ugābhogas on the other hand which were—रागप्रधान. The style of music represented by the latter came to light for the first time during the Vijayanagara period. The composers of the Dāsakūta have left to us a great treasure in the form of their numerous compositions which are even to-day a part of every household in Karnāṭaka.

32

The Brahma Sutra Vrtti of Praudhadevaraya

BY

DR. V. RAGHAVAN, M.A., PH.D.

University of Madras.

TO THE vast Sanskrit literature of the Vijayanagara times produced by the kings themselves or by poets and scholars patronised by them, which is known to us, it is my good fortune to have been able to add the work which forms the subject of this note. In the supplementary catalogue of the Sanskrit Manuscripts in the Government Oriental Library, Mysore, published in 1928, I found on page **22** the entry :

ब्रह्मसूत्रवृत्तिः प्रौढदेवराय (4950) : ना. 191 प.

Immediately I applied to Mr. M. S. Basavalingayya, M.A., B.L., Curator-in-charge of the Mysore Oriental Library, for extracts from this interesting manuscript and he kindly supplied me with them. The work is fortunately completely available in this manuscript which contains 191 folios. It is a gloss on the Brahma sūtras of Bādarāyaṇa, following the Advaita of Śaṅkara. The colophon ascribes the work to king Prauḍhadevarāya. I give below the beginning, end and colophon of the work :—

ब्रह्मसूत्रवृत्तिः प्रौढदेवरायः 4950 नागरी 191 पत्र

उपक्रमः—

वागीशाद्यास्सुमनसः सर्वार्थानामुपक्रमे ।
यं नत्वा कृतकृत्यास्स्युस्तं नमामि गजाननम् ॥
स्थित्युद्भवं प्रविलया जगतो यतस्स्युः ।
यं प्राहुरजमव्ययमद्वितीयम् । तं हेमकूटनिलयं
.... भवानीपतिमव्ययम् ।
विरूपाक्षं महादेवं प्रत्यगात्मानमाश्रये ॥
यद्भाष्यामृतयानेन जरामरणवर्जितम् ।
पदं याता हि विबुधाः शङ्करं नौमितं गुरुम् ॥

अनुष्ठितधर्मविद (म) लितान्तःकरणस्य पुरुषस्य "तरति शोकमात्मवित्" "ब्रह्मवेद ब्रह्मैव भवति" इत्यादि वेदान्तवाक्येषु संशयो भवति, किमेतानि वेदान्तवाक्यानि सकलानर्थनिवृत्तिद्वारेण परमसुखस्वरूपब्रह्मात्मैकत्वलक्षणमोक्षप्रवृत्तिसाधनज्ञानाय आरम्भणीयानि उत नेति। तत्र देहेन्द्रियादि प्रपञ्चस्य जावेश्वरत्वजगदाकृतिभेदस्य च (?) सत्यत्वेन आत्मवत् ज्ञानेन निवृत्त्यभोगात्। देहेन्द्रियादेर्विषयादनात्मनो विषयिगश्चात्मनः स्वयंप्रकाशस्य तमःप्रकाशवत् प्रतीयमानत्वात् आत्मन्यध्यस्तत्वानुपपत्त्या मिथ्यात्वायोगात् तन्निवृत्तिसाधनब्रह्मात्मैकत्वज्ञानाय नारम्भणीयमिति प्राप्ते सिद्धान्तः ;

॥ अथातो ब्रह्मजिज्ञासा ॥

नित्यानित्यविवेकादिसाधनचतुष्टयसम्पत्त्यनन्तरं, यस्माद्वेद एव "तद्यथेह कर्मचितो लोकः क्षीयते एवमेवामुत्र पुण्यचितो लोकः क्षीयते" इत्यादिः कर्मणामनित्यफलतां दर्शयति ; ब्रह्मविदाप्नोति परमिति ब्रह्मज्ञानात् परमपुरुषार्थप्राप्तिमपि दर्शयति, अत एवेहामुत्रार्थफलभोगवैराग्यापपत्तेः, शमदमादिसाधनसम्भवाच्च मोक्षसाधनब्रह्मज्ञानायारब्धवेदान्तबाक्यविचारः कर्तव्यः ॥

उपसंहारः—

॥ दर्शयतश्चैवं प्रत्यक्षानुमाने ॥

दर्शयतश्च विकारावर्तित्वं परस्य ज्योतिषः श्रुतिस्मृती—"न तत्र सूर्यो भाति न चन्द्रतारकं नेमा विद्युतो भान्ति कुतोऽयमग्निः" इति श्रुतिः। "न तद्भासयते सूर्यो न शशाङ्को न पावकः" इति स्मृतिः। तदेवं विकारावर्तित्वं परस्य ज्योतिषः प्रसिद्धमित्यर्थः ॥

॥ भोगमात्र साम्यलिङ्गाच्च ॥

अनेन भोगमात्रमेषामितरेण समानमित्युच्यते। भोगमात्रे ...... त्र साम्यं तत्र भोगमात्रसाम्यं लिङ्गं तस्मादिति विग्रहः। यथैतां देवतां सर्वाणि भूतानि अवन्ति एवं हैवंविदं सर्वाणि भूतानि प्राणिनः अवन्ति प्रीणयन्ति भोजयन्ति। एवमेव एवंविदं सगुणब्रह्मस्वरूप वेदिनं सर्वाणि भूतानि परमेश्वरप्रेरणया भोजयन्तीति श्रुत्यर्थः ॥

॥ अनावृत्तिः शब्दादनावृत्तिः शब्दात् ॥

ब्रह्मलोकं गतानां सातिशयैश्वर्याणामपि पुनरावृत्तिर्नास्ति, कुतः शब्दात्, " तयोर्ध्वमायन्नमृतत्वमेति ", " एतेन [चरति] पद्यमाना इमं मानव (मावर्त) मावर्तन्ते " इत्यादि शब्दप्रमाणादित्यर्थः । ब्रह्मणा सह तेषामपि सगुण-ब्रह्मविदुषां तत्समीपं प्राप्तानां महाप्रलये ब्रह्मात्मैकत्वज्ञानात् क्रममुक्तिः शास्त्रसिद्धा, अमृतत्वेनानावृत्तेः, कार्याध्यक्षेण सहित इत्यत्रोपपादितत्वाच्च । अनावृत्तिः शब्दादनावृत्तिः शब्दादिति सूत्राभ्यासः शास्त्रपरिसमाप्तिं द्योतयति ।

इति श्री राजाधिराज राजपरमेश्वर गजमृगयाधिराज श्री वीरप्रताप
प्रौढदेवराय महाराजकृतौ पम्पायां ब्रह्मसूत्रवृत्तौ
चतुर्थस्याध्यायस्य चतुर्थः पादः ॥
समाप्तश्चायं ग्रन्थः ॥

The brief commentary closely follows the Bhāṣya and the Bhāmatī and summarises, in the words of those two works themselves. As for instance, the comment on the sūtra **'दर्शयतश्चैवं प्रत्यक्षानुमाने'** given above is reproduced in toto from the Śaṅkara Bhāṣya. The only difference is while the Bhāṣya ends here with the words **'इत्यभिप्रायः'** this gloss ends with the words **'इत्यर्थः'**

The expression **'गजमृगयाधिराज'** found as a title of the author, King Praudhadevarāya in the colophon is a translation of the Telugu expression 'Gaja beṭa kāra,' 'elephant-hunter,' which was one of Devarāya II's titles.[1] The commentary is called in the colophon 'Pampā,' the name of the goddess in the city of Vijayanagara, whom Devarāya II specially worshipped. And this is attested to by a verse in an inscription on the basement of the Mukhamanṭapa of the Hazar Rāmasvami Temple.

श्री ॥ वाणीव भोजराजं त्रिपुराम्बा वत्सराजमिव ।
कालीव विक्रमार्कं कलयति पम्पाऽद्य देवराय नृपम् ॥

S. I. Ins. Vol. IV. No. 252.

Therefore it is natural that Devarāya II should have named his work after his patron-goddess. Further, in the introductory verses, there is reference to the temple in Hemakūṭa and god Virūpākṣa. These prove that this work is by Devarāya II, (1422-1446 A.D.).

1. Both these references were kindly supplied to me by Dr. N. Venkataramanayya, Madras University.

It is possible that it was some poet or scholar patronised by Devarāya II who wrote this gloss on the Brahma sūtras. There is as yet no evidence to find out its real author, who may be Śoṇādrinātha who seems to be the real author of the Mahānāṭakasūktisudhānidhi ascribed to this Immaḍi Devarāya, or even Kallinātha himself who wrote his Sangītaratnākara-kalānidhi while Devarāya was ruling, under the patronage of his son Mummaḍi Deva or Mallikārjuna. In the eleventh of his introductory verses Kallinātha refers to his great jñāna and vairāgya, inherited from his illustrious grandfather, one Tuttāleśvara,[2] shows his acquaintance with Vedanta in his comments on the preliminary portion of the first chapter of the Sangītaratnākara on Nādotpatti and here, quotes also the Bhāratī of Vācaspati. (p. 23 Ānandāśrama Edn.).

2. तुत्तालेश्वरदेवो हि यस्य साक्षात्पितामहः ।
असौ किं वर्ण्यते ज्ञानवैराग्यैश्वर्यसम्पदा ॥ १ ॥

Pl. 1.1 Hampi Ruins from Hēmakūṭam Hill

Pl. 1.2 Mātanga Parvatam and the Soolai Bazaar

Pl. 3.2 Large Linga in the ruined Śiva Shrine near the Narasimha Statue

Pl. 4.1 The King's Balance

Pl. 4.2 Metal Images of Krishṇa Rāya and his two queens, Tirupati Temple, Chittoor District

Pl. 5.1 Stone Water Channel near the Throne Platform

Pl. 6.1 Lepakshi Paintings

Pl. 7.1 Stone Trough, facing the King's Audience Hall

Pl. 7.2 Throne Platform from the south

a

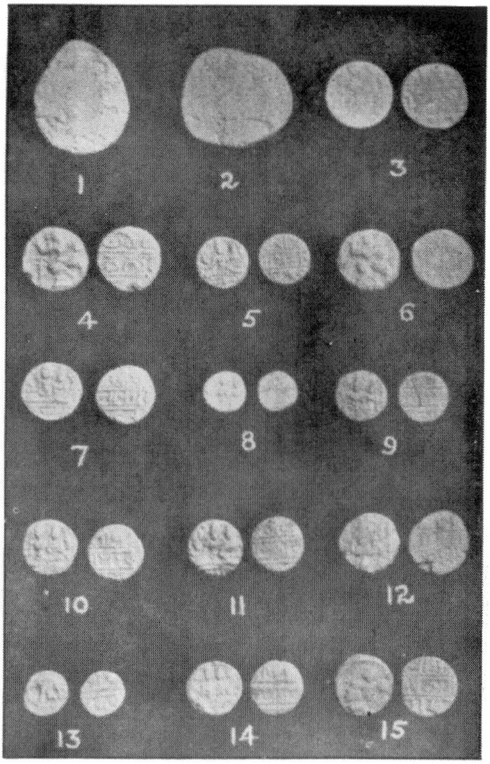

Pl. 8.1 (a&b) Vijayanagara Coins

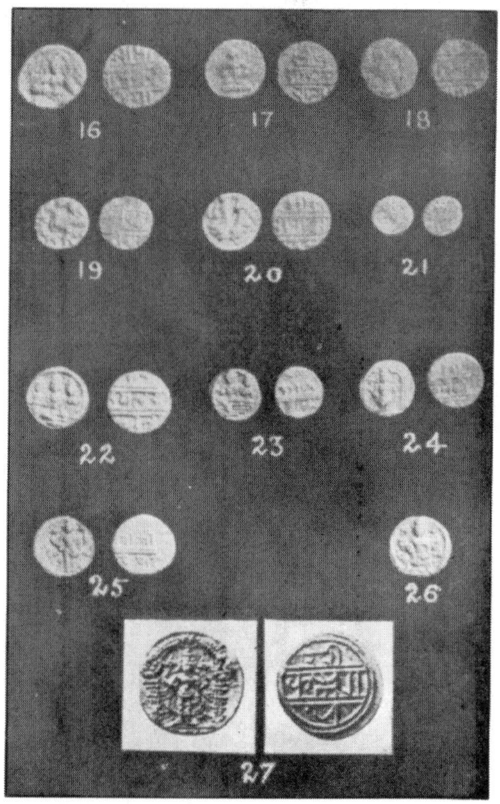

b

Pl. 9.1 Details of sculptures on the east wall of the steps on the south side of the Throne Platform

Pl. 10.1 King's Audience Hall

Pl. 10.2 Hazāra Rāma Temple, south-west view

Pl. 11.1 Carved balckstone pillar in the Hazāra Rāma Temple

Pl. 11.2 Southern Watch Tower, Zenānā Enclosure

Pl. 11.3 The Lotus Mahal

Pl. 12.1 The Elephant Stables

Pl. 13.1 Guards' Quarters

Pl. 14.1 Krishṇa Temple

Pl. 15.1 Sāsivikallu Gaṇēśa Statue

Pl. 16.1 Kadalaikallu Gaṇēśa Temple

Pl. 17.1 North view from Hēmakūṭam Hill

Pl. 18.1 Group of Jaina Temples, south of the Pampāpati Temple

Pl. 18.2 Hampi Bazaar from the east

Pl. 19.1 Achyuta Rāya's Temple

Pl. 19.2 Northern gateway of the inner courtyard of Achyuta Rāya's Temple

Pl. 21.1 Viṭṭhala Temple

Pl. 22.1 Viṭṭhala Temple, north entrance into main shrine

Pl. 22.2 Viṭṭhala Temple, interior view

Pl. 23.1 Viṭṭhala Temple, details of the plinth and cornice

Pl. 24.1 Viṭṭhala Temple, stone car

Pl. 25.1 Vidyāśankara Temple, general view

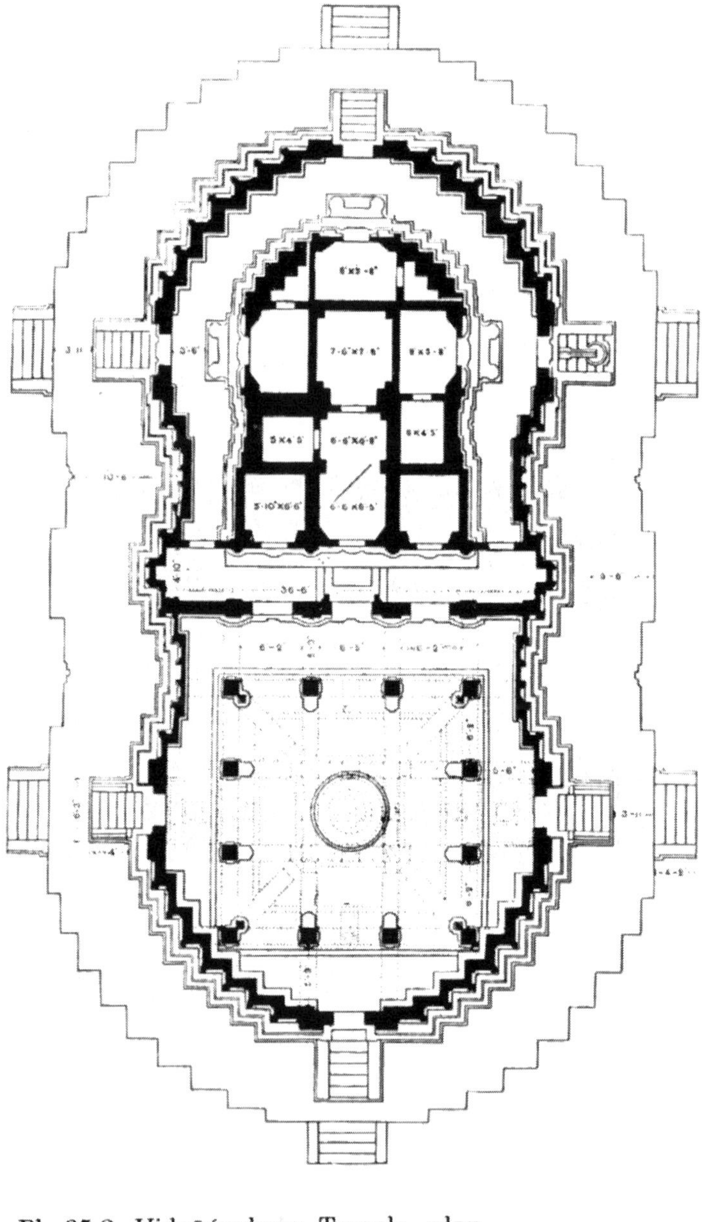

Pl. 25.2 Vidyāśankara Temple, plan

Pl. 26.1 Viṭṭhala Temple, Kalyāṇa Maṇḍapa

Pl. 26.2 Viṭṭhala Temple, Kalyāṇa Maṇḍapa

Pl. 26.3 Mālyavanta Raghunātha Temple, general view from the east

Pl. 26.4 Gāṇigiṭṭi Jaina Temple

Pl. 26.5 Pattābhi Rāma Temple

Pl. 28.1 Anantaśayanaga Temple, near Hospet

Pl. 29.1 Muhammadan Tombs at Kadirāmpuram